MW01602984

THE
LAW DOWN
— A CENTURY REMEMBERED —

by W. Edward Sell

A 100 Year History of the
University of Pittsburgh
School of Law

❧

The Law Down — A Century Remembered
by W. Edward Sell

ISBN: 0-9646415-0-X

Printed in the United States of America

ACKNOWLEDGMENT

Harold Obernauer, '13

Publication of this history has been
underwritten by a gift from
THE OBERNAUER FOUNDATION
in memory of
HAROLD OBERNAUER, '13
founder of the Pitt Law Alumni Association.

Proceeds from the sale of this volume will be
used to fund scholarships at the Law School.

To the thousands of students with whom I have shared a learning experience over forty-five years. They have provided me with a storehouse of treasured memories.

PREFACE

This is not a typical history. I have, with almost unbelievable effort, resisted the temptation to include footnotes. And so, this history is not written in law review style, but rather with a somewhat informal approach.

The history of the school divides itself, almost evenly, into two fifty year segments. The first fifty years—1895 to 1945—witnessed the school as local in nature. The faculty was composed largely of adjunct professors. The student body consisted largely of residents of Pittsburgh and the surrounding localities.

The archives of the University are rather meager with respect to materials dealing with the early years of the school. But, fortunately, much of the information I have used was found in the law school faculty records.

I arrived at the law school in September, 1947, and so have witnessed the last forty-eight years. I would note, however, that I knew two members of the first graduating class, Harry A. Jones and Charles A. Locke. Thus, in a sense, one way or another, I have had the good fortune to span the entire one hundred years of the school's existence. Contrary to comments made by some, I was not here at the inauguration of the school. It just may seem that way.

Because I was here for most of the second fifty years, portions of that history are presented as a somewhat anecdotal history.

I would be remiss if I did not extend sincere thanks to persons without whose help this history would not have been completed. The Word Processing Center of the law school, headed by LuAnn Driscoll and consisting of Karen Knochel, Darleen Mocello, Carolyn Rohan and Barb Salopek, did a tremendous job in the preparation of the various drafts. Always extremely competent and warm-hearted in cooperating with me, they deserve my deep appreciation and thanks.

My colleagues, Edward Symons and Mark Nordenberg, merit my thanks for their efforts in reading the manuscript and making valuable suggestions.

Maureen Polidori, of the law school staff, did a tremendous job of finding photographs for me. Without her help, there would have been few photographs, especially in the latter chapters. I deeply appreciate her assistance.

Terri Svidro has earned my thanks and appreciation for her efforts in compiling the tables dealing with faculty of the school (Tables 2 and 3).

My appreciation is extended to Lisa Delaney, External Relations in the law school, for her suggestions.

Libby Jacaszek, the law school receptionist, did her usual kind work in making certain that innumerable items were picked up and delivered.

And a special thanks goes to my colleague Karen Engro. Karen gave me a much needed title for this effort.

Frank Lucchino, Jr., of the Class of 1996, was of invaluable assistance. He read each chapter draft and made many excellent suggestions.

I researched the history as a personal labor. Therefore, any inaccuracies or errors are mine. This manuscript has been a labor of love, but then, I love this law school. I hope you will find it enlightening and entertaining. You may even be able to identify some persons unidentified in some of the photos.

W. Edward Sell
Dean and Distinguished Service
Professor of Law Emeritus

April, 1995

TABLE OF CONTENTS

CHAPTER
O·N·E
1895-1904

The year 1895 is generally said to mark the founding of the School of Law of the University of Pittsburgh. However, there were law graduates from the Western University of Pennsylvania as early as 1847. In fact, in 1843 the University announced classes in law at "thirty-seven and one-half dollars a term, payable in advance."

While the nation's first law school was established in 1784 at Litchfield, Connecticut, Harvard did not establish a law school until 1817. There were a handful of law schools established in the first half of the nineteenth century, but the chief method of education for the practice of law in the United States was the apprenticeship. Thus, the University was in the vanguard of university based legal education when it announced the establishment of law classes in 1843. Herman Dyer, dean of the faculty of the University, was appointed to succeed Robert Bruce as principal that year. He created the first department and law professorship. Dyer died in the Great Fire on April 10, 1845 when the University's hall at Third Street and Cherry Way was destroyed, along with all records, books, furniture and equipment.

The University then appointed Walter H. Lowrie to a newly created law professorship. At the time of this appointment, Lowrie was a professor of rhetoric and belle-lettres in the University. There are no known records as to the names of the students, which were few in number. However, the minutes of the trustees in 1847 indicate that the Bachelor of Laws degree was conferred on four individuals: Robert Finney, Matthew B. Lowrie, James C. McKibben and Matthew Stewart. There is no indication whether Matthew Lowrie was a relative of Walter Lowrie.

When Walter Lowrie was elected to the Supreme Court of Pennsylvania in 1851, the University's legal education program began to falter. With the start of the Civil War, ten years later, enthusiasm for educating attorneys took a back seat to such efforts as manufacturing munitions for the Union Army.

The vacant law professorship was filled in 1862 with the appointment of the Honorable Moses Hampton, President Judge of the District Court of Allegheny County, as Professor of Law. The next year, Henry Williams, Esquire succeeded him and delivered lectures in law. He subsequently became a Justice of the Supreme Court of Pennsylvania.

After the war, in 1870, the University attempted to reinstitute more formal legal education. A two-year course was designed, culminating in a Bachelor of Laws degree.

To effect this proposal, the University hired three prominent lawyers to conduct the program. Hill Burgwin, Esquire, was to lecture in practice and pleadings of common law and in real estate law. W. T. Haines, Esquire, was assigned criminal law, domestic relations, insurance, commercial law, and Pennsylvania law. William Bakewell, Esquire, was to cover equity, jurisprudence and practice, constitutional law, patent law, contracts, corporations and U.S. law.

Only three years later, the program collapsed. At this time, the

Walter H. Lowrie, first Professor of Law.

principal method of training lawyers was through an apprenticeship with an established lawyer, followed by a bar examination. When the University's program was instituted, it met with great opposition from some of the city's lawyers. One of these opponents was a University trustee. These individuals were opposed to any system which would

Pittsburgh Court House in 1843, when Western University of Pennsylvania appointed Professor Lowrie.

undermine the traditional system of "reading law" and training as law clerks to established lawyers. In addition, they charged that these faculty members managed the finances of the University for their personal interests and that no control over fiscal matters was exercised by the trustees. They alleged that the University had no right to seek consideration of the courts and that no special privilege should be accorded their graduates with respect to admission to the practice of law.

Moses Hampton, Professor of Law, 1862.

George Woods was Chancellor of the University. He and a committee of trustees met with the judges in an effort "to correct any wrong impression that may have been made," and to reach an agreement. But shortly thereafter the three professors resigned and the law program was abandoned in 1873.

By 1895, Pittsburgh was recognized as the steel capital of the United States. Two years earlier, a lengthy economic recession had ended, and an upsurge was in progress. This recovery brought both prosperity and a favorable climate for lawyers. However, the city's lack of a law school disturbed some prominent Pittsburghers, including the then Chancellor of the Western University of Pennsylvania, William Jacob Holland, Ph.D., Sc.D., D.D., LL.D.

In 1894, a University curriculum committee issued to the trustees a report in which it was stated: "Pittsburgh is the only large city in the United States as yet without a law school. It is manifestly the function of a university to provide such a school." Chief Justice Waite said: "The time has gone by when an eminent lawyer, in full practice, can take a class of students into his office and become their teacher. Once that was practicable, but now it is not. The consequence is that law schools are a necessity."

Dr. Holland was determined to establish a law school in the University. He invited the Allegheny County judges to a dinner at the Duquesne Club, which Dr. Holland had joined a year earlier. At that dinner, he asked the judges to appoint from

Chancellor William Jacob Holland.

among their number a committee to work with the trustees in establishing a law school as an integral part of the University. The suggestion met with almost immediate success and in October, 1895, the Department of Legal Instruction was established. A percentage of these first enrollees were college graduates and some were sons of prominent members of the bench and bar.

There was a determination that the first class would graduate after two years of study, with succeeding classes being required to follow a three-year course of study. This explains why there was a Class of 1897. Dr. Holland sought out his friend, John D. Shafer, to select the faculty and organize the school. Dean Shafer accepted the challenge. All of the faculty members were active respected practitioners who taught part time in the afternoon. This met with acceptance by those who were accustomed to the old apprentice program. The first faculty included Samuel Mehard, Thomas Herriott, Clarence Burleigh, James C. Gray, William McClung, Thomas Patterson and William Watson Smith. Alexander Marshall Thompson substituted from time to time for Mr. Smith.

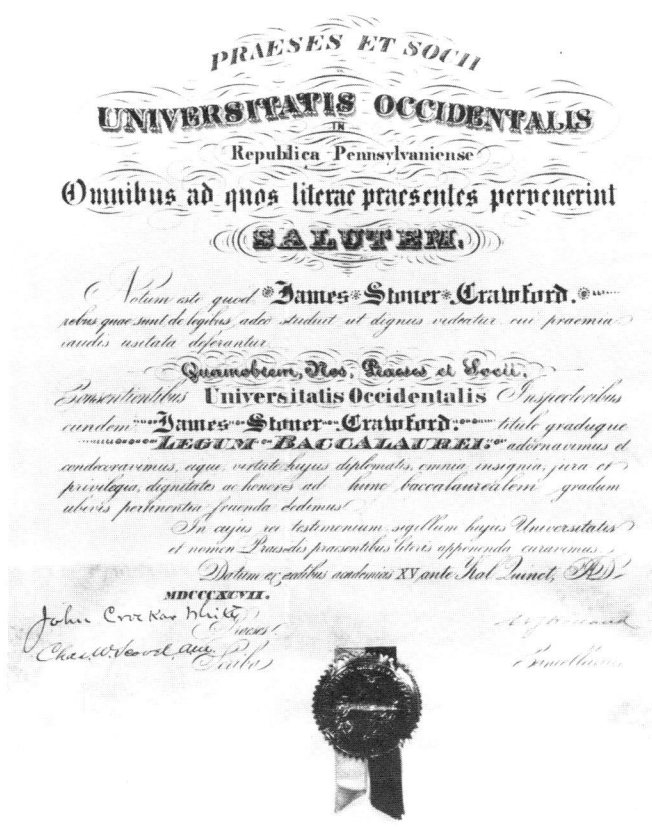

This is a copy of the baccalaureate degree awarded to James Stoner Crawford, a member of the first graduating class—1897.

The new dean, John Douglas Shafer, was born December 6, 1848 at Deer Creek, Allegheny County. His father was pastor of the Associated Reformed Church, which later became the United Presbyterian Church in Deer Creek. Judge Shafer received his early education in the country schools and in his home. In 1862, he entered Jefferson College and in 1866, he graduated from Washington and Jefferson College, first in his class. He spent a year in Allegheny Theological Seminary. After that, he taught Ancient Languages and German in local public schools and later in Westminster College. He then decided to study law and was registered in the offices of Kuhn and Evans. He was admitted to the Allegheny County bar in 1874. He soon became a recognized leader at the bar, particularly in the area of equity practice.

Portrait of Judge John D. Shafer.

In 1897, he was appointed by Governor Hastings to the Common Pleas bench of Allegheny County and remained an active judge until his death on October 12, 1926. He served as the presiding judge during the last few years. Although his interest in the law school never waned, he ceased teaching a few years after ascending the bench. In 1920, Judge Shafer became Dean Emeritus. In recognition of his preeminence as a legal scholar, he was awarded the degree of LL.D.

The first class had thirty-five students enrolled, and the first instruction day took place on October 14, 1895. Classes were held in rooms of the Allegheny County Court House, including one of the rooms of the Orphans' Court, through the courtesy of the Allegheny County Commissioners.

All applicants had to be of good moral character. There were two classes of students, those who were candidates for the degree of Bachelor of Laws and those who were not. Entering degree candidates had to be at least eighteen years of age. They could be admitted to the school upon the production of a certificate that they had passed successfully the preliminary examination required by the rules of the several courts of Allegheny County, or of the courts of any other county which required such a preliminary examination. In the alternative, they had to pass a similar examination administered by the faculty. The examination covered English grammar, geography, mathematics (including arithmetic, algebra, through quadratics and plane geometry), physics, English and American literature, English and American history and Latin (the grammar and two books of Caesar's Commentaries or an equivalent). The examination could be waived for students who were graduates of a "reputable college having a four year course" and requiring the studies set out above.

Non-degree students could enter as special students without any preliminary examination. Such students who attended all the lectures of any class paid the regular term fee. A special student who attended any one or more courses but less than the whole number paid for each course, $25 per term or $50 per annum.

The instruction took several methods. Much was by lectures and recitations based on the lectures. Some was based on textbooks, with recitations based thereon. The faculty also used selected cases, with recitation based on them. Finally, moot courts were utilized as instructional tools. Examinations were held regularly at the end of the spring term.

The school had no law library. The students used the Allegheny County Law Library.

The School's degree requirement was stated as follows:

"Students who have successfully completed the course and have prepared and submitted to the Faculty a thesis upon some legal subject sufficient in merit to satisfy the Faculty of the fitness of the candidates to receive a degree, will at the commencement of the University have conferred upon them the degree of Bachelor of Laws."

Special students were given certificates of attendance in elected courses.

The matriculation fee was $5, which was almost always required to be paid in advance. Tuition for degree students was $50 per term, which had to be paid in advance. The tuition

This full length view of the Allegheny County Court House, dedicated in 1888, was photographed when land was being cleared for the City-County Building.

refund policy stated that fees would be remitted only in cases where students were prevented by sickness or necessary absence from completing the studies of the term. No more than one-half of the term fee could be remitted.

Lectures and recitations took place from 3:30 to 5:30 p.m. Moot courts were held in the evenings. There was a ten-day vacation at Christmas. The Dean's Office was located at 184 Fourth Avenue.

Starting with the class entering in the fall of 1896, the prescribed course of study was:

First year: Real Property, Contracts, Torts, Crimes, Domestic Relations and Negotiable Paper.

Second year: Contracts, Partnerships, Bailments, Evidence, Equity, Equity Pleading and Practice, Real Property and Conveyancing, Criminal Procedure, and Pleading and Practice.

Third year: Equity, Corporations, Evidence, Constitutional Law, Pleading and Practice, Jurisdiction and Practice of United States Courts.

The list of textbooks used was not published.

The first term of the 1896-1897 academic year began on Monday, October 5 and ended February 5, 1897. The second term began February 8, 1897 and ended June 4, 1897. Examinations for admission were conducted on October 1, 2 and 3, 1897.

By 1897, the school occupied two rooms in the old University building, at the corner of Fourth Avenue and Ross Street and near to the Allegheny County Court House.

The law bulletin for 1897-98 contained the Rules for admission to the Bar of Allegheny County. They were as follows:

Admission to the Bar—
Rules governing admission to Bar of Allegheny County:

Rule 35.—Every student at law must be registered in the office of the prothonotary, and it shall be the duty of every attorney or judge of this Court so to register the name, age and place of residence of every person studying law under his direction; and the term of study shall be computed from such registration. No person shall be registered as a student at law until he shall have satisfied a board of examiners, appointed by the Court, that he is a graduate of a reputable college, having a four years' course, requiring the studies hereinafter mentioned, or shall have undergone an examination by the board of examiners on the elements of the Latin language and all the branches of a thorough English education, including algebra, geometry and the natural sciences, or fair equivalents therefor;

and shall file, with a prothonotary a certificate, signed by the majority of the board, that he is qualified to begin the study of law, and that the board has received satisfactory evidence of his good moral character.

The applicant shall give at least one week's notice to the secretary of said board of his desire to be examined for registration.

Rule 36.—No student shall be admitted to practice as an attorney of this Court except upon the following terms:

First.—He shall be a citizen of the United States, and of full age.

Second.—He shall first cause a notice to be published in the *Pittsburgh Legal Journal* of his intention to appear before the board of examiners, one week prior to the meeting of the board, and written notice shall be also be given to the board two weeks before its meeting. These notices shall set forth the name of the applicant; in whose office he has been registered: and at what time he will appear for examination.

Third.—First having been registered, he shall have served a regular clerkship in the office and studied under the direction of an attorney or judge of this Court for three years; provided, that the time actually spent in any law school of good repute shall be counted as a like term of study with an attorney or judge.

Any non-resident, however, who has been pursuing his studies in the office of some practicing attorney, or under some judge, of another county, or state, or at some law school of good repute, may be registered with a practicing attorney of this bar, as required in Rule 35, and after at least six months' clerkship and study in the office of said attorney, may appear for final examination for admission to the bar; provided, however, that his full course of study shall be at least three years.

Fourth.—He shall have undergone an examination in the principles and practice of law and equity, and file with the prothonotary at the time his admission is moved, a certificate signed by all the examiners who were present at his examination that he is qualified for admission to the bar and that they have received satisfactory evidence of his good moral character. Each examination shall consist partly of written questions to be answered in writing by the student; which questions and answers shall be reported to the Court, if required.

Rule 37.—No person admitted to practice in other Courts of this or other states shall be admitted to practice in this Court except upon the following terms:

First.—Having been in actual practice for five years, he shall have appeared before the board of examiners for final examination and filed, at the time his admission is moved, a certificate signed by all of the members present at his examination that they have received satisfactory evidence of his good moral character and professional qualifications, including at least five years' practice of the law.

Second.—Not having been in actual practice for five years, he shall have appeared for final examination upon compliance with the provisions of paragraph 3 of Rule 36, applicable to non-residents.

Third.—Written notice of his intention to apply for examination shall be given to the board at least two weeks before its meeting, and with said notice the applicant shall deliver to the examiners a certificate of the presiding judge of the Court wherein he last practiced, of his good moral character and of the length of time he has practiced in that Court. Provided, however, that notice shall be given by publication as in the case of students applying for final examination.

Provided, further, that this rule shall not apply to attorneys of other Courts seeking to be admitted for special cases.

These rules shall go into effect from this date, but nothing herein contained shall extend the time of study required of any students registered before April 1, 1896.

In 1897, a Law Club was organized by the students of the Middle Class. It was designed to provide a complete system of moot courts, with a prothonotary, sheriff and clerk. Once every two weeks, the courts sat for the entertainment of motions, and on alternate weeks to hear arguments on cases stated. At these meetings, a member of the Allegheny County Bar sat as presiding judge. Motions were made and papers filed as in regular practice, in order to familiarize the members with the practice in Pennsylvania. The Law Club was approved and supported by the faculty. A faculty member was the General Advisor and served on the Executive Committee.

One of the fascinating aspects from the history of those early years is an excerpt from the law bulletin which read:

"Attendance and Note Books

Unless excused, every student is required to attend every lecture delivered before the class of which he is a member, and to remain until the conclusion thereof; and to attend every recitation of his class, and to make such preparation as will enable him to take part therein. Students are required personally to take notes of all lectures, and any student may be called upon, at any lecture, to read before the class the notes taken by him of the lecture delivered, or of some previous lecture upon the subject."

In 1898, the school established an annual fellowship. At the close of each school year, a Fellowship was awarded to that member of the graduating class who had attended the full course of three years and who, in the faculty's judgment, was best qualified by scholarship and other attainments to perform the duties of the office. Each fellow was appointed for one year and performed such duties as were assigned by the faculty. The stipend for the fellowship was the sum of two hundred and fifty dollars. The first Fellowship (1899-1900) was awarded to John W. Chalfant, Jr. The 1900-1901 Fellowship was divided equally between W. B. Adair and F. W Miller.

In 1900, the Association of American Law School was founded. The law school joined 31 other schools as charter members of that organization.

In 1901, the matriculation fee was raised to $10, while tuition remained at $50 per term. In 1904, Rule 38 was added to the Rules of Admission to the Bar of Allegheny County. It provided:

"Every applicant for registration as a student of law, and every applicant for admission to practice law, without prior registration, shall at the time of filing his application, pay to the Secretary of the Board of Examiners a registration fee of five dollars, to be expended in payment of the salary of a clerk and other necessary expenses of the Board of Examiners."

The Rules Concerning Admission to the Bar of the Supreme Court of Pennsylvania were published in the school's bulletin as follows:

RULE I.—No person shall be admitted to practice as an attorney in this Court except upon the recommendation of the State Board of Law Examiners.

RULE II.—Any applicant for admission to the Bar of this Court, who is now in good and regular standing at the Bar of a Court of Common Pleas of this Commonwealth, and after he shall have practiced therein for at least two years, may be admitted, without examination, upon the certificate of the State Board of Law Examiners that he is eligible for admission under the provisions of the rules of this Court heretofore in force; and no such candidate shall be required to advertise or pay any fee for reporting upon his credentials; but this rule shall not apply to graduates of law schools, who shall have been admitted to a Court of Common Pleas, upon their diplomas, unless they shall have practiced at least two years in some one of the courts of this Commonwealth.

RULE III.—Any student who, on or prior to this date, has begun the study of the law, under the rules governing admissions to the Bar of the judicial district within which he resides, may apply to the State Board of Law Examiners for examination and admission to the Bar of this Court, at such date as he would have been entitled to apply for admission in such judicial district; and the certificate of the Board of Examiners shall be conclusive evidence of his eligibility for admission to the Bar of this Court upon examination.

RULE IV.—No person shall be registered as a student at law for the purpose of becoming entitled to admission to the Bar of the Supreme Court until he shall have satisfied the State Board of Law Examiners that he is of good moral character, and shall have passed a preliminary examination upon the following subjects: (1) English language and literature; (2) Outlines of universal history; (3) History of England and of the United States; (4) Arithmetic, algebra through quadratics, and plane geometry; (5) Modern geography; (6) The first four books of Caesar's Commentaries, the first six books of the Aeneid, and the first four orations of Cicero against Catiline.

Every such candidate shall pay to the State Board a fee of ten dollars, and, upon receiving a certificate recommending his registration and certifying that he is qualified to begin the study of the law, shall cause his name, age, place of residence, and the name of his preceptor, or the law school in which he proposes to pursue his studies, to be registered with the Prothonotary of the Eastern District.

RULE V.—Candidates for admission, who have spent at least three years after registration, in the study of the law, either by attendance upon the regular course of a law school, offering at least a three years' course eight months in the year and an average of ten hours per week each year, or partly in a law school and partly in the office of a practicing attorney, or by the bona fide service of a regular clerkship in the office of a practicing attorney, shall be eligible to appear for examination for admission to the Bar of this Court upon complying with the following requirements:

1. A candidate must advertise his intention to apply for admission in a law periodical or a newspaper designated by the Board, and published within the judicial district in which he resides, and in the *Legal Intelligencer*, once a week for four weeks immediately preceding the date of filing his credentials with the Board.

2. He must file the necessary credentials with the Board in such form as shall be prescribed at least twenty-one days before the date of examination and shall pay to the Board a fee of twenty dollars.

3. He must file a certificate signed by at least three members of the Bar in good standing in the judicial district in which he has resided or intends to practice, that he is personally known to them, and that they believe him to be of good moral character.

4. A certificate from the dean of the law school or preceptor that he has been regular in attendance and pursued the study of the law with diligence from the time of his registration.

RULE VI.—Every applicant for admission must sustain a satisfactory examination in Blackstone's Commentaries, constitutional law, including the Constitutions of the United States and Pennsylvania, equity, the law of real and personal property, evidence, decedents' estates, landlord and tenant, contracts, partnership, corporations, crimes, torts, domestic relations, common law pleading and practice, Pennsylvania practice, the Federal statutes relating to the judiciary and to bankruptcy, Pennsylvania statutes and decisions and the Rules of Court.

RULE VII.—Examinations for registration and admission to the Bar shall be conducted in writing, and shall be held simultaneously, after due notice, twice a year, in the cities of Philadelphia, Harrisburg, Pittsburgh, Williamsport and Wilkes-Barre.

RULE VIII.—The State Board of Law Examiners shall hold office during the pleasure of the Court, for a term not exceeding five years, except that of the members of the Board now appointed one shall withdraw at the end of each year, such withdrawals to be made in the order of seniority of admission to the Bar. The members of the Board shall serve without compensation, but shall be reimbursed their traveling and other expenses. The Board may, with the approval of the Court, appoint assistants to aid in securing compliance with the conditions preliminary to registration and examination, to superintend the conduct of the candidates, and to make a preliminary report upon the answers of the candidates; but the members of the Board shall be responsible to the Court for the enforcement of these rules, and the proper ascertainment of the results of the examinations, and no student shall be rejected except by a majority of the State Board of Law Examiners. The Board shall also have power to appoint a Secretary and a Treasurer, or the same person may hold both offices, and they may pay to each assistant examiner, and to the Secretary and Treasurer, out of the fees received, and after deduction of the necessary expenses, a reasonable compensation.

RULE IX.—It shall be the duty of the State Board of Law Examiners to prepare a paper for gratuitous distribution among intending applicants for registration or admission containing detailed information as to the subjects of examination.

RULE X.—Attorneys from other states, upon presenting satisfactory evidence that they are members in good standing of the Appellate Court of last resort of the state from which they came; that they have practiced in a Court of Record of that state for at least five years, and that they are of good moral character, may be admitted to the Bar of this Court without examination upon the recommendation of the State Board (provided, however, that the Board may, in its discretion, require any such applicant to take a final examination).

Attorneys from other states, upon presenting satisfactory evidence that they are members in good standing of a Court of Record of the state from which they came, and have practiced therein for at least one year, and that they are of good moral character, may, in the discretion of the State Board, be permitted to take a final examination without previous registration.

General Information for Intending Applicants for Admission to the Bar of the Supreme Court

1. The foregoing Rules apply solely to admissions to the Bar of the Supreme Court of Pennsylvania. Except in so far as the Superior Court and the Courts of Record of the several judicial districts of the state shall adopt rules providing for the admission of attorneys to practice therein upon the certificate of the State Board of Law Examiners, the Rules of the Supreme Court in no way affect admissions to the Bar of any of these courts.

2. On and after the first Monday of January, 1903, every applicant for admission to the Bar of the Supreme Court of Pennsylvania must present to the Court a certificate of the State Board of Law Examiners recommending his admission.

3. With the three exceptions, hereinafter noted and explained, every applicant for the State Board's certificate must pass both a preliminary and a final examination. A college diploma does not exempt one from taking the preliminary examination; a law school diploma does not exempt one from taking the final examination.

4. No special course of study in school or college is required as a pre-requisite for taking the preliminary examination. Every person who is a citizen of the United States, and who has filed the necessary credentials with the State Board of Law Examiners is eligible to take it. The examination will be held twice a year, simultaneously, in the cities of Philadelphia, Harrisburg, Pittsburgh, Williamsport and Wilkes-Barre. A candidate may be examined in any one of the above enumerated cities, but must make his selection at the time of filing his credentials. Due notice of the exact date of the examination and of the halls in which it will be held will be given in the *Legal Intelligencer* and other legal periodicals, and may be learned from the Prothonotaries of the several Courts of Common Pleas of Pennsylvania.

5. After he shall have passed the preliminary examination, the State Board will issue to the applicant a certificate directed to the Prothonotary of the Supreme Court for the Eastern District of Pennsylvania, certifying that he is qualified to register as a student at law. This is to be done by the applicant causing his name, age, place of residence, the name of his preceptor, or the law school in which he proposes to pursue his legal studies, to be registered with the said Prothonotary.

6. After registering as a law student, it is necessary for the applicant to spend three years in the study of the law, either in attendance upon the regular course of a law school, offering, at least, a three years' course, eight months in the year, and an average of ten hours per week each year; or partly in a law school and partly in the office of a practicing attorney; or by the bona fide service of a regular clerkship in the office of a practicing attorney.

7. After studying three years, as above provided, the applicant may come before the State Board for final examination. This examination will be held twice a year, simultaneously, in the cities of Philadelphia, Harrisburg, Pittsburgh, Williamsport and Wilkes-Barre. The candidate may take the examination in any one of the above enumerated cities, but must make his selection at the time of filing his credentials. Due notice of the date of this examination and of the halls in which it will be held will be given in the *Legal Intelligencer* and other legal periodicals and may be learned from the Prothonotaries of the several Courts of Common Pleas of the state.

8. After he shall have passed the final examination, the State Board will issue to the applicant a certificate directed to the Supreme Court of Pennsylvania, certifying that he has passed the examination prescribed by the Rules of Court, and recommending his admission to the Bar.

9. There are three classes of applicants who are exceptions to the system above described:

a. The Rules of the Supreme Court are not retroactive, and therefore it is provided in Rule III, that any person who, prior to the first Monday of January, 1903 (the date on which the present Rule of the Supreme Court went into effect), had commenced the study of law as a registered student, under the rules of the judicial district within which he resides, need not take the preliminary examination, but may take the final examination before the State Board at such date as he would have been entitled to take his final examination for admission in said judicial district. Such applicant, however, is required to comply with all the other rules governing applicants for final examination.

b. Those who, on the first Monday of January, 1903, were members of the Bar of a Court of Common Pleas of Pennsylvania, but who have not been admitted to the Bar of the Supreme Court, may, after practicing two years in a Court of Record of Pennsylvania, be admitted to the Bar of the Supreme Court, without examination, without advertisement and without paying any fee to the State Board. Upon receiving the necessary credentials from such applicant, the State Board will issue a certificate recommending his admission.

c. Attorneys from other states are to be admitted under the provisions of Rule X. They are divided by this rule into two classes.

Those who are members in good standing of the Bar of the Appellate Court of last resort of the state from which they came, and who have practiced in a Court of Record of that State for at least five years, may be admitted to the Bar of the Supreme Court of Pennsylvania without examination upon the recommendation of the State Board.

Attorneys from other states who are members in good standing of the Bar of a Court of Record of the state from which they came, and who have practiced therein for at least one year, may be admitted to the Bar of the Supreme Court of Pennsylvania upon taking the final examination only. In other words, applicants of this class are not required to take the preliminary examination.

APPLICANTS FOR EXAMINATION AND REGISTRATION AS STUDENTS AT LAW

Applicants for examination and registration as students at law must file with the Secretary of the State Board of Law Examiners, at least twenty-one days before the date of examination, an application for such examination accompanied by satisfactory proof of the good moral character of the applicant, which shall consist of a certificate to that effect signed by at least three members of the Bar in good and regular standing in the judicial district in which the applicant resides, or intends to practice.

The applicant must, also, at or before the time of filing the above credentials, pay to the Treasurer of the Board his examination fee of ten dollars. No credentials will be filed in any case until the examination fee shall have been paid.

All credentials must be made out on blank forms prepared and furnished to the applicant by the Board.

PRELIMINARY EXAMINATION

All applicants for registration should be prepared to pass a satisfactory examination upon the following subjects in accordance with the specifications herein given under each subject.

ENGLISH

1. No candidate will be accepted in English whose work on any subject is notably defective in spelling, punctuation, idiom, or division into paragraphs.

2. A short essay will be required to be written on a subject to be announced at the examination.

3. The applicant must have read the following works, and must be able to pass a satisfactory examination upon the subject matter, the style and the structure thereof, and to answer simple questions on the lives of the authors:

Shakespeare's *Hamlet* and *Merchant of Venice*.
The *Sir Roger de Coverly Papers* in the Spectator.
Scott's *Heart of Mid-Lothian*.
Thackeray's *Henry Esmond*.
First three books of Milton's *Paradise Lost*.
Longfellow's *Evangeline*.
Burke's *Speech on Conciliation with America*.
Burke's *Letter to the Sheriffs of Bristol*.
Autobiography of Benjamin Franklin.
Cooper's *Last of the Mohicans*.
Webster's *Reply to Hayne*.
Hawthorne's *Marble Faun*.

4. The applicant must also have such a knowledge of the general history of English Literature (including that of the United States) as can be obtained from a good standard text-book upon this subject.

HISTORY

1. OUTLINES OF UNIVERSAL HISTORY

Myer's *Ancient History*, and Myers' *Mediaeval and Modern History* or other equivalent works are recommended to those students who have not had the advantage of advanced academic instruction.

2. ENGLISH HISTORY

With special reference to social and political development. Students who have not had the advantage of advanced academic instruction should make a careful study of Montgomery's *Leading Facts of English History*, or Ransome's *Short History of England*, or Higginson and Channing's *English History for Americans*, or some other equivalent work; and all applicants are expected to read Green's *Short History of the English People*.

3. AMERICAN HISTORY

This will include Colonial History with a view to the origin and early development of our institutions, the story of the Revolution and of the formation and adoption of the Federal Constitution; and the political and social history of the United States down to the present time.

Students who have not had the advantage of advanced academic instruction should carefully study Channing's *Students' History of the United States*, or Johnston's *History of the United States for Schools*, or Thomas' *History of the United States*, or some other equivalent work; and all applicants for examination are expected to read:

A good general history of the United States.
Fiske's *Dutch and Quaker Colonies in America*.
Parkman's *Montcalm and Wolf*.
Fiske's *The Critical Period of American History*.

LATIN

(A) First four books of *Caesar's Commentaries*.
(B) First six books of *Virgil's Aeneid*.
(C) First four *Orations of Cicero against Catiline*.

This examination will include a general knowledge of the subject matter, history, geography and mythology of A and B; sight translations from the above works and sight translations taken at large from Virgil and Cicero adapted to the proficiency of those who have studied the prescribed works.

The student will also be required to render into Latin a short passage of English based on the first book of *Caesar's Commentaries*.

MATHEMATICS

ARITHMETIC.—A thorough practical knowledge of ordinary arithmetic. A careful training in accurate computation with whole numbers and fractions should form an important part of this work.

ALGEBRA.—Through quadratics.

GEOMETRY.—The whole of Plane Geometry as included in Wentworth's Geometry or any other standard text-book.

MODERN GEOGRAPHY

The student will be expected to have an accurate knowledge of the political and physical geography of the United States and such a knowledge of the political and physical geography of the rest of the earth as can be obtained from a careful study of the ordinary text-books of the schools.

_____

A circular, containing detailed information regarding final examinations provided by the State Board of Law Examiners, may be secured by application to the Prothonotaries of any of the Courts of Common Pleas in the State of Pennsylvania, or to the Prothonotaries of the Supreme and Superior Courts of Pennsylvania, or by application to Charles L. McKeehan, Secretary of the State Board of Law Examiners, 710 Bullitt Building, Philadelphia, Pa.

Any information in regard to the Pittsburgh Law School, or the rules governing admission to the Bar of Allegheny County, or to the Supreme and Superior Courts, will be cheerfully furnished on application to A. M. Thompson, Secretary of the Pittsburgh Law School, Room 728 Frick Building, Pittsburgh, Pa.

In 1904, students at the University, with the exception of the law school, voted to pay a $5 athletic fee to assist in the establishment of a football program.

In the early years of the school's existence, faculty meetings were held at noon at the Duquesne Hotel. It was located at the corner of Smithfield Street and Oliver Avenue, across the street from the then City Hall and it existed for only 31 years—from 1886 to 1917. In a colorful article, "Passing of Famous Hostelry," appearing in *The Pittsburg Dispatch* on Sunday, May 20, 1917, the writer stated:

"The hotel had, perhaps, the liveliest history of any Pittsburg hostelry in its short life of 31 years. Many political slates, local, State and national were fixed up by Republican leaders in secret conference, during the throne years of Quay, Magee, Flinn and others of lesser note. The silent walls here heard the first whispers of names that afterward were identified with Presidents of the United States. Gubernatorial candidates were picked in small secret conclaves...."

"But the old spot had its distinctive revelry betide. City Hall was just across the street, and the public servants drank the best. It was not a long way to Tipperary in those days, and the short straight line of that time has since become a catacornered one, not openly and with a sort of pride, as in the older days, but now with a slink and a disposition to sneak the thrilling cocktail. How times have changed in the public eye. The great leaders are gone, as well as the good whiskey. Alack and Alack."

The hotel had been sold to the Mellons, who razed the structure.

CHAPTER
T·W·O
1905-1914

Beginning in 1906, the faculty moved their meetings from the Duquesne Hotel to the Union Club. Most of the meetings continued to be held at noon, but some occurred at 5 p.m. or over dinner.

On May 9, 1907, Thomas Herriott, Esquire, one of the members of the original faculty, died. At a meeting of the faculty on May 16, 1907, the Reverend Dr. Samuel Black McCormick, Chancellor of the Western University of Pennsylvania, made appropriate remarks on the passing of Professor Herriott, who taught Orphans' Court, Bills and Notes and Domestic Relations.

Professor James Gray then presented the following:

> WHEREAS God, in his wisdom and love, has called home Mr. Thomas Herriott, who was a member of the Department of Law of the Western University of Pennsylvania since its organization in 1895, teaching the subjects of Orphans' Court, Bills and Notes, and Domestic Relations, and who, by reason of his noble qualities, his strong manliness, the strength and purity of his Christian ideals, the ripeness and thoroughness of his knowledge of the law, not only of those subjects which he taught but of the law as a whole; his ability in imparting to others the knowledge he possessed, and the great interest which he manifested in the young men who were preparing to enter the profession wherein he stood so high and which he had greatly adorned for so many years of his busy, useful life had greatly endeared himself to us all.
>
> *Therefore*, be it resolved, that we greatly mourn his loss, recognizing that to us it is irreparable and that while another may indeed take up the work which he has laid down and go in and out amongst us and also become endeared to us, no one can ever quite fill the place in our hearts and lives occupied by Mr. Herriott who was not only a brother to those of us who labored side by side with him in the practice of the profession which he loved and graced, but he was the instructor and friend of us all, being gifted not only in imparting a knowledge of the law, but gifted

beyond most men of our day and generation in that he was able to impart and did impart the knowledge of pure living and high thinking and that by the unconscious influence of his own true and noble living; and

Resolved, that whilst we mourn our loss, we yet recognize the fact that, having lived so well, he was ready to respond to the call and that we have no reason to mourn on his behalf, but rather to rejoice in that his was a full and complete life, for measured by its usefulness and its influence, he has lived much more and better than most men; and

Resolved, that these resolutions be spread upon the minutes of the Faculty of the Department of Law and a copy sent to the Board of Trustees to be filed with their records and a copy sent to the family of Mr. Herriott, as indicating in some faint measure the love and esteem we bore to our brother and friend.

On July 11, 1908, the Western University of Pennsylvania changed its name to the University of Pittsburgh. The University purchased the present campus in Oakland at that time. The Law Department officially became the Pittsburgh Law School. The opening

The Class of 1907

Front Row (left to right): James C. Dyer, John J. Heard, Christopher M. Anderson, Elder W. Marshall, Joseph T. Bell, Howard W. Douglass, Allen H. Kerr.

Second Row (left to right): Arthur V. McKee, Thomas F. Soles, H. Vaughn Blaxter, Sr., Hugh E. Fergus, Edwin P. Griffiths, William D. McBryar.

Third Row (left to right): Ralph B. Wakefield, James H. Duff, William H. Lacey, Abraham L. Goldstrohm, Clarence E. Sterret, Frank M. Painter.

week of law school in September, 1908, was postponed a week because of the City's Sesquicentennial celebration.

While there were no women students in the school at this early period, the women were not completely ignored by the law school. The school presented a series of four lectures on business law for women on Monday afternoons at the Twentieth Century Club. These lectures covered property rights of women, woman's legal status, investments and "Sociological and Economical Opportunities for Women." The program included an interesting bibliography listing magazine articles such as Susan B. Anthony's, "Woman's Half-Century of Evolution" and G.G. Cork's, "The Law's Partiality to Married Women."

A year later, Judge Shafer was given the power to arrange for a new location for the law school. A committee composed of Messrs. Gray, Hawkins and Thompson was appointed to confer with the County Commissioners with reference to continuing law school operations in the County building, located at the corner of Ross and Diamond Streets. In the event of failure to obtain the Commissioners' consent, the committee was to interview the Orphans' Court judges to obtain permission to use the Orphans' Court rooms temporarily.

The County Commissioners granted permission for the law school to occupy the old University building at the corner of Ross and Diamond Street until the building was torn down. The Law School was promised thirty days' notice to vacate.

The Faculty of 1908
Front Row (left to right): John T. Duff, Jr., Judge J.D. Shafer - Dean, E.W. Marshall.
Second Row (left to right): T.C. Noble, A.M. Thompson, Judge S.S. Mehard, Edmund Englert.
Third Row (left to right): Judge J.J. Miller, J.G. Houston, W.A. Blakeley, R.H. Hawkins,
   J.C. Gray - Vice Dean.

Robert L. Vann, Class of 1909, was the first black graduate of the school. He worked his way through law school serving dinner in a railroad dining car from Pittsburgh to Connellsville in the evening and breakfast on the return trip the next morning.

In 1910, Vann helped to found the Pittsburgh Courier. He used the newspaper to combat discrimination and promote better education, housing and employment opportunities for blacks.

Vann built the Courier into the most influential black newspaper in the nation. In the 1930s, its circulation reached 250,000 and by 1947 that number approached 400,000.

He served as an assistant city solicitor for Pittsburgh from 1917 to 1921. He developed a large

Robert L. Vann.

legal practice between 1909 and 1936, when he gave up his career as a lawyer.

President Roosevelt named Vann a special assistant United States Attorney, a position he occupied from 1933 to 1936. As war loomed in 1940, he switched political parties from Democrat to Republican and supported Wendell L. Wilkie.

Robert Vann died October 14, 1940 at the age of 61.

On May 11, 1911, the faculty voted to send three delegates to the Annual Meeting of the Association of American Law Schools in August in connection with the Annual Meeting of the American Bar Association in Boston. Each delegate was given a $50 expense allowance.

During the summer of 1911, the rooms theretofore occupied by the Law School in the Annex to the Court House were prepared for the use of the new County Court. The judges of the County Court expressed their willingness to have the Law School occupy these rooms at such times as would not conflict with the holding of Court therein. The faculty agreed to use the rooms under these conditions.

In October, 1911, the Secretary reported that there were over sixty students in the Junior class. A committee was appointed to study the desirability of sectioning that class. The committee reported back at a meeting on November 3, 1911 that a room had been secured, that it was being repapered and that it was being supplied with furniture to accommodate one of the sections.

William Blakeley

John D. Shafer

James Gray

Samuel S. Mehard

William McClung

Alexander Thompson

Law Faculty — 1909.

A proposed schedule was presented and approved.

Another interesting item in that faculty meeting was a report from the Secretary that he had communicated with the Association of American Law Schools with respect to its attitude toward night law schools. The reply indicated a feeling against night law schools. As a result, the faculty resolved not to undertake the holding of night sessions.

At a faculty meeting held January 27, 1912, the faculty adopted "Rules and Regulations of the Honor Board of the Pittsburgh Law School." The rules were presented by Mr. James J. Cosgrove, a member of the Senior Class.

J. Smith Cristy, Esquire, who joined the adjunct faculty in 1914.

Rules and Regulations of the Honor Board of the Pittsburgh Law School

I.   Composition of the Board.

1. The Board shall be composed of nine (9) members, three (3) from each class, who shall hold office throughout their course in the law school, and the members of the Senior Class shall hold office after their graduation until the members from the next incoming class are elected in the fall.

2. Three (3) members shall be chosen from each incoming class, one (1) by appointment by the Faculty and the other two by election by said class at a meeting of the class called by the President of the Honor Board and presided over by him. This meeting shall be held each year between November 10th and November 20th.

3. Vacancies caused by any reason except graduation shall be filled by election by the Board and such vacancy shall be filled from the class where the vacancy occurs.

II.   Officers and Election of Officers.

The officers of the Board shall be a President, Vice-President, and a Secretary, who shall be elected by the Board during the first week in May of each year to serve during the next ensuing year.

III. Duties of Officers.

1. The President shall call and preside over all meetings of the Honor Board, and shall explain the Honor System to each incoming class at least five days prior to the election of members by them.

2. The Vice-President shall perform all the duties of the President in his absence.

3. The Secretary shall keep the minutes of all meetings, record testimony at hearings, and notify a man accused of cheating, and witnesses, to appear before the Board. Minutes of Preliminary and Final hearings are to be destroyed as soon as a case is terminated.

IV. Meetings.

The Board shall meet at such time and place as shall be designated by the President, and a majority of the Board shall constitute a quorum at all meetings except as hereinafter provided.

V. Procedure.

1. Information shall be made secretly (either orally or in writing) to any member of the Board.

2. Upon receiving information, such member shall notify the President, who shall immediately call a meeting of the Board.

3. At this meeting a preliminary hearing shall be held and shall be conducted in the following manner:

   (a) The accuser shall be summoned and examined.

   (b) As far as possible all those that sat near the accused in the examination shall be summoned and examined.

   (c) Witnesses shall be examined separately, no other witnesses being present.

   (d) The examination papers and any other available evidence shall be examined.

   (e) The accused shall not be summoned to this meeting nor be informed of the hearing or accusation.

(f) The name of the accused shall not be mentioned to a witness unless he first mentions it himself.

(g) Any member of the Board may examine witnesses.

(h) This hearing may be continued from time to time as may be found necessary.

(i) At the close of the hearing a vote shall be taken as to whether or not a prima facie case has been made out against the accused. If five (5) or more members present vote that a prima facie case has been made out the Accused shall then be notified of the accusation. This notice shall be given to the accused personally in writing by the Secretary and shall be in substance as follows:

"You have been accused of cheating in _____ Examination held on _____ , 191 ___ and are required to appear before the Honor Board at _____ on _____ , 191 ___ to answer this accusation. If you do not appear as required or show good cause for not appearing your guilt will be presumed and unless you withdraw from the school within ten (10) days thereafter the Board will take steps for your dismissal."

4. The meeting at which the accused is summoned to appear shall be designated the Final Hearing and shall be conducted in the following manner.

(a) Seven (7) members of the Board shall constitute a quorum.

(b) The accused, if he appears, shall be examined at this meeting.

(c) The accused shall be permitted to offer any evidence tending to establish his innocence.

(d) The same rules as to the examination of witnesses shall apply as at the preliminary hearing, except that the accused shall have the privilege of being present at the examination of his own witnesses and of questioning them.

(e) The Board may, at its discretion, reexamine witnesses heard at the preliminary hearing, after hearing the testimony of the accused and his witnesses, and before pronouncing final sentence.

(f) This hearing may be continued from time to time as may be found necessary.

(g) After all the testimony has been heard and discussed, the Board shall take a vote as to the guilt or innocence of the party accused. A unanimous vote of those present shall be necessary to convict.

VI. The accused shall be immediately notified of the final action of the Board by the Secretary. If the Accused is convicted the notice shall be in writing and shall be served personally, shall be signed by the President of the Board as well as the Secretary and shall be substantially as follows:

> "It is the painful duty of the Honor Board of the Pittsburgh Law School to inform you that after due and careful deliberation upon all the facts in the case, you have been convicted of cheating in _____ Examination, held on _____ ;
>
> You are hereby given ten (10) days within which to resign from the School. If you fail to withdraw within the required time you will be officially dismissed by the Faculty and your name stricken from the roll.

The Secretary shall also at the same time notify the Secretary of the Faculty of the action of the Board.

VII. If the Accused when convicted does not withdraw from the school within ten (10) days from the service of the above notice he will be formally expelled by the Faculty.

VIII. All proceedings of the Honor Board shall be secret.

IX. The Board shall adopt such rules for the conduct of examinations as they may at any time deem proper.

X. Any necessary expenses incurred by the Board shall be paid by the Law School.

The Honor System of the School of Law
University of Pittsburgh

The Honor System in the University of Pittsburgh Law School is one of the ideals of the school. It is administered by the students themselves and every man who matriculates is expected not only to abide by it but to do all in his power to support it.

Duties of the Students

Every student, upon completion of his examination paper shall sign and attach the following pledge:

"I pledge my honor as a gentleman that during this examination I have neither given nor received aid, nor have I any knowledge of anyone having done so."

The students are expected to observe proper order and decorum during the examinations.

No examination paper shall be taken from the room.

A student may leave the room if he so desires, but only in case of absolute necessity shall he leave the building.

Each student is in honor bound to report to any member of the Honor Board any evidence of cheating that comes to his knowledge.

In reporting an offender against the Honor System, notice of the charge shall be given secretly to any member of the Honor Board.

All persons summoned to appear before the Honor Board, either as witnesses, or to answer an accusation, shall appear promptly at the time and place designated.

Duties of the Honor Board

It shall be the duty of the Honor Board to explain to each incoming Junior Class the Honor System here established.

It shall be the duty of the Board to administer the Honor System and to pass judgment in all cases.

All actions of this Board shall be secret.

Penalty

The penalty for the violation of the Honor System shall be permanent dismissal from the Law School, or such other penalty as to the Honor Board may seem meet.

In April, 1912, the faculty discussed the question of granting graduate degrees. It was the faculty's sentiment that no graduate degrees be granted except on a basis of adequate work and study, and that it was not desirable at that time to make provision for the same.

At that time, the three classes were referred to as junior, middle and senior classes.

A month later, the faculty adopted amended and corrected rules of the Law School as follows:

Rule I.
Admission to the Law School

Section 1. Students will be admitted to the Law School as candidates for degrees upon producing satisfactory evidence of their good moral character, and a certificate that they have passed the Preliminary Law Examinations, taken under the regulations of the Supreme Court of Pennsylvania, for admission to the Bar of that Court or upon a degree of a reputable college having a four year course, and whose requirements for entrance and curriculum are satisfactory to the Faculty of the Law School or upon passing an examination given by the Faculty of the Law School and covering the same subjects provided for the Supreme Court Preliminary Examination.

Section 2. An applicant for admission as a regular student to any other than the first year or Junior Class must present satisfactory evidence by examination or certificate from another law school, of having completed the course of study provided for prior classes in this school; but no new students will be admitted to the Senior Class, unless they present satisfactory evidence of having completed at least one year's work in another law school of recognized standing.

Note (a). The Law School of the University of Pittsburgh is a member of the Association of American Law Schools, and all its rules are to be read in harmony with the rules of that Association.

Note (b). Students who have been regularly admitted to the college or School of Economics of the University of

Pittsburgh and have pursued the regular course of study therein for three years and have received a certificate of satisfactory completion of the same will be entitled to enter the School of Law; and upon the completion of one year's work in the same to the satisfaction of the Faculty of Law will become eligible for a college degree.

Particular attention is called to the fact that no student is eligible to appear for final examination for admission to the Bar unless he has been registered as a student-at-law with the Prothonotary of the Eastern District of Pennsylvania for three years. Work in the Law School before such registration cannot be counted in computing the three year period. Students should read carefully Rules 4 and 5 concerning Admission to the Bar of the Supreme Court of Pennsylvania.

Section 3. In exceptional cases, subject to the approval of the Faculty, special students will be admitted to the Junior and Middle Class, but no special students will be admitted to the Senior Class.

Section 4. All candidates for admission to the Law School shall make application in the form prescribed by the Faculty.

Rule II
Classification of Students

Section 1. A regular student is one who has complied with the entrance requirements prescribed in Section 1 of Rule I and who is pursuing the full course of study prescribed by the Faculty.

Only regular students are eligible for the degree of Bachelor of Laws.

Section 2. A special student is one who is not pursuing the full course of study prescribed by the Faculty, or who has not complied with all the entrance requirements prescribed in Section 1, Rule I.

Section 3. A student may be permitted to change his status from that of a regular student to that of a special student upon making application in writing to the Faculty; but no student shall be permitted to make such a change and at the same time advance to a higher class unless at the time he applies he has satisfactorily passed all examinations given to his class up to that date.

Section 4. A special student who has taken the full course of study prescribed by the Faculty, and who has satisfactorily passed all examinations, may be permitted to change his status to that of a regular student at any time before entering the Senior class, upon making application in writing to the Faculty, provided he has satisfactorily complied with all the entrance requirements of regular students.

Rule III
Degrees, Promotions and Conditions

Section 1. On completing a year's work satisfactorily, a regular student of the Junior or Middle Class will be advanced to the next higher class and a regular student of the Senior Class will be granted the degree of Bachelor of Laws.

Section 2. The minimum percentage required for passing every examination shall be 60%. To complete a year's work satisfactorily, a regular student shall be required to pass every examination, make a general average of 75%, and to attend 80% of the lectures and recitations of the year.

Section 3. A regular student who has failed to pass not more than two examinations given during the year may continue with his class, provided he satisfactorily passes re-examinations in the subjects in which he is deficient before the first day of the next school year, and has attained, after such re-examinations, a general average of 75% for the entire year.

Section 4. A student who fails to pass examinations in three or more subjects during the year, or who fails to remove conditions, as provided in Section 3 of this rule, shall not be permitted to advance with his class, either as a regular or special student, but may take over again the work of the same year.

Section 5. In order to be advanced to a higher class, a special student shall be required to comply with the provisions of Sections 2 and 3 of this Rule with reference to required grades in the subjects which he is pursuing.

Rule IV
Tuition and Fees

Section 1. Before matriculating, all students must pay a matriculation fee of $10.00.

Section 2. The tuition fee required of all students in the Law School shall be $110 per annum, payable $60 in advance at the beginning of the first term and $50 at the beginning of the second term. If the tuition for the entire year is paid in advance, a reduction of $5 on the total payment will be made.

Section 3. Tuition fees will be remitted only in cases where students are prevented by sickness or necessary absence from completing the studies of the term, and in no case will more than one-half of the fee for the term be remitted.

Section 4. All students taking the law degree must pay a graduation fee of $10 before Commencement Day.

Section 5. Special examinations shall be allowed only on cause shown and a fee of $5 shall be paid for each special or re-examination.

Section 6. Students whose tuition or fees are in arrears 30 days will be denied the privileges of their classes.

Rule V
Conduct of Examinations

Section 1. All examinations shall be conducted according to the Honor System under the direction of the student body.

Section 2. The maximum time allowed for examinations shall be two and one-half hours.

CHAPTER
T·H·R·E·E
1915-1924

At a faculty meeting held on May 25, 1916, the faculty adopted the following resolution:

> That the attention of the Trustees be called to the desirability of granting Master's degrees to certain members of the Faculty of the Law School who have some years of service and do not possess that or a similar law degree.

The faculty also discussed the matter of acquiring new quarters for the Law School. On motion, it was resolved that the authorities of the University be requested to secure the proposed quarters in the B.F. Jones Law Building, or some other equally satisfactory location. After twenty years, the law students continued to use the facilities of the County Law Library since the law school had no separate library. The faculty discussed the question of acquiring a law library in accordance with the rules of the AALS, but it was resolved that the current policy regarding a law library be continued.

The tuition for the academic year 1915-1916 was increased to $150 per annum—$80 at the time of registration and $70 at the beginning of the second semester. A graduation fee of $10 was also added.

At a meeting of the faculty held on September 20, 1916, the committee assigned to look into the matter of suitable quarters for the school suggested that quarters be secured in the Union Arcade Building, if satisfactory arrangements could be made. The committee was given full power in the matter of securing more commodious and suitable quarters.

The faculty had earlier added as a requirement for admission to the law school the completion of two years of college work. The following resolution was passed by a majority of one vote in explanation of the two-year college requirement:

> RESOLVED, that in the interpretation and enforcement of the rule requiring two years of college work as a prerequisite to admission to the Law School, for the year 1916-17, it is the sense of the Faculty that concession by made as follows:
>
> That, in order to treat with the utmost fairness students who have been preparing to enter the School of Law, and who only lately learned

*Delta Kappa Nu charter
(forerunner of Delta Theta Phi) · 1916*

Top Row (left to right): Ira Houck, "Gal" Galbraith, Browny, Ed Newlin, Harry Richardson, Carson.
Middle Row: Jno. J. Bane, Dick Ahlers, Chas. Christler, Bill Campbell, Norwood Nelson, W.McN.,
*   George Hosack.*
Bottom Row: "Hans" Brinker, Ralph Miller, "Wick Wickersham, "Bob" Wettach, G. Scott Woods,
*   "Zinzy" Zinsmaster, "Stan" Douglass.*

of the change in admission requirements and not, therefore, prepared
to offer the two years of college work, such students be admitted with
conditions as follows:

1. For the student applying in 1916-1917 one college year, that he complete
    the second college year before he is advanced to the Middle standing.

2. For the student applying for admission in 1917-1918, lacking both
    college years,

    (1) That he complete at least thirty-eight credits of college work
         before he begins the work of the first year in the Law School.

    (2) That the remaining twenty-two credits be completed before the
         student is advanced to the Middle standing.

(3) After the year 1917-18, every student must offer at admission the full two years of college work.

Reasons for the above actions are:

1. The brief notice of the change, the first announcement being made in the Bulletin in the spring of 1915.

2. The inchoate right of the student who has advanced in his course of preparation under the old rule, and who may not be able to meet the larger requirement.

3. The obligation on the part of the University to be generously fair in all its dealings with the constituency it serves.

4. The concession made does not change the requirement of two years of college work, but for the present does extend the time during which the student may meet the conditions.

The graduation in 1916 was a landmark occasion for the law school. The first women to graduate were members of the Class of 1916. There were three in number—Marie Grace Clark Gallegher, Lily Virginia Pickersgill and Sara Mathilde Soffel. Ms. Soffel was the only one to have completed the full course of study in this law school.

Ms. Soffel was to later distinguish herself by being the first woman elected to a judgeship in Pennsylvania when she was elected a Judge of the Court of Common Pleas of Allegheny County. Forty years later, the Law Day Banquet of April 17, 1962 was held in Judge Soffel's honor. Professor Harry Kalven, Jr. of the University of Chicago Law School was the speaker.

The enrollment in 1916-17 was 149. This dropped to 61 the following year.

The faculty, at a meeting on October 5, 1916, moved to file a protest against the Executive Committee of the AALS with reference to the school's library situation. It was moved that the Dean appoint a library committee and that this committee be authorized and directed to purchase books for the Law School library during the current year to an amount not exceeding the sum of $5,000, appropriated for that purpose by the Trustees of the University.

Sara Mathilde Soffel.

Two months later, the faculty adopted a resolution stating it to be the sense of the faculty that:

(1) there be introduced into the faculty some full-time teachers;

(2) that it be the aim of the school to eventually have lectures during the morning hours as well as the afternoon; and

(3) that a building be secured for the law school as soon as possible.

It was a common practice in the early years of the school for the Chancellor of the University to attend law school faculty meetings. At the meeting of January 23, 1917, he spoke appreciatively of the work and record of the Law School.

Judson Adams Crane was hired by the Trustees as the first full-time instructor for 1917-1918 at a salary of $3,500 per year.

Judson Crane, a native of Massachusetts, graduated from Brown University and Harvard Law School, where he received his baccalaureate degree as well as an S.J.D. degree. He practiced law in Boston from 1909 to 1911. He was a professor of law at Pei Yang University, Tientsin, China, 1911 to 1914 and a professor of law at George Washington University, 1915-17. He served as a professor of law at the University of Pittsburgh from 1917 to 1954. He was Dean of the school from 1942 to 1949 and Acting Dean from February 1 to September 1, 1952. He later served as a Professor of Law at Hastings College of Law, University of California, from 1954 to his death. He was a visiting professor at the University of Southern California, 1928-29. Dean Crane authored several casebooks and textbooks, as well as law review articles. In addition to being the first full-time faculty member, he engineered the move of the school after World War II to develop a full-time faculty. He made many valuable contributions to the school.

I shall always hold fond memories of Dean Crane. He hired me as an instructor in law after interviewing me during my senior year at Yale Law School. I looked upon him as my mentor and role model. I had many discussions with him, dealing with the laws of corporations, agency and partnership.

Mrs. Lindsay, who served as Registrar from 1922 until her retirement in 1960, once said of Judson Crane:

Mrs. Marie G. Lindsay.

He came from Harvard—rough and ready. He put me in mind of Teddy Roosevelt. He was a good instructor, but the students called him 'the bulldog.' He handled the special lectures series. He was very good at that. Anyone of note that was in town he would drag over to talk to the students. He was an irascible man. In his later days, I made the mistake of telling someone that he'd mellowed, and he took me to task for that.

The majority of the law students in Pittsburgh not only attended classes but also spent a portion of the day in the law offices in which they were registered as students of law. This enabled students to become acquainted not only with the practice routine but also with the men with whom they would associate in the practice of law.

During this time, there continued to be a feeling that the law school deserved more desirable quarters. Judge J. J. Miller of the Orphans' Court, in defense of the law school, said that "the maintenance of the school was a labor of love; certainly the money that was in it was no object. . . . Others will say for it, and I need not, that it has always been a first class law school." He added that the trustees of the University were not able as yet, they had not come around yet, "to provide the Law School with the facilities which are desirable."

A. Marshall Thompson, Esquire, reported in 1918 that he expected to sail shortly for France to do YMCA work with the American Army during the period of the war. During Mr. Thompson's absence, Mr. Crane was appointed to serve as Secretary pro tem.

On April 24, 1918, the faculty adopted the policy that students joining the military or naval service after April 1, 1918 and who were in good standing and regular in attendance up to the time when it is necessary for them to leave, shall be given time credit for the year, and with the approval of their instructors, credit for courses as follows:

Law Students in the Service in 1917.

Seniors and middlers, unconditionally, and Juniors, provided they subsequently pass examinations on the work of the present year, and return and satisfactorily complete the second year.

In 1919, the faculty recommended to the trustees that a new full-time teacher be appointed, and that, beginning in the fall of 1920, at least three years of college or the equivalent thereof be an entrance requirement. It was agreed that the two year college requirement be waived in the case of students of mature age, apparently fitted to study law, whose college course was interrupted by military or naval service, provided they apply for entrance within one year from the date of discharge. At the faculty meeting of September 23, 1919, the following resolution was adopted on the death of Judge Samuel S.S. Mehard, one of the members of the first faculty of the school.

In Memory of Judge Mehard

The members of the Faculty of the Pittsburgh Law School are deeply grieved by reason of the death of Judge Samuel Smiley Mehard, which occurred on Wednesday, September 17th, 1919, at his old home in Mercer, Pa.

When the Pittsburgh Law School was organized in the month of October, 1895, Judge Mehard was one of the eight men who then composed the Faculty of the School. He continued in the active work of instruction in this School from the day of its organization until his last illness. During that interval of almost a quarter of a century he lectured upon the subjects of contracts, bailments, sales and part of the time upon insurance. He took an active part in an advisory way also in shaping the policy of the school and in determining the character of its curriculum and above all, in his influence upon the Faculty and Students alike in a measure which is beyond our power to express.

The successive generations of students at this School and the young men of this Bar have never had a more ardent champion or sympathetic friend than Judge Mehard, and the students who sat at his feet during these years have had the advantage of instruction from a man of broad knowledge, inspiring character and deep sympathy.

Teaching in this school was for Judge Mehard a labor of love and a constant exposition of the pure and undefiled Christian principles which controlled all his actions.

We mourn the death of Judge Mehard and we miss the presence today of a sincere friend of us all.

At a faculty meeting on November 26, 1919 at the Duquense Club, A. Marshall Thompson, Esquire, announced the plans to move the law school quarters to the Chamber of Commerce Building. He also proposed that the entrance requirement be raised to four years of college work and a degree. The matter was tabled. A report of a committee on revising the grading system made a report. The report was adopted, to go into operation for the current year's work. It provided:

1. 60% required to pass in all subjects, and a general average of 65%.

2. In computing the general average, credit to be given to courses according to approximate number of hours.

3. Credit to be given to review courses according to approximate number of hours.

4. Students to receive grades in each subject by letter only, and grade of average both by letter and percentage as follows:

> Below 60 . . . . E
> 60-64 . . . . D
> 65-74 C
> 75-84 . . . . B
> 85-100 . . . . A

5. Give cum laude degree to students having an average of "A."

6. Publish in annual catalogue list of degrees conferred, including those cum laude.

On February 12, 1920, the faculty approved a resolution that, beginning with the school year 1921-22, a bachelor's degree from an approved institution be required as a condition of entrance to the law school. At the same meeting, a discussion was had of a third full-time faculty member. The time for classes was changed as follows:

> First Class   — 1:30-2:20
> Second Class   — 2:20-3:10
> Third Class   — 3:15-4:05
> Fourth Class   — 4:05-4:55

A. Marshall Thompson, Esquire, succeeded Judge John Shafer as Dean in 1920. Tuition was raised to $210 a year, $110 being payable at registration for the first semester and $100 at the beginning of the second semester.

Mrs. Marie G. Lindsay was employed by the School in 1922, originally as Law Librarian. A year later, she was given the position of Registrar, which she held for the next thirty-nine years, until her retirement. Over the years, I have been amazed at the number of graduates who told me of kindnesses she showed to them at various times while they were students.

After her retirement, she ended up in Kane Hospital. My wife and I would visit her. After her death, I attended her funeral. There were four of us present, two of them her relatives. While she had her critics, there is no doubt that she was a very loyal and dedicated employee. She loved the law school.

A. Marshall Thompson.

For the school year 1920-1921, the school was moved to the tenth floor of the Chamber of Commerce Building. This new location included a law library. Dr. Crane was elected Secretary of the Faculty, succeeding the recently installed dean.

In 1921, Chancellor McCormick, who was retiring, wrote this letter to the Director of the Carnegie Foundation in New York:

> "The School of Law of the University has made very remarkable progress in these last years. Not only have we permanent quarters for the school, but we have three full-time men, and have advanced our entrance requirements to four years of college work."

At a meeting held on the evening of April 19, 1921 at the home of Dean Thompson, the faculty approved the effort to cooperate with the University of Pennsylvania in publishing a law review.

During the last year, the Faculty had, on more than one occasion, discussed the formation of an alumni organization. To that end, Mr. Garfield Houston undertook to organize a committee to work on the matter.

By the school year 1921-22, the school had three legal fraternities—Phi Delta Phi, Delta Theta Phi and Phi Delta Delta—plus the Shafer Law Club. It also had three full-time faculty members.

In September, 1922, when Marie G. Lindsay was hired as the Law Librarian, the Library had more than 5,000 volumes. Two years later, she also became the Registrar of the School.

The School received accreditation by the American Bar Association on August 28, 1923, when the ABA began to accredit law schools.

For the academic year 1924-25, the time of afternoon classes was changed to 2 until 4:00 p.m. Also, Marie Lindsay was assigned the additional title of Registrar, a title she retained until her retirement.

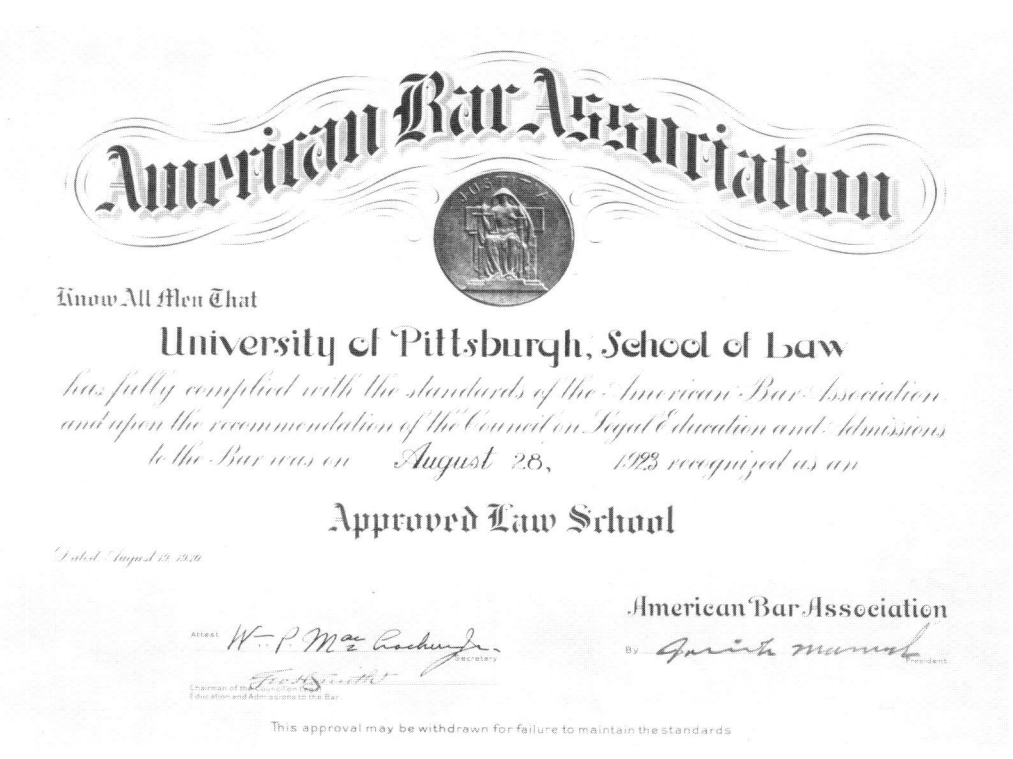

American Bar Association

Know All Men That

University of Pittsburgh, School of Law

has fully complied with the standards of the American Bar Association and upon the recommendation of the Council on Legal Education and Admissions to the Bar was on August 28, 1923 *recognized as an*

Approved Law School

Dated August 19, 1920

American Bar Association

Attest W.P. Mac Cracken Jr. *Secretary*

Chairman of the Committee on Legal Education and Admissions to the Bar

By *President*

This approval may be withdrawn for failure to maintain the standards

It is interesting to note that at a faculty meeting held February 15, 1924 the matter of a J.D. degree for graduates of the Law School was discussed and referred to a committee. There is no record in later meetings in which the committee reported. In any event, the idea was not implemented at that time or for about forty more years.

At a faculty meeting on March 19, 1925, the matter of the new space acquired in the Chamber of Commerce Building was discussed. The faculty at the same meeting gave permission for the establishment of a Jewish fraternity.

For 1925-1926, tuition was raised to $212.50, $112.50 due at the start of the school year and $100 at the start of the second semester. The school also established a $10 diploma fee.

I had a delightful interview with John D.S. Truxall of the Class of 1925. Mr. Truxall is one of the outstanding benefactors of the school. He has had a most interesting career at the bar. He told me that he taught Latin at

John D.S. Truxall.

Shadyside Day School and at Pittsburgh Academy in the evenings when he was young.

When he entered the school, there was no requirement that the applicant hold

a Bachelor's degree. He pointed out that the faculty, composed almost entirely of successful lawyers and judges, was an inspiration to the students. They were persons who had a great love for the law and were masters at communication of it to the students.

In discussing the individual faculty members, he pointed out that J. Garfield Houston, Esquire, was outstanding, as was James Smith Cristy, Esquire. He reminisced about John Taylor Duff, Esquire, later a judge. Mr. Duff taught conveyancing and common pleas practice. He was especially noted for his humor in the classroom. John Grier Buchanan, Esquire, taught taxation and constitutional law.

Another faculty member that Mr. Truxall remembered well was "Colonel" Hawkins, who taught Pennsylvania Real Estate. He was a partner in the firm of Dalzell, Fisher & Hawkins and was an excellent teacher. He published a set of notes which were a valuable source for practicing lawyers.

CHAPTER
F·O·U·R
1925-1934

After the school's move to the Chamber of Commerce Building, it established its own law library. In the fall of 1925, a reading room was opened off the library. Almost immediately difficulty arose when the Evening School of the University informed the Law School that it was scheduling classes for this reading room four nights a week. The faculty instructed the Dean to discuss the problem with the Chancellor, pointing out that unless the school was given the exclusive use of the room, it became useless space for the law school.

I interviewed Ralph Demmler, Esquire, '28, and William H. Webb, Esquire, '29, regarding their recollections of law school. Following that joint interview, Mr. Demmler shared with me an excerpt from a family history he wrote some years ago. Since it well summarized the sentiments I gained from these two distinguished alumni, I am quoting the excerpt here:

> Return to real life at the end of that summer was like a plunge into cold water. My father put me to work at Demmler Brothers at my old clerking job for the three weeks before classes started at Pitt Law School. Then when I did start law school I learned quickly that I was embarked on a course of study and a way of life entirely different from college. Moreover, living at home after four years at Allegheny represented a considerable change from the lifestyle of a fraternity house. The first few months of studying law were a period of intellectual confusion. It was at least eight weeks before I began to gain some perspective—the relationship of legal procedure to substantive law, the conceptual difference between a relationship governed by law, like marriage or parenthood, and a relationship governed by contract, the difference between a tort and a crime, the relationship of causation to legal liability. But by Christmas of the first year things began to clear up.
>
> Some of the law students were old friends of mine and I made some new ones. Bill Dale, Ted McQuiston (old Allegheny roommates) and I soon teamed up for study and occasional social life with Russell O'Malley from Scranton (later President of the Pennsylvania Bar Association) who

reflected in his character and manner the discipline of his Jesuitical undergraduate training at Fordham University, Wray Connolly, an extrovert with quick wit and more common sense than deep learning, and Don England, a Bucknell Phi Gam who questioned everyone's conclusion about anything.

Generally speaking, until Catherine came back to Pittsburgh in 1927 after finishing at Hood, I had precious little social life during the years in law school. The school was in the Chamber of Commerce Building in downtown Pittsburgh. We studied all morning, went to class all afternoon and studied all evening. About twice a week a group of us would go to a movie around the corner from the school over the noon hour. We had moot courts within and among the legal fraternities. Those were held in the evening and there would invariably be a dinner beforehand. It was a pretty constricted existence.

There is an old saying that in the first year of law school you are scared to death, in the second year worked to death and in the third year bored to death. There is some truth to the statement. However, the boredom of my senior year was eliminated by the fact that Catherine was back in Pittsburgh. We could see each other over weekends and occasionally during the week. The boredom was replaced by impatience—to start practicing law instead of going to class, to earn a living, to get married. I had the good fortune in the summers after my first and second years of law school to have a job at $150 a month as a claim adjuster for Hartford Accident and Indemnity Company. That enabled me to apply some of the law of negligence which I had learned in law school and it provided training in negotiating, an important aspect of a lawyer's work but something which is learned through on-the-job training not through lectures in law school.

Pitt Law School in the late 1920's was a Pennsylvania, as distinguished from a national, law school. The record of its graduates in passing the Pennsylvania bar examinations was excellent. It had several full-time professors: Judson Crane, trained at Harvard, who was as good and as tough as any Harvard Law School professor whom I have audited in subsequent years; George Jarvis Thompson, later of Cornell Law School, who drilled the law of contracts into our heads principle by principle in the manner of an English schoolmaster; Laylin K. James, later to become a picturesque fixture at Michigan Law School, trained at the Cravath firm in New York, who had one tone of voice—loud—and who was impatient with anyone who did not grasp on first hearing the more esoteric concepts of corporation law. Then there was Colonel Dick Hawkins, a hard drinking patrician, son of the first judge of the Orphans Court of Allegheny County. Hawkins was opposed to prohibition and opposed to any legal rationalizations supporting efforts to enforce the same. Having once been a trial lawyer defending negligence cases, he was opposed to plaintiffs in general. He did not teach by asking questions in the manner of Crane nor was he precise like Thompson. He would illustrate principles by stories: "Did I ever tell you of the scandal of Scottdale?" And then would follow the tale of Grandfather Overholt deeding property to Henry Clay Frick to keep it safe from Overholt's creditors and Frick's successful opposition to Overholt's suit to get the property back when the financial crisis passed. The principle is that a person must accept the consequences of his own attempted fraud.

Most of our teachers, however, were local lawyers and judges—all of them effective and thorough. President Judge John J. Miller of the Orphans Court, Judges Dick Martin and Elder Marshall of Common Pleas Court, Dean, later Judge, A. Marshall Thompson, John G. Buchanan, J. Garfield Houston, John D. McIntyre and Bill Eckert. Marshall and McIntyre later become partners of Reed Smith. I think that when, in attempting to comply with the requirements of the American Association of Law Schools which reflect the view of the full-time faculty establishment of the national law schools—Pitt Law School curtailed its part-time faculty and augmented its full-time faculty, the quality of both faculty and instruction suffered significantly for a number of years. Fortunately, having built up the hard way a larger full-time faculty, the law school has now achieved both national status and effective instruction.

In February, 1926, the faculty took some interesting actions affecting special students. First, it voted to ask the trustees to raise the fee for special examinations and reexaminations to $10. Second, the faculty voted that special students should be admitted, not over 5% of any one class on admission, only with the consent of the faculty. Special students were defined as persons over 25 years of age and showing a special reason for admission. Third, it was resolved that students applying for admission from colleges of whose standing little was known were admissible only if they were within the upper-third of their respective classes.

One of the graduates in 1927 was Anne X. Alpern. Born in Russia, she was raised in Scenery Hill near Washington, Pennsylvania. At an early age, she was encouraged to become a lawyer by her father, who operated a wholesale hosiery business on Penn

Avenue in downtown Pittsburgh. He was a great admirer of Clarence Darrow because of Darrow's defense of the poor and the unfortunate.

Honorable Anne X. Alpern, '27.

As an undergraduate, she was elected to Phi Beta Kappa. Following graduation, she began her legal career with the firm of Cunningham, Galbreath & Dickson. After practicing a couple of years in the firm, she became an Assistant City Solicitor. Later, she became First Assistant and in 1942 City Solicitor, becoming the first woman solicitor of a major city in the United States. In that capacity, she became the first woman to argue before the Federal Power Commission and the first woman attorney to argue a case before the Pennsylvania Public Utility Commission, which she once labeled "The Public Futility Commission." It was during these years that she became an expert in consumer matters, winning statewide recognition in rate battles before the Public Utility Commission. The electric companies were sometimes the target of her attacks. In one such case, she coined the phrase, "The Overcharge of the Light Brigade." Another of her targets was the Pittsburgh Railways Company.

In 1953, Anne Alpern won both nominations for the Court of Common Pleas and assumed the judgeship in 1954. In 1959, Governor and former Pittsburgh Mayor David L. Lawrence named her the first Commonwealth Attorney General. During her tenure in that office, she led the battle for discount prices for milk sold in gallon jugs, for a Court Administrator plan to speed up state court actions and opened the $500 million art collection at the famed Barnes Museum in suburban Philadelphia to the public, which had been closed to the general public for thirty-eight years.

In 1961, she was named to the Pennsylvania Supreme Court, the first woman to sit on that tribunal. In a bid for election to that court, she was defeated by the Honorable Henry X. O'Brien. Governor Lawrence then appointed her to the seat on the Court of Common Pleas of Allegheny County vacated by the elevation of Judge O'Brien.

Her last and most famous case was "Stop Skybus" in which she halted the Skybus plans by issuing an injunction against the Port Authority of Allegheny County, a decision later reversed by the Pennsylvania Supreme Court.

She served as President of the National Institute of Municipal Law Officers, which presented her with its distinguished service award in 1953. She also served in the House of Delegates of the American Bar Association. In 1952, she was named a Distinguished Daughter of Pennsylvania. Later, she received the Pittsburgh Junior Chamber of Commerce award for distinction in the field of law.

She retired from the bench on January 1, 1974. She died February 2, 1981.

J. Warren Madden, then dean of the West Virginia University Law School, was named a professor of law beginning with the 1927-28 academic year. Laylin K. James was also appointed to the full-time faculty. Following graduation in 1927, Mahlon E. Lewis, a member of the graduating class, was elected the fifth full-time Faculty member. In May, 1927, the School of Law was granted a charter in the Order of the Coif. The Order of the Coif is a national organization which charters local chapters. It is designed to give recognition to graduating law students who have attained superior academic records. A chapter of the Order can elect up to the top ten percent of the graduating class to membership.

Beginning in the fall of 1927, all members of the second year class were required to take a course in legal bibliography. A committee was formed to consider an increase in the number of courses in the curriculum and a change in the number of electives.

Despite the move to the Chamber of Commerce Building, the continued sentiment on the faculty was that the committee on a new building should continue its search.

Beginning in the fall of 1928, classes were conducted from 9:30 a.m. to 4:40 p.m. One interesting practice during this period followed a suggestion of Colonel Hawkins, a member of the faculty. Third year class members who had below 70% average for the previous year were listed in red ink in the professors' roll books, with the urging that such students be called upon for recitation more often.

Charter for the Pittsburgh Chapter of the Order of the Coif.

Class of 1925 Testimonial Dinner in Honor of Judges Richard W. Martin and Elder W. Marshall — PAA — February 13, 1930.

In the fall of 1929, Dr. Bowman, then Chancellor of the University, had the faculty as his guests for a meeting at the Duquesne Club. At that meeting, he mentioned the possibility of providing for law school quarters in the Cathedral of Learning, then under construction. He pointed out that adequate space could be provided for enlargement of the library, and said the matter should be decided by the spring of 1930. A discussion followed, with no action taken.

At a meeting of the faculty on May 22, 1930, it was announced that Professor Madden was granted a leave of absence for the next academic year in order to teach at Stanford Law School. Mr. Steele Gow, Secretary of the Board, who attended the meeting, announced that the faculty had until January 1, 1931 to make a decision regarding a move into the Cathedral of Learning. The faculty, a couple of weeks later, directed the Dean to communicate with the proper authorities its endorsement of Dean Wigmore for the Permanent Court of International Justice.

No further reference to a move to the Cathedral of Learning is found in the minutes of the faculty until February 7, 1936, although it is almost certain that the faculty had given an affirmative response before that time. At a meeting held on that date, it was resolved that the space proposed for the law school in the Cathedral of Learning would be adequate for the present, but that certain details as to partitions and provisions of lockers should be considered.

A eulogy prepared by Garfield Houston, Esquire was presented and adopted at a meeting on September 27, 1930 for Richard Wilson Martin, Judge of the Court of Common Pleas of Allegheny County and Professor of Law in the law school. Judge Martin graduated from the law school in 1904 and joined the faculty in 1911. The eulogy read as follows:

Richard Wilson Martin
1882-1930
Judge of the Common Pleas Court of Allegheny County
Professor of Law, University of Pittsburgh

Richard Wilson Martin was graduated with honors from this law school in 1904. Upon his admission to the Bar, his ability, integrity, and personality soon brought him a large general practice, and he was recognized by his colleagues at the Bar as a well read lawyer and a skilled advocate. His experience was broadened by terms of service as an Assistant District Attorney of Allegheny County, as Solicitor of the City of Pittsburgh, and as a member of the Public Service Commission of Pennsylvania. He was appointed a Judge of the Common Pleas Court of Allegheny County in 1926; and his performance of the duties of that high office so commended him to the lawyers, that, in a referendum of the Bar to endorse candidates for the Bench, he received the highest vote.

He took a keen interest in public affairs and sought both by precept and example to banish the atmosphere of futility and squalor that too largely characterize the political life of our times. He was all the word "gentleman" connotes—a man of honor, of high ideals, of broad and liberal culture, courteous, loyal, sincere.

He was deeply interested in this Law School and was eager to help and guide students and junior members of the Bar. He joined this Faculty in 1911; and at different times taught Criminal Law and Procedure, Partnership, Quasi Contracts, Public Utilities, and Legal Ethics.

Law students will find his professional career an example to imitate, and his all too brief but useful life as a source of inspiration."

The enrollment for 1931-32 numbered 377. This consisted of 102 third year students, 101 second year, 164 first year and 10 unclassified students.

During the depression, since there were no jobs available, parents tried to keep their children in school. The school expanded throughout most of the tenth floor of the Chamber of Commerce Building and started holding classes for the first time in the morning, as well as in the afternoon. Lawyers needed jobs, too, and some joined the faculty part-time.

At a meeting on May 25, 1932, the Curriculum Committee presented a report which was adopted by the faculty. In the first year, Criminal Law was changed to a one-semester course of three hours and Agency was placed in the second semester for three hours. The second year curriculum was retained but Equity II in the second semester was redesignated as "Trusts," and made an elective. In the third year, all courses except Legal Ethics were made electives, but the selection of

Left to right: Charles H. English, Chairman, Pennsylvania State Board of Law Examiners; Honorable R. Heber Dithrich; Dean Hitchler, Dickinson Law School; Dean A. Marshall Thompson.

courses by students was subject to approval of a committee appointed by the Dean.

June 3, 1932, all members of the faculty were admitted to the Order of the Coif. At that same meeting, the Faculty directed Dean Thompson to express to Chancellor Bowman the sentiment of the faculty that it is important for the School of Law to have research assistants to aid in the work being done for the American Law Institute and in the preparation of law books.

ANNUAL BANQUET–SENIOR LAW CLASS.
UNIVERSITY of PITTSBURGH LAW SCHOOL.
FACULTY CLUB,–FEB, 13th, 1930

Senior Class Annual Banquet — Class of 1930 — February 13, 1930.

Members of the Phi Delta Phi — Class of 1932

Front Row: Waltenbaugh, Howell, Marker, Fitch, Sensenich, Downie, Ralston, Brothers, Colonel Hawkins, Allison, Moore, Miller.

Second Row: McIlvaine, McKee, Davidson, Pensyl, Fritchman, Sanders, Gifford, McKenna, Christman, McCaskey.

The results of the Pennsylvania Bar Examination was a topic of discussion by the Faculty from time to time when the Board of Law Examiners would release the results. In a meeting on December 9, 1932, the Dean was authorized to appoint a committee to visit other law schools, examine their methods of admission, academic rules and other matters bearing upon preparation for graduation and bar examinations.

During the academic year 1932-33, there were 362 students in the School—92 third year, 135 second year, 129 first year and 6 unclassified. That number dropped significantly the following year, when the total enrollment was 290—104 third year, 85 second year, 93 first year and 8 unclassified. And in 1934-35, there was a further dramatic drop to 225—68 third year, 57 second year, 89 first year and 11 unclassified. The records fail to disclose any explanation for the enrollment declines. Perhaps one explanation was the effects of the depression being experienced in the nation.

Beginning with the 1934-35 academic year, seniors were given a comprehensive examination.

The Moot Court program, previously a required activity, was made voluntary for the academic year 1933-34. At a faculty meeting held on November 17, 1933, the Honor Board was requested to arrange for a meeting of the student body and to present to them the matter of theft and mutilation of library books.

By 1934, the matter of a law review became a serious topic with the Faculty. While there had been earlier comments about the school having a law review, by June, 1934 the faculty appointed a committee of Professors Putman, Madden and Crane to confer with students on the matter. After a year of study, the faculty approved in principle the establishment of a law review. It was the opinion of the Faculty that the amount of $5 should be allocated from the student activity fee collected.

The University of Pittsburgh Law Review was first issued in March, 1935. The Editor-in-Chief of Volume 1 and Volume 2 was Milton I. Baldinger. Volume 1 contained one issue. Beginning with Volume 2, there were (and still are) four issues to each volume. Harold R. Schmidt was Editor-in-Chief of Volume 3. The amount of $5 was allocated from the student activity fee collected from law students to support the publication of the law review.

Following issuance of Volume 8 of the Law Review during the academic year 1941-1942, the publication suspended operations because of the war. Publication was resumed as Volume 9 in October, 1947. James C. Kuhn, Jr. served as Editor-in-Chief of that volume. It has been published continually since then.

J. John Lawler, University of Texas, was hired for the academic year 1936-37 to replace J. Warren Madden on the Faculty.

CHAPTER
F·I·V·E
1935-1944

In the spring of 1936, the school's lease was up on its space in the Chamber of Commerce Building and the Cathedral of Learning was under construction. The University decided to move the school to Oakland, with quarters in the still uncompleted Cathedral.

From a discussion with C. Bryson Schreiner, '38, I learned that the move wasn't heralded with overwhelming approval. Many of the faculty opposed it because of the difficulty in getting from their offices in downtown Pittsburgh to Oakland for afternoon classes, and the students who commuted by train were inconvenienced because the line terminated downtown. In an interview, Mrs. Lindsay, the then Registrar, once remarked:

> If ever a school had a schedule rigged up to fit a railroad schedule, the law school was it. So many of the students came in from places like Washington, Pennsylvania, and we had to give them time to get from the Union Station. For most of them, their biggest expense was carfare—just the problem of getting to school.

The move to Oakland apparently signaled the end of an era in which the convenience of commuters was a serious consideration.

Other changes also were underway at this time.

An anonymous grading system was instituted with the spring semester examinations in 1937. In those exams, only the first and second year classes used the new system.

The cornerstone in the Commons Room of the Cathedral of Learning was laid on June 4, 1937. The faculty met following that ceremony, and the principal item on the agenda was the presentation by Dr. Crane of a new set of rules for students. After discussion and some minor changes, the new rules were adopted. The records did not disclose the nature of those rules.

At a faculty meeting on June 3, 1938, a resolution was adopted expressing to Professor Madden regret over his resignation from the faculty and wishing him well. It was agreed, at the same meeting, that academic credit be given for law review work as follows: two semester hours credit for work done during the second year and one semester hour for work done during the senior year. The faculty also conditioned election to The Order of the Coif upon willingness to participate in law review work.

Room 1428 in the Cathedral of Learning (the big upperclass room).

Professor Crane conducting a class.

Law students leaving the Cathedral of Learning.

During the 1940s, the School would have several deans. Dean Thompson resigned in 1940, replaced by Eugene Allen Gilmore, who served as dean for two years. Judson Adams Crane became dean in 1942 and served until 1949.

In October, 1940, the first-year class was apportioned among full-time faculty as advisees. It was also agreed that as soon as possible all recitations, both morning and afternoon, should begin on the hour and close at ten of the hour. It is obvious from the minutes of the faculty during this period that great concern was felt for first year students. For example, at the October 14, 1940 meeting, it was agreed that each instructor having a first year course would, between then and Christmas, give a written quiz either during the regular class hour or some other period, and that the results of the quiz be made the basis of a discussion with the class or individual members thereof concerning the character of the work being done.

At a meeting on November 15, 1940, it was the consensus of the faculty that a schedule of norms should be adopted indicating a desirable maximum of grades of each classification. Dean Gilmore requested Professors Blackburn and Lawler to prepare such a schedule. A discussion took place about carrying over excess credits from one year to another and the minimum hours required for any semester. It was agreed that the following rules should govern:

Eugene Allen Gilmore.

Judson Adams Crane.

(1) That the practice of carrying over excess credits from one year to another be discontinued.

(2) With respect to the Senior class, excess credits not to exceed three may be used to satisfy the requirement of the total necessary credits for graduation but not to reduce the minimum number of classroom hours required each semester, as specified below.

(3) That for the present Senior class a minimum of not fewer then eleven classroom hours be required each semester.

(4) Credit for Law Review work may be allowed as follows: in the third year, one credit applicable to the first or second semester at the option of the student; in the second year, two credits, both applicable in one semester or one each semester. Credits for Law Review work may

Senior Class — Class of 1936 — April 1936.

Michael Hanna, Carl Punzak, Dean Gilmore.

be counted in computing the minimum number of classroom hours required each semester.

(5) Members of the present third year class who are carrying during the first semester of this year more classroom hours than the minimum prescribed may reduce their classroom schedule for the second semester but not below the requirement for graduation.

(6) All the work of the first year is required for graduation; in addition, 26 credits in the second year and 26 credits in the third year.

(7) In order to count a semester for full time credit, not fewer than 12 hours of classroom work are to be carried except for the present third year class, as noted above. Not more than 14 classroom hours may be carried in any one semester without the written approval of the Dean.

While a discussion took place in the faculty meeting of December 3, 1940 as to whether the grade on the final examination should be based on the written examination alone or whether class work, class participation, interim quizzes and written work should be taken into account, no decision was made at that meeting. At the next meeting, two weeks later, in affirming the anonymous grading system, the faculty agreed that the grade on the exam shall be the final grade. To the present, where there is a written final examination, it alone is the basis for the final grade in the course. No student was eligible to take the final examination in a course if he had attended less than 80% of the classroom hours.

One of today's problems for policymakers, smoking, also caused difficulty more than fifty years ago. Initially, the law school encompassed floors 14 to 16 of the Cathedral. Later, the 16th floor was vacated and parts of 13 were occupied. At the time of the move to the new building, the law school occupied floors 15, 14, 13, 12 and a room on the fifth floor. No smoking was allowed on the 15th floor, except in the law review office. Smoking was permitted on the 16th floor and on the 14th floor, except in the classrooms.

By this time, war clouds were beginning to appear on the horizon. The draft had begun. At a meeting of the faculty held March 3, 1941, it was agreed that the following statement should be issued in the view of the national emergency:

> During the academic year of 1941-42, and longer if necessary, the faculty will endeavor, so far as possible, to arrange the program of instruction and examinations so that no student shall suffer a loss of academic standing by reason of service in the forces of the United States. To this end, mid-year examinations will be held in 1941-42 in all courses running through the year. Final examinations covering the second half year in such courses will be given at the end of the academic year. Weight will

Class of 1940 dinner.

Dean Thompson discussing a case with students.

Library in the Cathedral of Learning.

be given to the grade received on the mid-year examination in determining the final grade in any year course. Examinations in semester courses will be given at the end of the semester in which the course is scheduled.

A student leaving the school to enter the military forces of the United States may return to the school in any succeeding year to continue his courses from the point where they were interrupted. If he leaves the school between the mid-year and the final June examinations, he will need to take examinations upon his return only upon the work of the second half year in his courses.

Modifications were made in the admission rules. Paragraph 1 was modified to read:

Candidates for admission to the School of Law are required to submit evidence of having received a Bachelor's Degree upon the completion of a four-year course in a college or university approved by the faculty.

Paragraph 2 was modified to read as follows:

Admission is subject to the approval of the faculty. Any applicant whose record does not indicate sufficient aptitude, achievement, or academic training to pursue the study of law successfully may be denied admission.

Judd Poffinberger, Dean Eugene Allen Gilmore, William J. Copeland.

Marjorie Matson, Genevieve Blatt and Mary Jo Lippert performing at their class dinner in 1937.

Professor Judson Crane, Marjorie Matson and Carl Brandt.

The 14th Floor hallway (looking toward the Dean's office.)

At a meeting on March 24, 1941, the faculty agreed that the examination schedule should be available at the opening of the academic year to benefit the students as they elect courses.

The international situation continued to alter law school policy. On May 13, 1941, the faculty approved the following statement:

In order to reduce to a minimum the loss of school time resulting from service in the armed forces of the United States arising as the result of the officially declared unlimited national emergency, the Faculty of the School of Law recommend the following changes in the calendar and in the arrangement of courses, beginning with the academic year 1941-42. These will continue in effect until the termination of the present emergency and so long thereafter as may be necessary to enable students returning to the School to re-establish themselves in their former positions.

The academic year is divided into four terms instead of two semesters but the outside limits of the calendar and the holiday and recess periods correspond approximately to the general University calendar. Each term consists of approximately eight weeks of classroom work, exclusive of examination periods and holidays. The weekly minimum of work devoted to each course has been doubled, although the total weekly load of each student remains substantially the same. Under this plan no course extends longer than two terms, and some courses extend for only one term. Existing year courses are converted into two term courses. Existing semester courses are converted into one term courses. In two term courses, each term is independent and separate examinations are given for each term. Passing a satisfactory examination given at the end of each term insures credit for the work completed that term, whether the work be in a one term course or in a two term course.

Studying in the Law Library in the Cathedral.

Judge Elder Marshal teaching a class.

A group of students coming to classes in the Cathedral.

Library in the Cathedral of Learning.

George Davis, Marion Kamin (Finkelhor), A. Knox Harper studying in the Law Library.

Students arguing a moot court case before Honorable William McNaugher, Albert C. Hirsch, Esquire and Wayne Theophilus, Esquire.

Bar Exam time.

These proposed calendar changes and curricular re-adjustments do not make any change in the existing requirements for admission to the School nor in the requirements for graduation. All the existing regulations regarding attendance, classroom work, scholarship, examinations, and credits remain in force.

There is annexed hereto a detailed statement showing calendar changes and curricular adjustments. Consistent with these changes and adjustments, tuition in the School of Law will be based upon the term instead of the semester; that is, $75 the term rather than $150 the semester. If it is necessary for the student to leave school during a term, the tuition will be pro rated and, upon the student's return, he will be given credit for the unused portion of such term tuition. A student who leaves during a term to enter the military service of the United States may re-enter upon completion of his service at the point where his work was interrupted.

The existing matriculation fee of $5, the late registration fee of $5, and the graduation fee of $10 remain as heretofore.

On June 2, 1941, the faculty proposed a summer session, with a tuition of $150, to be offered only if there are at least twenty-four full session registrations, such registrations to be completed and satisfactory arrangements regarding tuition payments made on or prior to June 9, 1941. This was designed to enable students facing entry into the military the opportunity to attempt to complete their studies more rapidly. Approximately thirty students registered for the session beginning on June 16 and extending through September 11. The courses offered were: Taxation, Federal Judiciary, Evidence and Corporations.

Professor Blackburn conducts a seminar in trusts. Small group discussion around the table is an effective method of law teaching. Faculty members divide large classes into such groups.

Professor John Lawler conducts a class in Room 1418 in the Cathedral of Learning.

Professor J. Putman meeting with students.

In October, the faculty concluded that the school should administer an aptitude test and used materials prepared by the University of Iowa. This decision followed a practice that was beginning to develop in American law schools. Professors Blackburn and Crane were appointed to conduct the examinations.

While there was a no-smoking rule in effect, the minutes of the faculty indicate that smoking in the classrooms was continuing to be a problem.

In December, the dean and full-time faculty considered the status of seniors who enter the armed forces before fully completing their degree requirements. The Bar Examiners had indicated they would recommend to the Supreme Court admission without examination for students who by reason of enlistment or draft were prevented from taking the Bar Examination and who had been recommended for graduation by the law faculty. In the light of that information, the faculty adopted principles to be followed in recommending students for the Bachelor of Laws degree:

> The Faculty of the School of Law will recommend for graduation students who would normally graduate at the end of January, 1942, who, before completing the January examinations, are actually inducted into the armed services as a result of draft or enlistment, provided they have a satisfactory record to the date of their leaving and have continued to do their work satisfactorily until they are required to leave for immediate entry into service.

Norman Landy, Paul L. Friedman and Carl "Pete" Brandt performing at their graduation party.

By January, 1942, a month after the bombing of Pearl Harbor, the war's impact on the law school became ever more evident. Courses began to be omitted. Law arguments were discontinued for the time being. The faculty recommended to the administration and trustees a plan for the acceleration of the law school course and certain modifications in pre-law requirements.

When Judson Adams Crane became Dean in 1942, the University indicated that overtime pay would be given for the slight overloading of some faculty due to the reduced teaching schedule of Dean Crane.

The faculty voted to require attendance at the May 31, 1944 graduation exercises for those residing in Allegheny County on that date. Those outside the county had the option of attending.

The war years were critical in the history of the school. The enrollment had been greatly reduced and the school could have faced temporary closure. The end of the war was a seminal event for the law school because it marked the beginning of a new era which would see an expansion of the full-time faculty and a wider geographical distribution of students, both as to residence and as to undergraduate education. This was accomplished through the leadership of Deans Crane and Nutting.

The Class of 1938 — 50th Reunion

Front Row (l to r): Daniel B. Dixon, William A. Herd, Jr., August A. Iurlano, Arnold D. Wilner, Howard O. Husband, Wayne S. Luce, Alexander H. Lindsay, C. Bryson Schreiner.
Second Row (l to r): Solomon Abrams, Frank S. Lucente, Merle Howard Hildebrand, Joseph Solomon, John M. Duff, John P. Roche, Saul Weisberg, Leroy L. Lewis.

CHAPTER
S·I·X
1945-1954

After the war, the law school hummed with activity. Men who had been called into the service were returning to complete their legal studies. Others who now had the G.I. Bill as a means of funding began their studies in the school. The end of the war also signaled a significant change in the faculty makeup in the school.

Prior to World War II, the full-time faculty was very small. Part-time faculty of lawyers and judges rounded out the faculty, which taught a limited curriculum. Following the war, the school embarked on a new policy of manning the basic law school curriculum with full-time faculty members.

To accommodate returning servicemen who had partially completed their studies and those about to begin their law school careers, the school admitted students in both September and January. Further, there was a summer session to permit an acceleration of the law school program. Students were completing their requirements for the degree at various times during the year—January, June and August—depending upon when they entered the school and whether or not they accelerated their studies.

While the classes entering following the war were relatively large, considering the very limited amount of space occupied by the school on the fifteenth, fourteenth, and thirteenth floors in the Cathedral of Learning, the attrition rate academically was high, reaching almost 50% in at least a couple of classes.

It would not be until the sixties, when the entrance requirements were elevated, that there would be a dramatic drop in the attrition rate.

In October, 1946, the faculty voted to set the matriculation deposit at $15, payable when the student's application was accepted. This sum would not be refundable but credited to the tuition if the student actually registered. At a meeting on December 10, 1946, proposed amendments to the articles of association of the Association of American Law Schools were discussed. Delegates from this law school were instructed to oppose two proposals. One was a proposed requirement that a library expenditure of $20 per year per full-time student and $15 per part-time student in excess of 125 students be made. The other was a proposed amendment to require that in no case shall the number of full-time teachers be fewer than one for every 50 full-time students.

During this period, discussions were begun concerning the resumption of publication of the University of Pittsburgh Law Review, which had been suspended during the war.

Dean Crane appointed a committee to consider the problem, to report a plan of resumption of publication, and to prepare a draft of an announcement.

The lighting arrangements in the law school were also a topic of discussion, culminating in the installation of better lighting in the classrooms and the law library.

A new set of rules supplementing those in the law school bulletin, distributed to prospective students, was promulgated and adopted July 23, 1947, effective September 15, 1947. These rules were as follows:

I. A student who has been neither readmitted nor advanced on condition and who, in a term [a semester or a summer session] passes every course in which he is examined and makes a weighted average of not less than 70 is advanced unconditionally.

II. Exclusion of students.

A student shall be excluded from the Law School if in any term:

(a) Having passed all courses in which he is examined, he has a weighted average of less than 69,

(b) He fails more than one course,

(c) He fails one course and his weighted average in all courses in which he has made a passing grade during such term is less than 72, or

Mrs. Marie Lindsay in the Main Office of the law school in the Cathedral of Learning with the school secretaries.

(d) He fails to meet any condition imposed upon him under Rule V.

III. Advancement on Condition.

A student shall be permitted to advance on condition if in any term:

(a) He has received a passing grade in all courses in which he is examined and his weighted average in such courses is less than 70 but not less than 69, or

(b) He fails a course but is not excluded under Rule II(c).

IV. Readmission of Students.

A student who has been excluded from the Law School under Rule II may be readmitted:

(a) If he petitions the faculty in writing, setting forth the reasons why he failed to do satisfactory work and the reasons why he believes he will do satisfactory work if readmitted, and

(b) If the faculty concludes that the exclusion was caused by factors beyond the control of the student which have been eliminated and that the student has the will and capacity to do satisfactory work in the future.

V. Conditions Applicable to Students Advanced on Condition or Readmitted after Exclusion.

A student who is advanced on condition or who is readmitted after exclusion shall

(a) Thereafter pass all courses undertaken and shall maintain a weighted average of at least 70 for all courses taken in any term, and

(b) Comply with any other condition or requirement imposed by the faculty, including, but not limited to, the requirement that the student retake or stand reexamination in any designated course or courses.

VI. Second Examinations.

When a student is required or permitted to take a second examination under these rules, the grade made on the second examination shall be the final grade in the course and shall be treated as a grade made in the term in which the examination was first taken.

VII.   Permission to Students to Withdraw from a Course or Courses.

The Dean may, in his discretion, permit a student to withdraw from any course or courses before taking the examination therein, subject to such conditions as he may impose.

VIII.   Permission to Take an Examination When the Regular Examination is not Taken.

(a)   Each student is required to take the regular examination in each course for which he is registered, unless excused by the Dean. An unexcused failure to take any examination is regarded as a failure in the course.

(b)   A student who fails to take an examination because of extraordinary circumstances not involving fault on his part and who desires permission to take an examination in the course shall notify the Dean in writing, setting forth the reasons for such failure and requesting permission to take the examination. If the Dean concludes that permission should be granted, he may permit the student to take the examination when next regularly given or, in special circumstances, at some other time.

When I joined the faculty in September, 1947, I found that the next youngest member of the teaching faculty was about twenty years my senior. I had been recruited by Dean Crane, who visited the Yale Law School in the spring of 1947 to interview candidates. In those days, there were no appointments committees. The dean carried out the interviewing and hiring. Thomas S. Checkley had arrived a few months earlier to assume the position of law librarian, the first time that position was held by a professional librarian.

The faculty I met upon my arrival was a group of impressive scholars. Of course, Dean Crane had published casebooks on partnerships and damages. He was associated with the Pittsburgh law firm of Moorhead and Knox, and engaged in consulting in the business associations area. While he possessed an outward appearance of gruffness, which scared some students, he had an inner warmth and a keen intellect which attracted me to him almost immediately. We enjoyed many times together discussing legal matters.

The Vice-Dean, Charles B. Nutting, was also impressive. He taught constitutional law and administrative law. He had previously taught in the law schools of the University of Texas and the University of Nebraska. He served as Associate Solicitor of the U.S. Department of Agriculture from 1942 to 1946. He had a casebook on administrative law. One of his characteristics I remember well was his constant attire in a vested suit, with a watch chain from which dangled a Phi Beta Kappa key. Charles became President of the Association of American Law Schools in 1953, the only member of this school's faculty to be so honored.

Charles Wilson Taintor was a natural scholar. A devotee of Latin, he would usually be quoting it extensively in conversations dealing with legal problems. One memorable experience took place after Herb Sherman had joined the faculty in 1948. Herb and I approached Charlie with a property problem. Charlie taught the property courses and conflict of laws. He began the discussion in English but suddenly began speaking in Latin. When Herb and I confessed our inability to understand the Latin portion of his answer, he bitterly complained that today's students do not know Latin.

Charlie was a warm person. I thoroughly enjoyed his friendship and the many discussions we had, especially during the period when we had adjoining offices in the Cathedral of Learning.

Robert Coleman Brown was the resident expert in taxation, local government and some aspects of trusts and estates. He was a good natured friend who was able to take a lot of kidding from Herb Sherman, Bill Schulz and me. A dedicated teacher and scholar, he was a highly respected colleague. He authored a casebook in taxation.

When annual law review banquets were instituted, the non-law review students, feeling excluded from such events, organized the non-law review banquets. What fun events they were! I recall one at the Millvale Moose, where the program included a belly dancer and a speech by a justice of the peace. Of course, the law review banquets always had a judge, often a Pennsylvania Supreme Court justice, as the speaker. In a skit at one of these events, a student impersonated Bob Brown. He wore a pork-pie hat and gave a hilarious performance. Bob took it in stride and with a laugh.

The youngest was Fred Dewey, who taught evidence and torts. Fred moved on to the University of Cincinnati Law School after my first year on the faculty. One recollection I have of Fred occurred on Good Friday in 1948. In those days, that was a University holiday. Fred came in that morning and at 10 a.m. went into Room 1409 to meet his Torts class. After waiting for some time and finding no students entering the classroom, he stormed into the Registrar's Office, complaining about the total lack of attendance in his class. Mrs. Lindsay explained that it was Good Friday and no classes were scheduled. When she explained to him that this holiday was listed in the university calendar and on the bulletin board, Fred confessed that he never read either of them.

The new librarian, Tom Checkley, faced many problems when he arrived. There had never been a full-time librarian before this time. Faculty members had been given the assignment. Consequently, it was no great surprise to find many advance sheets and pocket parts not properly docketed. Tom did a fine job of taking care of the backlog and of organizing the library, including the reserve room. He was the only full-time person on the library staff, the library being staffed by part-timers, many of whom were law students.

I should mention that just before I arrived on the faculty, Dwight Malcolm Anderson, a very promising younger full-time faculty member, resigned to return to his father's practice because of the serious illness of his brother, who also practiced with his father.

One of the most colorful part-time faculty members was Charles A. ("Quizzer") Woods, Jr. He taught decedents' estates. He had several noticeable characteristics. He very often wore a bow tie. He never entered a classroom without carrying six or more books. In fact, in a student skit at one of the dances, a student wearing a huge bow tie and juggling a stack of about twenty books imitated Charlie going into class. His nickname, "Quizzer," fit him perfectly. Both in and out of the classroom, he could ask more questions than any other person I ever knew. Some students claimed he never answered any questions in the classroom, only asked them. He later moved to Harrisburg where he practiced law. He passed away in 1994.

While Tom Checkley was only a few years older than I, he was married. Outside of the academic side, I had little in common with my colleagues on the social side. While we did some socializing as a faculty, I spent what time I could devote to social life with some of the students. There were almost weekly parties on Saturday evenings. Some of the students I spent those times with were Earl F. ("Skip") Reed, Edgar Reed, Tom Welsh and Harry Kramer. In fact, it was at one of those parties that I met my wife on a blind date, arranged by one of the group.

I also remember fondly going with Walter ("Bud") McGough and Walt Howarth down to the old Pittsburgher Hotel where Ownie McManus had a room. We would spend evenings playing bridge. Both Walt and Ownie have passed away but Bud and I, when we see each other, reminisce about those evenings together.

One of the diversions of some students from the rigors of law study at this time was a form of table shuffleboard played in the law library. Two of the "champion" players at this time were John L. Laubach, Jr., '50 and William H. Knoell, '50. The game consisted of the two contestants sitting at opposite ends of one of the long, large tables in the Law Library. Using either a 50¢ coin or a silver dollar, they would, in an artistic manner, slide the coin down the table in the direction of the opponent. The one whose coin came closest to the end without falling off the table would win the point. I was never certain just what the point score required for victory was, although I vividly recall witnessing some of those games. I must say that this pastime certainly did not have an adverse effect on either Jack or Bill and was a source of entertainment for some of the observers.

In the spring of 1948, Dean Crane told me that he had just returned from a trip to Harvard and had hired a young colleague to keep me company. His name was Herbert L. Sherman, Jr., a graduate of Brown University and a third year law student in the Harvard Law School. When Herb arrived in September, 1948, there began a deep and lasting friendship between us which exists to this day. He taught a section of Torts his first year on the faculty. I taught the other section. He also taught Labor Law and Negotiable Instruments.

On May 11, 1948, the faculty adopted a Student Bar Association proposal that Moot Court competition be compulsory in the first year as part of the Legal Bibliography course.

The program was to be worked out substantially in compliance with a memo prepared by Tom Checkley, the Law Librarian and me.

On January 25, 1949, after a discussion of the Legal Bibliography course, the faculty adopted the following rules:

> A student who entered the School of Law in February, 1948, and who failed to present an acceptable brief in Legal Bibliography will not be permitted to advance in his Law School course unless he files an acceptable brief during the present semester or before a date to be fixed by the Law Librarian.

> A student who entered the School of Law in September, 1948, and who filed on time an unacceptable brief in Legal Bibliography will not be permitted to advance into the second year unless he files an acceptable brief during the present semester on or before a date to be fixed by the Law Librarian.

> A student who entered the School of Law in September, 1948, and (1) who failed to file any brief in Legal Bibliography, or (2) who failed to file a brief before examinations began will not be permitted to advance into the second year unless he (a) files an acceptable brief during the present semester on or before a date to be fixed by the Law Librarian and (b) files in addition a legal memorandum under such terms and conditions as may be prescribed by the Law Librarian.

> A student entering the School of Law in September, 1949, and thereafter shall not be permitted to take the examinations at the end of the first term unless he has filed a brief in Legal Bibliography in accordance with such terms and conditions as may be prescribed by the Law Librarian. A student failing Legal Bibliography, having filed a brief, shall, if otherwise entitled to advancement, be advanced on condition that he file an acceptable brief during the second semester on or before a date to be fixed by the Law Librarian. Failure in Legal Bibliography shall be regarded as failure in a course for the purposes of the rules relating to scholastic requirements approved July 23, 1947.

> It is the understanding of the Faculty that the Law Librarian in fixing the date for the filing of briefs will fix a date in the semester early enough to allow the briefs to be examined and returned and to permit a student to present a revised brief for consideration before the end of the semester.

By action of the faculty on February 14, 1949, the Curriculum Committee recommendation was adopted to the effect that graduation requirements should be increased by requiring attendance at the eight-week summer session. The following statement was adopted with the understanding that it would be applicable to students entering in September 1949 and thereafter:

Degree

The degree of Bachelor of Laws (LL.B.) is granted to students who, having met the entrance requirements before beginning Law School, have completed three full academic years of resident study (the last of which, including the required Summer Session, must be in this School), who have satisfactorily demonstrated their ability in courses totalling 84 credit hours, of which not less than six credit hours shall have been earned in the summer session and shall have satisfactorily done such other work as may be prescribed from time to time. The work of the first year is all required and calls for 27 credit hours—approximately 14 classroom hours per week in one semester and 13 classroom hours in the other. In the fall and spring semester of the second and third years no less than 12 nor more than 14 hours weekly may be carried, except with the permission of the Dean.

On February 14, 1949, following discussion, the faculty adopted the following Library Rules:

1. No book shall be removed from the Law School premises without express permission.

2. No book shall be defaced, or otherwise damaged, by underlining, checking or mishandling. Any book so defaced or otherwise damaged shall be charged for at replacement cost.

3. All books shelved in the Reserve Room (1524) are on 2 hour reserve, and shall be overdue if not returned within two hours from the time of charging out, unless express permission to the contrary is given. Evidence of such permission is limited to the showing that the Librarian on duty has placed his initials opposite the borrower's name on the charge card of said book.

4. Reserve Room books which may be taken out overnight are subject to the following rules:

   (a) Two copies must remain in the Reserve Room at 4 p.m.

   (b) One copy must remain in the Reserve Room at 9 p.m.

5. Reserve Room books which may be taken out over weekends are subject to the following rules:

   (a) Two copies must remain in the Reserve Room at 4 p.m. Friday.

   (b) One copy must remain in the Reserve Room at 2 p.m. Saturday.

6. All books taken out overnight are due before 10 a.m. the following morning.

   All books taken out for a weekend are due before 10 a.m. the following Monday.

7. Special rules will be formulated and posted for holiday chargeouts.

8. A fine shall be levied against the borrower of an overdue book in the amount of:

   (a) Fifty cents for the first hour or fraction thereof that the book is overdue.

   (b) Thereafter, ten cents an hour or fraction thereof that the book is overdue; provided, however, that the hourly fine under this subdivision shall be suspended in the event that the book is returned in the borrowers' first free hour as determined by his schedule filed in the Law School offices. If the offender cannot within the hour get and return the book, allowance shall be made therefor at the discretion of the Law Librarian.

   For a second offense the student shall be subject to any disciplinary measures prescribed by the Law School Faculty.

9. A book which has been lost shall be charged for at the replacement cost, plus one dollar ($1) for handling.

10. In any case where there is evidence of repeated or conscious and intentional violation of the rules, the borrower shall be subject to disciplinary action over and above the fine levied. Such evidence of conscious and intentional violation might be the failure to report promptly to the Law Librarian the losing of a book, or the retention overdue of a textbook (e.g., hornbook) shortly before an examination in that subject.

Charles Bernard Nutting.

In 1949, Charles B. Nutting, who had been Vice-Dean since 1946, became the Dean. He received his Bachelor of Arts degree from the University of Iowa in 1927. He received the Bachelor of Laws, Master of Laws and Doctor of the Science of Jurisprudence degrees from Harvard University. He previously taught in the law schools of the University of Texas and the University of Nebraska. He came to Pitt from the position of Associate

Solicitor of the U.S. Department of Agriculture, where he served from 1942 to 1946.

In June, 1949, at the request of the Honorable David L. Lawrence, mayor of the city of Pittsburgh, and his Director of Public Health, Dr. I. Hope Alexander, the School of Law undertook research into the health laws, regulations and ordinances of the Commonwealth of Pennsylvania and the city of Pittsburgh. The project was made possible by a generous grant from the A.W. Mellon Educational and Charitable Trust to the school. Dean Charles B. Nutting placed the work of the project under the direction of Professor Harold Gill

Dean Nutting discussing a case with Franklin Blackstone, Jr., '52.

Reuschlein. James C. Kuhn, Jr. and David Stahl, recent graduates of the School undertook the task and saw it to completion. Both men were very well equipped for the careful research required by the project. As the project progressed, the compilation of the research was expedited and augmented by the work of David W. Craig, Harry W. Fawcett, Grace D. Moore and Nancy Welfer, also graduates of the School. Secretary of the project was Mary Frances Wagner. The stenographers were Peggy A. Graftan and Mary P. Roman. The volume was published in October, 1950.

Revision and improvement of the health laws of both the Commonwealth and the City of Pittsburgh were the ultimate objectives of the Public Health Law Research Project. To a considerable extent the objectives were achieved.

In September, 1949, William Frederick Schulz, Jr. joined the faculty. He had been teaching at Stetson University College of Law. A graduate of the University of Illinois, he was welcomed by Herb and me. For many years, we three enjoyed a close personal relationship. Just before Bill retired, the three of us represented over a hundred years of teaching in the law school. Bill has passed away

David Stahl, Professor Harold G. Reuschlein and J. Craig Kuhn with a copy of the Public Health Laws research study.

Craig Kuhn and David Stahl at work on the project.

but I still miss him very much. He was a warm, loyal and devoted colleague.

At the beginning of 1950, the School received a grant from the Allegheny Conference on Community Development to establish the Housing Law Research Project. Dean Charles B. Nutting appointed David W. Craig, upon the completion of his law school studies, as full-time research fellow under the general supervision of Professor Harold Gill Reuschlein. Ms. Norma Rudert served as secretary, with Ms. Peggy Grafton and Ms. Martha Allison assisting in publication.

During the first part of 1950, the project staff developed the main body of the report. After receiving reactions to the draft from interested agencies, the A.W. Mellon Educational and Charitable Trust provided the funds for its publication in book form in 1951. It was to serve as: (1) a legal handbook for municipal officials; (2) an outline of countywide or regional action; (3) a reference as to relevant state legislation; and (4) a text for use by lawyers and law students. The project examined in complete detail all the building codes in the 53 municipalities which had adopted them, and all of the 72 zoning ordinances adopted by that number of local governments.

Comments by municipal officials, local government solicitors and other lawyers have indicated that this Housing Law Project study by the law school provided some information and analyses usable in their legislative and administrative actions, as a result of its distribution to the law libraries of the county, the universities and elsewhere.

State and local legislation in the twc decades after the study was directed toward solving many of the problems identified. The most significant legislation has been the Pennsylvania Municipalities Planning Code, Act No. 247 of 1968, extensively revised in 1988 to authorize, among other innovations, joint municipal zoning.

Although the Housing Law Project research cannot be credited with motivating those subsequent improvements in the field, its identification of some problems and solutions has been confirmed by the later attention given to them by the public and private leadership.

On December 2, 1949, the School of Law held a dinner in honor of the Honorable Arthur T. Vanderbilt, Chief Justice of the New Jersey Supreme Court, in the Breakfast Room in the University Club.

Professor Taintor was granted a leave of absence for the academic year 1949-1950.

The Law Student Dinner was held on March 9, 1950 at 7 p.m. at the Webster Hall Hotel. Harold J. Gallagher, Esquire, President of the American Bar Association, was the speaker.

School of Law Faculty — 1949-50

Seated (l to r): W. Edward Sell, Judson A. Crane, Charles B. Nutting, Robert C. Brown, Harold G. Reuschlein
Standing (l to r): William F. Schulz, Jr., Thomas S. Checkley, Herbert L. Sherman, Jr.

Dean Nutting presenting a copy of the Pittsburgh Public Health Law study to Mayor David Lawrence, as Dr. I. Hope Alexander, Director of Public Health, and Anne X. Alpern, Esquire, City Solicitor, look on.

By faculty action, the school switched from the Iowa test for admission to the test offered by the Educational Testing Service.

On May 3, 1950, the faculty adopted the Scholarship Committee's Report on the Comprehensive Examination. The following rules were adopted with respect to such examination:

1. The honor system is to be used in the examination.

2. The examination shall be given in one day of two four-hour sessions (9 to 1; 2 to 6).

3. Eleven courses to be covered in the examination.

4. Committee empowered to consult with the Dean and decide on the kind of examination paper to be used in the examination.

Student Bar Association meeting in 1950.

Law Review members at work in 1950. (l to r): Meyer J. Herman, (at typewriter), Vincent L. Matera, Harry W. Fawcett, Warren S. Reding, Vincent J. Pepicelli and Gene K. Lynch.

5. Each faculty member should decide whether to go over the examination questions for which he is responsible in a meeting of the group or to write annotations on each examination paper listing the errors of commission and omission. It is also optional with each instructor whether he desires to mimeograph answers for distribution.

6. Each question to be graded on the basis of 100; the grades for the questions to be totaled and then divided by 14—the number of questions to be given in the examination.

David Craig reviewing manuscript of the Housing Law Research Project with his secretary, Norma Rudert.

7. A failure in this examination will appear on the student's record.

At a meeting on October 5, 1950, the Committee on Tuition recommended that tuition for the academic year be raised from $302.50 to $402.50 and that the summer session tuition be raised $22.50 to $100.

Classes for the week of November 27, 1950 were suspended because of a snowstorm that began the Friday after Thanksgiving and blanketed the city with over 36 inches of snow.

By 1951, the Korean War was in progress. Dean Nutting called the attention of the faculty to the fact that there were a few students in the law school who would be called to active duty either late in the Spring Term or during the summer session for a period of two weeks. The faculty discussed the procedures to be followed with respect to exams. At a faculty meeting on March 27, the Dean also outlined some of the problems the school may face in 1951-1952 in the light of an anticipated drop in enrollment. The Curriculum Committee was advised to draw up a proposal for such changes should they be required. Such a proposal would merely serve as a guide for the Dean in making his decisions on the matter.

At this time, there was a proposal in the state legislature to require professors to take an oath of loyalty to the nation and to the Commonwealth. At a special meeting on April 16, 1951, the faculty unanimously approved the following statement regarding the loyalty oath as a statement of the law faculty position on the matter:

Law Review Banquet, 1950. (l to r): Mrs Harold G. Reuschlein, Willard Wirtz, speaker, Harry Fawcett, Editor-in-Chief, Miriam Fawcett and Dean Nutting.

The faculties of the University of Pittsburgh would welcome an opportunity to demonstrate their loyalty to the Nation and the Commonwealth through subscribing to the oath which Article 7, Section 1 of the Constitution of Pennsylvania requires of all senators and representatives and all judicial, state and county officers.

These faculties believe, however, that Senate Bill 27, considered as a whole goes far beyond a loyalty oath and has a dangerous tendency to give to an administrative official power of definition amounting to thought control. Individual Attorneys-General might thus have the power to destroy the basic freedoms which all Americans prize.

Accordingly, while affirming their vital interest in preventing the spread of Communism in and out of places of education and public employment, the faculties respectfully urge the disapproval of Senate Bill 27. They also urge that no bill of this character should be passed without public hearings at which representatives of educational groups may appear.

The bill requiring such oath was not passed.

The Annual Law Alumni Dinner was held on June 10, 1951 in the Alumni Room of the University Club. The address was delivered by the Honorable James H. Duff, '07, United States Senator from Pennsylvania.

Dean Nutting's tenure was shortened by his elevation to the position of Vice-Chancellor of the University in 1951. From the time he assumed the deanship, he was being called into consultation with the then Chancellor, Dr. Rufus Fitzgerald, on numerous University problems. The frequency of those occasions no doubt led to Dr. Fitzgerald creating the position of Vice-Chancellor and recommending Charles for the position. While his time in the deanship was brief, he brought continued excellence to the law school program. Several grants were awarded to the law school for research projects during this period. He carefully assembled teams to carry out these efforts with great success.

When a new administration assumed leadership of the University under Dr. Edward Litchfield, Charles Nutting became the Director of the Buhl Foundation in Pittsburgh, a position he held until he assumed the deanship of the National Law Center at George Washington University in 1960. He passed away in 1994.

It should be noted that during this period the Association of American Law Schools was entertaining proposals for revision of certain standards of the Association. Two proposals during this period dealt with the size of the library staff and study space for students. Faced with tight budgets and severe space limitations, the faculty continued to oppose such proposals.

On April 17, 1952, Justice Felix Frankfurter spoke at the Law Day Dinner. He earlier participated in a seminar on opportunities in the law, held in the law school. The Annual Law Review Banquet was held May 1, 1952 at the Hotel Roosevelt. The

A Moot Court Argument — Law Day, 1952.

speaker was Edwin Dickinson.

By action of the faculty on June 10, 1952, a new set of Scholastic Requirements, supplementing those in the current bulletin was adopted:

I. A student who has been neither readmitted nor advanced on condition and who in a term [semester or summer session] passes every course in which he is examined, makes a weighted average of not less than 70, and who has not accumulated five or more Ds or Fs by the end of his second year, is advanced unconditionally. Final examination grades of the first semester of the freshman year (e.g., Criminal Law) will be counted in determining the first year average.

II. Automatic Advancement on Condition. A student not previously in scholastic difficulty shall be permitted automatically to advance on condition, if in any term:

    (a) He has received a passing grade in all courses in which he is examined and h.s weighted average in such courses is less than 70 but not less than 69, or

    (b) He fails a course but is not excluded under Rule IIIA(3) or (4).

Provided that, at the end of the first semester of the second year, a regular second year student, not in previous scholastic difficulty, shall be automatically advanced on condition if he did not fail more than one

Afternoon panel discussion — Law Day, 1952

Dean Charles B. Nutting, Honorable Felix Frankfurter, Justice, United States Supreme Court and Dean Emeritus Judson A. Crane.

course at the end of the first term of that year and is not excluded under the "Cumulative D" rule.

III.   Exclusion of Students.

    A.   A student shall be excluded if in any term (subject to the proviso to Rule II):

        (1)   Having passed all courses in which he is finally examined, he has a weighted average of less than 69, or

        (2)   He fails more than one course, or

        (3)   He fails one course and his weighted average in all courses in which he has made a final passing grade during such term is less than 72, or

        (4)   He has accumulated five or more Ds or Fs by the end of his second year or before, or

        (5)   He fails to meet any condition imposed upon him under Rule V.

B. The Faculty shall determine as it sees fit the weight to be given to the freshman course examinations taken, for the first time, at the end of the first semester.

IV. Standard conditions applicable to Student Advanced on Condition or Readmitted after Exclusion.

A student who is advanced on condition shall:

(a) Thereafter pass all courses undertaken and shall maintain a weighted average of at least 70 for all courses examined in any term, and

(b) Not accumulate five or more Ds or Fs by the end of his second year or before, and

(c) Comply with any other condition or requirement imposed by the Faculty, including, but not limited to, the requirement that the student retake or stand re-examination in any designated course or courses.

V. Readmission of Students.

A student who has been excluded from the Law School for failure to meet scholastic requirements may be readmitted:

(a) If he petitions the Faculty in writing, setting forth the reasons why he failed to do satisfactory work and the reason why he believes he will do satisfactory work if readmitted, and

(b) If the Faculty concludes that the exclusion was caused by factors largely beyond the control of the student which have been eliminated, and that the student has the will and capacity to do satisfactory work in the future.

VI. Re-Examinations.

When the student is required or permitted to take a re-examination under these rules, the grade made on the re-examination shall be considered the final grade in the course and shall be treated as a grade made in the term in which the examination was taken.

VII. Permission to Students to Withdraw from a Course or Courses.

The Dean may, in his discretion, permit a student to withdraw from any course or courses before taking the examination therein, subject to such conditions as he may impose.

VIII. Permission to Take an Examination when the Regular Examination is not Taken.

(a) Each student is required to take the regular examination and to submit any required work in each course for which he is registered, unless excused by the Dean. An unexcused failure to do so is regarded as a failure in the course.

(b) A student who fails to take an examination and to submit any required work because of extraordinary circumstances not involving fault on his part and who desires permission to take an examination in the course or to complete the required work shall notify the Dean in writing, setting forth the reasons for such failure and requesting permission to take the examination or to complete the work. If the Dean concludes that permission should be granted, he may permit the student to take the examination when next regularly given or, in special circumstances, at some other time and to complete any other required work under such conditions as he may see fit to require.

When Dean Nutting became Vice-Chancellor, Dean Crane was named Acting Dean. He sometimes, in a jovial manner, referred to his position as DEAD—Dean Emeritus Acting Dean. Dr. Nutting immediately set out to find a dean for the school.

He approached Brainerd Currie, an established authority in the area of conflict of laws. He received his undergraduate and law degrees from Mercer University and his masters and doctorate degrees in law from Columbia University. Currie was a Professor of Law at the University of California at Los Angeles (UCLA) School of Law. He agreed to become dean but stated that he had a commitment to teach summer school at the University of Chicago Law School. It was arranged that he would come to Pittsburgh upon the completion of that summer commitment. When he arrived in Chicago, a lovefest developed between him and the law school. He was offered a chaired professorship. When he decided he would rather continue as a professor than as a dean, he asked to be relieved of his commitment to come to Pitt as dean. The University officials indicated that they expected him to honor his commitment. The officials at Chicago indicated they would hold the position for a year. Consequently, when he arrived in Pittsburgh, he immediately submitted his resignation, effective at the end of the academic year. At the end of the year, he returned to Chicago until 1961, when he became the Williams R. Perkins Professor of Law at Duke University School of Law, where he remained until his tragic death.

Brainerd Currie.

At a meeting on December 8, 1952, the faculty instructed the dean to vote against a proposal of the Association of American Law Schools that Federal Civil Service be extended to cover lawyers.

R.B.ACKELSON A.P.BARTIROMO M.J.BERMAN S.S.BLAUFELD W.J.BLENKO JR. M.BRAUNSTEIN E.A.BRISELL A.D.CAPOZZI E.C.CARROLL M.I.COHEN R.M.CRUM

S.DAVIS D.L.DIGBY A.H.ERVING D.B.FAWCETT JR. J.M.FEENEY JR. H.S.FEINBERG T.FLOOD T.M.GUINEY W.C.HART J.B.HECHT M.HLADIO

F.E.HOLAHAN H.J.HOTCHKISS N.H.JACOBS K.S.JOHNSTON L.W.KAPLAN W.L.KIMMEL

UNIVERSITY OF PITTSBURGH
SCHOOL OF LAW
CLASS OF 1953

E.L.KOHLER H.C.LABBIE J.B.LANDIS D.L.LICHTENSTEIN J.LIND R.B.LUBIC

J.R.LUKE J.H.McDANIEL J.L.McGUIGAN A.L.McLAUGHLIN E.R.McMILLIN II C.W.MARGOLF R.MARKON M.M.MERMAN J.W.MOORE P.R.OBERT J.M.PATTON

R.B.PEABODY R.W.PIPER J.M.POTASHMAN L.E.PRICE R.W.RIEHL D.E.ROGERS J.I.ROSENBAUM W.PRUDDOCK R.H.SABEL R.F.SCANNELL P.D.SCHURGOT JR.

M.H.SHEINMAN R.E.SMITH W.I.STALEY J.A.STEEDLE J.J.SWEENEY JR. T.J.TERPUTAC W.W.THOMSON W.C.URLING JR. A.C.VAN GORDER L.J.WENDEKIER S.W.ZANOLI

During the academic year, J. Henry O'Neill gave a gift of $300 to the school to be expended for books to be selected by the Librarian. The selection was to be reported to the Dean for communication to the Chancellor and Mr. O'Neill.

One of the events that took place in the post-World War II era was the annual law school dance. This event attracted a large number of students and most of the faculty. Intermission was marked by the presentation of entertainment by students, sometimes in the form of a skit. I treasure many happy memories of some of those skits.

In one of the first of them, the Honorable John Brosky played the part of Dean Nutting, with a Phi Beta Kappa key made from a cigar box and a flashlight bulb inside, which John flashed on and off as he gave an inane lecture on mens rea in common law marriages. And then there was the late Judge Harry Kramer, who portrayed Dean Crane. I shall never forget how Dean Crane's wife laughed so much at that presentation.

In another year, the Class of 1953 gave a great skit and then some songs, allegedly written by Larry Kaplan (now His Honor). The following are examples of what they presented (and which they repeat at their reunions).

Pitt Law School Class of 1953 Songs

1. Milton Berle Show Theme
   ("We Are the Men of Texaco")

   We are the Class of '53
   About to start our destiny
   A law practice can't be too
        very far

   We've filed all our petitions
   We have met all the conditions
   All we have to do is pass the
   Pennsy Bar.

   But— if we don't pass it
   We'll still have this: "A
        smash hit!
   And tomorrow we'll be servicing
        your car.

2. "Four Leaf Clover"

I'm looking over
A case in trover
That I overlooked before

One is in "Trespass"
The other in "Case,"
But in Wisconsin it's the law
        of the chase

No need explaining
The one remaining
It's res ipsa loquitor

I'm looking over a case in trover,
That I overlooked before.

3. '53 Class Anthem

Respondeat Superior
Res ipsa loquitor
De minimus non curate lex
Our whole damned class
Is over-sexed.

In 1968, Bart McGuire, a young member of the faculty, suggested to me that the time was ripe for the faculty to strike back. He suggested that at that year's dance the faculty surprise the students by asking that evening (in the middle of their program) for equal time for the faculty. He wrote about six verses to the tune of the Battle Hymn of the Republic. In those verses, he managed to take off on student activities and some students. We secretly rehearsed it, accompanied at the piano by my Associate Dean for Academic Affairs, John E. Murray, Jr. Not only were the students surprised that evening, but they were thoroughly entertained by our obvious amateur effort.

Unfortunately, the tradition died out when the school became larger. With the sectioning of many courses, faculty were no longer able to develop close relationships with many of the students. Dances became a time for students to enjoy some time away from the school and the faculty.

Under the leadership of Dean Currie, the faculty adopted new Requirements for Degree and Scholarship Rules, effective immediately, as follows:

Requirements for Degree and Scholarship Rules

1. The degree of Bachelor of Laws is granted to students who, having met the entrance requirements before beginning law school, have completed three full academic years of resident study (the last of which must be in this School); who have received a passing grade (60 or more) in courses totaling 86 semester hours; who have completed in this school a summer session program of at least 6 semester hours; who have satisfactorily done such other work as may be prescribed from time to time; and who have complied with the scholarship requirements set out below.

2. The scale of grading is as follows:

90-100	A
80-89	B
70-79	C
60-69	D
Below 60	F

3. No student shall be granted the degree of Bachelor of Laws whose weighted average for the entire law school course, computed on all work undertaken, is less than 70.

4. Any grade less than 70 signifies that the work of the student is unsatisfactory. If at any time a student receives a grade less than 70 in a course he is thereby put on notice that his performance in that course has been unsatisfactory. If in any semester or summer session a student's weighted average, computed on all work undertaken in that time, is less than 70, he shall be warned by the Dean in writing that his work for that semester or session has been unsatisfactory.

5. Every student whose cumulative weighted average, computed on all work undertaken, is less than 70 at the end of his first year in residence, or at the end of his third semester in residence, or at the end of his second year in residence plus one summer session, shall be excluded.

6. A student excluded under the terms of paragraph 5 may be readmitted on probation if, in the judgment of the faculty, he will be able in the following semester, year or session to raise his cumulative weighted average, computed on all work undertaken, to at least 70; Provided, that no student shall be admitted to his third year in residence on probation.

7. a. A Student on probation will be finally excluded if, at the end of his probationary period, he fails to raise his cumulative weighted average on all work undertaken to the required level of 70, or if he fails to comply with any condition of probation imposed by the faculty, including any restriction on the amount of time which may be devoted by the student to outside employment.

b. A student on probation is not eligible to hold office in the Student Bar Association nor to participate in Law Review work, legal aid work, or the Moot Court program.

8. Any student whose record at the end of his first semester in residence indicates lack of capacity, interest, or diligence may be excluded or placed on probation at the discretion of the faculty.

9. Any student who has been admitted to his third year in residence may be excluded at the discretion of the faculty if his record indicates lack of capacity, interest, or diligence or if in the judgment of the faculty he will be unable to meet requirements for the degree within a reasonable time.

10. In computing the weighted average, grades less than 50 shall be treated as 50.

11. It is the policy of the faculty not to permit a student who has received a grade in a course to take a reexamination or to repeat the course for the purpose of raising his grade. Normally, a student who has received an unsatisfactory grade in the course will be expected to make up the deficiency in hours of credit and in his cumulative average by the grades and credits received in other courses. This policy does not apply to courses which are designated by the faculty as courses which must be successfully completed as a condition of graduation, and the faculty may relax the policy in other exceptional cases; but in all such cases the

cumulative average shall be computed by including both the original grade and the grade on reexamination or repetition of the course; the latter grade will not be substituted for the original.

12. A student may withdraw from a course in which he is registered only with the permission of the Dean.

The Student Bar Association's Law Day Banquet was held on April 30, 1953 in the Grand Ballroom of the Hotel William Penn. The speaker was the Honorable Calvert Magruder, Chief Judge of the United States Court of Appeals for the First Circuit.

Honorable Calvert Magruder.

With Currie's resignation in hand, the University officials set out to find a dean for the school. Again, in this era, there were no dean search committees. Arthur Larson, who was a professor at Cornell Law School, was offered the position. He accepted and began his tenure on July 1, 1953. He was a graduate of Augustana College (1931). He received his law degrees from Oxford University during his three years as a Rhodes Scholar.

I had resigned from the faculty in the summer of 1951 to accept a position in the Law Department of United States Steel Corporation. Having spent two years there and missing my real love—legal education—I indicated to University officials my willingness to return to the faculty. Dean Larson offered me an Associate Professor position and I accepted.

One note of particular interest is from the faculty minutes of January 12, 1954. The Dean announced that the law school's share of the Alumni Fund receipts was $1,337, which was being

Arthur Larson.

expended in making improvements or additions to the law school plant. This was a practice that had long existed, whereby the receipts from the Annual Alumni Fund were divided among the various schools and units. The school was never given any information as to the formula or method of distribution of the receipts. During my deanship, I joined with a couple of professional school deans in campaigning for a radical change in this process. Finally, the university inaugurated the present system whereby contributors can earmark contributions for a particular school, unit or project.

One of the highlights of the 1953-54 academic year was an Institute on the Uniform Commercial Code recently adopted in Pennsylvania. It was held on February 12, 13 and 27.

At a special faculty meeting called on March 23, 1954, it was announced that Dean Larson had received an appointment as Undersecretary of Labor in the Eisenhower Administration and would have to leave for Washington as soon as confirmed. While he tendered his resignation at that time, it was not accepted by the University. Dr. Nutting announced that effective at the beginning of the Fall Semester, Professor Charles W. Taintor, II would be the acting dean. This arrangement was to continue until the appointment of Thomas M. Cooley II as dean in August, 1957.

In the latter stage of Charlie's term as Acting Dean, the Litchfield administration accepted Arthur Larson's resignation, which had been in its hands since his departure for Washington. After the government service, Larson joined the faculty of the Duke University School of Law. He died in 1994.

In retrospect, I think it was a mistake to continue an acting deanship for such an extended period. First, Charlie Taintor never had an administrative aspiration and was, admittedly, not very adept at it. Second, any acting deanship means a period of waiting until a permanent dean comes aboard. To stand still in legal education is to regress and I felt we experienced a bit of that during this period.

The Student Bar Association's Annual Law Day Banquet was held on May 6, 1954. The occasion honored Judson A. Crane. It was held in the Sylvania Room of the PAA. The address was given by the Honorable Ralph H. Demmler, '28, chairman of the Securities Exchange Commission.

In 1955, an incident in my Corporations class proved to be more dangerous than originally anticipated.

A group of students, representing a moot court project, came to ask my permission to stage an incident in my class as the basis for a mock jury trial. I told them I had no objection so long as it was done near the beginning or end of the class period.

Weeks went by and I had forgotten the matter. One day, when John L. Bailey,

A seminar meeting with Professor Reuschlein in 1950.

Class of '56, was reciting, a rap came on the classroom door. When no on attempted to answer two different raps, the door opened and a young man stood in the doorway. He looked quite angry as he asked if John Bailey was in the class. Bailey acknowledged that he was John Bailey. The young man told him he wanted to see him in the hall. John told him he was reciting. The man told him that he didn't care, that he wanted to see him then. I still did not realize this was the staged incident and that by coincidence Mr. Bailey was reciting at the time.

John asked me if he could be excused and I agreed. When John got in the hall, we heard a loud exchange of voices. Suddenly a shot rang out and we saw, through the translucent glass in the door, Bailey's body sliding to the floor. Two students near the door ran out of the room. Bailey was moaning. The one fellow classmate attempted to render assistance while the other chased the gunman, tackling him between the 14th and 13th floors and putting him in Presbyterian Hospital with an injured knee. The gunman was a drama student from then Carnegie Tech.

A member of the group staging the incident then entered the classroom, announced that it was a staged incident and asked the students to cooperate if asked to be a witness.

The event made the Post-Gazette the next morning with a headline: "Student Shot in Professor Sell's Corporation Class."

Needless to say, it was the last such "staged" incident. The trial was held in an evening in a Common Pleas courtroom. I attended and was interested in listening to the witnesses—how different persons had a different perception of what had occurred.

Class of 1953 at a 1986 Reunion.

A Law Review Banquet.

A moot court argument in the School. (l to r): Robert W. Lewis, Harry W. Kramer, Allen D. McCrady, J. Craig Kuhn, Albert McBride, Jr. and Franklin Blackstone, Jr.

Class of 1954.

Law Day 1952.

CHAPTER
S·E·V·E·N
1955-1964

The Annual Law Day Banquet was held on February 24, 1956 at the Hotel Webster Hall. The principal speaker was the Honorable Herbert F. Goodrich, Judge of the United States Court of Appeals for the Third Circuit. Dr. and Mrs. Charles B. Nutting were guests of honor. Dr. Nutting, former dean of the law school and former vice chancellor, was serving as acting chancellor of the university.

"When the Saints Come Marching In"

In the spring of 1956, I was experiencing a practice of third-year students coming in late for the first five or ten minutes of the class. Pleas for the cessation of the practice proved futile. Finally, I announced that beginning the next Monday, I was going to lock the door when the bell rang and if they were not then in the classroom they should go up to the library and study.

The Monday morning I intended to institute the practice, I had gone down to the Tuck Shop in the basement of the Cathedral of Learning for coffee. While there, John P. Flaherty, Jr., an underclassman (Class of 1958), came in carrying a trumpet case. While I wondered why a law student would be bringing a musical instrument to law school, I thought no more about it.

My class was held in Room 1428. I was able to enter that classroom from my office through a separate door. I often used that door to enter Room 1428. However, on this morning, I decided I would go out through the hall and enter the room through the door used by the students in order to be certain the lock was on the door. As I entered the hall, I noticed that a very sizeable group of the class was standing around laughing and talking. I concluded they were going to test me. As the bell rang, I entered the room and placed the lock on the door. I instructed the student next to the door not to open the door under any circumstances. When I began the class, there was a small percentage of the class present.

About five minutes later, I heard a commotion in my office. This puzzled me since I always kept my office locked. Suddenly that door opened and in walked the rest of the class, led by Richard T. Wentley, Class of 1956, later a Judge of the Court of Common Pleas and now a partner in Reed, Smith, Shaw & McClay. Dick was playing "When the Saints Come Marching In" on John Flaherty's trumpet. John, now a Justice of the Pennsylvania Supreme Court, has steadfastly maintained that when he entertained Dick's request to borrow his trumpet, he knew nothing about the prank.

Well, the parade marched across the front of the room in front of me, down the side of the room and stood in the back until the rendition was completed. They then took their seats.

Apparently fearful that I would not get angry but even, they behaved marvelously the rest of the term. In fact, I nearly needed sunglasses for the shining of their halos. For several years thereafter, at law school dances, the orchestra was requested to play "When the Saints Come Marching In" in my honor.

Honorable John P. Flaherty, Jr., '58, first University of Pittsburgh School of Law graduate to be elected to the Pennsylvania Supreme Court.

Effective with the first-year class entering in 1956, the scholarship rules were changed to require an average of 71 to enter the second year and an average of 72 to enter the summer

Class of 1956 at a reunion in 1985.

session following the second year. The average required for graduation was raised to 72.

On February 25, 1957, the faculty met to discuss its position on two questions presented to it by a committee composed of representatives of the Board of Trustees, the administration and the faculty. The two questions were:

1. In a modern university, what part should the faculty play in the determination of university policy?

2. What would be the most effective structure for such faculty participation in policy-making? That is, what kind of faculty organization, how constituted and how operating, would best develop and communicate faculty thinking on policy matters?

After considerable discussion, the faculty tentatively set forth the following ideas, subject to further discussion and modification prior to a meeting of the faculty with Dr. Putnam Jones:

1. The University Faculty or the Faculties of the several subdivisions of the University should have the power to decide all matters which have direct and actual impact on the educational functions of the University.

2. The general Faculty should have the power, for example only: to determine the admission policy of each school, the intellectual level of instruction in each school, the entire athletic policy.

3. The faculty of each subdivision involved should have the power, for example only: to determine the requirements of academic standards to continue as a student and to qualify for a degree, for establishment of research projects, to establish the policy of the selection of members of the Faculty and the selection of the Members themselves.

Seymour J. Schafer, '58, Professor Clare B.McDermott, Jr., '52, and John J. Scuillo, '56 discussing research.

In the spring of 1957, I experienced a humorous and yet significant event. In my class in Sales, I had, among others, Sam DiFrancesco, Derrick Bell and Norman Rubash as students. One day, a student came into my office and announced that Sam was quitting law school because he had received a poison pen letter. I immediately sought out Sam and asked to see the so-called poison pen letter. After some reluctance on his part, he shared it with me.

In fact, it wasn't a poison-pen type of letter. The writer merely pointed out that Sam was asking so many questions in my class that he feared the course would not be completed by exam time. It suggested that Sam be circumspect about his questions. It was signed, "A Friend."

The next day, when I attempted to end the matter by explaining the problem created by asking too many questions, Derrick Bell raised his hand. He publicly apologized to Sam, explaining that before writing the note he had spoken with Sam about the problem. Since those conversations had apparently failed to ameliorate the problem, Derrick resorted to the anonymous note. Sam accepted the apology and I thought the matter was settled.

A few days later, every member of the class received a hectographed note, signed "A Friend." The note congratulated the recipient on asking the most intelligent questions and giving the most brilliant recitations. I remarked to the class that I received the letter, signed "A Friend." And since the "Friend" had identified himself earlier, we know who was responsible.

In fact, I knew Derrick, who at that moment protested his innocence, was not the sender of this letter. I knew it had to have come from Norm Rubash since I knew he worked part-time for Consolidation Coal Company and that he had available to him a hectograph machine at work.

The next day, Derrick asked for equal time. I obliged. He pulled from under his table a guitar and sang several original verses to the effect "I was only foolin' you."

I shall always remember that event. It was a mixture of humor and sensitivity. The participants and I enjoy recalling the incident whenever we are together.

Thomas M. Cooley, II, Esquire was named Dean of the School of Law in August, 1957 and I was named Associate Dean. Thomas M. Cooley, II, was a graduate of the University of Michigan and Harvard Law School. Upon his graduation from Harvard in 1935, he spent the next year as a graduate fellow. When he was selected as dean, he was a practicing attorney in Washington, D.C. I was in charge of administration of the Office of the Dean during that time.

At the September 16, 1957 faculty meeting, the new dean greeted the faculty and urged it to give him a list of the problems that demanded immediate attention.

The faculty approved Professor Sherman's taking the position of Chairman of the

Board of Arbitration of United States Steel Corporation and the United Steelworkers for a period lasting no later than September 1, 1958.

On December 6, 1957, Morris Ernst, Esquire, visited the law school to meet informally with faculty and students.

Law Day ceremonies were observed in the law school on February 18, 1958. The Law Review Banquet was held on March 27 at the Webster Hall Hotel. Dean Robert J. Farley of the University of Mississippi School of Law was the speaker.

Dean Cooley had, upon assuming the deanship, requested that the Scholarship Rules be reviewed. After considerable discussion, the new rules were adopted at a faculty meeting on April 23, 1958. They were as follows:

Thomas McIntyre Cooley, II

I.

(a) Any student whose record at the end of his first semester in residence indicates lack of capacity, interest, or diligence may be excluded or placed on probation at the discretion of the faculty.

(b) A student must attain a cumulative average of at least seventy-one (71) percent in all of his work in the first year in order to be advanced to the second year. Failure to attain this average will work an automatic exclusion from the school.

II.

(a) A student must receive an average for the work of the first semester of the second year of at least seventy-one (71) percent. A failure to attain this semester average will automatically place the student on probation and require his presence at a meeting before the Dean and the Scholarship Committee.

(b) A student must receive an average for his work in the second year of at least seventy-two (72) percent. Failure to attain this yearly average will work an automatic exclusion from the school.

(c) Further, a student must attain a cumulative average of at least seventy-two (72) percent in all of his law school work in the first two years in order to be advanced to the third year. Failure to attain this average will work an automatic exclusion from the school.

III.

(a) A student must receive an average for the work of the first semester of the third year of at least seventy-two (72) percent. A failure to attain this semester average will automatically place the student on probation and require his presence at a meeting before the Dean and the Scholarship Committee.

(b) A student must receive an average for his work in the third year of at least seventy-two (72) percent. Failure to attain this yearly average will subject the student to whatever conditions or actions, if any, the faculty shall deem appropriate and advisable under the circumstances of the particular case.

(c) The student must maintain a cumulative average of at least seventy-two (72) percent in all of his law school work in order to be eligible for graduation from the school.

IV.

For purposes of these rules, the work in the summer session after the second year shall be considered as work in the first semester of the third year. In the event the summer session is taken after the third year, it shall be considered as work in the second semester of the third year.

Upon exclusion for any of the reasons set forth herein, readmission may be obtained only upon the granting of a written petition to the faculty, which is granted in the discretion of the faculty for good cause in the particular circumstances of the individual case.

Any student whose record in grades, attendance or classroom performance at the end of any semester in residence, including his first, indicates lack of capacity, interest or diligence may be excluded or placed on probation at the discretion of the faculty.

At a faculty meeting held on July 23, 1958, the faculty recognized the retirement of Professor Robert C. Brown with best wishes to him and his wife for a happy, healthy and long period of retirement.

Dr. Elvis J. Stahr, Jr., who had been vice chancellor of the Social Professions resigned to accept the presidency of West Virginia University. The law faculty tendered him a farewell party on January 23, 1959, at 4:30 p.m. in Room 801, Bruce Hall.

One of the significant events took place in January, 1959 when the law school was officially excused from participation in the Trimester Program.

The Trimester Program had been proposed by Chancellor Litchfield. The academic year was divided into three equal terms. Designed to better utilize the university facilities and to enable students to shorten the time required for degrees, it enabled students to go year-round and graduate, in the undergraduate situation, in less than three years. The law school faculty had not embraced the program for at least two reasons. First, the law faculty was so limited in number that it would have required every faculty member to teach in all terms, leaving no time for substantial research and writing. Second, the law students generally used the summer to earn money for the next year of school. As a result, unless very significant amounts of financial aid were infused into the school, few students could afford to take the third trimester, roughly comparable to the summer term.

On March 12, 1959, the Law Alumni held a luncheon in connection with the regional meeting of the American Bar Association in Pittsburgh. The luncheon was held at the Penn-Sheraton Hotel with Chancellor Edward Litchfield as the speaker.

On March 18, the Annual Law Review Banquet was held. The honored guests were Anne X. Alpern, Esquire, '27, Attorney General of Pennsylvania and David Stahl, Esquire, City Solicitor of the City of Pittsburgh. Ms. Alpern was the first woman to serve on the Pennsylvania Supreme Court and the first woman Attorney General of the Common-wealth. The speaker was the Honorable J. Edgar Murdock, Chief Judge of the Tax Court of the United States.

Class of 1932 at their 25th Reunion — June 12, 1957.

The Annual Law Day Banquet of the Student Bar Association was held on May 1, 1959. The Honorable Hubert I. Teitelbaum, United States Attorney for the Western District of Pennsylvania served as toastmaster. The preliminary address was given by the Honorable Stuart L. Udall, Congressman from Arizona. The principal address, "The Bill of Rights Today" was given by the Honorable Simon E. Sobeloff, Chief Judge, United States Court of Appeals for the Fourth Circuit.

The Law Alumni Dinner was held on June 9, 1959 in the PAA. The Honorable Genevieve Blatt, '37, Secretary of Internal Affairs for the Commonwealth of Pennsylvania was the speaker.

On June 30, 1959, the faculty, after considerable discussion, voted to abolish the required summer session effective with the first year class entering in September, 1959. The principal reason for the action was a feeling on the part of the faculty that because other Pennsylvania law schools did not have a similar requirement the school was at a distinct competitive disadvantage.

Mrs. Marie G. Lindsay, Registrar, retired on January 1, 1960, having served the law school faithfully for 37 years, initially as law librarian and then, after two years, as Registrar.

In January, 1960, Professor Clare B. McDermott, one of five young professors, announced that he was resigning from the faculty at the end of the current academic year to accept a position with the Board of Arbitration of United States Steel Corporation and the United Steel Workers.

The Law Review Banquet took place on March 15, 1960 at Gateway Plaza. The Address was given by Russell J. O'Malley, Esquire, '28, President of the Pennsylvania Bar Association.

The Law Alumni Dinner was held on May 18, 1960 at the Penn-Sheraton Hotel.

While the compulsory summer session was abolished beginning with the 1961 session, there were questions raised about alternative experiences counting as credit for the problem course requirement. The faculty voted that work by a student in the United States Attorney's Office shall satisfy the problem course requirement. Also, satisfactory completion of one year of legal aid work was deemed a satisfaction of the problem course requirement.

On October 31, 1960, Professor Charles Wilson Taintor, II died. At a faculty meeting on November 3, the following resolution was adopted.

Charles Wilson Taintor, II, died on October 31, 1960 at the age of sixty-four. Professor Taintor came to the legal profession at a later age than most individuals, having spent several years in business after graduation from Harvard College. He returned to Harvard and received his Bachelor of Laws degree in 1935, his Master of Laws degree in 1936 and his Doctor of Science of Jurisprudence degree in 1939. During the academic year 1938-1939, he held a Brandeis Fellowship. Although he spent less than a quarter century in legal education, he put into those years the productive scholarship seldom equalled by one enjoying a much longer period of activity in the field.

Concentrating his interest on the law of property and conflict of laws, he made significant contributions in both fields. His authorship of casebook material and other writings is illustrative of a scholarly mind and a deep insight into the problems in his fields of interest.

As a teacher and scholar, Charles Taintor displayed an intense interest

in property law and conflicts. Moreover, he had an acute awareness of the whole of jurisprudence and its function. His wide knowledge of the common law and the feudal system imbued him with a great enthusiasm for the derivation of our modern laws and their application.

As a man, he was a gentleman in every sense of the word. He was a wise, generous and affectionate colleague and friend. A devotee of the arts, he found much enrichment in art and music. Always willing and eager to discuss the law, he was a sage opponent in any debate on a point in controversy. Whether won to his view or not, one always felt that he had profited by the experience. He never attempted to win his point by any means other than hard legal analysis and reasoning. In the process, he was always willing to listen with open mind to the presentation of the other side.

He loved to teach and did it superbly. His faith in and deep liking for students, his intense interest and enthusiasm for the subject matter and his animated classroom presentation made him a favorite of all students. His missionary zeal for the development of the legal mind has left its imprint on all of his host of former students. He enjoys a position of esteem and gratitude with all of them.

We, the Faculty of the University of Pittsburgh School of Law, pay our deep and affectionate respect to Charles Wilson Taintor, II, our departed colleague and friend. This school, the legal profession and all who were privileged to know him are better for having had him with us.

The faculty set up a Taintor Memorial Fund.

Dr. Litchfield and Dr. Van Dusen attended a faculty meeting on November 28, 1960 at which the Faculty Recruitment Committee reported. Dr. Litchfield pointed out that it might be possible to make an appointment which might also be helpful to some other school or department within the University.

Despite having received earlier an excuse from participation in the trimester program of the University, the university administration was again seeking the law faculty's approval of the trimester program for the school. In March, 1961, it was decided that a special meeting should be convened to consider a possible trimester arrangement for the law school. April 10, 1961, the faculty voted tentative approval of a Trimester Plan proposed by the Trimester Committee, as amplified by the Sell Memorandum, subject to obtaining satisfactory commitments from the administration. These conditions included the addition of scholarship aid for students since in a trimester program they would not have an opportunity to earn money for their education. There was also the condition that additional faculty positions be created in the school. The trimester program would give faculty no opportunity for scholarly work or any significant time off from teaching.

The Annual Law Day Dinner was held April 4, 1961, at the PAA. The dinner honored Charles Alvin Jones, Chief Justice of Pennsylvania. The speaker was Dudley R. Bonsal, Esquire, a partner in Curtis, Mallet-Prevost, Cold & Mosle, New York City. Mr. Bonsal was a member of the International Commission of Jurists and the Immediate Past President of the Association of the Bar of the City of New York.

The Alumni Dinner was held on May 17 in the Urban Room of the Penn-Sheraton Hotel. The Alumni Award was presented to Joseph Widmar, '61. The address was delivered by the Honorable James M. Landis, Special Assistant to President John F. Kennedy.

At a meeting of the faculty on May 2, 1961, the Dean explained that present information given to him was to the effect that the law school budget for 1961-62 would represent a substantial reduction from the current budget. The faculty then passed the following resolution:

> Resolved, that the faculty of the Law School believes the objectives of the school cannot be reconciled with budget reduction, that the faculty endorses the position taken by the Dean and the Associate Dean on the question of reduction, and that the faculty directs the Dean to invite the appropriate University officers to discuss the question of reduction with the whole faculty in order that our position can be demonstrated in detail.

The Trimester Committee met with David Henderson of the central university administration. He made suggestions to the Committee with respect to the listing of specific conditions and commitments. Generally, these conditions were ones voiced earlier by the faculty. They included the allocation of significant additional amounts of scholarship aid for students and additions to the faculty. The committee expressed its willingness to follow Henderson's suggestion but felt that while conditions might not be met, any willingness on the part of the faculty to go on the trimester would be taken as a commitment by the school to adopt the program.

On May 26, 1961, the faculty voted to raise the requirement for graduation for the class entering in September, 1961 to 86 hours from 84 hours.

Friends of the late Louis Caplan, Class of 1912, distinguished member of the Allegheny County Bar Association and former president of the Allegheny County Bar Association, established a lecture fund in the School of Law for the purpose of holding lectures by distinguished lawyers, jurists and professors. The inaugural lecture, held in 1962, was delivered by the Honorable Archibald Cox, who spoke on "Understanding the Supreme Court."

At a meeting held October 2, 1961, the Committee on University Use of Segregated Facilities presented its report. After discussion and several defeated amendment proposals, the faculty approved the following resolution:

> The University of Pittsburgh as an institution of higher learning attracts students, professors and visiting scholars of all colors, creeds and races who become a part of its educational endeavor. In the course of its activities, the University holds meetings, institutes, lectures, ceremonies and other functions in private clubs, and in restaurants, hotels and other places of public accommodation, resort or amusement, in which students, professors and visiting scholars should and do participate.

> Therefore, the Faculty of the School of Law of the University of Pittsburgh resolves that no meeting, institute, lecture, ceremony or other function of the School of Law shall be held at any private club, or any restaurant, hotel or other place of public accommodation, resort or amusement which discriminates because of race, creed, color, national origin or nationality.

Class of 1961 at a reunion.

The Faculty of the School of Law of the University of Pittsburgh directs the Dean to bring this resolution to the attention of the Administration and the Faculty of the University and recommends that there be established a University policy against the holding of any meeting, institute, lecture, ceremony, athletic contest, or other function, sponsored or supported, wholly or in part by the University, at any private club or any restaurant, hotel or other place of public accommodation, resort or amusement, which makes any distinction, restriction, exclusion or discrimination on the basis of race, creed, color, national origin or nationality.

On March 23, 1962, the faculty, following lunch in the Faculty Club, adjourned to Room 1418 where Dr. Van Dusen discussed building plans for a proposed law building. This appeared to be a perennial topic of discussion in faculty meetings. One started to get the feeling that such discussions were held to diffuse the faculty unrest over lack of a separate facility for the law school, a matter which held the attention of the faculty for a very long period of time.

Professor Henry Foster resigned from the faculty in the spring of 1962 to accept a position on the faculty of the New York University School of Law.

The Annual Alumni Dinner was held on May 17, 1962 at the PAA. The address was given by Professor Herbert Wechsler, Harlan Fiske Stone Professor of Constitutional Law at Columbia University Law School.

Dean Cooley sent a memorandum to the faculty members dated May 30, 1962 on the trimester subject. That memorandum read as follows:

I have read and reread all of the analyses which various faculty committees and I have made of the proposal that the Law School convert to some form of trimester.

These comprise, so far as my files show, the following:

1. Faculty response to the Chancellor's inaugural address (for)

2. My memo to the University Committee on Trimester (January 16, 1958—against)

3. The Bookstaver-McDermott study of the effects of trimester—expenses, benefits, detriments (against)

4. Bookstaver-Schulz-Sherman report of July, 1960 (for, with one member dubitante)

I conclude, needless to say, that I was right all the time. The negatives and the unassessable dangers seem to me far to outweigh any provable advantages other than the awards conformity may bring. True, conformity to views held in high places is often the better part of valor (whatever that means); but recent events in the electrical industry suggest that sturdy adherence to simple values may sometimes (by hindsight) appear the sounder course.

However this may be, I am persuaded by advisors whose sincerity and devotion to the School I cannot doubt that mere resistance is no longer possible. Accordingly, I suggest the maximum concessions compatible with my view of honorable capitulation the following:

A colorable trimester system involving

1. A Fall trimester conforming to the undergraduate calendar, and a Spring term including a trimester and one-half--all included within the present one-year tuition charge.

2. A Fall trimester as before, and a Spring trimester conforming to the undergraduate calendar—this to be followed by a (purely optional) one-half trimester running until June 15 (approximately), to be paid for separately.

Either alternative would involve added compensation for instructors who put in extra time to carry it out. Each would present genuine problems of curriculum arrangement. Both (to be acceptable) would have to enable those who took maximum advantage of their offerings to complete their law study by Christmas of the third year.

Either plan could be accompanied by a ½ trimester of orientation work preceding the opening of the Fall term. This would require some tuition payment and might be made available to undergraduates who would like to see what the study of law is like and, perhaps, to borderline applicants. Enrollees would not be degree candidates and could obtain credit only if later accepted. There may, of course, be better ways of doing what seems to be required. Please be prepared to discuss on Monday any which occurs to you, remembering:

a. The fate that overtook compulsory summer school.
b. The problem of charging tuition for partial terms.
c. The basic question—is this good for legal education (regardless of its expediency)?

On June 4, 1962, the faculty voted to approve the following memorandum to Dr. Litchfield:

Memorandum to Dr. Litchfield

After careful and extended consideration the faculty of the School of Law is prepared to frame for early adoption an experimental program under which the School will conform to the general University policy respecting the utilization of student time for the full year. This decision constitutes an opportunity to extend the influence of legal education within the University. However, it is the faculty's opinion that several basic considerations underlie any plan which is adopted.

If the Chancellor agrees it is feasible to prepare a plan based on the considerations below, the School of Law will submit such a plan by November 1, 1962.

1. The plan adopted must allow experiment in calendar and instruction to realize fully the aims of the University and the School of Law and must be grounded on the principle that the duty of the School of Law is to educate students for service to the community and the profession, that all other considerations are secondary to this duty and that the faculty must bear primary responsibility for successful accomplishment of this task.

2. The plan adopted will require that the School of Law receive a larger budget to operate under the extended program and to permit it to attract students and visiting faculty which will enlarge the intellectual horizons of the School and permit increased interdisciplinary activity. Adoption of a new program poses a challenge for the faculty to investigate the expanding role the School of Law may play in the University. Fiscal planning must be a facet of this investigation. Preliminarily, a figure of $35,000 will be needed. The exact requirements may be substantially more depending on the final plan adopted, but will increase in succeeding years. The Law School has accepted a responsibility to add to its own resources but suggests that as its role expands, an increasing call upon general University funds will be required.

3. It is the unanimous opinion of the faculty that under no circumstances should an extended session be made compulsory.

4. It is expected that the plan adopted will improve the University's program in legal education, but it should be recognized as experimental. It will be subject to continuing evaluation and modifications will be made as dictated by experience. If it is found that the quality of legal instruction or the quality of students is adversely affected, and modifications prove unsuccessful, the present calendar would then be restored.

5. After a detailed plan with careful cost estimates is drafted, the faculty will meet with the Chancellor after November 1 to answer his questions, raise any further considerations and consider with him whether the plan as presented can be implemented.

The faculty was convened for a meeting on June 5, 1962 in the Office of Chancellor Litchfield for the purpose of discussing what the law school faculty was doing in the direction of a fuller utilization of the student's time and mind during a greater portion of the calendar year. He made the following comments with respect to the faculty memo under date of June 4, 1962:

1. Paragraph #1 is not needed in such a memorandum. It is a statement of the obvious.

2. Paragraph #2 is also obvious. It is expected the institution of any additional programs will cost more money.

3. Paragraph #3 is not acceptable to him at this point, before a plan has been studied. If, after the working out of a plan the faculty feels it should not be made compulsory, he will accept this judgment. However, he does not wish to be bound before any plan is ever worked out.

4. He stated that with respect to Paragraph #4, it is always understood that new programs are experimental and that they will be abandoned or changed if they prove unsatisfactory or detrimental to the highest principles of education in the University.

5. With respect to Paragraph #5, the Chancellor stated that he is always willing to discuss matters with faculties and he will be pleased to discuss with the law faculty any plan they may evolve.

The Chancellor emphasized that he had no preconceived notions. He stated that it is possible that after full study the law faculty will conclude that there is nothing that it can or should do. If this is so, he will accept the well-considered judgment of the faculty.

On November 6, 1962, a proposal for an integrated law and business program was presented to the faculty, which voted to approve it. The proposal presented was as follows:

Proposal for an Integrated Law and Business Program

This proposal emanates from a conference held at Tumble Run on July 24. The participants were the Chancellor, Dr. Van Dusen, Deans Cooley and Robinson, and Professors Horty, Zoffer and Holahan. It was preceded by preliminary conferences in June and July at which the other participants exchanged views and framed an agenda for the meeting with the Chancellor. This memorandum is an effort to reduce the product of serveral long meetings to its basics. A full set of minutes is available in Dr. Van Dunsen's office.

The proposal contemplates:

(1) A combined program under which students of strong leadership potential, who might be viewed as the corporate statesmen of the future, would spend four years at Pitt and earn, in that time, the degrees of LL.B. and M.B.A. These students would spend the first two years in the conventional law school course. They would spend the third year in the M.B.A. program (three trimesters). The fourth year would send them back to the law school for administrative purposes. The fourth-year program, while satisfying the basic law school third-year requirements, would have a business orientation, using presently available electives. Any new joint offerings which the two faculties might develop, such as a "capstone" seminar, would be available to these fourth-year students. A "capstone" seminar would call for highly selective admission to participation, very substantial faculty effort, and recruitment of outsiders who are themselves "corporate statesmen."

(2) The numbers to be accommodated in this program would be small. Quality of the program would be pitched at the highest level at the expense of supposed recruiting desiderata. The Tumble Run meeting spoke in terms of "twenty or twenty-five students ten years from now."

(3) A dual admission procedure would be evolved for combined-degree candidates. This might be done by a joint admissions committee of the two schools. Or it might be done by the exchange of policy

statements. Coordination in this area would not imply departure from conventional faculty control of admissions, and business school admission might be revoked where a student's law school record established a lack of ability or motivation.

(4) Students in the combined program would be counseled by faculty of both schools working in cooperation.

(5) A joint curriculum committee would be established to consider areas where integration might be advantageous.

On October 8, 1962, the Trimester Committee issued another memorandum. There was a discussion of this memo at a faculty meeting on October 11th. At the conclusion of the discussion, the Dean asked each faculty member to prepare a memorandum covering possible alternatives to the trimester set-up. There was further discussion of the trimester plan at a meeting on November 15, 1962.

On March 8, 1963, a faculty meeting convened to discuss the various proposals that

University of Pittsburgh School of Law 1962

ORRIN G. HATCH   JACK E. MC GREGOR   GEORGE E. FOWKES   PETER F. MC NEISH   GORDON GORDON   PETER H. BLOCK   STANFORD A. SEGAL   ROBERT W. MANDELL   ROBERT A. LANGHAM   IRWIN M. STEIN   ROBERT B. BOWYTZ   SHOLOM D. COMAY   DAVID O'HANESIAN   RALPH F. KRAFT   JAN C. SWENSEN   WILLIAM K. HERRINGTON   ROBERT A. LEBOVITZ   ROBERT B. SHUST   ROBERT REED   GENE E. ARNOLD   JOHN R. PRUGER   CHARLES E. WITTLIN   GRETCHEN REED   ARNOLD B. SILVERMAN   JOSEPH R. ROYSTON, III   DAVID J. ASKIN   THOMAS L. COOPER

resulted from the extended discussions of the trimester program or other programs designed to utilize more of the students' calendar year. For the first time, there was an issue which was appearing to become a devisive factor in the faculty ranks. At the outset of the meeting, I made the following statement:

> I would like to make a statement at the outset of this meeting and then I intend to refrain from restating points which we have reviewed ad nauseum.

> The general topic which we are meeting to discuss today has been a topic of many, many meetings over the last few years. Varying positions have been stated and, from time to time, the attitudes of the faculty and its individual members have seemingly shifted. Changes in faculty personnel have had some effect on this shift.

> As we begin these deliberations, I would only ask that you consider the following points:

> 1. In my fourteen years on this faculty, we have never been cursed with a divided faculty. It is true that there has often been a situation of divided opinion. However, this has never spilled over into the area of personal animosity or the fear of later reprisal by any one against any other member of the faculty. Through extended discussion and debate over these several years on this general topic, I seem to sense the distinct possibility that the subject matter is beginning to become a dangerous weapon which could serve to cut deep personal wounds. Gentlemen, I plead that we avoid this at all costs.

> 2. After this meeting, I sincerely feel we should bury our personal differences, accept gracefully the decision and then, as mature individuals, work our heads off to insure the workability of whatever arrangement is settled upon. By this, I do not mean to indicate a desire to thwart individual freedom of thought. However, after the democratic process has been utilized, there is no room for outside manifestations of remorse, regret or dissension. I will not be a party to any minority report to be sent outside this school. I will not enter into any discussions with students on the matter of alternatives rejected. I will not name those in favor of or against any proposal.

3. I am frankly appalled and disappointed at the tremendous amount of valuable time this faculty and the Dean have expended on this matter. Had we this time back and were we to put it to productive scholarly effort, we would doubtless be much further ahead of the game. This cannot be, I realize. However, I implore you to join me in a genuine effort to get this matter out of our systems today and then move on to a more glorious and fruitful future of this law school which it has if we will only capture and use the opportunity. We owe this to the alumni and to the students going through.

4. Lastly, and this to me is superfluous, may we exercise our franchise in this meeting in good conscience and in accord with our individual sincere convictions.

I have great confidence in this faculty's ability to do a job and do it well, even when it isn't exactly what we might like. Now let's go to it and when we are done, let's close ranks, if indeed they be presently breached, and work for the common good. To do less would be something less than honorable."

After considerable discussion and several votes, the final vote was in favor of a program that basically rejected the trimester plan as being proposed by the general university administration.

After the decision reached by the faculty was conveyed to the central administration, I was called and asked to come to an administrator's office. I was asked to divulge the names of those who voted against the trimester. I explained that after a vote was taken by the faculty, there were no opposing views. Further, I told him that faculty votes were confidential items not to be disclosed to outsiders. It was obvious to me that retribution was a distinct possibility. Upon my refusal to disclose, I was summarily dismissed and returned to my office.

The Law Day Dinner in 1963 was held on Monday, April 29, at the Webster Hall Hotel. The speaker was Harvard Law Professor Paul A. Freund, who spoke on "The Supreme Court Under Attack."

In the spring, 1963, Professor William F. Schulz was appointed to a four-year term on the Pennsylvania State Forest Commission.

I have a fond recollection of the Secured Transactions class in 1964. There seemed to be an inordinate number of "unprepareds," even for seniors. One day, I pointed out to them that I thought they were taking the course in a rather cavalier manner.

The morning after the final examination in the course, I arrived at the law school at my usual 6:30 time. On the student bulletin board outside the main office on the

14th floor was posted an 8 x 11 paper on which was drawn a cartoon. At this time, Cavalier cigarettes were being sold, with the picture of a cavalier on the box.

The cartoon, produced with a red ball point pen, depicted a cavalier lying on the ground. His plumed hat was off at the side. Standing over him was a ghost identified as "Secured Transactions." The ghost had taken the cavalier's sword and stabbed him in the back.

I was so impressed that I took it down lest someone might remove it. I have often tried to find it in my files. It was the work of Harry A. Thompson. It was a masterpiece and I congratulated Harry for it, lest anyone might think I was offended by it. Whenever I see Harry, I have a warm remembrance of it.

The 1963 Caplan Lecture was delivered on December 18 in Foster Memorial Auditorium by the Honorable Thomas E. Dewey. His lecture topic was "Progress Toward World Peace Through Law."

On February 4, 1964, the faculty met with Chancellor Litchfield. The meeting was requested by the faculty to discuss some of the acute problems the law school faced. Professor Holahan made a presentation on behalf of the faculty. The chancellor responded, explained the present financial problems of the university and suggested that perhaps the only immediate source of relief was the law alumni.

At this time, the student body was becoming irritated over the physical conditions in the law school. The library space was inadequate. The tables and chairs in the classrooms were those used thirty years earlier when the school moved into the Cathedral of Learning. Students were complaining about the condition of the furniture, some of which was in a very shaky condition. Others produced splinters and damaged clothing.

The Student Bar Association decided that it should attempt to bring the matter to the attention of the University administration. To this end, Dr. Albert C. Van Dusen, Vice Chancellor of the Social Professions, was invited to come up to the law school and engage in a dialogue with the students.

The faculty were specifically barred from the meeting, which took place in the first-year classroom—Room 1409, in the Cathedral of Learning. Since I was obviously not at the meeting, I can only state what was told to me. Enough persons have corroborated the story to make it acceptable as fact. From all accounts, there were students wall-to-wall in the room, with many standing in the back and on the sides of the room.

Dr. Van Dusen proceeded to explain how much better off the law school was than some other segments of the University. He was in the midst of explaining how much better our furniture was when there was a sudden crash. Cyril A. Fox, jr., Class of 1965, was on the floor, his chair having disintegrated under him. Reports are that he picked himself up and, waving a piece of the broken chair in the air, vociferously agreed with Dr. Van Dusen that we had great furniture in the law school.

There are many who will never be convinced that this was a truly coincidental occurrence. They feel that Cy Fox hunted a chair which was in a state of near collapse and used it as the vehicle to prove his point.

In January, 1965, financial problems were of such magnitude that the law school had difficulty purchasing a new, badly needed mimeograph machine. Three Pittsburgh firms' contributions made the purchase possible. The firms were: McArdle, Harrington & McLaughlin; Reding, Blackstone, Rea & Sell; and Wilner, Wilner & Kuhn.

Later in the spring, the faculty considered limiting the first year class to 70 because of the financial situation. This was followed by the resignation of Thomas Cooley as dean of the School on May 11, 1965. He was given a leave of absence for the academic year 1965-1966 in order to accept a Visiting Professorship at the University of Illinois Law School. With this announcement by Dean Cooley, the faculty became concerned about leadership of the school for the coming academic year. It was obvious that while I was a logical choice for acting Dean, having served as Tom Cooley's associate dean for five years, I would not be appointed because I had earlier refused to disclose to the Litchfield administration the way individual faculty members of the faculty had voted on the trimester issue.

As I recall, Eugene Holahan suggested that we end-run the administration by setting up a method for running the school during the academic year 1965-1966. It was suggested to the University that a committee of full professors be in charge. The administration acquiesced.

The committee immediately elected me as chair and made it clear to me that they expected me to administer the school. They agreed to become involved only if I got into difficulties with the university and I needed some "fall guys." The plan worked very well and I think we progressed during the year while a search was being conducted by Dr. Van Dusen for a dean.

"Moot court" was a part of the educational experience in the School from the early years of its existence. Most of the experience was in moot appellate arguments, although from time to time a mock jury trial was presented. This usually depended on the energy or imagination of someone who would organize it. Mock trials attained a more structured level when the Academy of Trial Lawyers of Allegheny County organized a yearly competition between the law school and the Duquesne University School of Law in the spring of 1964.

In the first couple of years, KDKA radio personalities were involved in a "staged" incident which became the basis for the suit. These personalities were the litigants and witnesses. The trial was held in a federal courtroom and was broadcast by KDKA.

The Academy named its competition, which continues to this day, after the then Chief Judge of the United States District Court for the Western District of Pennsylvania, Wallace S. Gourley.

In the early years, the School won with some consistency. In 1965, the winners were

The Faculty conducting the annual seminar.

Seated (l to r): W. Edward Sell, Dean Thomas M. Cooley, II, Charles A. Woods, Jr.
Standing (l to r): Lee Silverstein, Herbert L. Sherman, Jr., David R. Bookstaver, Jack Rappaport,
 William F. Schulz, Jr., Charles B. Nutting and Clare McDermott.

William Alvah Stewart and Joseph Yablonski. The 1966 competition was won by James R. Blackwood and John J. Dean. In 1967 James A. Wymard and David F. Dunn were triumphant. Harry J. Gruener and Helen M. Witt won in 1968 and Vincent J. Bartolotta, Jr. and John A. Miller in 1969. Robert L. Potter and Edward C. Schmidt were the winners in 1971. The 1975 winning team was composed of Paul M. Pohl and Ivan S. Abrams.

Then the Academy enlarged the competition to include schools in addition to Pitt and Duquesne. Among those law schools competing at one time or another were Cleveland State University, Case Western Reserve University, the University of Buffalo, West Virginia University, the Dickinson School of Law, Widener University, Villanova University, Howard University, Catholic University and George Washington University. Presently, twelve schools are involved.

At the University of Pittsburgh School of Law, the competition proved to be very popular and students sought out the opportunity to represent the School long before the American Bar Association mandated the teaching of professional skills. The untimely death of Murray S. Love, a distinguished trial lawyer and a 1954 graduate of the school, resulted in his family, friends and law firm creating a fund to underwrite a Trial Moot Court Competition in his honor from which the Gourley Competition team is chosen.

The Murray S. Love Trial Moot Court Competition took effect in 1981 when its winners, Mark A. Nadeau and Michael J. Chutz, were the Gourley team. Team members since then chosen from the Love Competition were Thomas M. Fallert and Vicki L. Kuftic in 1982, Daniel J. Siegal and Dawne E. Sapanski Hickton in 1983, Steven E. Mackey and Patrick A. Milberger in 1984, Nora A. Hackett and Rex Regula in 1985, Amy Keim and Miles Kirshner in 1986, Jeffrey S. Horwitz and Laura A. Meaden in 1987, Sean M. Coleman and Kathy D. Miller in 1988, Jeffrey A. Schwartz and Anita J. Amato in 1989, Paul Walsh and Kevin Harkins in 1990, Andrew O'Hara and Kim Watterson in 1991, Gregory Silver and Shawn Reed in 1992, and Bethann Lloyd and William Pastorich in 1993. The 1994 Love champions are William Pastorich and Chris Ludmer.

Given that there are twelve schools competing, the success of the Murray S. Love champions of the University of Pittsburgh School of Law in the Gourley competition has been outstanding. Our 1983, 1987 and 1992 teams were victorious.

Even when not winning, the team wins. The Academy of Trial Lawyers attempts to pick the best plaintiff team and the best defendant team to move into the finals. It is not a round robin competition since obviously the Federal Court in downtown Pittsburgh

Donald Stock, Nathan Hershey and Eric Springer at work on the Hospital Law Research Project.

cannot afford such dedication of courtroom resources or trial judge time. The school's most recent attempts have been victories over the strongest team on the other side. Pitt brought in verdicts from the jury on the weak side of the case and outscored their opponents in courtroom skills.

This exercise underwritten by the Murray S. Love Competition has provided students with training in courtroom skills beyond what might be reasonably expected. The move into the law building provided the opportunity for formal curricular efforts in trial advocacy. Every afternoon save Friday sees a two-hour course in the Teplitz Courtroom taught by skilled adjunct faculty members who are outstanding courtroom attorneys or distinguished trial judges. Students today want more than the classroom experience and they get it in the Murray S. Love Competition. Each student participating will try a three-hour case before a judge or practitioner. The four who participate in the final trial will have tried at least four cases. Presiding at the final trial each year has been Murray S. Love's long-time friend, the Honorable Lawrence Kaplan, Class of 1953. This is one of the many ways Judge Kaplan, from time to time, serves the law school and its student body.

There is a tremendous investment of student time and effort in this non-credit activity. The enthusiasm of the students, supported by the friends of Murray S. Love, bodes well for the future of the legal profession. It is yet another example of the unique

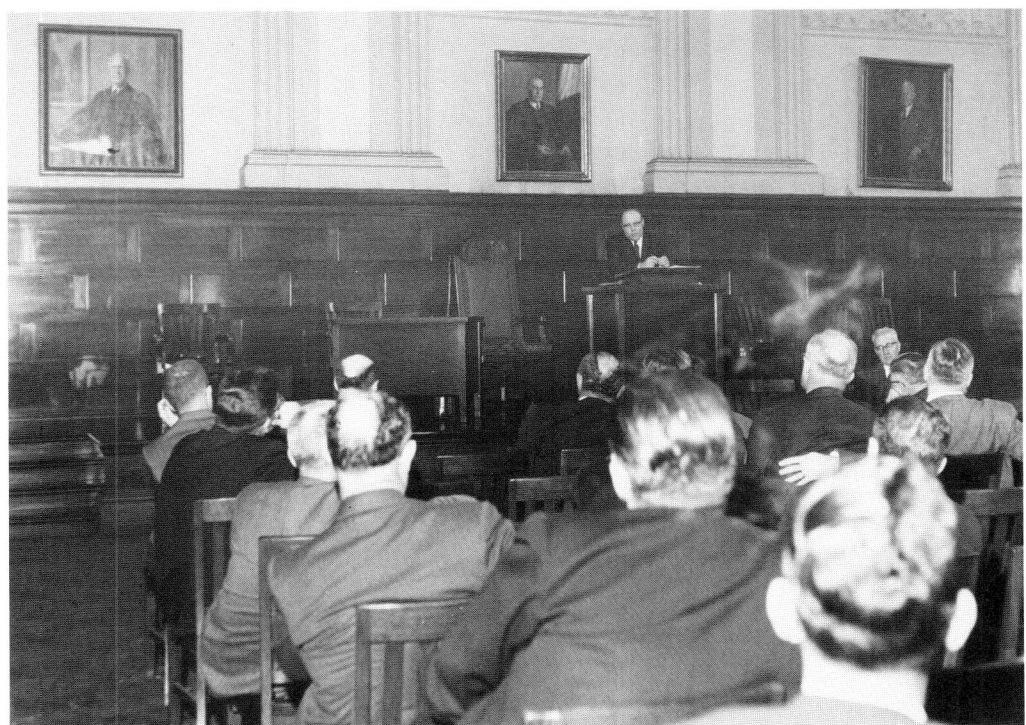

Professor Herbert Sherman discussing developments in tort law at the annual seminar on developments in Pennsylvania law.

opportunities that the University of Pittsburgh School of Law provides for those students who want to do well for themselves and by their profession.

I would be remiss if I didn't note with deep appreciation and thanks the yeoman effort that Professor Richard H. Seeburger has made in directing this activity. Unlike the appellate moot court program, administered by a student board, Professor Seeburger has the administrative responsibilities for the moot jury trial program. He expends vast amounts of time in running this very worthwhile program and the school is in his debt for those efforts.

The Annual Law Day Banquet of the Student Bar Association was held on April 15, 1964 at the Webster Hall Hotel. Dr. Arthur Larson, former dean of the law school, spoke on "A Practical Program for Peace, World Rule of Law."

On December 2, 1964, the Caplan Lecture was delivered by the Honorable Nicholas deB. Katzenbach, Acting United States Attorney General. The lecture, entitled "Civil Rights—Yesterday, Today and Tomorrow," was held in the Stephen Foster Auditorium.

CHAPTER
E·I·G·H·T
1965-1974

At a faculty meeting on September 8, 1965, the faculty was advised of the untimely death of former Dean Brainard Currie. The law school was being administered by an administrative committee chaired by myself. I proposed a 10-year plan for the law school. Professor Holahan was appointed to chair a committee to develop such a plan.

I was able to arrange for Edward Levi, former dean of the University of Chicago Law School and then with the Ford Foundation, to discuss with the faculty our situation. I felt it would be beneficial for the faculty to sit down with a very respected former law school dean to elicit his views and opinions concerning our situation and any suggestions he might make. At this time, I felt that the administration had questioned our position on goals for the school and our methodology for reaching them, as well as our feeling of inadequate treatment of the school. The faculty found the meeting, held at the Duquesne Club, to be very fruitful. We felt vindicated in the position we were taking with the administration.

One of the seminal events in the progress of the law school was the famous "Columbus Day Dinner" in 1965. The fall term of 1965 had started. During the first week of classes, I was leaving the Cathedral of Learning one evening about 6 p.m. At the same time, the late Gwilym A. Price, Class of 1917, retired CEO of Westinghouse Electric Corporation and at that time Chairman of the University's Board of Trustees, was coming out of the Cathedral of Learning. We stopped to chat briefly. As we left each other, I suggested to him that it would be worthwhile to have a meeting of the full-time faculty with the lawyer members of the Board of Trustees to discuss the law school and its future. At this time, I was chairing the Administrative Committee of the law school. I received no immediate reaction from Mr. Price.

Shortly thereafter, Dr. A.C. Van Dusen, Vice Chancellor of the Social Professions, called me about setting up such a meeting. It was scheduled for Tuesday, October 12, 1965, "Columbus Day."

Prior to this dinner meeting, I drafted a confidential appraisal of the law school's current status and its prospects for the future. This was hand delivered by me to the lawyer members of the Board of Trustees of the University. The trustees included George Lockhart, William Wallace Booth, Gwilym A. Price and Harbaugh Miller.

The report was as follows:

"Status of the School of Law"

The quality of a law school is hard to measure. It rests on many considerations which can be tested only by those who are intimately involved with the operation of the school and may for that reason be lacking in perspective or by those who, having considerable knowledge of legal education, devote time and effort to looking into the school's records, talking with its faculty and students and assessing the quality of the instruction and of such extracurricular programs as the law review.

There are, though, some tangible indices of quality that can be made available to those having a legitimate interest in the future of the school. They are summarized here, but should not be publicized.

The faculty believes, on the basis of this material and on its own evaluation of less tangible considerations, that the school has reached a juncture at which some hard decisions must be made concerning its

future. If certain needs can be met, existing opportunities can be seized and exploited to insure the growth and academic prosperity of the school. The meeting of these needs can be viewed as an investment with a prompt payout and a considerable return in prestige and quality of education. If these needs cannot be met, the law school faces a bleak future and consideration should be given to terminating its operation. The amount of money required is small in terms of the university budget. The means exist for generating it from tuition revenues and other sources. The factual basis for these assertions can be investigated quickly.

Students. Owing to the limited physical plant, the number of students in the school this year exceeds the number permissible under our accrediting standards. These students have been more and more carefully picked, as our admissions standards have been forced up beyond the point dictated, in our judgment, by purely educational values. While the school had more students than at present in the immediate postwar period, they were not so well selected as the present student body. Applications are at an all-time high, exceeding even the postwar period. Had the faculty request for space been granted late last winter, the school would presently be matriculating students at a rate calculated to produce a school population of three hundred. From now until 1969, we may anticipate a further increase in applications owing to an increase in the birth rate from 1943 to 1947 (most law students are twenty-two upon matriculation).

Student Performance. Bar examination results are now excellent, second only to Harvard's on the Pennsylvania examination, and superior to those of the other Pennsylvania schools (though Penn and Duquesne are also doing well). This is perhaps an unreliable index of the quality of education at a school, but it is a concrete one and has an important impact on the attitude of prospective students and the bar toward the school. Attrition has declined, though this is of course in part a reflection of the increasing selectivity of our admission standards. The faculty judges the performance of the students in class as well as in examinations to have improved up until last spring, when difficulties between the dean and the university administration, coupled with an airing of overall university problems, appear to have deleteriously affected student morale. It is somewhat improved over last spring and the favorable trend, it is felt, can be completely restored with assurances that the law school's needs will be met.

Faculty. The faculty is small (10 full time members) but of proven ability and dedication. The core of the faculty is the group of four full professors, including the librarian, who were appointed in the last years of the deanship of Judson Crane. It should be noted that no present member of the faculty has risen through the ranks at the university since that time. The faculty has suffered from rapid turnover and serious recruiting difficulties in recent years. It is presently below its traditional authorized strength, though, that strength is keyed to its old curriculum rather than the new curriculum which has resulted in faculty expansion at other schools. Recent experience suggests that newly-recruited faculty members will stay two years, then leave because of inadequate career expectations. None have stayed more than two years since 1960. Experienced people can be recruited only in extraordinary circumstances, usually alumni with strong local ties. Even these men are obtained only by paying them salaries in excess of those being paid to the men who taught them in law school. In matters of recruiting, the school cannot do as well as it did in past years, for example, the late 1940s, when many

experienced men were hired as well as beginners. The school is feeding on the reputation it built in past years in order to do as well as it does. The reason for the law school's problems with faculty recruitment and retention is inadequate career expectations. The erosion of the faculty, amounting to an average annual turnover of twenty to twenty-five percent depending upon the base used for computation, must be stopped. The faculty must be brought up to strength—an embarrassing share of the instruction is now in the hands of part-time teachers, of whom we have the best, but whose primary obligation, of course, is to the client and the firm. The faculty is united on its educational values. It appreciates, even reveres, the traditions of the school. Personal relationships are excellent, in part because would-be prima donnas have no time to quarrel with their colleagues. Salaries, however unbecoming it may be for the faculty to point this out, are a crucial problem. The average salary paid by the law school is less than the published figure for the average salary paid at the University of Pittsburgh. This is so though the law faculty is relatively senior (six full professors, three assistant professors, and one instructor-assistant to the dean, with a median age over forty). Further, it is usually felt necessary to pay a professional school differential, however unjust this may be to our more strictly academic brethren in the arts and sciences. This last problem is a fact of the academic marketplace, recognized, and it is not to be overcome by any amount of leadership. In salaries, Penn's law school has completely out-distanced Pittsburgh, as have the big-ten schools. Even Duquesne recently hired a thirty-two-year-old Professor of Law at a salary well in excess of what we pay our highest paid faculty member who is sixty.

The Library. The library is comfortable for those who can find seats and is run on a service principle, rather than on the principle of keeping the books on the shelves. It is prepared to meet most of the demands made upon it. It is too small in respect to accommodating both people and books, however. This is one respect in which the school is already violating minimal accrediting standards. The book-space problem is mitigated by the modesty of the acquisitions budget, the lowest of any law school library in Pennsylvania. In fact, the cost of continuation of existing sets is not assured. Some relief from the space problem is promised when seventh-floor space is available for classroom purposes.

The Physical Plant. The physical plant is the worst of any law school in Pennsylvania. It must be improved by allocation of space convenient to the present accommodations if law school expansion is not to await the erection of a law building in the distant future.

Costs and revenues. Law school is graduate education and cannot be cheap. At the same time, a law school can offer a considerable prestige, furnish an alumni body of influence and even wealth, and do this with considerably less expenditure than most graduate programs. Law schools offer more education per dollar because they have enormous faculty productivity. The best of the faculty is put to teaching large sections of freshman students rather than small seminars of illuminati. Our law school tuition revenues presently cover all direct costs charged to the law school budget. Costs will not increase proportionately to increase in revenues if the size of the student body can be substantially expanded. The law school can then make a contribution to general university overhead. It should be noted that the university contribution to the law school budget, i.e., the law school deficit, has been declining in recent years because tuition increases and growth in enrollment have exceeded increases in the law school budget. It should further be noted that the present budget and the proposed budget for the law school are smaller than the budgets of the law schools with which we are competitive, and smaller than the budgets of all other professional schools at the university.

What is to be done? The school cannot be continued on the present basis without fatal aggravation of its problems. Minimum academic standards are no longer being maintained in fact, although the school is still respectable and is still in a position to render important, needed service in training future lawyers. But faculty retention and recruitment, physical plant, and library difficulties threaten to overwhelm it. It has no dean and no prospect of securing one without a substantial increment in its budget. At the same time, the amount of money required to meet immediate problems is small, a small fraction of one percent of the university budget. With this increment in budget, the school can prepare to expand and can finance its own improvement out of increased revenues. The trustees and administration of the university should therefore be invited to arrange for such inspections and evaluations as will substantiate these claims before the end of the calendar year, with the aid of a committee of the Association of American Law Schools or, possibly, of the Ford Foundation Study Committee, which includes Edward Levi, former dean of the University of Chicago School of Law, and which has staff and funds to do a proper job.

The dinner was held in the Venetian Room of what was once the Schenley Hotel and was now the Student Union. Following dinner, I made an oral presentation, expounding somewhat on the written materials earlier distributed to the trustees. A frank discussion ensued with both faculty and trustees participating.

In my remarks, I had pointed out just how poorly the law school had been treated by the university administration in relation to other schools and departments. It was then that I told the trustees they had but one basic decision to make—"feed it or shoot it." I noted that the school was blessed with too many wonderful alumni to have their law school being subjected to a slow and painful demise. I declared that I needed an immediate infusion of $60,000 into the law school budget.

The Annual Meeting of the Association of American Law Schools was to be held between Christmas and New Year's in Chicago. This meeting used to be called the "slave market." I pointed out that there was a seller's market for law professors and we felt confident we could relocate should they elect to close the school. In any event, I stated that we needed a definite answer to the request by December 15 at the latest. Although there was a soft murmur about the needs of other units in the university, I indicated my lack of concern for their plights, especially in view of the fact that during the preceding years of the Litchfield Administration, these others expressed no concern about the treatment accorded the law school.

It should be noted that one reason for the lack of support of the school arose out of an unwillingness of the law school faculty to embrace the trimester system. There were several reasons for this position. First, the faculty was so small that a trimester would have resulted in no scholarly productivity from the faculty. Second, most students needed to work in the summer to gain money for the academic year. The law school's scholarship fund was pathetically small. In any event, the law school faculty rejected the trimester program and we paid the price.

After I made the presentation of the law school's problems, expressions of surprise came from some of the trustees, who stated they were never aware of the law school's situation. As the meeting ended, Mr. Price expressed the hope that some help would be forthcoming for the law school.

On November 18, 1965, Dr. Van Dusen called me and asked me to convene a meeting of the faculty. I did so that day and he announced to the faculty that the trustees had granted an immediate increment in the law school budget of $60,000.

Needless to say, that grant provided the impetus for the faculty to remain intact and work on improving the overall condition of the school. I was able to adjust some salaries and make some badly needed adjustments in the budget generally.

The fall of 1965 again saw suggestions by the University Administration that the law school move to the 4th, 5th and 6th floors of the Cathedral of Learning. Most discussions and studies concluded that the school would not benefit substantially from any relocation within the Cathedral. Further, any move of this type would relieve the pressures for a separate law building and probably delay the achievement of such goal.

Dr. Stanton Crawford, formerly Dean of the College and then Acting Chancellor of the University following the departure of Dr. Litchfield, passed away in January, 1966. Dr. David Kurtzman, who served in Governor Lawrence's cabinet and who returned to the University to work on the project of making the University of Pittsburgh a state-related institution, succeeded Dr. Crawford and served until the appointment of Dr. Wesley W. Posvar as Chancellor.

During this academic year, a search was underway to obtain a successor to Dean Cooley.

The Annual Survey of Developments in Pennsylvania law published in the University of Pittsburgh Law Review was terminated by faculty action. The position of the faculty in making this decision was that faculty research and writing could better be directed to broader problems in their particular areas than limiting their efforts to Pennsylvania law, as was the case in producing the annual survey.

On December 15, 1965, the Honorable Thurgood Marshall, Solicitor General of the United States, delivered the Caplan Lecture in Carnegie Music Hall.

By April, there appeared a feasibility study run by the University architects regarding the relocation of the law school to the fourth, fifth and sixth floors of the Cathedral of Learning. A review by the faculty led to its being referred back to the architects for reconsideration.

My term as Chair of the Administrative Committee of full professors for the '65-'66 academic year proved to be very interesting. The famous Columbus Day Dinner was the start of what was to be a series of unusual events. A dean search was mounted. It was not conducted the way dean searches are conducted at the University today. Apparently, the vice chancellor was conducting the search. Various candidates were brought to the school, culminating with a chiropodist from Cleveland, Ohio, who had graduated from a night law school.

At this time, Dr. David Kurtzman was occupying the position of chancellor, following the sudden death of Dr. Stanton Crawford, acting chancellor. Apparently some faculty members were distressed over the search and some of the candidates brought to them. They made their feelings known to Dr. Kurtzman.

I was called down to Dr. Kurtzman's office in the early summer. In a long conversation, he told me he wanted to appoint me dean of the school. I told him I wasn't interested and that I was leaving for vacation the next day with my family. I felt there were some individuals still in the administration of the university who found me unacceptable because of my earlier refusal to cooperate in "ratting" on my colleagues. Dr. Kurtzman made me promise not to make any final decision. We agreed to meet when we were both back on the campus, he being ready to leave for a trip to South America.

In August, we met. He and Dr. Van Dusen were present and stated they wanted to make the announcement before the start of the fall term in the law school. I accepted.

On August 24, 1966, Dr. David Kurtzman announced my appointment as dean of the School of Law. The following is the press release issued by the University.

William Edward Sell.

W. EDWARD SELL NAMED
PITT LAW SCHOOL DEAN

PITTSBURGH, August 24—W. Edward Sell, who has served as chairman of a faculty executive committee administering the University of Pittsburgh School of Law for the past year, today was named dean of the School.

The appointment was announced by the University's acting chancellor, Dr. David H. Kurtzman. "Professor Sell's long service with the University, his demonstrated ability as associate dean from 1957 until 1962, and as chairman of the Law School Executive committee, make clear the desirability of his appointment now to the permanent post of dean," Dr. Kurtzman said.

Born in Hanover, Pa., Mr. Sell received the bachelor of arts degree from Washington and Jefferson College in 1944 and the bachelor of law degree from Yale University Law School in 1947.

He became instructor in law at Pitt in 1947 and served successively as assistant and associate professor before becoming a full professor in 1954. From 1951 to 1953, he also served as an attorney for the United States Steel Corporation. He was a visiting professor of law at the University of Michigan School of Law in the summer of 1957.

He was associate dean of the School from October, 1957 to September, 1962.

An Executive Committee of the Law School faculty was created in August 1965 to administer the affairs of the School after the resignation of the former dean, Thomas M. Cooley III. Mr. Cooley, who has returned to teaching, now is a professor of law in the School.

Mr. Sell is a specialist in commercial and business law. He is the author of a text, Fundamentals of Accounting for Lawyers, used in the University's law curriculum, and of various articles in legal periodicals.

He is a member of Phi Beta Kappa; Order of the Coif; American Law Institute; the American, Pennsylvania and Allegheny County Bar Associations, for which he is active on a number of committees; and the Commission on Race and Religion of the Pennsylvania Synod of the Presbyterian Church.

Professor Sell and his wife, the former Cordelia Fulton, and their son, Jeffrey Edward, 12, make their home at 106 Seneca Drive, Mt. Lebanon.

Bartlett McGuire, Esquire, and R. Stanton Wettick, Jr., Esquire, were welcomed to the faculty for the 1966-67 academic year.

When law schools developed in the United States in the nineteenth century, most of them required no previous academic work past high school graduation. Accordingly, the law degree was the baccalaureate degree. By the early twentieth century, law schools began to require some college education—first a year or two, then three years, and eventually the requirement was a college degree.

When a college degree began to be required, it seemed redundant to receive two bachelor degrees. The law school faculty in 1924 considered changing the degree to juris doctor. Although a faculty committee was appointed to study the matter, there is no indication in faculty minutes that such committee ever reported back to the faculty.

The question of the title of the law degree arose in American law schools in the 1960s. The impetus for this move to change the degree to juris doctor (J.D.) was the differential in the federal pay scale between the LL. B. and the Ph.D. When the law schools were unable to convince the federal authorities to equate the two degrees for salary purposes, law schools began to change their degree.

A significant action at the November 30 faculty meeting was to set the maximum enrollment in any law school course at 120 students. That rule is still in effect in the school.

The Louis Caplan Lecture was delivered on December 13, 1966, by the Honorable Leonard Meeker of the State Department. The title of his presentation was "Vietnam and the International Law of Self-Defense."

On October 31, 1966, Professor Norman Anderson, dean of the London University Law School and director of the Institute of Advanced Studies, was a guest of the law school.

In November, the school received authorization to recruit two additional faculty members for the academic year 1967-1968. Later that month, the school received a grant from the Ford Foundation in the amount of $6,000 to increase the international law collection.

In December, 1966, Professor David Cohen was awarded a grant from the International Dimension Committee under the Ford Foundation Grant for a summer project in England to study various problems of British entry into the Common Market.

At a faculty meeting on January 23, 1967, I announced the appointment of Professor John E. Murray, Jr. to the faculty. Professor Murray was at that time a faculty member at the Duquesne University School of Law.

The Annual Law Review Banquet was held on March 21 at the Park Schenley Restaurant. Justice Samuel Roberts of the Pennsylvania Supreme Court was the speaker. Some other members of the Court were in attendance as guests.

The Law Alumni Dinner was held at the Hilton Hotel on April 26, 1967. The speaker was Dr. Richard C. Bates, a medical director of General Motors. He spoke on how to get a heart attack. The address was obviously a satire. He was pointing out those practices and habits that can lead to heart attacks. The talk was very effective in making his points. Asserting that lawyers can be likely candidates for heart attacks, he drew the particular attention of the spouses of lawyers present.

A sad note during the 1966-67 academic year was the passing of Paul B. Wilson, Jr., a member of the second-year class. The faculty adopted a resolution of condolence on his death at a meeting on June 19, 1967.

As the year wore on, continued discussions of the law school's major space deficiencies took place. Although the school was promised some additional space on the thirteenth floor of the Cathedral of Learning, it would not be available until the following November or December.

September 15, 1967, Dr. Wesley W. Posvar announced a reorganization of the top administration of the University of Pittsburgh.

The key change was the creation of the office of Provost. Dr. Charles A. Peake was the first appointee to the position. The office of Vice-Chancellor-The Professions was abolished. Instead of reporting to the Vice Chancellor, the law school now reported to the Provost.

Despite the rigors of law school study, students still found a bit of time for humor.

Mr. Seeburger's first-year class presented him with the following, supposedly authored by Helen Witt, '69:

> We've certioraried
> And habeas corpused
> Through Powers and Duties and Rights.
> We've peered microscopically
> (Granted, myopically)
> At Jehovah's Witnesses' plights.
> But Mr. Seeburger,
> We have to inform you
> That 1200 pages cause pain.
> In truth, it's like reading
> Our highest court's holdings
> On Burma-Shave signs from a train!

The 1967 Glick Memorial Seminar was held at 8:15 p.m. on November 9 at the Duquesne University School of Law. Professor David Cohen and Paul M. Singer, a third-year student, participated in the discussion following a presentation by Professor Milton Katz of Harvard Law School: "The Cold War and the Peaceful Settlement of Disputes: The Relevance of International Adjudication."

While discussions occurred through the years in legal education circles about the law degree, it never became a serious problem until the 1960s, when government salary scales accorded the Ph.D. about three or four grades higher than a Bachelor of Law degree. While law school deans pointed out to the government the inequity in the salary differential, it was to no avail. Consequently, encouraged by law student petitions, the law schools rapidly began to convert their degrees.

On December 12, 1967, the faculty, by a 7 to 6 vote, empowered the dean to take the necessary steps to effect the change of degree from Bachelor of Laws to Juris Doctor beginning with the 1968 graduating class and to apply the same retroactively.

Within a year, the faculty had reversed itself from its decision of November 10, 1966, when a student petition for the change was denied.

At this point in time, a number of law schools had changed the degree from Bachelor of Laws to Juris Doctor. Given this trend and the salary implications flowing from the change with respect to government service, the faculty deemed it crucial that the school follow this trend in transforming the degree.

At this time, the law school was in a serious financial situation. The budget had not kept up with the basic needs of the school. The library was so short of budget that the law librarian was forced to discontinue some periodicals. Having received approval for the degree change from the trustees, I wrote to the alumni, offering to convert the degree they held for a $25 charge. Most alumni quickly responded. All monies so received were placed in the law library budget. A very large majority of our alumni chose to so convert their degrees. The new diploma, signed by W. Edward Sell, Dean, carried a legend on the bottom indicating it was issued in substitution for an initial degree awarded on a particular date. This was a significant action by the faculty and deserves some background information.

The funds so collected enabled the Librarian to resubscribe to those periodicals that had been discontinued.

The annual Law Review Banquet was held on March 12, 1968 at the Park Schenley Restaurant. Marvin Comisky, Esquire, former chancellor of the Philadelphia Bar Association (1965) and general counsel of the Pennsylvania Constitutional Convention, was the principal speaker.

Two weeks later, on March 27, Dr. Posvar was inaugurated as chancellor in the Carnegie Music Hall. When the annual Law Alumni Dinner took place on April 6, 1968, at the Chatham Center Ballrooms, Dr. Posvar was the principal speaker.

On April 9, classes were suspended from 10 a.m. to 1 p.m. in memory of Dr. Martin Luther King, Jr., who had been assassinated five days earlier.

As a result of the efforts of William K. Unverzagt, Esquire, Class of 1937, Vice President and General Counsel of Alcoa, the Alcoa Foundation made a grant for the establishment of a scholarship in the school for 1968-1969.

On October 17, 1968, the Honorable William P. Bundy, Assistant Secretary of State for East Asian and Pacific Affairs, delivered the Caplan Lecture in the Auditorium of Lawrence Hall.

A University-sponsored international conference was held October 20-25 at the William Penn Hotel on "Interdisciplinary Aspects of the Application of Engineering Technology to the Industrialization of Developing Countries." Professor David Cohen was a reporter and Professor Larry Lee was a discussant.

The University administration adopted a plan for each school to have a Board of Visitors. The chair of each board was to be a trustee. The dean and faculty could make recommendations to the Chancellor for membership on the board. Each board was to consist of outsiders who were involved in that area or field. Out initial board was comprised of lawyers, judges and legal educators from other institutions. The board meets once or twice a year. It reviews the school's program and meets with faculty, students and the administrative staff. At the conclusion of its meeting, it meets with the Provost and/or the Chancellor, reporting on its reactions and recommendations. A Board of Visitors meeting was held on November 7, 1968. The members of the first Board of Visitors were: Harbaugh Miller, Chair; William W. Booth; Rev. Dr. Robert M. Carson, Jr., Ralph H. Demmler; William H. Eckert; Professor Ralph Fuchs; the Honorable A. Leon Higginbotham; James M. Houston; William H. Knoell; the Honorable Thomas F. Lansberry; R. Heath Larry; Professor Robert B. McKay; the Honorable John L. Miller; J. Quint Salmon; William K. Unverzagt and Edward T. Tait.

A highlight of the fall was the success of Edward L. Symons, Jr., a third-year student, and Allan McClain and Michael P. Malahoff, second year students, in winning the regional eliminations of the National Moot Court Competition. The team went on to place second in the national finals in New York. The Chief Justice of the panel hearing the final argument was the late Justice Thurgood Marshall.

I thought a faculty retreat would afford an opportunity to discuss matters affecting the school and legal education without the time constraints faced in regular faculty meetings. The first retreat was held on January 9 and 10, 1969 at the Mountain View Inn outside Greensburg. It was agreed that no actions would be taken. Matters such as class attendance, grading and curriculum were discussed. Faculty members were selected to lead particular discussion topics. We held these retreats for about four years. By then, the faculty had expanded in size to the point where law school funds could not bear the expense, although I thought the retreats were very worthwhile.

A practice developed with certain members of the Class of 1969 during their senior year. Atlantic Richfield was distributing red styrofoam balls to place on auto antennas.

(l to r): Edward L. Symons, Jr., '69, Justice Thurgood Marshall, Allan McClain, '70 and Michael P. Malakoff, '70.

Some students, apparently in an effort to work off steam, developed a game known as "Red Ball." These seniors, depending on the person with whom you talk, were headed by Frank E. Yourich, Jr., Ed Symons or Harry Greuner. Others in the group included Ted Brooks, Rich Davis, Wayne DeLuca, Norm Green, Mike Kelly, Gerry Marcovsky, Bernie Marcus and Sam Orr. A bench was used and they hit the ball against the wall, similar to racquetball.

I had just had one of the classrooms repainted (and no one will ever appreciate the effort that took). Every time the ball was hit against the newly-painted wall, it left a red dot. I happened into the room while a game was in progress. There sat Wayne DeLuca on a chair placed on top of a table. He was the "judge," making rulings in accordance with the rules set up for the "game." Upon looking at the wall full of dots, I asked what they were doing. After seeing Harry Gruener and Ed Symons present, I lost any thought of anger. Instead, I suggested the wall needed painting. It was repainted. By whom I do not know.

There were a couple of other "athletic events" by this group. In one, I understand that Frank Yourick and Ted Brooks were engaging late one evening in a game of red ball. One of the players ran into the door and broke the glass. They realized they were in trouble and so took the door to the eighth floor and exchanged it for a door from that floor. After the exchange, they realized that the new door had painted on it the room number from the eighth floor. Although I never heard of the outcome (mainly because I only heard of the event years later), I understand the gentlemen worked out a solution with my associate dean.

In the other incident, Mr. Brooks and Ray Baum were playing soccer in the hall on the fourteenth floor, using an empty milk carton as the ball. During the game, Ray ran into one of the bulletin boards on the fourteenth floor breaking the glass in the door.

But lest you think this group of students put all of their energy into these athletic contests, I assure you some of their "games" had a slight relationship to the academic side. They were in Dave Bookstaver's class in decedents' estates. Dave had a reputation for issuing strings of citations for many propositions. Some of these citations were from English reports. Apparently the students conducted pools, selecting a number. The one whose number was closest to the last citation Professor Bookstaver gave for that class period would be the winner. I understand that some times one who earlier had the winning number would ask Dave to repeat the earlier citation at the bell so as to be the last. At least all of this demonstrates how some overactive students decided to work off the

excess energy in these extracurricular activities.

After the arrival of Dr. Posvar as chancellor, I began to suggest to him and his administration that in order to develop a first-rate law school, it was essential that the school have its own building.

At this time, the school had only sixty seats in the law library. Students were not permitted in the library unless they were doing actual legal research. Merely studying between classes had to take place in a room on the fifth floor of the Cathedral, which contained only tables and chairs—no law books.

At this time, I was concerned about the lack of minority students. Efforts I had made to win some highly promising minority students met with failure when the larger law schools with many more resources were able to outbid me successfully. I had an idea for a program for minority students in which we would take a limited number of such students who demonstrated promise and motivation but who did not possess the traditional qualifications. The faculty accepted my suggestion for the program, which would permit this group of students to spread their program out over more than the normal three year span. While they were able to spread the academic program over another semester or two, I want to emphasize that in every course they took the same examination and with the same anonymous grading system in place as the students who were regular admits to the school.

Unable to secure funds within the University, I sought the aid of The Carthage Foundation. To inaugurate the program, that fund gave me an initial grant of $10,000. They made additional grants in succeeding years, as did the Alcoa Foundation. While I had hoped to have a success rate of at least 40%, we actually enjoyed a rate of almost 80%. Graduates of the early years of the program have distinguished themselves in the profession. And I think the school is better for having put the program in place.

On January 30, 1969, the law alumni held a luncheon at noon at the Hilton Hotel in conjunction with the annual meeting of the Pennsylvania Bar Association being held in Pittsburgh.

The Glick Memorial Seminar was held on Wednesday, February 5 at 4:30 p.m. in the Frick Fine Arts Auditorium. Professor Harold Berman of the Harvard Law School spoke on "The Comparison of Soviet and American Law: Its Significance for International Relations." Hal had been a classmate of mine at Yale Law School.

Professor David M. Cohen received a Congressional Fellowship under a grant from the Ford Foundation through the American Political Science Association. Professor Wettick took a leave of absence for the next academic year in order to serve as Executive Director of the Neighborhood Legal Services Association.

The annual Law Review Banquet was held on April 29 at the Park Schenley Restaurant. Byrd R. Brown, Esquire, was the speaker.

The annual Law Alumni Dinner was held on May 10 at the Chatham Center.

For the academic year 1969-70, Cyril A. Fox, jr., Esquire, joined the full-time faculty.

A faculty retreat was again held at the Mountain View Inn on January 13 and 14, 1970. Ideas dealing with admissions, curriculum, grading, faculty development and budget were discussed. No formal action was taken on any topic.

The Law Review Banquet was held on March 19, 1970 at the Park Schenley Restaurant. David Stahl, '49, deceased, Judge of the United States Court of Appeals for the Third Circuit was memorialized. The Honorable Richard L. Thornburgh, United States Attorney for the Western District of Pennsylvania, was the speaker.

The Law Alumni Dinner took place on May 2 at the Chatham Center Ballroom. The Honorable Leon Higginbotham was the speaker.

The Glick Memorial Lecture was delivered by Professor Paul A. Freund of Harvard Law School on May 15, 1970 in the Pittsburgh Room of the William Penn Hotel.

Early in the academic year 1970-71, the Chancellor informed me he wished to visit the school for the greater part of a day. Dr. Posvar visited the school on October 13, 1970. The Chancellor came with no agenda. His main purpose was to become better acquainted with the faculty, the students and the program of the school. He visited a couple of classes, spoke with students and met with the faculty.

Again, the matter of finding a home for the law school became a topic for faculty discussion. At this time, a suggestion had been advanced that the law school might be moved to Pennsylvania Hall, near Pitt Stadium. That facility had been vacated by the medical school. The faculty expressed substantial reservations. I opposed the idea because I thought it would foreclose getting a law school building erected for the school.

During this period, the question of clinical education was advanced. An ad hoc committee of faculty and students was appointed to study the matter. While there was considerable support for the idea, there was a feeling that present budget and space limitations made the institution of such programs impractical.

On January 21, 1971, there was a one-day off-campus faculty retreat held at the Holiday Inn West at the Parkway West. The discussions covered class scheduling, model answers for examinations, admissions, seminars and the law school calendar.

The entire space allotted to the school was grossly inadequate. Student Bar Association leaders were constantly criticizing the quarters. While I understood that the university administration had other priorities in terms of space and facilities, I would not wait for what might be a very long period until the school attained a space priority position.

I proceeded on my own to meet with Pitt Law Alumni in the state legislature, especially K. Leroy Irvis, Eugene Scanlon, Edward Zemprelli and John B. McCue. My dear friend, Dr. Bernard Kobosky, was my helpmate in this effort. The result was the introduction of a bill in the Legislature to authorize the General State Authority to issue $6.9 million of general revenue bonds for the purpose of erecting a School of Law building.

The site selected was the corner of Forbes Avenue and Bouquet Street. But that wasn't the end of the effort. The exercise of eminent domain to take the site of the Civic Motel ran into procedural delays. And then, when that appeared to be settled, the city balked at closing Gurtz Way, which was an alley behind the Civic Motel and Stuckert's Service Station, used primarily to service the motel. Eventually, that problem was solved and we were ready to schedule a groundbreaking after the motel and service station were razed.

For many years, a student hoping to practice law in the Commonwealth of Pennsylvania after graduation was required to register with the Pennsylvania State Board of Law Examiners and to have a preceptor. The preceptor was a practicing lawyer. The student had to serve a six-month internship with the preceptor, at least three months of which had to be taken after the bar examination. In theory, during this preceptorship, the student was to be made aware of many facets of practice, including the operation of the courthouse and many basic matters involved in the practice of law, such as a title search, a real estate closing and similar transactions. Unfortunately, while the preceptorship had lofty goals and practical advantages, there were many variations and some abuses, resulting in increasing criticism of the plan as it then existed. The criticisms led the Pennsylvania Supreme Court to abolish the system on February 1, 1971.

The Law Review Banquet was held on April 8 at the Student Union. The Law Alumni dinner was held on May 8 at the Student Union Ballroom. The University Commencement took place on May 29 in the Civic Arena. Following that event, the law school held its own graduation program in the Student Union. The Honorable Alfred P. Murrah, Director of the Federal Judicial Center, was the speaker at the separate program. He spoke on "The Seven Lamps of Advocacy."

I mention this because this marked the first time the law school had a separate graduation following the University Commencement. Later, when the University Commencement began to be held earlier, the law school participated in that event in only a token way. Two law students would ceremonially go through the University program. The law school now conducts its own graduation ceremony late in May each year.

Beginning in the fall of 1971, the Journal of Legal Education was published out of this law school, with Associate Dean John E. Murray, Jr. serving as Editor.

The Journal of Legal Education is a publication of the Association of American Law Schools. It is published in collaboration with the West Publishing Company. It contains materials dealing with legal education. The Editorship of the Journal is rotated every several years. We were fortunate in being offered the opportunity and in having John agree to be the Editor. Richard Seeburger served as Book Review Editor.

At the first faculty meeting in the next academic year, I discussed the on-going space problem and the delay in the construction of a new law building.

A meeting of the Board of Visitors was held on Friday, November 5, 1971. While a number of problems were discussed, much of the meeting was centered on the law school budget, faculty development and space needs.

One of the sad moments for me was the announcement by Professor Bartlett McGuire of his resignation from the faculty to return to the practice of law in New York City. He was bright, energetic and creative, and I felt he had a brilliant future in legal education.

On March 15, the Law Review Banquet was held at Chatham Center. The speaker was the Honorable Benjamin R. Jones, Chief Justice of Pennsylvania.

The annual Law Alumni Dinner was held on May 6 in the Student Union. The dinner was held in the Supper Room and Ballroom of the Student Union. The speaker was Richard K. Donahue, president of the Massachusetts State Bar Association.

Solis Horwitz, Esquire, university professor, who served on the law school faculty in addition to being University Counsel, died on April 25, 1972. At a special faculty meeting held on May 11, 1972, the following resolution was unanimously adopted:

> Solis Horwitz, colleague, friend, public servant, lawyer, passed away
> Tuesday evening, April 25, 1972. His passing leaves a void in our ranks.
> While he joined the faculty only four years ago, his association with us
> and with the students was a rich and rewarding one. We benefitted from
> his advice and the wisdom of his wide experience in administration. We

valued his friendship and those precious times when he would recount his experiences in government. We recognize the stabilizing influence he often exerted when difficult problems were before us for decision. He was interested in us and in the school. In his death, we sense the loss of this influence. We adjourn this meeting out of respect for the memory of this gentle, wise and kind man.

The graduation speaker at the June 3 ceremony in Lawrence Hall was the Honorable Edward D. Re, Judge, United States Customs Court.

The 1972-73 academic year began with our new additions to the full-time faculty—Professor Jackie Kanovitz and Professor Robert B. Harper. Professor Francis E. Holahan had taken retirement.

One of the highlights of the fall took place on Thursday, November 2, 1972, at 4 p.m., when ground was broken for the new law school building. Chancellor Wesley W. Posvar presided at the site of the new six story, $7.9 million building located at the corner of Forbes Avenue and Bouquet Street. It was a joyous occasion after so many years of longing for a separate law school building.

(l to r): William J. Copeland, '47, Harry W. Scott, '73, (Student Bar Association), Representative of General State Authority, Dean Sell, William Rea, Chair, Board of Trustees, Representative of Jedoco Construction Co. and Chancellor Posvar.

Dean Sell delivering remarks at Groundbreaking.

Participating in the short program which preceded the actual groundbreaking, in addition to the chancellor, were: William Rea, chairman of the Board of Trustees; William J. Copeland, Esquire, who chaired the $3.5 million Capital Funds campaign; Max Barth, architectural advisor to Governor Milton Shapp; Charles M. Blum, Deputy Executive Director, General State Authority; Harry Scott, President of the Student Bar Association and myself.

Approximately 125 people attended the ceremony on a cool, damp afternoon. The scheduled completion date was late fall of 1975. The building was completed on time and the move was effected over the holiday recess.

A reception followed in the Ballroom of the Student Union.

I would be remiss if I did not acknowledge the support I received from Senators Eugene Scanlon and Edward Zemprelli and Representatives K. Leroy Irvis and John McCue, all alumni of the school. I also received encouragement and guidance from my friend, Bernie Kobosky, who was at that time Vice

Dr. Esther Teplitz, donor of the Teplitz Memorial Courtroom.

Chancellor of External Affairs of the University of Pittsburgh.

At a faculty meeting on December 5, the report of an ad hoc committee chaired by Professor Seeburger was unanimously adopted. The other members of the committee were Shyameshwar Das, John E. Murray, Jr. and William F. Schulz, Jr. This was a comprehensive report by a committee appointed by me in response to faculty concerns over a possible disparity between the resources made available to the school and the mission the school was being asked to fill. I charged the committee to make a thorough study of the role the school had created for itself and how it had been performing in that role. Particular reference was to be made to the impact of the recent growth in the size of the student body and its likely impact for the future given present conditions. The committee was to recommend whatever changes it considered desirable.

Law school graduation took place on May 19, 1973, at 10:30 a.m. in Lawrence Hall.

The National Center for Juvenile Justice, created by the National Council of Juvenile Court Judges, selected the law school as its location. It was provided space on the

13th floor of the Cathedral of Learning.

The Law Alumni Association's annual dinner was held on September 28, 1973, at the William Penn Hotel. The Honorable Ruggero J. Aldisert, '47, received the Distinguished Alumnus Award.

In January, 1974, one of the first-year law students was selected as "Person of the Year" for 1973 by The Pittsburgh Forum. The annual Forum Award is given to an individual in Pittsburgh who has received little public recognition for positive contributions to the community.

Pat Miller, '76, was chosen primarily because of the impact of Women's Health Services, Inc., of which she was a founder. This organization operated an abortion clinic in Pittsburgh. She also engineered the Pennsylvania Abortion Clinic, a grassroots campaign which spread into other states.

On February 11-14, 1974, Gilbert Nurick, former president of Pennsylvania Bar Association, was in residence. He delivered some lectures on professional responsibility and conducted individual conferences with interested students. He enjoyed the time with us and we all profited from his being here.

During the latter period in the Cathedral of Learning, Patricia Miller of the Class of 1976 was one of a group of women who found it unwise for the women to have to travel the dimly lit stairways from the law library on the fifteenth floor to the women's room,

Dr. Rhoten Smith, Judge Silvestri Silvestri and Dean Sell.

originally on the fourteenth but later on thirteenth floor. Pat was selected as the one to approach Professor Herbert Sherman and plead for the conversion of the fifteenth floor men's room to a women's facility since there was a men's room on the fourteenth floor. I have never been able to ascertain why they went to Professor Sherman instead of me.

In any event, Herb came to see me and pleaded for the requested change. I found the request perfectly justified and took immediate steps to effect it. While there were suggestions for an enfeoffment ceremony and an invitation for the TV news to be brought in, the change was quietly carried out.

Mr. Sherman relayed my decision to the group which then took steps to erect a sign outside the fifteenth floor facility, giving Professor Sherman due credit. While I never checked it out, there were rumors that flower pots had been installed in the urinals.

With the move to the new building, facilities for both sexes were installed on the fifth, fourth, third and ground floors, as well as the second floor. In 1994, an additional restroom for women students was built on the first floor.

On March 13, 1974, Chesterfield H. Smith, Esquire, president of the American Bar Association visited the school. He spoke to the student body; there followed a question and answer session.

At a faculty meeting held on April 16, 1974, the following rule was adopted:

> As a condition for graduation each student shall be a full-time student in residence for a period of not less than six semesters. To receive residence credit for a semester, a student must be enrolled in a schedule requiring a minimum of ten class hours a week and must receive credit for at least nine class hours. Regular and punctual class attendance is necessary to satisfy residence and class hour requirements. Regular means attendance at not less than eighty (80) per cent of the classes held in each course. A failure to meet the requirement of regular attendance will result in the student being automatically certified out of the course, which means that the student will not receive credit for the course. As these attendance requirements are absolute minimums, the instructor in any course may require a greater percentage of class attendance for a student to be eligible to receive credit for that course. A student is not eligible to receive credit for a course in which the instructor in charge certifies that the student has been deficient in preparation for class or in participation in classroom discussion. The procedure for recording attendance will be set out in detail in September. This notice is to apprise you of the changes prior to the end of this school year.

By 1973, I was becoming frustrated with respect to faculty additions. I would put in a request for an additional faculty position or two. Months would pass with no word.

By spring, the request would be granted, obviously too late to recruit for the coming academic year. However, we would begin early in the fall to recruit—before the recruiting season had actually begun. But just when we were about to make an offer, the University's budget office would come through and take back all vacancies. Then, it would be back to requesting again the position or two. At a Board of Visitors meeting in the spring of 1974, I criticized the practice of delaying the granting of my requests for faculty positions. When asked by an administrator what I really wanted (implying that I was always asking for something for the law school), I told him I wanted a plan whereby I would be given faculty slots and other items upon an increase in the enrollment.

Shortly thereafter, I was asked by the provost whether I had anything concrete in mind. I asked to be excused from the meeting for five minutes, went to my office and returned with a twelve-column accounting sheet. On the left columns I had the current law school budget. I then had columns for five successive years, showing proposed increments in budget items as the enrollment increased. Over the next month or two, there were short discussions with the provost and associate provost over certain items and some suggested amendments were effected.

Just before the fall semester of 1974 began, I received a joint memorandum from the

Presentation of award to Professor Bookstaver upon his retirement.

chancellor and the provost approving my five-year plan as earlier modified.

As I look back I conclude that that was a very significant move on my part. It turned out that in the next few years, deans were experiencing budget cuts. I escaped that only because I had a five-year plan approved by the chancellor and the provost.

On May 23, 1974, the third annual Black Law Student Benefit Banquet was held in the Student Union Ballroom. The speaker was the Honorable Henry Smith, Judge of the Court of Common Pleas of Allegheny County. His talk was titled, "The Role of the Black Attorney in the 1970s."

Professor Herbert L. Sherman, Jr. was elected chair of the Labor Law Group, a body of thirty labor law professors across the country.

The law school graduation was held on May 25, 1974, in David Lawrence Hall. Dr. Andrew Watson, Professor of Law and Psychiatry at the University of Michigan, was the speaker.

On Monday, June 10, 1974, the School of Law and the South Hills Child Guidance Center co-sponsored a program, "Children and Families in Crisis."

On July 16, 1974, Mrs. Marie G. Lindsay died at Kane Hospital at the age of 85 years. As I mentioned earlier, Mrs. Lindsay served the school with devotion and aided innumerable students while they were in the school.

The David Glick Memorial Lecture was held on September 19 at 4 p.m., with Archibald Cox, the Samuel Williston Professor of Law at Harvard Law School, the speaker.

The Law Alumni Dinner was held on September 27 in the William Penn Hotel.

The Journal of Legal Education editorship was retained at the law school for another five years by the Executive Committee of the Association of American Law Schools. Associate Dean Murray was retained as Editor and Professor Seeburger as Book Review Editor.

Professor Curtis J. Berger, 1981 Mellon Scholar.

The Sarah Scaife Foundation pledged a quarter-million dollar gift in support of the School of Law's library. The pledge was in response to the School's, "Partners for Preeminence" campaign in connection with the construction of the new law school building.

At the time of the receipt of the pledge, I remarked: "The law library is the very heart of the law curriculum, which is based largely on readings of case histories in law. Right now we have an invaluable community and University resource packed into spaces scattered over four floors of the Cathedral of Learning, with thousands of books in storage. We simply do not have enough shelf space and, in consequence, we have had to limit our collection."

The graduation speaker on May 24, 1975, was the Honorable Joseph F. Weis, Jr., '50, Judge, United States Court of Appeals for the Third Circuit.

One of the long-serving dedicated members of the faculty, David R. Bookstaver, retired in July, 1975 and was granted the status of Professor of Law Emeritus. He was honored by the creation of a David R. Bookstaver Award, to be awarded annually in the form of a cash prize to the member of the graduating class who has the most distinguished record in the areas of wills, trusts and estate planning. He taught here for eighteen years and continued to teach part-time for several years after his formal retirement.

A graduate of Cornell University and Yale Law School, Dave was one of the most dedicated, selfless faculty members with whom I have had the privilege to associate. Always willing to step in and help where needed, I consider him one of my very dear friends. He had a long career in private and government practice, as well as legal education.

Dave now lives in Port Orange, Florida.

Telethon for law school at Webster Hall Hotel, February, 1971.

The late Judge David Olbum, talking with Dean Sell.

CHAPTER
N·I·N·E
1975-1984

The ninth decade began with the annual dinner of the Law Alumni Association held on September 26, 1975 at the William Penn Hotel. For many years, the law alumni dinner was held in the spring. That pattern was changed in 1973, when the dinner was held in the fall. The practice continued for the remainder of the first century of the school's existence.

One of the law faculty, Professor William J. Brown, was elected President of the University Senate, a body composed primarily of faculty members. The University Senate proposes to the administration programs and policies.

Judge Ruggero Aldisert attended the faculty meeting on October 9, 1975. He sought suggestions for membership on the newly constituted Board of Visitors. Three members had already been appointed to the Board: Judge Aldisert, William J. Copeland, Esquire, and Professor Robert McKay of New York University School of Law.

The long-delayed accreditation inspection of the law school by the American Bar Association and the Association of American Law Schools was scheduled for March 29-31, 1976. These inspections occur every several years. The inspection team is composed of persons representing either of the two associations. For me, this was a critical event. The school had been scheduled on several earlier dates over the previous few years. I was very fearful that an inspection while we were still in the Cathedral of Learning would result in a quite negative report, given the inadequate space, particularly in the library, and the size of the student body, which were expanding in anticipation of a move to the new building. Therefore, I was very happy each time the scheduled inspection was postponed. However, now that we were moving to the new building before the second semester, I encouraged the setting of inspection dates by Professor James White, Consultant to the American Bar Association's Section on Legal Education. That inspection took place as scheduled. The report from that inspection was a very positive one.

The new law school building was completed by December, 1975. The faculty was moved from the Cathedral of Learning into the new building immediately following the last classes for the fall semester.

What had seemed to be the biggest challenge, relocating the law library, was accomplished with little difficulty. We rented many wooden crates designed to transport books. The crates were the size of a shelf of books. We hired a number of law students

THE UNIVERSITY OF PITTSBURGH LAW SCHOOL BUILDING

The Faculty Lounge.

Law library.

Seminar room.

Rooms 111 and 113 and Courtroom (view from the bench with walls open).

Room G-12.

First floor lobby.

Room 107.

The Dean's office.

to assist in the move. Some of them dusted and vacuumed books, placed them in crates and affixed labels indicating their location in the law library on the third, fourth and fifth floors of the new building. Trucks transported the books to the new building. Other students took the crates by dollies to the labeled location in the new library and placed the books on the designated shelves. When classes began in January, the library was in full operation, as were the remainder of the building's facilities.

Toasting the new building are Dean Sell, Justice White and Chancellor Posvar.

The dedication ceremonies of the new law building took place on Friday, April 30, and Saturday, May 1. After eighty years housed in other buildings, the school had its own building and one that was designed and built for the teaching of law.

The ceremonies of the two-day program began on Friday morning, April 30, at 10 a.m., when the United States Court of Appeals for the Third Circuit convened a session in the court room of the new building. The panel consisted of Chief Judge Collins J. Seitz and Judges Ruggero J. Aldisert and Joseph F. Weis, Jr. Over two hundred attorneys were admitted to practice before that court, followed by the hearing of two arguments. From 1 to 4 p.m., tours of the building were conducted for the many representatives of other law schools who were in attendance.

The day's events concluded with the largest banquet in the history of the Law Alumni Association. Held at the Pittsburgh Hilton Hotel, more than 950 persons were in attendance.

Law Faculty — 1975.

DEDICATION CEREMONY OF LAW SCHOOL BUILDING

Phillip Werner Amram, Esquire.

Honorable William Scranton.

Honorable Ruggero J. Aldisert.

Honorable Byron R. White delivering dedication address.

(l to r): Judge Aldisert, Justice Byron R. White, Dean Sell, Chancellor Posvar, James Morton, Esquire, President of Law Alumni Association.

Judge Harry Kramer, who was released from the hospital only to attend the dedication ceremony.

The keynote address was delivered by Phillip Werner Amram, Esquire, chairman of the Civil Procedural Rules Committee of the Pennsylvania Supreme Court. In his remarks, Mr. Amram described the new School of Law building as "breathtaking," adding that he doubted whether there was anything to equal it. He observed: "But beautiful brick and mortar cannot make a great law school such as you have at the University of Pittsburgh. That only comes by having a distinguished dean, a distinguished faculty, and a distinguished student body." He presented an interesting address on some of his speculations about the practice of law in the year 2001, given the proliferation in new areas of the law and the impact that new technological advances in electronic equipment is likely to have on the practice.

DEDICATION
SCHOOL OF LAW BUILDING
University of Pittsburgh
May 1, 1976

Dedication program.

Also present were the Honorable William Scranton, former Governor of Pennsylvania and now U.S. Ambassador to the United Nations, the Honorable Byron R. White, Justice, United States Supreme Court, who delivered the dedication address the next morning, Chancellor Wesley W. Posvar, Judge Aldisert, James Morton, Esquire, President of the Law Alumni Association, and myself. My remarks at the banquet were as follows:

> Since September, 1947, when I first joined the faculty, I have longed for the day when the school would be housed in a building constructed to provide an opportunity to carry out the program of the school with efficiency and effectiveness. There has been much work and waiting since 1947 for this event. Tomorrow morning, we will dedicate that building, a truly magnificent structure. For the first time in the eighty-one year history of the school, it is housed in its own building—one especially constructed for law school use. The faculty, students and administration of the law school are deeply appreciative of all the efforts put forth by many to make this a reality.
>
> This has turned out be both a good and a bad time to hold the dedication. It is a fitting time since it is Law Day, 1976, the Bicentennial year. However, it is a bad time in that many who might otherwise have

been with us on this occasion were precluded from doing so because of other commitments in connection with Law Day. This is particularly true of some of the law school deans who are tied up with their own Law Day programs. To those law school representatives in attendance, we extend a hearty welcome and a thank you for being with us on this occasion.

Chief Justice Jones of the Pennsylvania Supreme Court had hoped to be with us this evening. He called me about a week and a half ago to express his regret at being unable to attend because of court business. We have also received regrets from many other members of the judiciary, government officials and other invitees who were unable to be present.

Present this evening are many who worked hard on the building, including legislators, representatives from the Department of General Services (formerly General State Authority), architects, contractors and university personnel. I would be remiss if I did not single out the tremendous work of my Associate Dean for Administration, Thomas O. White, who worked with the architects and contractors over the last three or four years. He was responsible also for working out the furnishing of the building, as well as the move from the Cathedral into the new structure.

Tom has resigned as Associate Dean, effective July 1, when he will begin a three-year leave of absence. He will become Executive Director of a consortium being formed among the Law School Admission Test, Multistate Bar Examination, Law School Data Assembly Service, Pre-Law Handbook and Competent Lawyer Study Projects, to be located in Princeton, New Jersey. After working with him closely for the last eleven years, I will miss him very much. I want to take this opportunity to again thank him for his support and efforts on behalf of the school. We all wish him well in this new and important opportunity.

I also want to pay respects to the three living former deans of the School of Law, all of whom are with us this evening and seated on the dais—Charles B. Nutting, Arthur Larson and Thomas M. Cooley, II. We are happy to have you with us.

It is a great pleasure for me to have Justice Byron White and his wife, Marion, with us this evening. He will deliver the dedicatory address tomorrow morning. Our friendship dates back to law school days at

Yale, when he and I took Debtors' Estates together and where we spent some pleasant times together. He honors me and all of us by being with us.

This is by far the largest turnout for a Law Alumni Dinner in the history of the organization. For the alumni, this must be a great moment, one in which all can take great pride. It is tempting to view this accomplishment as the end rather than an end. That temptation is one that must be avoided.

This new building marks an end to twenty years of work for many who first were asked and gave to a law school building fund in the late 1950s. It marks an end to years of work for many others who were supportive of our efforts to secure the facility during the past dozen years or so.

What is important to remember is that the end—the resulting building—amounts to a means to the larger end—a program of unparalleled quality in legal education.

As you know, legal education has never been supported by government funds, nor has legal education received great financial assistance from the profession. At any time, this circumstance poses a great challenge to a school striving to achieve and maintain an excellent professional education program. At this time, when resources available to other segments of the university are being reduced, it results in the need for each of us to seize every opportunity to enhance the support given to the school.

We recognize and are deeply appreciative of the support that our alumni have given the school in recent years, with an alumni group whose composition is largely younger people from whom we cannot expect large amounts of personal contribution. However, we can and would hope that when the occasion arises for those of you who have the opportunity to exert influence upon others capable of supporting our program you will think of the School of Law and do your best to secure support for it.

The capital funds drive—Partners for Preeminence—taught us much about the potential for this type of support and we believe that if assistance of this nature would constantly be on the minds of our alumni, we would get much of the support we will need during the next few years to cause the program to continue its development and progress.

I urge you to celebrate our success in reaching this point of unprecedented excellence in legal education in this area. Celebrate the completion of our new home. Celebrate the achievement of our alumni in contributing to the school and to the profession and society. And of most importance, celebrate our potential. Collectively and cooperatively we have done much and we can do more. With your continued interest and help, we will.

On Saturday morning, a continental breakfast was served in the Faculty Lounge for law school representatives and other special guests. At the dedicatory program held in the Lawrence Hall Auditorium, following greetings from Judge Aldisert, Chancellor Posvar and me, James Morton spoke on behalf of the law school alumni. Frederick Hill, Class of 1978, and President of the Law Student Bar Association, spoke of the student body's appreciation for the new building.

Ronald Lench, Class of 1957, Secretary of the Department of General Services of the Commonwealth of Pennsylvania, successor to the General State Authority, which built the facility, presented the symbolic key to the law school to Chancellor Posvar, who spoke briefly.

Justice White spoke about the pressures on the law school curriculum created by a more qualified faculty and student body and the rising tension between law schools and the practicing bar over what constitutes the best training for future lawyers. Like previous speakers, Justice White insisted that "this country depends on the law schools to sustain the rule of law." He concluded that "legal education is in some very good hands at Pittsburgh."

I concluded the program with the following remarks:

The School of Law of the University of Pittsburgh has perceived its mission as one designed to fulfill three societal needs. The first of these needs is to provide training for persons to serve both as practitioners in the traditional sense and in roles dependent on, supported by or ultimately involved with the law. The second need is for the conduct of research in the law, the objectives of which are to understand the present state of the law, and to provide for the orderly and well-founded changes in the law to meet the demands to be made on the law. The third need is to provide a repository where the accumulated scholarship, learning and practices of the law over the centuries can be gathered and made available to both the specialized and general public for its use.

We dedicate this beautiful new building today in the expectation that it will provide the ideal environment for carrying out those objectives.

We feel that this facility will enable us to institute and carry out new and innovative programs in the area of continuing education for the bar and the bench.

Our new library, with the program to increase its research capability, will provide the ideal arrangement for conducting research and significantly contributing to the improvements in the law and its role in our society. Further, it will provide a repository for such accumulated scholarship.

The beautiful courtroom gives us an opportunity to train students in court proceedings in a setting designed to acquaint them with the trial and appellate surroundings they will encounter as practicing attorneys.

The classrooms and seminar rooms are designed to provide the maximum opportunity for dialogue and discussion between faculty and students and among students.

I hope that when you tour the building you will note that one of the primary objectives of its design is to immerse the students and faculty in a constant teaching-learning environment.

While it is obvious that a physical plant cannot insure quality education, it is an important element. To all who labored to make it a reality, we express our sincere appreciation and thanks. In so dedicating this building, we rededicate our efforts for continued improvement of the school's program and its contributions to the profession and society generally.

From noon to 4 p.m., tours of the law building were conducted.

A week later, graduation ceremonies took place in David Lawrence Hall. The address was delivered by Honorable Richard L. Thornburgh, Assistant United States Attorney General—Criminal Division, and a member of the Class of 1957. The title of his remarks was "Today's Challenge to Law—And Lawyers."

On July 1, 1976, the university announced a grant of $500,000 to the law school from the Richard King Mellon Foundation. The grant was to be used for the establishment of distinguished professorships in the school. The grant put the capital funds drive near the $2.1 million goal of the campaign. Seward Prosser Mellon, chairman of the executive committee of the Foundation, said, "The University of Pittsburgh School of Law has shown its commitment to excellence in legal education by recently completing the newest and one of the finest law school buildings in the country. We have a personal involvement in this in that my great-great-grandfather, Judge Thomas Mellon, received a diploma from Western University of Pennsylvania, the predecessor institution to the University."

It was later decided, with the concurrence of the Foundation, that the income from the fund be used for a Mellon Scholar program, whereby distinguished academicians, judges and lawyers would be invited to give lectures, etc., in the school.

An event occurred the morning before Labor Day, 1976, that sent shock waves through me. On that Sunday morning, about 5 a.m., I received a telephone call from the university police, informing me that there had been trouble in the law building and suggested that I come to the school.

I dressed and left for the law school. As I walked into the building, I heard water cascading down the elevator shafts, and a couple of inches of water were on the ground floor of the building.

With the elevators out, I walked up to the fourth floor to find the library under a couple of inches of water. The water was almost up to the bottom shelves of the stacks. The water was running down to the third floor through the stair wells. Water, water, everywhere. I almost cried to see the building I had worked so hard to get in such a water-soaked condition.

University of Pittsburgh School of Law Class of 1975

FIRST ROW: C. Dewitt, T. Hennessy, J. Krey, J. Spangler,
F. Holland, T. Geary, J. Newborg, M. Heintzman.
SECOND ROW: F. Hill, M. Pohl, G. Travalio, B. Wolf, R. Hartman, M. Hruska, D. Young, W. Yang, F. Meister,
F. Heintz.
THIRD ROW: R. Staudenmaier, M. Weber, S. Evans, K. Sable, M. Buchwach, R. Krasnow, J. Cascio, A. Rogal,
T. Donahoe, R. Siegel, J. Stets, S. Metosky, K. Judson, E. Wechsler, D. Murdoch, A. Verduci, G. Otto.
FOURTH ROW: J. Grubor, M. Murphy, G. Kefalos, H. Mattern, N. Wright, D. King, K. Boring, G. Pettrone,
C. Manseli, N. Cafardi, R. Hamill, N. Conway M. Quigley, L. Metz, P. Kushner, G. Werfel, J. McCue,
J. McAneny, R. Flaherty, E. Das.
FIFTH ROW: F. Dougherty, S. Dugas, G. Faban, K. Neyland, T. Junker.
SIXTH ROW: S. Paskoff, J. Hart, K. Kemp, D. Reed, M. Yost, W. Samuelson, C. Gainor, P. Glasser, D. Megnin,
C. Garris, J. Lee, P. Boschini, C. Vater, D. Marcucci, E. Purviance, F. Little, S. Stern, B. Coughenour,
R. Kotulak, H. Wein, E. Smith, J. Barrett, J. Silvestri, J. Belliveau.
SEVENTH ROW: A. Jones, M. Vadnal, R. Durrant, T. Murphy, C. Ross, T. Stanton, M. Wolak, R. Simpson,
M. Hughes, C. Vollmer, T. Martin.

It turned out that the trouble occurred when the deluge water heads on the fourth floor let go. No one was ever able to ascertain what caused it. The deluge heads are designed to flood the floor with water in order to slow a fire from going to the floor below. In addition to the deluge heads, there are normal sprinkler heads. Luckily, they did not go off.

The university maintenance people did a marvelous job. Despite it being a Sunday morning on Labor Day weekend, they were able to call out most of their personnel. Using pumps, water vacuums, etc., they were able to get most of the water off the new carpets and floors by early afternoon. The building was then closed tightly and the air conditioners shut down. By the time I arrived at the building at my usual 6:25 a.m., the carpets were dry and we were ready to start classes at the normal time. A few books were damaged by water but the library staff did their usual yeoman job in drying them out with a minimum of permanent damage.

October 15, 1976, I announced my resignation as Dean in letters to the Chancellor and the Provost. My resignation was effective before the beginning of the 1977-78 academic year. In an open letter to faculty and students, I stated: "I am in my eleventh year in this position and that is long enough." I pointed out that I had achieved the goals I had set after my appointment in 1966. "Now it is time for a new dean, with new goals and aspirations, to take over the leadership of the School." I cited as major achievements the new $8.5 million law building, and the growth of the school from 9 faculty and 130 students in 1966 to 25 faculty and 632 students. During my deanship, the Law Alumni Association was strengthened, and I was very pleased with the inspection reports for accreditation by the American Bar Association and the Association of American Law Schools.

I announced my resignation early because I wanted to afford the University ample time to find my replacement and avoid an acting deanship situation for the law school. I had observed first-hand the effects of earlier acting deanships in the school. Generally, an acting deanship is a holding operation. Every decision, except the most urgent, is made to await the appointment of a new dean.

I sent an explanatory letter to the student body on October 15, 1976.
This is that letter:

October 15, 1976

To the Student Body of the School of Law:

For some time, the rumors have been circulating that I was resigning as Dean. These were just that at the time they began. However, I have concluded that the time has arrived for me to step down as Dean. I am in my eleventh year in this position and that is long enough.

When I assumed the Deanship in 1966, I had set certain goals for the School under my leadership. These were: (1) to get a law building for the School, which was being housed in inadequate facilities and which never had a building of its own; (2) to build the faculty and student body in size and quality (when I assumed the Deanship we had 130 students and nine faculty); (3) to strengthen and expand the Law Alumni Association into a body which would be supportive of the School and its efforts to improve; and (4) to obtain a good inspection report for reaccreditation by the American Bar Association and the Association of American Law Schools. These objectives have, in my opinion, been achieved. The later goal—the Capital Funds Drive—is within $125,000 of its goal of $2,100,000.

Now it is time for a new Dean, with new goals and aspirations, to take over the leadership of the School. Consequently, I have submitted to the Chancellor and Provost of the University my resignation as Dean, effective before the start of the 1977-1978 academic year. I am taking this action now so that there is ample time to find my replacement and thus avoid an Acting Deanship situation for the School.

In my opinion, the School is in a very strong posture. Our report from the American Bar Association was most gratifying to us. I am very proud of this School, even though it is not my own alma mater. I think the students here are receiving as good a legal education as they could find anywhere. The success of our graduates is testimony to that fact. And I have always been very proud of our student body.

I did want to take this opportunity to inform you of my decision, lest you be forced to find it out by some indirect method. You deserve to know. I had always determined that once I made the decision, the students would know immediately.

In the meantime, it will be business as usual.

Sincerely,

W. Edward Sell
Dean

In November, 1976, I sent a similar letter to the Alumni.

At a meeting on April 20, 1977, the Faculty agreed that no credit would be given for a course taken at another law school unless the student earns at least a "C" or its equivalent.

In the summer of 1977, Professor John E. Murray, Jr. was appointed to succeed me as Dean of the School of Law. He had served as my Associate Dean for Academic Affairs for eight years.

Dean Murray received his Bachelor of Arts degree from LaSalle University in Philadelphia, his Juris Doctor degree from Catholic University and his Doctor of the Science of Jurisprudence from the University of Wisconsin. He joined the faculty of Duquesne University School of Law as an Assistant Professor. He later became a full professor and served, for a period, as Acting Dean.

John E. Murray, Jr.

While he was at Duquesne, I heard that he was unhappy and was going to leave. Knowing of his excellence in teaching and scholarship, I approached him about joining our faculty. He was very receptive and we had some sessions to discuss the details. One day, I received a call from Chancellor Kurtzman, inquiring whether I had been talking to Professor Murray about joining this faculty. I acknowledged that I had. He told me to cease the effort since the Duquesne University administration was upset at my effort to entice him away from Duquesne. John called me one day and

Law faculty — 1976.

asked why he hadn't heard anything further from me. I told him I had been instructed to cease negotiations and the reasons for it. John then went to the administration at Duquesne and impressed upon them the fact that he was leaving Duquesne and that, while he wished to stay in Pittsburgh, he would leave if he couldn't move to Pitt. At this point in time, the administration at Duquesne called Chancellor Kurtzman and told him that we were free to negotiate with John.

He joined the law faculty in September, 1967. He held a joint appointment in the Graduate School of Business. At the time of his appointment, he had authored eight books and a number of law review articles. While serving as Associate Dean, he was appointed Editor of the Journal of Legal Education, the official publication of the Association of American Law Schools. He also served as mayor of the Borough of Pleasant Hills for four years—1970 to 1974.

At a meeting on September 9, 1977, the faculty was informed that the widow and daughter of Judge Samuel Feigus established a $1,000-a-year scholarship in his honor. Professor Meisel, on behalf of the Curriculum Committee, presented a proposal for a Developmental Disabilities Law Project. After discussion, the faculty voted to accept the program provided a suitable person was first found to administer it. Later, Ms. Ilene Shane was appointed to head the project.

Other events of note during the 1977-78 school year including the following:

- The annual Law Alumni Dinner took place on October 14, 1977.

- On October 20, 1977, Dean Roger C. Crampton of Cornell University School of Law was a guest of the school.

- A ceremony to present Dean John E. Murray, Jr. took place in the courtroom on March 17, 1978.

- The 1978 Caplan Lecture was delivered by Dean Albert Sacks of the Harvard Law School on March 30, 1978.

- Martha Hartle Munsch resigned from the faculty, effective at the end of the academic year, to return to law practice in the firm of Reed, Smith, Shaw & McClay.

- The 1977 Client Counseling team of Charles R. Conway and James R. Fiorentino won the regional competition. Professor Mark Nordenberg served as their faculty advisor.

The 1978 graduation program was held on May 27, 1978, in David Lawrence Hall. The speaker was the Honorable Harry A. Blackmun, Justice of the United States Supreme

Court. The program included an In Memorium for Robert J. Christina, who passed away December 11, 1977. He was a member of the class of 1978 for five semesters.

In June, 1978, the School of Law, in cooperation with the Allegheny County Bar Association, conducted the first Intensive Course in Trial Advocacy. I served as Program Director for the two-week program, which was limited to twenty-eight registrants. Most of the individuals had been in practice less than six years and had had limited trial experience. The faculty consisted of approximately thirty trial lawyers and judges. The faculty members donated two days to the program. The students were given instruction in various aspects of trial practice, including opening and closing statements, examination and cross-examination of witnesses and expert witnesses. The class was divided into two groups of fourteen each. The teaching team leaders were Professors Mark A. Nordenberg and William V. Luneburg. Each day was devoted to some aspect of trial practice. The program culminated in a full-day set of trials in downtown courtrooms, with sitting judges presiding. The success of the program was, to a large extent, the result of the participation by the outstanding faculty of judges and trial attorneys.

The course was so successful that it has been repeated a number of times. The tenth such offering took place in June, 1991. To give an idea of the faculty, the 1991 faculty was composed of: Vincent J. Bartolotta, Jr., '70, Donald W. Bebenek, Eugene G. Berry, '80, the Honorable Alan N. Bloch, '58, Bruce R. Brown, the late Franklyn E. Conflenti, '52,

Justice Blackmum, U.S. Supreme Court.

Thomas L. Cooper, '62, the Honorable Gustave Diamond, the Honorable Richard DiSalle, '51, David B. Fawcett, Jr., '53, Nora Barry Fischer, the Honorable Judith K. Fitzerald, '73, Stanley W. Greenfield, '59, Robert S. Grigsby, Amy Reynolds Hay, '82, Dawne S. Hickton, '83, Thomas Hollander, '61, Joseph A. Katarincic, '60, W. Gregg Kerr, '52, Alexander H. Lindsay, Jr., '71, Roslyn M. Litman, '52, Thomas L. Livingston, '56, Paul A. Manion, the Honorable Carol Los Mansmann, Howard F. Messer, '71, Jack H. Olender, '60, Wilbur McCoy Otto, Robert L. Potter, '72, Herbert N. Rosenberg, '51, Daniel H. Shapira, Kathleen L. Simpson, the Honorable Joseph F. Weis, Jr., '50 and the Honorable I. Martin Wekselman.

In addition, there were model demonstrators. They were: Thomas E. Crenny, John P. Gismondi, '78, Philip A. Ignelzi, '81, Dennis St. J. Mulvihill, '72, Lynette Norton, Russell J. Ober, Jr., '73, Neil R. Rosen, '76, and Christine A. Ward, '82.

I am planning for the eleventh presentation of the program in June, 1995.

The annual Law Alumni Dinner was held on October 13, 1978 at the Hyatt Hotel in Chatham Center. Ambassador Elliott Richardson was the speaker.

During the 1978-79 academic year, Dean Murray announced the institution of another dual-degree program, which was to be a joint effort of the School of Law and the Graduate School of Public and International Affairs.

Judge Louis Pollack, former dean of Yale Law School and the University of Pennsylvania Law School and then District Judge for the United States District Court for the Eastern District of Pennsylvania, was the graduation speaker. The ceremony was held in Soldiers' and Sailors' Memorial Hall. Lou had been a classmate at Yale Law School. When I chaired the Federal Judicial Nominating Commission set up by Senators Heinz and Schweiker, one of the persons we recommended for nomination to the federal district court for the Eastern District of Pennsylvania was Louis Pollack. I was very happy to see him nominated by the President.

The annual Law Alumni Dinner for 1979 was held at the Hilton Hotel on October 19. The speaker was William H. Webster, Director of the Federal Bureau of Investigation.

In the fall of 1979, the school conducted two six-week continuing legal education courses. The courses met on Monday evenings from 6:30 to 8:30 p.m. and were team taught by a professor and a practitioner. Students were expected to participate in the classroom discussions. I conducted one program in bankruptcy with Hillard Kreimer, Esquire, who has since deceased. We covered the new Bankruptcy Reform Act of 1978. The other course covered Estate and Gift Tax and Tax Planning. It was given by Professor William J. Brown and Dixon Rich, who also has since deceased. Both courses were well received. While no further courses of that type were offered by the School, the faculty is now embarking on an extensive continuing education program to provide courses for Pennsylvania lawyers who are now faced with mandatory continuing legal education requirements.

In 1980, the Law Student Division of the American Bar Association instituted an Appellate Advocacy Competition. The competition begins with regional events, roughly laid out by circuits. The winning team or teams, depending on the number of teams in a regional competition, advance to the national finals, conducted in conjunction with the annual meeting of the American Bar Association. I served as faculty advisor and sent two teams into the regionals consisting of Mark A. Nadeau, Ann Elizabeth Baldwin, Russ Warner and David J. Hickton. They won the regional competition and advanced to the

Professor Jesse H. Choper.

finals. The team of Beth Baldwin and Dave Hickton should have been in the national finals but was deprived by a scoring error. I later received a written apology for it.

The initial meeting of the Mineral Law Resources Institute was held at the law school on March 6 and 7, 1980. The organization elected Samuel L. Douglass, Class of 1958, as the first president and Professor Cyril A. Fox, jr., Class of 1965, was elected as Assistant Secretary-Treasurer. The organization is now the Eastern Mineral Law Foundation.

The 1980 Louis Caplan Lecture was held in the law school courtroom on April 10, 1980. The lecturer was Professor Jesse H. Choper of the University of California School of Law.

Volume VIII of the Bulletin of the American Academy of Psychiatry and the Law was published out of this school. This is a scholarly publication which is moved when there is a change of editorship. Herbert E. Thomas, M.D., a member of the adjunct faculty, was editor.

At its meeting of May 20, 1980, the faculty approved a recommendation of the dean for the creation of a second law review, devoted to the areas of business and commercial law. The new review, to begin publication in the next academic year, would be called the Journal of Law and Commerce. The impetus behind the creation of a second law review was two-fold. There was a feeling that there was a need for a law review devoted to business and commercial law matters. And with the size of the student body, there was not an opportunity for a sufficient number of students to gain the benefits of work on a law review when the only publication was the University of Pittsburgh Law Review.

Justice William Rehnquist delivered the address at the 1980 graduation ceremony.

Ms. Jenni Parrish was welcomed as the new Law Librarian at the start of the 1980-81 academic year.

The 1980 annual Law Alumni Dinner was held in the law school on October 24.

The speaker was the Honorable Bruce W. Kauffman, Justice of the Pennsylvania Supreme Court. He was introduced by the Honorable John P. Flaherty, Jr., '58, also a Justice of the Pennsylvania Supreme Court.

Questions having been raised about the length of time allowed for earning the Juris Doctor degree, the faculty, at its meeting on November 12, 1980, ruled that the maximum time is six years.

The Northeast Regional Conference on "Women and the Law" was held at the school from October 31 to November 2. Workshops included: sexual harassment, domestic relations, welfare rights, pornography, reproductive freedom, and confidentiality of discussions with rape counselors and the state. It is worth noting that fifteen years later, these are visible issues of concern not only to the bar but to society generally.

Professor Zygmunt Plater of Wayne State University Law School visited the school on February 19 and 20, 1981 as a Mellon Lecturer. His principal areas of teaching are environmental law and administrative law.

Curtis J. Berger, Lawrence A. Urin Professor of Real Estate Law at Columbia University, was the Mellon Scholar in March, 1981. Professor Berger is one of the foremost legal scholars in the field of real estate law. In 1993, he served as President of the Association of American Law Schools.

A team from the law school won the Regional Competition of the American Bar Association Young Lawyer's Appellate Advocacy Competition. The team was composed of Christine Ward, Thomas M. Fallert and Donna Jean Tocco. Christine Ward won best

Professor Francis Allen.

Fred Graham.

oralist in the competition. The team then competed in the finals, conducted during the annual meeting of the American Bar Association. This was the second year in a row in which the school's team placed first in the regional competition. As faculty advisor of the team, I was very proud of their accomplishment.

Professor Frank Allen, Sunderland Professor of Law at the University of Michigan, delivered the Caplan Lecture on Friday, April 10, 1981.

The graduation speaker, at the ceremonies held on May 23, 1981, was Fred Graham, Law correspondent/CBS News.

The 1981 annual Law Alumni Dinner was held in the law school on October 9, 1981. In November, the faculty approved the proposed dual-degree program with the School of Industrial Administration of Carnegie Mellon University.

On October 31, 1981, the school held a program entitled, "The Economic Tax Recovery Act of 1981—How It Affects You." The speakers were Professor William J. Brown, LeRoy L. Metz, II, Esquire, '75, William J. Smith, Esquire, and Richard E. Brock, manager of the planned giving program, University of Pittsburgh.

The faculty held a seminar on January 14, 1982. Drs. Henry Bonson and Thomas Starzl, transplant surgeons at Presbyterian University Hospital and on the medical school faculty, gave a most interesting slide presentation. This was followed by a discussion concerning some of the legal and ethical issues involved in transplantation of body organs.

In February, 1982, the law school announced plans to establish two dual degree programs—one with the Katz Graduate School of Business of the university and the other with Carnegie-Mellon University's Graduate School of Industrial Administration. Both required the approval of the Board of Trustees of the University. Under the plan, a student could possibly complete the dual-degree program with the Katz School in three and a half years. The Pitt-CMU program would take four years to complete because CMU's Graduate School of Industrial Administration does not offer summer courses.

It also was indicated that other programs between the law school and other graduate or professional schools were contemplated.

In announcing the program, Dean Murray stated "We are confident that the new program is an appropriate and timely response to the changing needs of the marketplace. Knowledge of both law and business is in demand more than ever."

One enrolled in the Pitt-CMU program attends law school much the same as a typical first year student. The second year is dominated by business courses at CMU, with the third and fourth years concentrating again on law courses. Graduates completing the program receive two degrees—master's in business administration and the Juris Doctor degree.

Since the fields of business and law are interrelated, this type of dual education is an advantage for a person contemplating entry into the business world as either a lawyer or an executive. The program has an additional advantage of saving the student time.

The total number of credits required is fewer than those needed if a student seeks separate law and business degrees. To be accepted into the program, the applicant must be accepted for admission to both the law school and the graduate school of business.

There were two other joint degree programs already in place. A joint law-graduate urban and public affairs degree program was offered by the law school in conjunction with Carnegie-Mellon University's School of Urban and Public Affairs. Another joint degree program was offered by the law school and the University of Pittsburgh Graduate School of Public and International Affairs.

Professor Willard H. Pedrick.

On February 17 and 18, 1982, Justice Ellen Peters of the Connecticut Supreme Court and former Professor of Law at Yale visited the school as the Mellon Lecturer.

At the faculty meeting of March 4, 1982, it was announced that the firm of Eckert, Seamans, Cherin and Mellott had established an annual prize for an outstanding student writing in memory of William H. Eckert of the Class of 1924.

Two events during the spring brought scholars to the school for significant lectures. Professor Sylvia Law of the New York University School of Law served as the Mellon Lecturer on March 29 and 30, 1982. Her formal presentation was titled, "Work, Women and Welfare." The 1982 Caplan Lecture was delivered by Professor Richard E. Speidel of Northwestern University School of Law on April 15. He is the former Dean of Boston University and is now Beatrice Kuhn Professor of Law at Northwestern. His teaching and scholarship are in the commercial law field.

Professor Willard H. Pedrick, founding Dean of Arizona State University College of Law, spoke at graduation on May 29, 1982. The annual Law Alumni Dinner was held on October 23, 1982 at the Press Club.

The American Bar Association and the Association of American Law Schools conducted a periodic accreditation inspection of the law school on November 10-12, 1982. While the reports are kept confidential and not to be distributed, they are shared with the faculty and administration. Again, we received a very good report.

At the Faculty Meeting on December 2, 1982, the dean announced the receipt of a $16,000 grant from the Alcoa Foundation to support a Law and Economics Program in the school.

At a meeting held on March 17, 1983, the Faculty voted to add to the curriculum a course in environmental law if a proper, qualified person could be located to teach the course, and sufficient student interest was manifested.

The graduation speaker on May 28, 1983 was Derrick A. Bell, Jr., of the Class of 1957, Dean of the University of Oregon School of Law.

In August 1983, Dean Murray announced that he was resigning at the end of the academic year to head the Villanova University School of Law. Some apparent disagreements over the law school budget led to his decision to resign.

At the beginning of the 1983-84 academic year, Ms. Fredi G. Danzinger was named director of admissions.

On October 6, Professor G. Edward White of the University of Virginia School of Law delivered a Mellon Lecture.

At the 1983 Law Alumni dinner on Friday, November 11, Dean Murray announced the establishment of the Harold Obernauer Computerized Legal Research Center in the law school. Support for the Center has come from the Obernauer Foundation, created by the will of Harold Obernauer, a 1913 graduate of the law school.

Dean Murray, in announcing its establishment, stated: "The Center is tremendously exciting because it puts the total body of contemporary law at the fingertips of students and faculty, and prepares students for the law offices of the future. These computerized research systems are wonderful supplements to the time-consuming process of manual legal research."

Foundation support helped to defray the costs of WESTLAW, a computerized legal research service. WESTLAW, developed by West Publishing Company, was added to the existing LEXIS facility, developed by Mead Data Central. The center is housed on the fourth floor of the law school building.

Richard J. Pierce, Jr.

Professor Alan Farnsworth of the Columbia University School of Law presented the Caplan Lecture on April 5, 1984.

At the 1984 graduation on May 26, 1984, the graduating class requested that Dean Murray be the speaker. This was John's last ceremonial activity as Dean of the School of Law.

On April 23, 1984, Chancellor Wesley Posvar and Provost Roger Benjamin announced the appointment of Richard J. Pierce as dean of the School of Law. He was W.R. Irby Professor of Law at Tulane Law School in New Orleans.

In my opinion, John Murray's deanship was very successful. John worked closely with me during my tenure as dean. I had recruited him from Duquesne and, within a year, I named him my Associate Dean for Academic Affairs. During our time together, we developed programs for faculty development, student recruitment and strengthened alumni ties.

I had to spend a significant amount of time working on the project of getting a law school building. There was a great amount of time spent not only on getting a new building but on resisting efforts to put the law school in other space in the Cathedral of Learning or in some abandoned building. Consequently, I depended heavily on John to implement the programs we had planned.

One such program was looked upon with amazement by some other deans in the university. It was our belief that if we were to develop a first-class law school, we needed a faculty of good teachers and good scholars. Not willing to rely solely on the evaluations of faculty by the students, we developed a program for class visitations by other faculty members.

At the outset, I explained to the student body that this was not a "spying" effort. We were not bringing onto the faculty persons we did not feel had the potential for being better than average classroom performers. In order to realize their potential, they were visited in class by a committee of senior professors whose obligation was to critique the class with the professor and aid him or her in improving classroom performance. The process continues to this day and has been invaluable in developing a strong teaching faculty. It is now implemented in other parts of the university, although it has not met with enthusiasm in all quarters.

While John and I worked together, both of us were also busy with our own scholarship. It was our feeling that if we could produce scholarly work in addition to our own classroom work (and both of us taught almost a full teaching load all the time we were administrators) it was not unreasonable to expect the same from the rest of the faculty.

When John became dean, he continued these programs. In fact, I look upon his tenure as the period when the faculty development took its greatest strides.

During John's tenure, the School created a second law review—the Journal of Law and Commerce. This effort resulted in giving more of our students the experience of working on a scholarly journal. With an increased budget, he was able to offer summer stipends to faculty, which included not only grants to some faculty members themselves, but also available summer research assistance for many of the faculty. The school was also able to bring in more speakers with scholarly reputations to speak to not only the students and faculty but also, in many cases, to alumni and friends of the school.

I will always have a warm spot in my heart for the deep friendship I enjoy with John. During parts of my deanship, things were not always pleasant. There was the period in the late sixties when students were demanding in many respects. I was threatened more than once with being locked in my office. I could always find support in John. Such adversity seemed to be the cement for a lasting friendship and mutual respect.

It should be noted that during John's deanship he continued to produce books and articles with a magnitude that was amazing. He also served, during part of the time, as

Editor of the Journal of Legal Education, published by the Association of American Law Schools with the cooperation of the West Publishing Company and located in the University of Pittsburgh School of Law.

John's replacement, Richard Pierce, served as director of the Energy Law Program at Tulane, where he also served one semester as acting associate dean. Prior to coming to Tulane, he held appointments at the University of Virginia and the University of Kansas School of Law. His background included military and corporate experience.

He received his undergraduate degree in economics from Lehigh University and his law degree from the University of Virginia School of Law, where he served as managing editor of the Virginia Law Review. His principal area of scholarship is energy law. He served as a consultant to the Louisiana House and Senate on energy issues.

In announcing his appointment, Provost Roger Benjamin said: "One of Professor Pierce's major, initial undertakings will be the guidance of the law school through our new planning process. His experience at Tulane, as well as other positions he has held, make him very well qualified for this important position."

The annual Law Alumni Dinner was held on October 19, 1984, at the Carnegie Music Hall. Dean Richard J. Pierce, Jr., addressed the alumni.

On November 12, 1984, at 3 p.m. Frank Seamans, Esquire, of Eckert, Seamans, Cherin & Mellott spoke to the students on changes in the practice of law and the effect of lawyer advertising.

In 1985, Professor Arthur Hellman was appointed to the Board of Directors of the American Judicature Society.

Law Fellows — April, 1985.

At the meeting of April 4, 1985, the Dean announced that Professor Mark Nordenberg had agreed to accept the position of Associate Dean for Academic Affairs, replacing Richard H. Seeburger, who resigned to return to full-time teaching.

The 1985 Caplan Lecture was given on April 19, by the Honorable Stephen G. Breyer, Judge, United States Court of Appeals for the First Circuit. Judge Breyer is now a Justice on the United States Supreme Court.

Graduation was held on May 25, 1985. The graduation address was delivered by the Honorable Robert N.C. Nix, Jr., Chief Justice of Pennsylvania.

William Wallace Booth, Esquire, at 1982 Law Alumni Dinner.

Professor Thomas Morgan - Mellon Distinguished Lecturer - 1981.

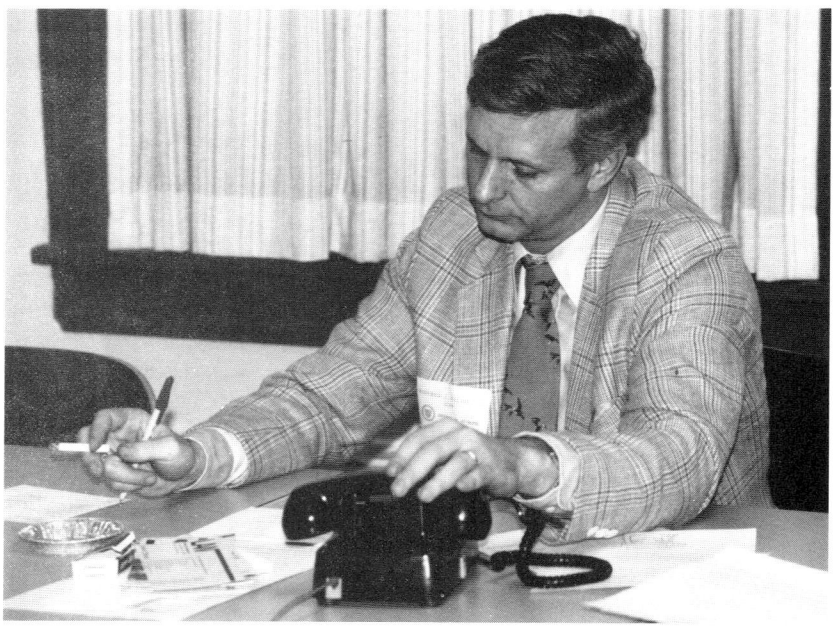

Dean Pierce at Phonothon.

Class of 1951 reunion.

Class of 1956 reunion.

CHAPTER
T·E·N
1985-1994

The United States Court of Appeals for the Third Circuit sat in the Teplitz Courtroom from October 1-4, 1985. Cases being argued before the court had been summarized for the law students in writing so they would understand the arguments being presented. The students and faculty were free to enter the courtroom and witness the arguments. At the end of the sessions, the judges spoke to the students about the process of arguments before an appellate court. Among the judges sitting for the cases were Chief Judge Ruggero J. Aldisert, Class of 1947, and Judge Joseph F Weis, Jr., Class of 1950.

At the October faculty meeting, it was announced that Talbert Fowler, the law librarian, would retire effective January 1, 1986. At that same meeting, disclosure was made of efforts being advanced to remove course registration and scheduling, student records and transcript generation from the law school to the central registration office. The faculty voted unanimously to oppose any such attempts.

On October 28, 1985, Richard L. Fischer, Esquire, Class of 1961, Senior Vice President and General Counsel of Alcoa, spoke to interested students on careers in corporate law. The Alcoa Foundation announced a grant of $65,000 to the School of Law to be used for library acquisitions in support of the school's international business transactions program. Mr. Fischer worked with Professor Ronald Brand in the development of the program.

The Annual Law Alumni dinner was held at the Westin William Penn Hotel on November 2, 1985.

The School was faced with another deanship vacancy when Dean Pierce announced at the November 7 faculty meeting that he had tendered his resignation. He had failed to agree on an acceptable level of funding for the law school with University officials. At the time of his resignation, he stated, "I pressed them to give me some idea of the amount of funding that would be available for next year, and they did. We had several unsuccessful discussions about it."

After he told the faculty of his decision to resign at the end of the academic year, there was a feeling that leadership of the school should immediately be turned over to the Associate Dean, Mark A. Nordenberg, who would serve as Acting Dean while a Dean Search was organized. The University officials agreed and Chancellor Posvar made the appointment in November, 1985.

Dick Pierce served out the year as a member of the law faculty and then accepted a chaired faculty appointment at Southern Methodist University Law School. He now holds a chaired professorship at Columbia Law School.

In the Fall, 1985 Law Notes, Dean Pierce wrote the following farewell:

As many of you know from press accounts, I have resigned as Dean of the University of Pittsburgh School of Law effective November 25. I was initially attracted to this School by its outstanding faculty, dedicated staff, and supportive graduates. My experience as Dean has served only to reinforce my initial feelings of respect and admiration for all three groups. Notwithstanding the uniformly high quality of the members of the Law School community with whom I have had the pleasure of working, I felt it was time for someone else to undertake the task of establishing a productive dialogue with the University administration. I was able to make no apparent progress toward resolving a serious and protracted disagreement with the administration concerning the level of tuition and budgetary support appropriate for the School of Law. Indeed, during my brief stewardship, the University increased the School's tuition substantially and reduced its level of budgetary support relative to other law schools.

I am pleased to announce that Mark Nordenberg, who agreed to serve as Associate Dean for Academic Affairs at the beginning of this academic year, has now agreed to serve as the School's Interim Dean. I have total confidence in Mark's ability to lead the School. The School could not be in better hands during this difficult period. He and the School need and deserve your continuing support.

I have consistently declined to discuss publicly the details of the School's budgetary dispute with the University. I do want to take this opportunity, however, to deny one false story. At least one press account of my resignation attributed it to University reallocation of money donated to the School of Law. I do not know the source of that story, but it is totally false. I have had many disagreements with the University administration, but I firmly believe they have credited to the Law School's account every dollar that a donor designated for the benefit of the School of Law. I hope that you will be particularly generous in your giving to the School of Law to enable it to retain its outstanding faculty and educational program during the period necessary for Dean Nordenberg to resolve satisfactorily the continuing budgetary dispute between the University administration and the School of Law.

It has been a pleasure to work with you to maintain, and to build upon, the extremely high quality law school created by the efforts of my predecessors, John Murray and Ed Sell.

Mark A. Nordenberg.

Dean Nordenberg is a graduate of Thiel College and a 1973 graduate of the University of Wisconsin Law School. Upon graduation, he practiced in Minneapolis, Minnesota in the firm of Gray, Plant, Mooty & Anderson. He entered law teaching at Capitol University Law School in Columbus, Ohio. He came to the school as a visiting professor for the academic year 1977-78. His excellence in teaching became readily evident and he was offered a position in the tenure stream. He was widely regarded as one of the school's finest teachers, having been the initial recipient of the senior class's Excellence-in-Teaching Award in 1984 and the Chancellor's Distinguished Teaching Award in 1985. He was involved in a number of professional organizations. His administrative experience was limited to four months' service as Associate Dean under Dean Pierce.

He pursued his new responsibilities tirelessly. He appointed Professor Margaret M. Mahoney as Associate Dean for Academic Affairs. This was another distinction for Margaret, who earlier had been the first woman awarded tenure and appointed to the rank of full professor in the school's history. She then became the first woman to hold the post of Associate Dean. Following the completion of a national search, Mark was named Dean of the School in May, 1987.

Among the most pressing concerns facing the new dean was the need to shore up relations with two important constituencies—the leadership of the University and the alumni of the school. Probably the most critical need was the establishment of an effective partnership within the University. The fact that significant friction had been developing between the law school and those in the Cathedral of Learning had not been fully understood by the faculty until Dean Pierce's resignation made it a public matter. However, Dean Murray, at the time of his resignation, had felt that the school was both underappreciated and underfunded.

At an early point in his administration, Dean Nordenberg won University commitments to increase dramatically the funding for the law library, to create a development office within the school, to upgrade the school's placement office, to increase modestly the size of the faculty and staff and to add new tuition-remission scholarships for non-resident students. In all these efforts, he was assisted greatly by the Provost, Dr. Donald Henderson, the Vice Provost, Dr. Jack Daniel and the Executive Assistant Provost, Robert E. Dunkelman, who is now Secretary of the University and one of my very best friends. This all resulted in a changing attitude toward the school within the larger University. By the mid-point of Dean Nordenberg's administration, both the Provost and the Chancellor had publicly proclaimed that the School of Law was "one of the jewels in the University crown."

A great amount of time and attention was also directed at strengthening the ties between the school and its alumni, as well as the larger practicing profession. In certain respects Dean Nordenberg was well qualified for this task. His professional involvements were substantial, including service on both the United States Advisory Committee on Civil Rules and the Pennsylvania Civil Procedural Rules Committee. This work, plus his involvement with me in the school's intensive trial advocacy programs, had garnered for him respect from the bench and bar.

During this period of financial stringency for colleges and universities, fundraising became an important function for all deans. During Dean Nordenberg's tenure, contributions to the school's annual fund grew dramatically. The most visible sign of progress in this area was the expansion of the Law Fellows. That program, instituted by

The Honorable Dennis W. Archer,
Justice Supreme Court of Michigan,
Martin Luther King Day Address.

Justice William J. Brennan, Jr.,
United States Supreme Court.

Dean Pierce, constituted as Law Fellows those individuals who contributed at least $1000 annually to the school. At the departure of Dean Pierce, this group numbered about thirty. By 1990, membership had grown to more than 150. Much of this was a testament to the strong leadership of a succession of chairs of the Law Fellows Committee—Harold R. Schmidt, '37; Marvin S. Lieber, '58; W. Gregg Kerr, '52 and Thomas P. Lutz, '74.

The second semester of 1985-86 saw several lectures delivered in the school. On January 22, 1986, the Honorable Dennis Archer, Justice of the Michigan Supreme Court delivered the Martin Luther King, Jr. Day address.

Harold R. Schmidt, '37.

On January 31, the Honorable William J. Brennan, Jr., Justice of the United States Supreme Court gave the Mellon Distinguished Lecture. The lecture itself was a "standing room only" event. Following the lecture, students stood in long lines hoping that Justice Brennan would autograph their constitutional law casebooks. The evening concluded with a dinner in the William Pitt Union.

Professor Stephen A. Saltzburg of the University of Virginia School of Law

Professor Stephen A. Saltzburg,
University of Virginia School of Law.
1986 Louis Caplan Lecturer.

Honorable Edward D. Re, Chief Judge,
U.S. Court of International Trade,
Graduation address — 1986.

Seated (l to r): Dr. James Farmer and Professor Robert B. Harper.
Standing (l to r): Deans Sell and Nordenberg.

delivered the 1986 Caplan Lecture on April 10.

The Honorable Edward D. Re, Judge, United States Court of International Trade, spoke at graduation ceremonies on May 24 in Soldiers and Sailors Memorial Hall.

John E. Murray, Jr., former Dean and Professor of Law, rejoined the law school faculty at the start of the 1986-87 academic year as a Distinguished Service Professor of Law.

Dr. Roger Benjamin, Provost of the university, resigned to return to the University of Minnesota. He was succeeded as Provost by Dr. Rudolph Weingartner.

The Honorable Alfred T. Goodwin, Chief Judge of the United States Court of Appeals for the Ninth Circuit, was a Distinguished Jurist in Residence October 27-29, 1986. He was available to both students and faculty.

The annual Law Alumni Dinner took place on November 1, 1986.

Dr. James Farmer delivered an inspiring address for the School's Martin Luther King, Jr. observance on Friday, January 23, 1987.

On February 26 and 27, 1987, the School of Law held a special symposium in connection with the 200th birthdays of both the United States Constitution and the University of Pittsburgh. The program explored the Constitution, judicial review and foreign affairs.

The keynote address was delivered of Senator Orrin Hatch, Class of 1962, United States Senator from Utah, and only the second United States Senator who graduated from the law school, the other being Senator James H. Duff, Class of 1907, senator from Pennsylvania. Senator Hatch was a charter member of the Law Fellows. He was presented with a Bicentennial Medallion by Wesley W. Posvar, University President.

The second portion of the program featured Judge Frank Easterbrook of the Seventh Circuit Court of Appeals and Chief Judge John Gibbons of the Third Circuit Court of Appeals. Judge Ruggero J. Aldisert served as moderator of the discussion of differing views of judicial review of the Constitution.

The final segment of the symposium consisted of a debate between Robert B. Owen, Esquire, who served as legal adviser to the Department of State during the Carter administration and Davis R. Robinson, Esquire, who served as legal adviser to the Department of State during the first term of

Senator Orrin G. Hatch, '62, returned to deliver the Louis Caplan Lecture as part of a program celebrating the Bicentennial of the United States Constitution. A charter member of the Law Fellows, he also attended the annual gathering of that group.

President Reagan. The topic was whether and under what circumstances foreign affairs issues are the appropriate subjects of legal review. Professor Jules Lobel moderated this session.

On Tuesday, March 17, Nora Astorga, the Nicaraguan ambassador to the United Nations, delivered an address at the school. The visit was co-sponsored by the School of Law, the University's Center for Latin American Studies, and the Pittsburgh-San Isidro Sister City Project. The address was followed by a lengthy question-and-answer period.

On Friday and Saturday, March 20, and 21, the school hosted the Niagara International Moot Court Competition, sponsored by the Canada-U.S. Law Institute. The competition features student teams representing law schools from throughout the two countries. The 1987 competition was based on a problem focusing on the extraterritorial application of United States discovery rules.

The 1987 graduation program was held on May 30 in Carnegie Music Hall. The Honorable Ruggero J. Aldisert, Chief Judge, United States Court of Appeals for the Third Circuit, spoke on "Remembering Who We Are: Toward an Enlightened Professionalism." Special tribute was paid to George J. Barco, Class of 1934, for his many contributions to the legal profession, the University and the School of Law.

The computer laboratory, funded in part by the Harold Obernauer Foundation,

George J. Barco, Esquire, '34.

(l to r): Dean Nordenberg, Patrick Latham, University of Brussells, Volker Behr, University of Augsburg and Professor Ronald Brand.

was opened for use by the students at the start of the academic year.

In July of 1987, the School of Law was awarded a grant from the United States Information Agency to fund a faculty exchange with the Faculty of Law at the University of Augsburg. It was the result of a special competition celebrating the bicentennial of the United States Constitution. The selection of the school reflects the faculty strength in the area of constitutional law.

The grant funded visits to the law school by faculty members from the University of Augsburg in September and October for each of three years and visits from our faculty to Augsburg in May and June during the same period. The visits were for approximately eight weeks each. The program has continued and the two faculties enjoy a close relationship.

On Monday, September 21, 1987, Mr. Justice Ernst Benda, former President Judge of the West German Constitutional Court delivered a lecture at the school. Two days later, Professor Derrick Bell, Class of 1957, of the Harvard Law School delivered a lecture on civil rights. The title of his address was, "Blacks as Victims and Heroes of the Constitution." The presentation was based on his new book, And We Are Not Saved: The Elusive Quest for Racial Justice, which had been released a week earlier on the date of the national celebration of the Constitution's bicentennial. During his visit, recognition was given his contributions to both legal education and civil rights. He was presented with the University Bicentennial Medallion of Distinction by President Wesley W. Posvar.

On Friday, October 9, Dr. Vasil Tuperkovski, member of the Yugoslavian Presidency, delivered a lecture regarding constitutional reform in his country.

In the fall of 1987, George J. Barco, '34, and his daughter Yolanda G. Barco, '49, announced a gift of a million dollars for the library. The gift, the largest in the history of the school, was used to create a permanent endowment for the library. Since then, by combined gifts, by gifts from his daughter after George's death, and by provisions in his will, the total gift amounts to approximately two million dollars, ensuring the long-term strength of the library.

The objective of the endowment "is to provide funds in addition to the regular University support in order that the law school

George J. Barco, '34.

Yolanda Barco, '49 and Dean Nordenberg.

George and Yolanda Barco surrounded by friends.

may attain and maintain excellence in law library services to respond fully to the teaching and research missions of the law school as well as to provide a continuing learning resource for practitioners in the law."

The Barcos shared a strong interest in the University of Pittsburgh, George having served as a trustee until his death. His daughter, Yolanda, now serves on the board. She has followed in her father's footsteps. Both served at one time as President of the Crawford County Bar Association.

The annual Law Alumni Dinner took place on Saturday, November 7, 1987.

The School of Law participated in the University's $225 million capital campaign, "Campaign for the Third Century." The law school's campaign was co-chaired by David B. Fawcett, Jr., '53, and Edward A. Perlow, '51. Mr. Perlow unexpectedly passed away before the completion of the campaign, to which he was a major contributor. Over $2.1 million was raised from individuals, corporations, foundations and law firms.

The 1988 graduation was held on Saturday, May 28, 1988 in the Soldiers' and Sailors' Memorial Hall. The speaker was Robert D. Raven, President-Elect of the American Bar Association.

On September 15 and 16, 1988, Professor Karl Meessen of the University of Augsburg visited the school.

The Honorable A. Leon Higginbotham, Jr., Judge of the United States Court of Appeals for the Third Circuit, spoke at the Martin Luther King, Jr. Day program on Friday, January 27, 1989.

Edward A. Perlow, '51.

David B. Fawcett, Jr., '53.

At the March meeting of the faculty, it was announced that Dr. Rudolph Weingartner had resigned as Provost of the University.

A Pitt Law School team, composed of Bruce Jamison, Waldo Jones and Eric Schumann, won the first National Corporate Moot Court Competition in the spring of 1989. The same team repeated as national champions in 1990. I was very proud of this team with whom I worked as faculty adviser.

For me, one of the high points of my many years on the faculty occurred on Friday, April 7, 1989 at the Pittsburgh Hilton. The law school, the Pitt Law Alumni Association, the Allegheny County Bar Association, the Pennsylvania Bar Association and the Pennsylvania Bar Institute sponsored a testimonial dinner in my honor.

Over six hundred of my friends and former students attended what turned out to be a masterfully executed semi-roast. Dean Nordenberg, who was the Master of Ceremonies, moved the program, interspersed with the dinner, in clockwork fashion.

That afternoon, in the Teplitz Courtroom of the law school, four of my former students presented a panel discussion on "The Changing Face of Corporations: Takeovers, Mergers, Buyouts." The four panelists were: Richard L. Fischer, Esquire, Senior Vice President and General Counsel of Alcoa; Joseph A. Katarincik, Esquire, partner of the then Katarincik, Salman & Steele law firm; William H. Knoell, Esquire, President and CEO of Cyclops Corporation; and Joseph S. Schuckert, Jr., managing partner of Kelso and Company.

Dr. Jeffrey E. Sell, Dean Sell, Cordelia F. Sell.

The evening dinner program was as follows:

W. EDWARD SELL

TESTIMONIAL DINNER

———————

A TRIBUTE TO
MORE THAN FOUR DECADES
OF DISTINGUISHED AND
DEDICATED SERVICE TO
LEGAL EDUCATION AND
THE LEGAL PROFESSION

———————

The Pittsburgh Hilton
Pittsburgh, Pennsylvania
Friday, April 7, 1989

The entire evening was a deeply emotional experience for me. The high point was the announcement by James J. Flaherty, Esquire, of the creation of the W. Edward Sell Professor of Business Law position in the law school. He announced that over $275,000 of the $500,000 required to fund a professorship had been raised. Since then, the minimum amount has been raised and the school is currently seeking applicants for the position.

My son, Dr. Jeffrey E. Sell, a pediatric cardiac surgeon gave the final tribute. I must say that he drew some of the greatest laughs—at my expense.

At its meeting on May 23, 1989, the faculty approved a dual Juris Doctor/Master of Public Health degree program with the Graduate School of Public Health.

Graduation ceremonies were conducted at 10 a.m. on Saturday, May 27, 1989 in Soldiers' and Sailors' Memorial Hall. The Honorable Carol Los Mansmann, Judge, United States Court of Appeals for the Third Circuit, spoke on "The Successful Lawyer: Warrior or Peacemaker?"

In June, 1989, as part of the University's Campaign for the Third Century, the Alcoa Foundation presented the University with a $1.5 million grant to be used toward various scientific and humanities prógrams. Two hundred fifty thousand dollars of the grant was earmarked for the law school. Part of the law school portion was for financial aid for minority students. Fifty thousand dollars was directed to the W. Edward Sell Professorship of Business Law and one hundred thousand dollars was for continuing development of the school's legal writing program.

On December 28, 1989, the Honorable Ralph J. Cappy, '68, was inducted as a member of the Pennsylvania Supreme Court, joining Justice John P. Flaherty, as the only two graduates of the school elected to the highest court in the Commonwealth.

The Provost, Dr. Donald Henderson, delivered the 1990 Martin Luther King, Jr. Day address on Friday, January 10.

On March 18-20, 1990, the American Bar Association and Association of American Law Schools conducted a joint on-site evaluation of the school. Again, the school received commendation from the inspection team. As noted previously, the reports prepared by the accreditation inspection teams are deemed confidential. While shared with the faculty, they are not to be made public.

On April 3, United States Attorney General Dick Thornburgh, '57, returned to the school to deliver the 1990 Caplan address. A former two-time governor of Pennsylvania, he was nominated by President Ronald Reagan to head the Justice Department. He was sworn into office in August, 1988 and retained by President Bush.

The title of his lecture was "The Rule of Law in Russia: How Democracy Might Work." He dealt with the prospects for democratic reform in the light of both cultural traditions

Dean Sell and Justice Ralph J. Cappy, Pennsylvania Supreme Court.

and what he called "seismic disruptions" in that part of the world. He pointed out that ultimately what is required for these upheavals to result in positive outcomes is for changes that result and new systems created to be grounded in a true commitment to the rule of law.

The attorney general had been hosted during a visit to Moscow by Soviet Justice Minister Veniamin Yakovlev, who had visited the law school in the fall of 1989 and gave Pitt law students his perspective on democratic reform in his country.

Graduation was held on Saturday, May 26, 1990 in the Syria Mosque Auditorium, which has since been purchased by the University and razed. The Honorable Ralph J. Cappy, Justice of the Pennsylvania Supreme Court, spoke on "The Ethical Component of Being a Lawyer, or Has the Legal Profession Become a Billable Event?"

The Honorable Richard L. Thornburgh (Pitt Law 1957), the Attorney General of the United States, delivered the 1990 Louis Caplan lecture. The Attorney General discussed "The Rule of Law in the Soviet Union: How Democracy Might Work."

The annual Law Alumni Dinner was held on November 10, 1990.

It was noted with sorrow at the faculty meeting on January 31, 1991, that former Dean Thomas M. Cooley, II and Professor William Frederick Schulz, Jr. had passed away.

The 1991 Martin Luther King, Jr. Day address was delivered by Professor Derrick Bell, Class of 1957.

Graduation took place on May 25, 1991, with the address given by the Honorable Dolores K. Sloviter, Chief Judge, United States Court of Appeals for the Third Circuit. The title of her presentation was "Remarks on the Independence of the Judiciary."

At the opening faculty meeting for the 1991-92 academic year, it was announced that Professor Paul Carrington of the University of Virginia would be the 1992 Louis Caplan Lecturer.

At the March 20, 1992 faculty meeting, Dean Nordenberg announced that he was resigning from the deanship, effective August 31, 1993. In making his announcement, he stated: "The summer of 1993 will be the 16th anniversary of my arrival at Pitt. Half of that time I spent in faculty positions; the second half will have been spent in the dean's office. I really felt, personally and from an institutional perspective, that it was a good time for a change."

In recounting his administration, he pointed out that there had been a continuing development of what is one of the country's finest faculties, a conversion of our library from an institutional embarrassment to an area of strength, dramatic improvement in research and writing programs and a reentry into the world of clinical legal education.

My own assessment of Mark's administration is that while the above areas certainly were strengthened under his leadership, the single most significant contribution was a strengthening of ties with the alumni and the practicing bench and bar. This was an area I found most enjoyable during my deanship, although I was unable to devote as much time to alumni affairs as I would have liked, mainly because of my preoccupation with the new building.

Professor Barbara Black of the Columbia University Law Faculty was the Mellon Distinguished Scholar for 1991-92. She visited the school from April 1 through April 3.

Graduation took place on May 23, 1992 at 10 a.m. in Soldiers' and Sailors Memorial Hall. Two hundred and twenty-eight graduates were awarded the Juris Doctor degree. The Honorable Joseph F. Weis, Jr., '50, Senior Judge of the United States Court of Appeals for the Third Circuit, spoke on "Innovation in the Legal System: Oxymoron or Prophecy?"

On October 1, 1992, Visiting Professor Volker Behr of the University of Augsburg delivered a lecture, "Codetermination Law in Germany: Worker Participation in Corporate Governance."

Earlier that day, at the monthly faculty meeting, Dean Nordenberg announced that Professor Jennifer Parrish, Director of the Barco Law Library, was resigning to accept the position of director of the law library at the Hastings College of Law of the University of California at San Francisco. Nickie Singleton assumed the position of Acting Director on November 30, 1992.

On October 22, Professor Robert A. Sedler, Class of 1959, of Wayne State University Law School delivered a Distinguished Alumni Lecture.

The 1993 Louis Caplan Lecture was delivered by Professor Geoffrey Hazard of Yale Law School on February 1, 1993. His address was entitled, "Dimensions of Ethical Responsibility: Relevant Others."

On Monday, February 8, Professor David Cole of the Georgetown Law School delivered the Marion Damick lecture, "Censoring Sex and Art in the Age of AIDS."

On Friday, March 19, 1993, an outstanding program was presented in the Teplitz Memorial Courtroom entitled, "A Mentor's Legacy: Charles Hamilton Houston, Thurgood Marshall and The Civil Rights Movement." The program was arranged by Kenneth Gormley, Esquire, first director of the Mellon Writing Program, and author of "A Mentor's Legacy," an article in the June, 1992 issue of the American Bar Association Journal, which was dedicated to Justice Thurgood Marshall. The special program was in honor of the tenth anniversary of the Mellon Writing Program and the genius of two great 20th century civil rights lawyers, Charles Hamilton Houston and Thurgood Marshall.

Charles Hamilton Houston was the vice dean of the all-black Howard Law School

◆ ◆ ◆

A Mentor's Legacy special guest speakers (l to r): Oliver Hill, Juanita Kidd Stout, Charles Hamilton Houston, Jr., Genna Rae McNeil, Charles Ogletree.

in the early 1930s. He transformed a floundering night school into a first-rate legal program, producing many of the foremost civil rights attorneys of the century, including Thurgood Marshall. He was the first African-American lawyer to argue and win a case before the United States Supreme Court, and architect of a string of school desegregation cases that led to ultimate victory in Brown v. Board of Education four years after his death in 1950.

The program was open to the public and followed by a reception. The special guest speakers were: Dr. Genna Rae McNeil, Professor of History at the University of North Carolina and author of Charles Houston's biography, Groundwork; Professor Charles Ogletree, Harvard Law School professor studying Mr. Houston's contributions to criminal law; Oliver Hill, Esquire, an 85-year-old classmate of Justice Thurgood Marshall at Howard Law School, who studied under Charles Houston and was an attorney in the Virginia portion of the landmark Brown v. Board of Education; retired Justice Juanita Kidd Stout, first African-American woman to serve on the Pennsylvania Supreme Court, who was secretary to Mr. Houston before enrolling in law school; and, Charles Hamilton Houston, Jr., only child of Charles Houston, who was pursuing a Ph.D. in history at the University of Maryland. The program was moderated by Professor Gormley, who was a visiting professor in the law school.

The program lasted for two and a half hours as the speakers recounted stories of the perfectionist Houston, as well as remembrances of Justice Thurgood Marshall, who would say of his unheralded professor before his death: "The school case [Brown v. Board of Education] was really Charlie's victory. He just never got a chance to see it." It was a very well attended affair.

The program concluded with the presentation of awards to five African-American graduates of the law school who have made unique contributions to the legal profession. The five are: Commonwealth Court Judge Doris Smith ('72) for her contribution to the Pennsylvania judiciary; Robert Berkley Harper ('71) for his contribution to legal education; K. Leroy Irvis ('54) for his distinguished career in government service; Garland McAdoo ('72), for his excellence in the private practice of law; and William Lynn Wallace ('80), former public broadcaster and then executive at National Geographic Society, for his work in the media.

The Mellon Distinguished Lecture was delivered on April 7, 1993 by Morris Dees.

The graduation speaker on May 29, 1993 was the Honorable A. Leon Higginbotham, Jr., now a Senior Judge on the United States Court of Appeals for the Third Circuit. His address was titled, "Lawyers' Values and Justice."

Upon the announced retirement of Dean Nordenberg, a dean search committee was formed by the Provost. The committee was chaired by Professor John Camillus of the Katz Graduate School of Business. The committee narrowed its list of candidates to five. The list become further reduced by withdrawals and other factors. Finally, two viable candidates were presented for faculty consideration. Neither candidate received substantial faculty support. Most of the law faculty signed a resolution requesting the Provost not to offer the position to either candidate, but to start a new search. The Provost, Dr. Donald Henderson, concurred and the search was voided.

Professor Richard H. Seeburger, who had served as Associate Dean for Academic Affairs under Dean John E. Murray, Jr., was named Interim Dean by Dr. Henderson. Dean Nordenberg agreed to serve as Interim Provost, the chief academic officer of the University for the 1993-94 academic year. This was prompted by the retirement of Dr. Henderson as Provost, effective June 30, 1993.

A new search committee was organized, with Dr. Randy Juhl, Dean of the School of Pharmacy, serving as chair.

Another of the outstanding programs conducted during its first century took place on Friday, December 3, 1993. It was the Inaugural Henry Shore Memorial Lecture. Mr. Shore was a 1934 graduate of the law school. For 44 years, Mr. Shore was employed by the National Labor Relations Board at its Pittsburgh regional office, first as field attorney, then as regional attorney, and beginning in 1947, as regional director, a position he held for 34 years until his retirement in 1981.

During his long career, Mr. Shore developed an outstanding national reputation as an expert labor law practitioner, teacher and public administrator. At the time of his retirement, he was the dean of all regional directors. Following his retirement from government service, Mr. Shore served as an arbitrator until his death in July, 1987. His many friends and associates established the lectureship in his memory.

The inaugural program was entitled "The Saturday Night Massacre, a 20-year

Retrospect." The program was arranged by Kenneth Gormley, Esquire, a visiting professor in the School of Law and the biographer of Archibald Cox. Featured in the program were Archibald Cox and Elliott Richardson, principals in the Watergate investigation and events leading up to the Saturday Night Massacre, when Elliott Richardson resigned and Archibald Cox was fired as Special Investigator.

The program was moderated by James Doyle, who was selected in 1973 to serve as press secretary and Special Assistant to the Watergate Special Prosecutor. He occupied a vital role as spokesman for Archibald Cox and his successor, Leon Jaworski, throughout the Watergate investigation.

Also on the program was the Honorable Philip Heymann, then Deputy Attorney General of the United States in charge of the Criminal Division of the U.S. Department of Justice. In the summer of 1973, Heymann volunteered to serve as Associate Watergate Special Prosecutor, working closely with Archibald Cox and Leon Jaworski over the next two years.

The University of Pittsburgh
School of Law

Is Proud To Present

**The Inaugural
Henry Shore Memorial Lecture**

The Saturday Night Massacre:

A 20-Year Retrospect

A special program marking the 20-year anniversary of the Saturday Night Massacre and other key events of Watergate, during the fall of 1973.

FRIDAY, December 3, 1993

Teplitz Memorial Courtroom
University of Pittsburgh
School of Law

The program consisted of a detailed, almost hour by hour, discussion of events of the week leading up to Saturday night's discharge of Cox as special prosecutor. This was the first time that Messrs. Cox and Richardson appeared together to discuss Watergate. At the conclusion of the formal program, a short question and answer period was held. Those in attendance found it a most interesting and informative presentation.

The 1994 Caplan Lecture was delivered on Monday, February 21, 1994 by Professor Julius "Jack" Getman of the University of Texas School of Law.

The annual Martin Luther King, Jr. address in the law school was delivered by Professor Robert B. Harper on February 25, 1994. Following Bob's presentation, there was a roast. There were musical and dance performances included in the program.

Bob is a wonderful colleague. After his graduation from the law school in 1971,

Professor Cox autographing his book after the Saturday Massacre Program.

Archibald Cox and Elliot Richardson.

he served as legal counsel for the Pittsburgh Police. I was looking for an assistant dean to serve in my administration. I approached Bob and he accepted. I thoroughly enjoyed working with him. I particularly enjoyed visiting pre-law college groups with him. After a few years, I felt it was unfair to Bob to have him both serving as an administrator and as a professor. It was obvious that if he were to succeed as a professor he would need to devote time to scholarship as well as the classrcom. After I had some discussions with Bob on the matter, he resigned as Assistant Dean to devote full time to teaching and scholarship. He was not only the first black in

Peter M. Shane.

the schocl's administration but the first black faculty member and the first black full professor.

The accolades given him at the February 25th program were certainly merited. Some members of his family were present to enjoy it with him.

On Monday, April 18, 1994 Interim Provost Mark Nordenberg announced that University of Iowa Law Professor Peter Shane would become the new dean of the law school. In his announcement, Mark Nordenberg stated: "I am very pleased with this appointment. Professor Shane has distinguished himself as a scholar and teacher. He also is an extremely thoughtful member of the community of legal scholars. He has demonstrated administrative ability in past leadership positions. I am certain he will make a contribution to progress at the University of Pittsburgh School of Law."

The University also extended an offer to Peter Shane's wife, Martha Chamallas, also a law professor at the University of Iowa. She is a graduate of Louisiana State University Law Center in 1975. She clerked for the Honorable Charles Clark in the United States Court of Appeals before becoming a professor at LSU and later at Iowa. She teaches torts, feminist legal theory and employment law. In announcing her appointment, the Interim Provost stated: "Professor Chamallas is a very distinguished scholar and accomplished teacher, and she will add greatly to the existing strength of the law school, both in the classroom and through her written work."

Dean Shane was born and raised in West Hempstead, Long Island, New York. He attended Harvard College where he obtained an interdisciplinary social science degree. He received his law degree from Yale in 1977, after which he clerked for Honorable Alvin B. Rubin in the U.S. Court of Appeals. He also worked for the U.S. Department of Justice before becoming a law professor. His fields of expertise are constitutional law, administrative law, law of Presidential power, legislation, and education law.

The new dean said there were a lot of reasons why he wanted to come to the University of Pittsburgh School of Law. Among those, he cited an ambitious faculty with a commitment to first-rate teaching and research. He said he was also drawn by the close relationship he saw between faculty and students.

Seeing his role as promoting a public service, Dean Shane stated: "If the dean is successful at strengthening a law school, it can have profound effects on the community, most directly on students who pass through it, but also it can make an impact on the legal community by using law to serve people's interests more effectively. If I'm good, a few years down the road, I can say that I helped contribute to some of that."

Herb Sherman.

On Friday, April 29, 1994, the school held a Sell-ebration. The program began at 5:30 pm. with a program in the Teplitz Memorial Courtroom. I was placed on trial before a court consisting of Dawne Hickton, John E. Murray, Jr., Mark A. Nordenberg, Gregg Kerr, Judge Lawrence Kaplan, Dean Joseph Harbaugh of the University of Richmond Law School and my son, Dr. Jeffrey E. Sell, a heart transplant surgeon at Children's National Medical Center in Washington, D.C. There were numerous charges, which I had some difficulty ascertaining.

I was very surprised after all these "impartial judges" addressed all of my wrongdoings, to find my counsel, Professor Herbert L. Sherman, Jr., who had assured me he had a good defense to all of these

---

The University of Pittsburgh -- School of Law

Invites You To Attend A

Sell-ebration

Former Dean W. Edward Sell will retire in May of this year, having completed 47 years of service to the University of Pittsburgh School of Law and Pittsburgh legal community. Celebrating this event, you are invited to attend a program of reflection and rememberance followed by a reception.

Friday, April 29, 1994

5:30 PM - Program
Teplitz Memorial Courtroom - Ground Floor

6:30 PM - Reception
Main Lobby - First Floor

University of Pittsburgh School of Law
3900 Forbes Avenue (Corner of Forbes and Bouquet)

charges, tearing up all of his papers, throwing them on the floor and pleading me guilty. I felt I had had inadequate counsel but since Herb was such a dear friend of about forty-six years I decided against raising the issue.

After the program, there was a reception in the first floor lobby. The emotional high point of the event occurred when Interim Dean Dick Seeburger unveiled a plaque in the lobby which reads as follows:

In Honor of

W. EDWARD SELL
BUILDER ... TEACHER ... SCHOLAR

W. Edward Sell joined the faculty of the School of Law in 1947 and served as a full-time Professor of Law longer than any other person in the history of the School. His personal vision as Dean (1966-1977) led to the construction of the present Law Building and to the enhanced national reputation of the School.

Great teachers touch the future. Ed not only touched, but shaped the future with his dedication, love of the law and sense of deep commitment to all who labored and learned with him. His impact on the Pitt Law School, on generations of law students and on the legal profession is indelible and will live in perpetuity. On the occasion of his retirement from the faculty and appointment as Emeritus Distinguished Service Professor of Law, the alumni, faculty and staff of the University of Pittsburgh School of Law hereby express their admiration, their appreciation and their friendship.

May 1994

The evening ended at the University Club where about two hundred friends paid me the honor of their attendance.

At the graduation on May 28, 1994, I became Dean Emeritus and Distinguished Service Professor of Law Emeritus. My very good friend, Mark Nordenberg, serving as Interim Provost, presented me with the appropriate indicia of emeritus status. A former student, Professor Derrick A. Bell, Jr., '57, delivered the graduation address.

Full-time Law School Faculty — 1994-1995.

Judges for 1987 Moot Court Finals. Justice John P. Flaherty, '58, Judge Maurice B. Cohill, Jr., '56, and Judge Joseph F. Weis, Jr., '50.

James M. Houston, '34.

Class of 1953's 35th reunion.

Honorable Richard Thornburgh, '57 and Richard L. Fischer, '61 upon receiving Bicentennial Plaques from University.

Elevation of Ruggero J. Aldisert to Chief Judge, U.S. Court of Appeals for the Third Circuit.

Judge J. Quint Salmon, '31 and his wife, Anne.

1986 Law Fellows (l to r): Prof. Stephen Saltzburg, Richard Brok, Joseph A. Katarincic, Richard J. Pierce, Jr., Harold R. Schmidt, Distinguished Service Prof. W. Edward Sell, Mrs. Sammuel Feigus, The Hon. J. Quint Salmon, John H. Morgan, Marvin S. Lieber, Acting Dean Mark A. Nordenberg, The Hon. Harry M. Montgomery, Blair S. McMillin and John P. Gismondi.

Some of the 1988 Trial Advocacy Faculty. Front row (l to r): Herb Rosenberg, Pete Dixon, Mark Nordenberg, Bill Luneburg. Back row (l to r): Al Lindsay, Gil Helwig, Ed Sell, Paul Manion, Gregg Kerr, Tom Hollander.

Chatting with a former student, Judge Weis, at the 1988 graduation.

Federal Judge Robert Keeton at a program on the Future of Federal Litigation, September 30, 1988.

Moot Court Judges — 1990.

A Moot Court final argument.

With my dear friend, Bill Schulz at the 1990 Caplan Lecture.

Class of 1962 30th Reunion. Front row (l ro r): William Herrington, W. Edward Sell, Gretchen Sohn Reed, Judge Robert C. Reed. Second row (l to r): Jan C. Swenson, Arnold B. Silverman, Francis E. Holahan, Robert B. Shust.

Class of 1953's 40th Reunion.

Judge James Rowley, '52, Judge Maurice B. Cohill, Jr., '56, Justice Ralph Cappy, '68 and Judge Timothy Lewis who served on the Panel for the intraschool moot court finals, 1994.

The 1993-94 Moot Court Board to which I served as Faculty Adviser.
Front row (l to r): Susan Herilla, Beth Lochmiller, Susan Sandoe.
Back row (l to r): Thomas Shultz, Stephen D. Moritz, W. Edward Sell,
Gerald Stubenhofer, John Jones.

Board of Visitors, 1986.

At the Sell-ebration. (l to r): Dr. Donald Henderson, Retired Provost, Dean Nordenberg, Dean Margaret Mahoney and Robert Dunkelman, Secretary of the University Board of Trustees.

My friend, Dr. Donald Henderson with whom I enjoyed working when I served as dean.

With two close friends and colleagues, Deans Murray and Nordenberg.

The author.

Deans of the School

John Douglass Shafer .... 1895 – 1920

Alexander Marshall Thompson .... 1920 – 1940

Eugene Allen Gilmore .... 1940 – 1942

Judson Adams Crane .... 1942 – 1949

Charles Bernard Nutting .... 1949 – 1951

Brainerd Currie .... 1952 – 1953

Arthur Larson .... 1953 – 1956

Thomas McIntyre Cooley, II .... 1957 – 1965

William Edward Sell .... 1966 – 1977

John E. Murray, Jr. .... 1977 – 1984

Richard J. Pierce, Jr. .... 1984 – 1985

Mark A. Nordenberg .... 1986 – 1993

Peter M. Shane .... 1994 –

—TABLE TWO—
Faculty Members by Year They First Joined the Faculty

YEAR	NAME	YEAR	NAME
1895	Burleigh, Clarence*	1926	McIntyre, John D.
1895	Gray, James C.*	1927	James, Laylin K.
1895	Herriott, Thomas*	1927	Lewis, Mahlon E.
1895	McClung, William H.*	1927	Madden, J. Warren
1895	Mehard, Samuel S.*	1927	Ringsdorf, Samuel D.**
1895	Patterson, Thomas*	1928	Wasson, Jr., Henry G.**
1895	Shafer, John D.*	1929	Demmler, Ralph H.**
1895	Smith, William Watson*	1930	Geiser, Dixon H.**
1898	Longnecker, Ralph*	1930	Putman, Francis J.
1900	Chalfant , Jr., John W.*	1931	Blackburn, James B.
1902	Miller, Frederick W.*	1931	Kelly, Edward F.**
1903	Noble, Thaddeus C.*	1932	Downie, Robert D.**
1903	Thompson, A. Marshall*	1933	Metz, Jr., John A.**
1904	Hawkins, Richard H.**	1934	Houston, James M.**
1904	Woodside, Robert G.*	1935	Lemon, W. Ernest**
1905	Blakely, William A.*	1936	Boreman, Leonard**
1905	Haber, DeWitt*	1937	Lawler, J. John
1906	Black, Alexander**	1937	Schmidt, Harold R.**
1907	Englert, Edmond*	1938	Marks, Leonard H.**
1907	Houston, J. Garfield**	1939	Sawyer, John N.**
1908	Marshall, Elder W.**	1939	White, James L.**
1908	Miller, J. J.*	1940	Dickerson, F. Reed
1909	Duff, Jr., John T.**	1940	Gilmore, Eugene Allen
1910	Moorhead, William S.**	1940	Lamproplos, Milton W.**
1911	Holland, Moorhead B.**	1940	Snyder, Jr., Daniel**
1911	Miller, Thomas A.**	1940	Teitlebaum, Hubert**
1912	Bell, James C.**	1940	West, Stanley
1912	Martin, Richard W.*	1940	Wilson, James R.
1913	Arensberg, Charles F. C.*	1941	Marsh, Edward W.**
1913	Caplan, Louis**	1943	Taintor, II, Charles W.
1913	Reed, John C.**	1946	McCann, John A.*
1914	Applegate, Robert A.**	1946	Nutting, Charles Bernard
1914	Christy, J. Smith*	1946	Woods, Charles A.*
1914	Reed, Harold F.**	1947	Brown, Robert Coleman
1915	Buchanan, John G.*	1947	Checkley, Thomas A.
1915	Wilson, John H.**	1947	Dewey, Fred E.
1916	Hirsch, Albert C.**	1947	Sell, W. Edward
1916	MacFarlane, James R.*	1948	Anderson, Jr., D. M.*
1917	Crane, Judson Adams	1948	Reuschlein, Harold G.
1917	Soffel, Sara M.**	1948	Sherman, Jr., Herbert Leroy
1918	Heiner, William G.*	1949	Rahauser, William S.*
1918	O'Neill, Henry J.**	1949	Schulz, Jr., William Frederick
1919	Thompson, George J.	1949	Wentling, Thomas L.*
1920	Isaacs, Nathan	1950	Helwig, Gilbert*
1923	Hawkins, Richard H.	1951	Stahl, David
1924	Eckert, William H.*	1952	Currie, Brainerd
1924	Herron, J. Pat	1952	Garrett, Sylvester*

YEAR	NAME	YEAR	NAME
1952	Gregg, Loyal H.*	1972	Harper, Robert Berkley
1952	Kuhn, Jr., J. Craig*	1972	Kanovitz, Jacqueline R.
1952	McKee, William R.*	1972	Lampl, Sanford M.*
1953	Larson, Arthur	1973	Farley, Andrew N.*
1954	Buell, Eugene F.*	1974	Choate, John I.
1954	Foster, Jr., Henry H.	1974	Gruener, Harry J.*
1954	McDermott, Jr., Clare B.	1974	Meisel, Alan
1957	Bookstaver, David Richard	1974	Yablonski, Steven K.
1957	Cooley II, Thomas McIntyre	1975	Frolik, Lawrence A.
1958	Litman, Roslyn M.*	1975	Hellman, Arthur D.
1958	Rappeport, Jack J.	1975	Holmes, Eric Mills
1959	Kahn, Arthur H.	1975	McCarthy, Francis Barry
1959	Milner, Alan	1975	O'Loughlin, Johanna*
1959	Silverstein, Lee	1975	Potter, Robert L.
1960	Bachrach, Jerome C.*	1975	Smith II, George P.
1960	Holahan, Francis Eugene	1975	Strassburger III, Eugene B.*
1960	Horty, John F.*	1976	Burkoff, John M.
1961	Hay, Peter H.	1976	Cohen, Charles C.*
1961	Hershey, Nathan (SA)	1976	Munsch, Martha Hartle
1961	Meiners, Robert G.	1977	Cooper, Carl G.
1961	Schafer, Seymour J.*	1977	Herbst, Karl P.
1961	Springer, Eric W.*	1977	Kennedy, Thomas J.
1961	Thomas, Herbert Edwin*	1977	Klein, Leonard E.
1962	Reisner, Ralph	1977	Nichols, Rosemary
1964	Blackstone, Jr., Franklin*	1977	Nordenberg, Mark A.
1964	Cohen, David M.	1977	Raphael, Robert*
1964	Greenspan, Robert S.	1977	Shane, Ilene (L)
1964	Seeburger, Richard Harry	1978	Gerety, Tom
1964	Shattuck, Jr., Leroy A.*	1978	Knapp, Andria S.
1965	Aldisert, Ruggero J.*	1978	Luneburg, William V.
1965	Mattern, Clara L.*	1978	Mahoney, Margaret M.
1965	McCreight, John C.*	1978	Patton, Robert F.*
1965	Wekselman, I. Martin*	1978	Rosenberg, Herbert N.*
1965	White, Thomas Owen	1978	Wilder, Joanne Ross*
1966	McGuire, Bartlett H.	1979	Blackmore II, Josiah H. (V)
1966	Ross, Eunice L.*	1979	Cercone, William F.*
1966	Wettick, Jr., R. Stanton*	1979	Chabon, Robert S.*
1967	Bravenec, Lorence L.	1979	Das, Eva Borsody (L)
1967	Murray, Jr., John E.	1979	Greenfield, Stanley W.*
1967	Newlin, William R.*	1979	Rothstein, Mark A. (V)
1968	Brown, William J.	1980	Barker, Robert S.*
1968	Lee, Lawrence D.	1980	Beard, Philip E.*
1968	White, Welsh S.	1980	Connolly, Mark Q.
1969	Baker, Joan E.	1980	Fein, Marvin A.*
1969	Fowler, Jr., Talbert B.	1980	Grigsby, Robert S.*
1970	Horwitz, Solis*	1980	Hummel, Lee*
1970	Levenson, Leonard H.	1980	Parrish, Mary J.
1970	Mullock, Philip	1980	Reicher, Harry (V)
1970	Symons, Jr., Edward L.	1980	Rothstein, Laura F. (V)
1971	Benett, Edward J.	1980	Torres, Gerald
1971	Das, Shyameshwar	1981	Appelbaum, Paul S. (SA)
1971	Fawcett, Jr., David B.*	1981	Finegold, Alan H.*
1971	Fox, jr., Cyril A.	1981	Samuelson, Pamela
1971	McLean, Jr., John J.*	1981	Snyder, Mary W.
1971	Very, Donald L.*	1982	Attanasio, John B. (V)

YEAR	NAME
1982	Brand, Ronald A.
1982	Dixon, F. Peter*
1982	Gormley, Kenneth G.
1982	Harvey, Calvin R.
1982	Hunter, James O.
1982	Kalis, Peter J.*
1982	Rowles, James P. (V)
1982	Smith, Charles R.*
1982	Vogel, Joan E.
1982	Wood, Jacques M.*
1983	LaPiana, William P.
1983	Lobel, Jules L.
1984	Cosetti, Joseph L .*
1984	Flechtner, Harry M.
1984	Pierce, Jr., Richard J.
1984	Ross, Thomas
1984	Tobias, Carl W. (V)
1985	Allen, Anita
1985	Barry, Francis A.*
1985	Cannon, David C.*
1985	Chew, Pat K.
1985	Gismondi, John P.*
1985	King, Paul M.*
1985	Thompson, Thomas M.*
1985	Wittenberg, Jeffrey D. (V)
1986	Brenner, Robert M.*
1986	Chaykin, Arthur A. (V)
1986	Elfenbein, Donald M. (V)
1986	Goldberg, Michael J.
1986	Henderson, Thomas J.*
1986	Lieber, James B.*
1986	Wasserman, Rhonda S.
1986	Zonn, Sidney*
1987	Cafardi, Nicholas P.*
1987	Cooper, Thomas L.*
1987	Deasy, Kevin M.
1987	Hoke, S. Candice
1987	Koniak, Susan P.
1987	Lee, Greg R.
1987	Mansmann, Carol Los*
1987	Messer, Howard F.*
1987	Schwartz, Frederic S. (V)
1987	Weis, Jr., Joseph F.*
1988	Alstadt, Lynn J.*
1988	Bevan III, William*
1988	Cohen, George M.
1988	Curran, Vivian
1988	Gelfand, Gregory (V)
1988	Hibbitts, Bernard J.
1988	Irvis, K. Leroy*
1988	Jordan, Sandra D.
1988	Kline, Michael J.*
1988	Weisblatt, Harold*
1988	Wilkinson, James A.*
1989	Ashley, Kevin D.
1989	Bowman, Forest J. (V)
1989	Brandon, Barbara H.*
1989	Brown, Edward G.*
1989	English, David M. (V)
1989	Friedberg, James J. (V)
1989	Hitt, Leo N.*
1989	Hornak, Mark R.*
1989	Katz, Howard E. (V)
1989	Richey, P. Jerome*
1989	Saunders, Kurt M.
1989	Stark, Shelley J.* (C)
1989	Steinberg, David E.
1989	Taylor, George H.
1990	Armour, Jody D.
1990	Boyle, Thomas E.*
1990	Brackey, Channing E. (V)
1990	Fure, Barbara A.
1990	Herring, David J.
1990	Krasik, Carl*
1990	Schiff, Anne Reichman
1991	Greer, Martha J. (C)
1992	Cichon, Dennis E. (V)
1992	Lindsay, Jr., Alexander H.*
1992	Lynd, Staughton*
1992	Montgomery III, J. W.*
1993	Bhandari, Jagdeep S.*
1993	Brostoff, Teresa K.
1993	Burke, Timothy F.*
1993	Colker, Ruth
1993	Engro-Fanberg, Karen (C)
1993	Hartman, Rhonda G.* (V)
1993	McWilson, Frank B.* (C)
1993	Smetanka, Stella L. (C)
1994	Arbogast, Thomas*
1994	Boehm, Frederick A.*
1994	Chamallas, Martha E.
1994	Diederichsen, Eva*
1994	Henson, Deborah M.
1994	Hickton, Dawne S. (C)
1994	Kerr, Thomas*
1994	Lieber, Penina K.*
1994	Mannix, Martha M. (C)
1994	Pike, III, George H.
1994	Shane, Peter M.
1994	Wang, Lu-in (V)
1994	Zipursky, Benjamin C. (V)

Faculty Members in Alphabetical Order
With Year First Joined the Faculty

<table>
<tr><td>CODE</td></tr>
<tr><td>*Part Time; **Teaching Fellow; (C) Clinic Faculty; (L) Lecturer;
(SA) Secondary Appointment; (V) Visitor</td></tr>
</table>

YEAR	NAME	YEAR	NAME
1965	Aldisert, Ruggero J.*	1913	Caplan, Louis**
1985	Allen, Anita	1979	Cercone, William F.*
1988	Alstadt, Lynn J.*	1979	Chabon, Robert S.*
1948	Anderson, Jr., D. M.*	1900	Chalfant , Jr., John W.*
1981	Appelbaum, Paul S. (SA)	1994	Chamallas, Martha E.
1914	Applegate, Robert A.**	1986	Chaykin, Arthur A. (V)
1994	Arbogast, Thomas*	1947	Checkley, Thomas A.
1913	Arensberg, Charles F. C.*	1985	Chew, Pat K.
1990	Armour, Jody D.	1974	Choate, John I.
1989	Ashley, Kevin D.	1914	Christy, J. Smith*
1982	Attanasio, John B. (V)	1992	Cichon, Dennis E. (V)
1960	Bachrach, Jerome C.*	1976	Cohen, Charles C.*
1969	Baker, Joan E.	1964	Cohen, David M.
1980	Barker, Robert S.*	1988	Cohen, George M.
1985	Barry, Francis A.*	1993	Colker, Ruth
1980	Beard, Philip E.*	1980	Connolly, Mark Q.
1912	Bell, James C.**	1957	Cooley II, Thomas McIntyre
1971	Benett, Edward J.	1977	Cooper, Carl G.
1988	Bevan III, William*	1987	Cooper, Thomas L.*
1993	Bhandari, Jagdeep S.*	1984	Cosetti, Joseph L .*
1906	Black, Alexander**	1917	Crane, Judson Adams
1931	Blackburn, James B.	1988	Curran, Vivian
1979	Blackmore II, Josiah H. (V)	1952	Currie, Brainerd
1964	Blackstone, Jr., Franklin*	1979	Das, Eva Borsody (L)
1905	Blakely, William A.*	1971	Das, Shyameshwar
1994	Boehm, Frederick A.*	1987	Deasy, Kevin M.
1957	Bookstaver, David Richard	1929	Demmler, Ralph H.**
1936	Boreman, Leonard**	1947	Dewey, Fred E.
1989	Bowman, Forest J. (V)	1940	Dickerson, F. Reed
1990	Boyle, Thomas E.*	1994	Diederichsen, Eva*
1990	Brackey, Channing E. (V)	1982	Dixon, F. Peter*
1982	Brand, Ronald A.	1932	Downie, Robert D.**
1989	Brandon, Barbara H.*	1909	Duff, Jr., John T.**
1967	Bravenec, Lorence L.	1924	Eckert, William H.*
1986	Brenner, Robert M.*	1986	Elfenbein, Donald M. (V)
1993	Brostoff, Teresa K.	1907	Englert, Edmond*
1989	Brown, Edward G.*	1989	English, David M. (V)
1947	Brown, Robert Coleman	1993	Engro-Fanberg, Karen (C)
1968	Brown, William J.	1973	Farley, Andrew N.*
1915	Buchanan, John G.*	1971	Fawcett, Jr., David B.*
1954	Buell, Eugene F.*	1980	Fein, Marvin A.*
1993	Burke, Timothy F.*	1981	Finegold, Alan H.*
1976	Burkoff, John M.	1984	Flechtner, Harry M.
1895	Burleigh, Clarence*	1954	Foster, Jr., Henry H.
1987	Cafardi, Nicholas P.*	1969	Fowler, Jr., Talbert B.
1985	Cannon, David C.*	1971	Fox, jr., Cyril A.

YEAR	NAME	YEAR	NAME
1989	Friedberg, James J. (V)	1982	Kalis, Peter J.*
1975	Frolik, Lawrence A.	1972	Kanovitz, Jacqueline R.
1990	Fure, Barbara A.	1989	Katz, Howard E. (V)
1952	Garrett, Sylvester*	1931	Kelly, Edward F.**
1930	Geiser, Dixon H.**	1977	Kennedy, Thomas J.
1988	Gelfand, Gregory (V)	1994	Kerr, Thomas*
1978	Gerety, Tom	1985	King, Paul M.*
1940	Gilmore, Eugene Allen	1977	Klein, Leonard E.
1985	Gismondi, John P.*	1988	Kline, Michael J.*
1986	Goldberg, Michael J.	1978	Knapp, Andria S.
1982	Gormley, Kenneth G.	1987	Koniak, Susan P.
1895	Gray, James C.*	1990	Krasik, Carl*
1979	Greenfield, Stanley W.*	1952	Kuhn, Jr., J. Craig*
1964	Greenspan, Robert S.	1972	Lampl, Sanford M.*
1991	Greer, Martha J. (C)	1940	Lamproplos, Milton W.**
1952	Gregg, Loyal H.*	1983	LaPiana, William P.
1980	Grigsby, Robert S.*	1953	Larson, Arthur
1974	Gruener, Harry J.*	1937	Lawler, J. John
1905	Haber, DeWitt*	1987	Lee, Greg R.
1972	Harper, Robert Berkley	1968	Lee, Lawrence D.
1993	Hartman, Rhonda G.* (V)	1935	Lemon, W. Ernest**
1982	Harvey, Calvin R.	1970	Levenson, Leonard H.
1923	Hawkins, Richard H.	1927	Lewis, Mahlon E.
1904	Hawkins, Richard H.**	1986	Lieber, James B.*
1961	Hay, Peter H.	1994	Lieber, Penina K.*
1918	Heiner, William G.*	1992	Lindsay, Jr., Alexander H.*
1975	Hellman, Arthur D.	1958	Litman, Roslyn M.*
1950	Helwig, Gilbert*	1983	Lobel, Jules L.
1986	Henderson, Thomas J.*	1898	Longnecker, Ralph*
1994	Henson, Deborah M.	1978	Luneburg, William V.
1977	Herbst, Karl P.	1992	Lynd, Staughton*
1990	Herring, David J.	1916	MacFarlane, James R.*
1895	Herriott, Thomas*	1927	Madden, J. Warren
1924	Herron, J. Pat	1978	Mahoney, Margaret M.
1961	Hershey, Nathan (SA)	1994	Mannix, Martha M. (C)
1988	Hibbitts, Bernard J.	1987	Mansmann, Carol Los*
1994	Hickton, Dawne S. (C)	1938	Marks, Leonard H.**
1916	Hirsch, Albert C.**	1941	Marsh, Edward W.*
1989	Hitt, Leo N.*	1908	Marshall, Elder W.**
1987	Hoke, S. Candice	1912	Martin, Richard W.*
1960	Holahan, Francis Eugene	1965	Mattern, Clara L.*
1911	Holland, Moorhead B.**	1946	McCann, John A.*
1975	Holmes, Eric Mills	1975	McCarthy, Francis Barry
1989	Hornak, Mark R.*	1895	McClung, William H.*
1960	Horty, John F.*	1965	McCreight, John C.*
1970	Horwitz, Solis*	1954	McDermott, Jr., Clare B.*
1907	Houston, J. Garfield**	1966	McGuire, Bartlett H.
1934	Houston, James M.**	1926	McIntyre, John D.
1980	Hummel, Lee*	1952	McKee, William R.*
1982	Hunter, James O.	1971	McLean, Jr., John J.*
1988	Irvis, K. Leroy*	1993	McWilson, Frank B.* (C)
1920	Isaacs, Nathan	1895	Mehard, Samuel S.*
1927	James, Laylin K.	1961	Meiners, Robert G.
1988	Jordan, Sandra D.	1974	Meisel, Alan
1959	Kahn, Arthur H.	1987	Messer, Howard F.*

YEAR	NAME
1933	Metz, Jr., John A.**
1902	Miller, Frederick W.*
1908	Miller, J. J.*
1911	Miller, Thomas A.**
1959	Milner, Alan
1992	Montgomery III, J. W.*
1910	Moorhead, William S.**
1970	Mullock, Philip
1976	Munsch, Martha Hartle
1967	Murray, Jr., John E.
1967	Newlin, William R.*
1977	Nichols, Rosemary
1903	Noble, Thaddeus C.*
1977	Nordenberg, Mark A.
1946	Nutting, Charles Bernard
1975	O'Loughlin, Johanna*
1918	O'Neill, Henry J.**
1980	Parrish, Mary J.
1895	Patterson, Thomas*
1978	Patton, Robert F.*
1984	Pierce, Jr., Richard J.
1994	Pike, III, George H.
1975	Potter, Robert L.
1930	Putman, Francis J.
1949	Rahauser, William S.*
1977	Raphael, Robert*
1958	Rappeport, Jack J.
1914	Reed, Harold F.**
1913	Reed, John C.**
1980	Reicher, Harry (V)
1962	Reisner, Ralph
1948	Reuschlein, Harold G.
1989	Richey, P. Jerome*
1927	Ringsdorf, Samuel D.**
1978	Rosenberg, Herbert N.*
1966	Ross, Eunice L.*
1984	Ross, Thomas
1980	Rothstein, Laura F. (V)
1979	Rothstein, Mark A. (V)
1982	Rowles, James P. (V)
1981	Samuelson, Pamela
1989	Saunders, Kurt M.
1939	Sawyer, John N.**
1961	Schafer, Seymour J.*
1990	Schiff, Anne Reichman
1937	Schmidt, Harold R.**
1949	Schulz, Jr., William Frederick
1987	Schwartz, Frederic S. (V)
1964	Seeburger, Richard Harry
1947	Sell, W. Edward
1895	Shafer, John D.*
1977	Shane, Ilene (L)
1994	Shane, Peter M.
1964	Shattuck, Jr., Leroy A.*
1948	Sherman, Jr., Herbert Leroy
1959	Silverstein, Lee
1993	Smetanka, Stella L. (C)
1982	Smith, Charles R.*
1975	Smith II, George P.
1895	Smith, William Watson*
1981	Snyder, Mary W.
1940	Snyder, Jr., Daniel**
1917	Soffel, Sara M.**
1961	Springer, Eric W.*
1951	Stahl, David
1989	Stark, Shelley J.* (C)
1989	Steinberg, David E.
1975	Strassburger III, Eugene B.*
1970	Symons, Jr., Edward L.
1943	Taintor, II, Charles W.
1989	Taylor, George H.
1940	Teitlebaum, Hubert**
1961	Thomas, Herbert Edwin*
1903	Thompson, A. Marshall*
1919	Thompson, George J.
1985	Thompson, Thomas M.*
1984	Tobias, Carl W. (V)
1980	Torres, Gerald
1971	Very, Donald L.*
1982	Vogel, Joan E.
1994	Wang, Lu-in (V)
1986	Wasserman, Rhonda S.
1928	Wasson, Jr., Henry G.**
1987	Weis, Jr., Joseph F.*
1988	Weisblatt, Harold*
1965	Wekselman, I. Martin*
1949	Wentling, Thomas L.*
1940	West, Stanley
1966	Wettick, Jr., R. Stanton*
1939	White, James L.**
1965	White, Thomas Owen
1968	White, Welsh S.
1978	Wilder, Joanne Ross*
1988	Wilkinson, James A.*
1940	Wilson, James R.
1915	Wilson, John H.**
1985	Wittenberg, Jeffrey D. (V)
1982	Wood, Jacques M.*
1946	Woods, Charles A.*
1904	Woodside, Robert G.*
1974	Yablonski, Steven K.
1994	Zipursky, Benjamin C. (V)
1986	Zonn, Sidney*

Number of Graduates by Year of Graduation

YEAR		NUMBER OF GRADUATES	YEAR		NUMBER OF GRADUATES
1897	....	30	1948	....	66
1898	....	5	1949	....	94
1899	....	9	1950	....	76
1900	....	20	1951	....	72
1901	....	16	1952	....	63
1902	....	23	1953	....	71
1903	....	28	1954	....	65
1904	....	16	1955	....	51
1905	....	30	1956	....	55
1906	....	21	1957	....	45
1907	....	19	1958	....	51
1908	....	31	1959	....	38
1909	....	27	1960	....	27
1910	....	29	1961	....	28
1911	....	33*	1962	....	28
1912	....	53	1963	....	27
1913	....	35	1964	....	34
1914	....	39	1965	....	40
1915	....	37	1966	....	57
1916	....	45	1967	....	55
1917	....	42	1968	....	51
1918	....	19	1969	....	60
1919	....	13	1970	....	70
1920	....	37	1971	....	103
1921	....	26	1972	....	155
1922	....	39	1973	....	213
1923	....	43	1974	....	131
1924	....	46	1975	....	149
1925	....	62	1976	....	105
1926	....	48	1977	....	178
1927	....	60	1978	....	198
1928	....	75	1979	....	221
1929	....	75	1980	....	197
1930	....	68	1981	....	216
1931	....	86	1982	....	203
1932	....	101	1983	....	226
1933	....	92	1984	....	194
1934	....	104	1985	....	204
1935	....	68	1986	....	205
1936	....	53	1987	....	262
1937	....	48	1988	....	250
1938	....	47	1989	....	217
1939	....	38	1990	....	235
1940	....	38	1991	....	144
1941	....	34	1992	....	199
1942	....	45	1993	....	187
1943	....	30	1994	....	249
1944	....	7			
1945	....	11			
1946	....	1			
1947	....	24			*plus 9 special students

University of Pittsburgh School of Law Graduates

— Class of —
1897

AMEISEN, ARTHUR
ATWOOD, HENRY D.
BAILEY, SAMUEL G.
BRISLIN, JOHN M.
CALVERT, GEORGE H.
CHALFANT, GEORGE H.
CRAWFORD, J.S.
DAVIS, RALPH W.
DIAMOND, HARRY
DOAK, FRANK E.
GRIMES, WILLIAM D.
HIGH, JOHN L.
HIRSHFIELD, BENJAMIN L.
JONES, HARRY A.
KENNEDY, JOHN M., JR.
LOCKE, CHARLES A.
LONGENECKER, RALPH
MARSHALL, ALBERT A.
McCONEGLY, WILLIAM L.
MOORE, CHARLES T.
OVER, ARTHUR L.
PIERCE, WILLIAM T.
REAMER, CHARLES W.
STILLEY, HIGH M.
STONE, STEPHEN
SILVEY, HARRY S.
SPIRO, ALEXANDER
SACHO, CHARLES, II
THOMAS, JOHN W.
WRIGHT, J. MERRILL

— Class of —
1898

BOWN, CHARLES ELMER
FEIGEL, C.W.
GREER, THOMAS H.
LEGGATE, THOMAS
SHAFFER, GEORGE J.

— Class of —
1899

CHALFANT, JOHN W., JR.
COLVIN, A.G.
ELWOOD, R.D., JR.
HAZZARD, VERNON
HOLT, ALBERT E.
McCLAFFERTY, JAMES A.

MONTGOMERY, HOWARD
  DEANE
SAMPLE, H. GLENN
WALLACE, JOSEPH S.

— Class of —
1900

ADAIR, WATSON B.
BOCK, HARRISON W.
BOYD, WILLIAM C.
FITZHUGH, CARROLL H.
FORSYTH, ANDREW W.
KAMBACH, GEORGE J.
McDOWELL, WILLIAM S.
McKAY, JOHN E.
MILLER, FREDERIC W.
MILLER, JAMES McC.
MONAHAN, LAWRENCE P.
NEVIN, DANIEL E.
O'DAY, DANIEL, JR.
RIAL, WILLIAM S.
SAMPLE, ROBERT F.
SHERIFF, J. CHARLES
SMITH, EDMUND B.
WALLACE, CLARENCE E.
WEAVER, JAMES B.
WEDDELL, JOSEPH B.

— Class of —
1901

CHESS, ROBERT STERRETT
CLARKE, CHARLES MARSHALL
DUNLEVY, JEREMIAH VINCENT
ENGLERT, EDMOND
FLOOD, EDWARD HOUSTON
GIBSON, CARL
GREENBERGER, JACOB
HERRIOTT, GEORGE PATTERSON
KENNEDY, GEORGE BASYE
LOWRIE, MATTHEW
MEYER, ALBERT PETER
PHILLIPS, FERD HUGH
RODGERS, ARTHUR deVERRE
STEIN, ABRAHAM CASS
TIERNEY, THOS. JOSEPH
WHITEMAN, THEODORE C.

— Class of —
1902

BROWN, JOHN WILLOCK
CHRISTY, JAMES SMITH
CORT, JOHN SHAW
DAVIS, RALPH CARTER
DUNN, JAMES RAYMOND
EVANS, BERNE HOLBROOK
FLANNERY, JOHN ROGERS
HAMILTON, HARRY DAVID
HARTMAN, HARRY BENTON
LEE, ALFRED McCLUNG
LONG, RICHARD CARLYS
MARTIN, CHARLES EDWARD
McALINNEY, JOHN JAMES
McBRIDE, JOHN BAVINGTON
McKENNA, JAMES FRANCIS
NEELY, HOWARD
PEEBLES, GEORGE ELLIOTT
PHILLIPS, HARRY RALPH
RUSSELL, JOHN McBRIDE
SNEE, SYLVESTER JOHN
TEPLITZ, A. CHARLES
WEISBERGER, HARRY
WOODSIDE, ROBERT GAILEY

— Class of —
1903

BIALAS, JOSEPH HENRY
BRADSHAW, GEORGE CALVERT
CRISS, NICHOLAS
  RITTENHOUSE
DODDS, ROBERT JAMES
FRIEDMAN, BERNARD
GIBANSKY, HARRY AARON
GASTEIGER, WILLIAM
  HARRISON
HAWKINS, RICHARD HAYS
HILL, JOSEPH HALL
HINDMAN, J.E.
JARVIS, FRANK WASHINGTON
JENNINGS, DALE CRAWFORD
KOSSLER, AUGUSTINE MARTIN
LAUGHLIN, JOHN EDWARD
McCALMONT, JOHN E.
McCLELLAND, PAUL GEORGE
McKIM, SAMUEL JOHN
MILLER, WILLIAM LUDLUM
PATTERSON, WILLIAM
  WALLACE
PORTMAN, LOUIS JOHN

ROBINSON, WILLIAM McILWAIN
REED, DAVIS AIKEN
REILLY, PHILLIP BRENNEN
SECRIST, WILLIAM B.
SEIFERT, WILLIAM ALEX.
THOMPSON, WILLIAM HUSTON
WASSELL, HENRY
    BORNETRIGGER
WATSON, THOMAS

— Class of —
1904

CUNNINGHAM, ANDREW
FLACCUS, GEORGE EDWARD
FRAZIER, JOHN GILFILLAN
HABER, DeWITT
MARTIN, RICHARD WILSON
McGUIRE, PATRICK HENRY
METZ, JOHN ALFRED
SCULLY, CORNELIUS DECATUR
STADTLANDER, WILLIAM
    FREDERICK
SOFFEL, H.E.
TIM, JOHN FREDERICK
WALLACE, GUIAN de YARMOND
WATSON, THOMAS WILLIAM
WEBER, PIERRE
WINGERT, SAMUEL TILDEN
WOLF, HAVEN VEATCH

— Class of —
1905

ADAMS, JAMES LEE
ARNOLD, HARRY IRWIN
BARRON, ALEXANDER J.
BELL, EDGAR DAWSON
BLACK, ALEXANDER
COPELAND, WALTER LEROY
CUMMINGS, ERWIN
DENNISON, WILLIAM REED
GILL, ALBERT A. GARFIELD
GRIER, ROBERT NICHOLL
HOOPES, CHARLES
HURST, LAWRENCE BARRETT
HUSTON, ROBLEY DUNGLESON
IRWIN, ERNEST CHESTER
JOHNSON, WILLIAM KERR
KRAUS, EDWARD ADRIAN, JR.
LINK, FRANK CHARLES
McBRIDE, ARTHUR BEVERIDGE
McCREIGHT, JOHN RALSTON
McKELVEY, JOHN SAMPLE
MEHARD, CHURCHILL BROWN
RIGGS, WALTER LEE

SHOEMAKER, LOUIS M.
SILVERMAN, GEORGE
SIMON, ABRAHAM MARCUS
SLOAN, ANDREW EARL
SMITH, ARTHUR CLYDE
STEINMEYER, WILLIAM
    AUGUSTUS
THOMPSON, DONALD
YINGLING, ORVIN C.

— Class of —
1906

BULLOCK, JAMES CUNLIFFE
CANCELLIERE, PIETRO
CHESS, JOHN PARKE
FREW, WILLIAM
GUTHRIE, JOHN ANDREW
HAHN, HERBERT RAYMOND
HOUSTON, JAMES GARFIELD
KEIL, LAWRENCE HAWLEY
KLINE, EDWIN
LEVY, VICTOR HARRIS
McAWLAY, WILLIAM JAMES
MELLON, THOMAS
MILLER, JAMES ROBERT
ROBB, JOSEPH ALLAN
SCHEIN, SAUL
SHARMAN, GEORGE HERBERT
SPEER, GARNET ROY
THOMPSON, JOHN WILSON
WALDSCHMIDT, CHARLES
    AUGUSTUS
WILSON, WILLIAM ARNOT
ZEHNER, GILBERT FRANCIS

— Class of —
1907

ANDERSON, CHRISTOPHER
    MAGEE
BELL, JOSEPH TURTURICE
BLAXTER, HENRY VAUGHN
DOUGLAS, HOWARD WEDDLE
DUFF, JAMES HENDERSON
DYER, JAMES CHESTER
FERGUS, HUGH ERNEST
GOLDSTROHM, ABRAHAM
    LINCOLN
GRIFFITHS, EDWIN PATTERSON
HEARD, JOHN JAY
KERR, ALLEN HUMPHREYS
LACEY, WILLIAM HART
MARSHALL, ELDER WATSON
McBRYAR, WILLIAM DANA
McKEE, ARTHUR VINCENT

SOLES, THOMAS FRANKLIN
STERRETT, CLARENCE EARLE
WAKEFIELD, RALPH BENTHAM
WHITE, HOWARD JOSEPH

— Class of —
1908

BECK, JOSEPH ALBERT
BOSTWICK, ROY GRIER
BURNS, HARRY PHILLIPS
BRADSHAW, SAMUEL
    HAMILTON
CAMPBELL, LEIGHTON
    HERRIOTT
CARTER, PASCO BILLINGS
DUFF, JOHN TAYLOR, JR.
D'ZMURA, VICTOR PETER
ECKLES, ALEXANDER EDWIN
EUWER, EUGENE COURTNEY
FELDSTEIN, BERNARD HARRY
FLEMING, MONTGOMERY
    WARD
HAGUE, WILLIAM EDWARD
HARTMAN, WILLIAM WALTER
HAYS, EDWARD FLORENCE
HILL, HALE
IAMS, JESSE DORSEY
KAY, FREDERICK WARREN
LITTLE, JAMES EDGAR
McCLUNG, SAMUEL ALFRED, JR.
McCRORY, WILLIAM BRUCE
McILVAINE, RICHARD BIDDLE
MEYER, JOHN D.
MOORE, ERNEST EPHRAIM
NEVIN, JAMES GORDON
PRICE, OBED K.
SCULLY, ARTHUR MARTLAND
SHIELDS, FRANK SLOAN
SWAN, GEORGE MYRON
WARMCASTLE, KARL WATSON
WEIL, GEORGE

— Class of —
1909

BENN, JOHN KIRKER
BOWMAN, ALFRED WILLIAM
BUCHANAN, ISAAC VICTOR
BURGWIN, HILL
CHAITKIN, MAURICE
COOPER, BENJAMIN
DELP, FRANK SEBASTIAN
ENGLAND, MILES HICKS
GLOECKNER, JOHN FABIAN
GRAHAM, WILLIAM JOSEPH

HARBISON, FRANCIS ROY
HETHERINGTON, JOSEPH
HULL, CHARLES MAURICE
IMHOFF, JOSEPH DOCK
KULAMER, JOHN
LECHNER, HARVEY LOUIS
LITTLE, JAMES EDGAR
MARGOLIS, JACOB
MARKUSKY, JOSEPH CHARLES
McCANDLESS, ALEXANDER
    WILSON
McGINNESS, SAMUEL WILSON
MICHAEL, WALTER FREASE
MOORHEAD, WILLIAM SINGER
REESE, FRED EDWARDS
ROBERTSON, ANDREW WELLS
SUNSTEIN, ELLAS
VANN, ROBERT LEE

— Class of —
1910

BOYLE, ANDREW I., JR.
FULLER, ALBERT M.
FULTON, OLIVER HENRY
HOLLAND, MOORHEAD
    BENEZET
JACKSON, EARLE R.
KAPLAN, FRANK RAPHAEL
    SELIG
KELLER, MORSE J.
KNOX, WILLIAM FRANCIS
LAUER, JOHN HENRY
LINDLEY, REX HAROLD
LITTLE, ALBERT KEIL
LLOYD, DAVID
McCLINTOCK, BOWDOIN
McCOMMON, WILLIAM ROSS
McKELVIE, JOHN
McWHINNEY, HARRY EARL
MILLER, JEROME ALEXANDER
MILLER, THOMAS ALAN
PATTERSON, HERBERT
PATTERSON, SIMON TRUBY
REED, ALEXANDER PRESTON, JR.
REMINGTON, PAUL D.
ROSE, ROY
SCHMERTZ, JAMES SIDNEY
SCHMIDT, ARTHUR F.
TOWNSEND, RICHARD
    RODERMOND
WEGER, ROBERT F.
WELDON, JAMES L.
YOUNG, CLYDE FULTON

— Class of —
1911

ADAIR, EARLE TAYLOR
AUTENREITH, EDWIN EARL
BECHMAN, WILLIAM GEORGE
BELL, JAMES CLARKE
BERGER, GEORGE REIS BART
COLVIN, WILLIAM HENRY
CURRAN, JAMES LEO
CURRY, GRANT
DENNY, HARMAR DENNY, JR.
DIHM, FREDERICK ULYSSES
FERREE, DELMONT KENNEDY
FRANK, RALPH HERBERT
GARDNER, SAMUEL HILL
GLICK, PETER
HAMROCK, FRANK, JR.
HERRCHEN, WILLIAM JOHN
HORVITZ, SAMUEL JOSIAH
JACOB, WILLIAM CARL
KNOELL, WILLIAM FREDERICK
MARSHALL, THOMAS MERCER
McCOBB, CARLETON LEROY
MORTON, EARL AUSTIN
NEESON, ALBERT RICHARD
RITCHIE, CHARLES LOTHROP
ROE, JACOB
SCHUMAKER, FREDERICK
SEIDEL, HARRY CLYDE
SEITZ, HARRY ROBINSON
SESSA, THOMAS GAETAN
SHAPIRA, MYER AARON
WALTERS, JOSEPH WILLIAM
WERLE, ROBERT RALPH
WILSON, ARTHUR EDWIN

— Class of —
1911
SPECIAL STUDENTS

KOUNTZ, GEORGE PHILIP
LYON, STANLEY
MILLER, ARTHUR DEVOE
    POWELL
MILLER, ARTHUR GILBERT
MORAN, JAMES LINUS
PATTON, ROBISON BRAUFF
ROBERTS, THOMAS
    PASCHALL
ROHRER, JOHN WISE
TYRELL, FAYETTE JOEL

— Class of —
1912

AILEY, MONT LESLIE
ALLEN, SAMUEL HARPER
ARROWSMITH, EDWARD
    EMMERSON
ASKIN, WILLIAM JAMES, JR.
BARCHFIELD, ELMER
    ANDREW
BIRMINGHAM, LEWIS
    ZEDIKER, JR.
BLAKELEY, WILLIAM JONES
BRIGHTWELL, WILLIAM
    DELANCEY
BROWN, JOSEPH BAILY
CAPLAN, LOUIS
CHRISTIANSEN, ARTHUR
    CLAUS
COBER, PETER GARFIELD
COSGROVE, JAMES JOSEPH
CUNNINGHAM, KENNETH
    REESE
DAVIES, FREDERICK LINCOLN
DEAN, HARRY ALVA
DITHRICH, WILLIAM HEBER
DONNAN, ALVAN EWING
ESLER, JOHN RUSSELL
GOLLMAR, FRANK IRWIN
HAGGERTY, JOHN FRANCIS
HAZLETT, ELMER EMERSON
HENDERSON, ARTHUR
    WADDELL
HENNING, GEORGE PHILIP
KENNEDY, JOSEPH EUGENE
KRAUS, MAURICE JOSEPH
LANGFITT, GEORGE FRANCIS
    PHILLIP
LYON, ADDISON
MacCONAUGHY, DAVID
    LEMAN
MACHESNEY, GLEN NICOL
MARTIN, FRANK PAYNE
McKNIGHT, JOSEPH
    LEANDER, JR.
METZ, GRAYSON MELVILLE
MOHN, EARL JOHN
NEEL, PAUL VINCENT
PEARLMAN, BENJAMIN
RECTENWALD, HENRY JOHN
REED, JOHN MOORHEAD
SCHUTZMAN, JOSEPH
SCOTT, GEORGE WILSON
SHAFFER, ADAM BEN. CHAS.
SILVERMAN, ABRAHAM LOUIS

SMART, WALTER PEARSON
SNYDER, GEORGE PHILIP
SOLOMON, ELI
SPATZ, JULIUS
STEFFLER, ROBERT MEHARD
STEINBERG, BENJAMIN LEON
STEVENSON, PHILIP HENRY
SWEARINGEN, WILLIAM VAN
TAYLOR, WOODWARD MILLER
WICKS, ELVERTON HAZLETT
WILLIAMS, LAWRENCE ALBERT

— Class of —
1913

ABRAHAM, PAUL JAMES
APPLEGATE, ROBERT
    ASHWORTH
ARONSON, HARVEY MILTON
ARTHUR, WILLIAM CATHCART
BERNSTEIN, ISADORE AARON
BIRMINGHAM, HARRY ROBERT
CLUNK, ROY TAYLOR
ELY, JOHN WILFRED
ESTEP, HARRY ALLISON
HUMPHRIES, THOMAS
    BERTRAM
KAHANOWITZ, WILLIAM
    MORDECAI
KAUFMAN, ABRAHAM HARRY
LATIMER, JOHN LEROY
McCUTCHEON, FREDERICK
    COLLIER
McNEES, STERLING GLENN
MEYER, GEORGE YOUNG
MILLER, WILLIAM EVANS
OBERNAUER, HAROLD
OVER, JAMES PEEBLES
PARK, ANDREW THOMAS
PATTON, HUGH McKEE
REED, HAROLD FRANCIS
REICHMAN, SAMUEL HARRY
RICHARDS, GEORGE
    WASHINGTON, JR.
ROSENBERG, NICHOLAS
    WHITEMAN
SCHMIDT, ERHARD
SHEARER, HORACE FRANTZ
SPANN, MAX JOSEPH
SPRIGGS, JOSEPH VAN
    COURTLANDT
STEWART, WILLIAM DENNING
STRELITZ, JULIUS MALCOLM
TRITSCHLER, JOSEPH
    ALOYSIUS
WALTER, A. ROSS

WHARTON, WILLIAM
    BAKEWELL
YOST, RUSSELL RAYMOND

— Class of —
1914

BARMEN, LOUIS ALBERT
BODE, CHARLES HENRY
CALHOUN, NOEL ALEXANDER
CANNON, JOSEPH LLOYD
CHANTLER, DAVID EVERETT
CHERSKY, SAUL
COLLINS, JAMES LEO
DONLEY, CHARLES MORRIS
DUFF, JOHN BOYD, JR.
EVANS, GEORGE EDWARD
FRIEDMAN, ARMIN HARRY
HAMILTON, DAVID BOYCE
HART, LLOYD OSCAR
HEARD, JAMES DRAYTON
HELBLING, ALPHONSUS GALE
HENRY, SAMUEL LOWRY
KNOX, R. JAMES
LANGFITT, EPHRAIM WALTERS
LEFKOFSKY, SAMUEL
LEVIN, ABRAHAM
LITTLE, LOUIS
MARSH, JAMES INGRAHAM
MARSHALL, JAMES JOHN
    FIELDING
McCLURE, DANIEL WESTLAKE
McCRADY, ROLAND ALLEN
MILHOLLAND, JAMES
MORRIS, THOMAS LYNN
PIPES, CLYDE STEPHEN
SANGSTON, WILLIAM
    JEFFERSON, JR.
SCHLESINGER, WILLIAM LOUIS
SEFLER, ERNEST ABRAHAM
SILVEUS, JOHN T.
SNOWDEN, FELIX BRUNOT
TAYLOR, THOMAS GALLAGHER
WATKINS, ROY WALKER
WEISS, HARRY MAXWELL
WHITWORTH, SMITH NESBIT
WICK, GEORGE DeWITTE
WILSON, JOHN HOWARD

— Class of —
1915

AIKEN, WILLIAM JAMES
BLAIR, LAWRENCE DILWORTH
BLOCH, LOUIS J.
BOTHWELL, EDWARD GRAHAM

BRADSHAW, THOMPSON
CAMPBELL, WALTER
    FREDERICK
COGHLAN, WILLIAM
COLBERT, JAMES LEE
FOSTER, DAVID PAULSON
GIFFEN, BENJAMIN HARRISON
GOTTLIEB, SIDNEY
GRAFF, JOHN FRANCIS, JR.
GRATZ, ABRAHAM
GREENBAUM, MEYER
HARRISON, BRUCE
HARRISON, DAVID MATHEIS
HIRSCH, ALBERT CARL
LEFTON, SAMUEL
LEITCH, HAROLD KING
LEONARD, HARRY WHITE
LEVY, MORRIS GOLDSMITH
LEWINTER, SAMUEL M.
LORE, CHARLES LAWRENCE
LUCCOCK, EUGENE
    COURTNEY
McFALL, WILLIAM BAILEY, JR.
MURDOCK, WILLIAM
    INGHRAM
POLLOCK, LLOYD EDWIN
RAVICK, HARRY
REED, J. ALBERT
SCOTT, CHARLES LINN
SELIGSOHN, JACOB
SHEFFLER, JACOB
SHEINBERG, EDWARD
SLONE, VICTOR
WALTER, GEORGE LEONARD
WOLK, ABRAHAM
ZEMAN, ADOLPH LEBEAU

— Class of —
1916

ALLSHOUSE, HARRY L.
APPLESTEIN, HARRY JACOB
ATWOOD, FREDERICK
    HARMAN
BANE, JOHN JOSEPH
BLUMENTHAL, ROBERT JOHN
BRADEN, ALFRED GOODRICH
CALDWELL, WILLIAM JAMES
CAMPBELL, CLYDE WILLIAM
CARSON, ROY IRWIN
CHILDS, WILLIAM ST. CLAIR
CLASTER, LOUIS
COHEN, SAMUEL DICKSON
COLMERY, HARRY WALTER
CONNELLY, WILLIAM JAMES

CUNNINGHAM, EDWARD
GILMORE
DARRAGH, JAMES DONALD
FORSYTH, WILLIAM DAVID
FREY, ERNEST
GALBRAITH, WILBUR FLOYD
GALLEHER, MARIE GRACE
CLARK
GOLDSMITH, EDWIN BERNARD
GOODE, OTIS SHEPARD
HALL, JAMES HOUSTON
HAMILTON, GEORGE MURRAY
HOGE, GUY BENTON
HORN, JOHN MacPHERSON
LAPPE, WILLIAM JACOB
LUTHER, WILLIAM ZELLERS
LYNCH, THOMAS
McWHERTER, GEORGE HOMER
MURPHY, OWEN JOSEPH
NICHOLS, THOMAS
OLIVER, ALWINN McNEILL
PICKERSGILL, LILY VIRGINIA
PLUMMER, WILLIAM CLIFFORD
ROSENBAUM, JOSEPH S.
SELIGSOHN, SOL AARON
SOFFEL, SARA MATHILDE
THOMAS, DONALD STEADMAN
THROCKMORTON, FRANK
VAN KIRK, JAMES ROY
VAN KIRK, WARREN HATHAWAY
WEIL, FERDINAND THEOBALD
WILBERT, FRANK, JR.
WYMARD, NORMAN
LAWRENCE

— Class of —
1917

AHLERS, RICHARD WILLIAM
AVERBACH, BENJAMIN ROBERT
BALDRIDGE, RALPH BAYARD
BLACKBURN, JAMES
BRECKENRIDGE
BRINKER, FREDERICK CHARLES
BROIDO, LOUIS
BROWN, WILLIAM ELBRIDGE
BUFFINGTON, KENNETH
BURGWIN, GEORGE
COLLISON, JR.
CHRISTLER, CHARLES
MORRISON
CLARK, ARTHUR
DUFF, WILLIAM BOYD
EMERY, GEORGE TEMPLE, JR.
FERGUSON, FRANK BAMFORD
GOLDFARB, MEYER

GROSSMAN, ARTHUR
MATTHEW
HEINER, WILLIAM GRAHAM
HEPPS, ABRAHAM CHARLES
HOFFMAN, CLEMENT ROSCOE
HOUCK, IRA CHAUNCEY
HURWITZ, SAUL SENIOR
KNOX, J.R. IRWIN
LOWE, HAROLD CLIFTON
LUBIC, BEN
MANDELBAUM, MAX
MATTHEWS, CHARLES, JR.
McCARTHY, DANIEL
FRANCIS, JR.
McNAUGHER, WILLIAM HARPER
MURRAY, THOMAS DAVITT
NEWLIN, EDWIN BENSON
O'NEILL, J. HENRY
PANTON, HOWARD RANDALL
PRICE, GWILYM ALEXANDER
RUBIN, HARRY
SAUL, WILLIAM GEORGE, JR.
SIKOV, MEYER
SMITH, VINCENT W.
SNIDERMAN, MAYER J.
TEPLITZ, BENJAMIN HENRY
WETTACH, ROBERT HASLEY
WRENSHALL, ABRAHAM
KIRKPATRICK
ZINSMASTER, WARREN
WOODLING

— Class of —
1918

BOWDEN, FRANCIS JOSEPH
BRUNSTETTER, ROSCOE H.
BUCKLEY, MINNIE ZIEGLER
CALLAN, MARY LOUISE
FELDMAN, HARRY GILBERT
GLICK, HARRY IRWIN
HERMAN, ABRAHAM
KATTEN, ESTHER ISRAEL R.
KIER, SAMUEL MARTIN
LENCHER, BENJAMIN
LUTHER, WILLIAM ZELLERS
McDONALD, G. MALCOLM
McNAMEE, FRANCIS LEO
MOTHERAL, PHILANDER
KNOX
REPLOGLE, ARNOLD MILLER
RIEHL, WALTER WALDORF
SAUERS, H. RALPH
SOWASH, JAMES RAYMOND
STEVENSON, ARTHUR
DANIEL

— Class of —
1919

ABEL, ROBERT
CONLEY, JOHN FRANCIS
CREE, WILLARD HERMAN
HAMMER, EDGAR THOMAS
HERRON, JAMES PATRICK
McCANCE, PRESSLY HODGE
MONK, REGINALD RATTRAY
NIXON, CLARENCE BOVAIRD
RUFF, FRANK S., JR.
SILVERMAN, SIDNEY LEO
WEAVER, GEORGE WILLIAM
WEST, GEORGE WALTER
ZECKHAUSER, JULIUS
NATHANIEL

— Class of —
1920

ALLISON, R.W.
BARRISH, ROBERT
BEISTEL, CLYDE DAVID
BOCK, WILLIAM EARL, JR.
BROWN, OLIVER WELLINGTON
COHEN, PAULA H.
DOUGLASS, HARRY STANLEY
DOUGLASS, WILBUR
CHALFANT
EDWARDS, ROBERT MILLER
FINKELHOR, MAURICE
FREED, MORRIS M.
GABLER, RAYMOND B.
GLOCK, CARL EDWARD
GOEHRING, LOUIS M.
HAMILTON, LEON ALDRICH
HARBISON, ROBERT LELAND
HOEHL, SIDNEY SEBASTIAN
HOSACK, GEORGE M., JR.
IMBRIE, BOYD VINCENT
KELLER, NORMAN DANIEL
KLEIN, PRESSLEY BIRGER
McWHINNEY, ROBERT RUSSELL
MELNICK, ISRAEL A.
MOORE, WINFIELD SCOTT, JR.
PERVIN, ABRAHAM
SCHARPF, CARL FAWCETT
SCOTT, CRAWFORD
THOMAS, HORACE, JR.
THOMAS, SUMNER EVANS
TOLOCHKO, MAURICE LEON
VAN KIRK, JOHN SCOTT
VIROSTEK, JOHN A.
WEAVER, GEORGE WILLIAM

WEDDELL, CLINTON LEE
WOLFENDEN, CHARLES
GILBERT
YODER, ALBERT STEEL
ZIMMERMAN, GEORGE LESLIE

— Class of —
1921

ALTER, SAMUEL GUY
BONIDY, JOSEPH
CHAITKIN, JACOB
DeCASTRIQUE, ARCHIBALD
BENJAMIN
FLA HAVEN, HOLLAND
FLETCHER
FRAZIER, GEORGE ORION
GERDTS, ROBERT BERTRAM
IVORY, HELENA AGNES
JOHNSON, OLIVER
LIVINGSTON
KELLEY, WALTER HOWARD
LEVY, HARRY ROBERT
McBURNEY, BERNARD R.
McDONALD, DAVID
CAROTHERS
McINTYRE, JOHN DeWITT
McKEAN, FRANK WESLEY
MILLER, CLARK
MURDOCK, JOHN EDGAR
PACHTMAN, PERCY CHARLES
SAPPER, MAX LOUIS
SCHLUEDERBERG, HARRY
SORG, JOHN HENRY
SWARTZ, JOSHUA GOHEEN
TURNER, LAMBERT
WEIL, A. LEO, JR.
WILEY, JOHN FULTON
WOLFE, KIVIE

— Class of —
1922

ARNOLD, SIGMUND
ASHINSKY, MAURICE
BARNETT, ROBERT FULTON
BLOOM, ISAAC
BLOOM, ISRAEL CASTLE
BOOTH, WILLIAM WALTER
BRAHAM, WILLIAM WALTER
BROOKS, HAROLD KING
BURNWORTH, HAROLD
FRAZER
BYERLY, JOHN ALLISON
COOPER, ALEXANDER
COTTOM, HARRY VANCE

CRIBBS, HYATT M., JR.
CUNNINGHAM, ROBERT
ANDREWS
DAVIDSON, MOLLY
GAUT, JOHN GOEHRING
GOODMAN, BERNARD
HEID, LEO PAUL
JACOBSON, BENJAMIN
KAUFMAN, SAMUEL
MARKS, BENJAMIN HOMER
McALLISTER, DAVID IRONS
McCAMEY, HAROLD EMERSON
McCONNEL, STEWART PHILLIPS
McCREARY, JOHN ELLIOTT
McKEE, RALPH DYER
MITINGER, JOSEPH EDWARD
MORRIS, HUMPHREY
MURRAY, GEORGE PIERSOL, JR.
NICKLAS, JOHN BALZER, JR.
REED, PAUL REVERE
RUBENSTEIN, JOSEPH AULTAN
SCHNEIROV, MAURICE
SERENA, JOHN ROBERT
STERN, JOHN CORNELIUS
STUCKY, MELBA H.C.
SWOPE, THOMAS ALBERT
THOMPSON, MARY C.
WEINER, DAVID H.

— Class of —
1923

ANDERSON, DONALD C.
BAER, WILBUR J.
BAUER, EDWARD G.
BEAL, JAMES H., JR.
BREDIN, JOHN R.
BROWN, HOMER S.
BURSTIN, LOUIS C.
CAMPBELL, LOUDEN L.
CARMACK, HAROLD S.
CHECCO, CONRAD H.
EWING, MEREDYTH H.
FAUNCE, GEORGE, JR.
FEATHERMAN, ISADOR
FELDMAN, JOSEPH B.
FERGUSON, SCOTT D.
FLACK, JOHN S.
FULTON, HENRY W.
GOLDBERG, CECILE S.
GOLDING, JACOB D.
HAWORTH, ELWOOD B., JR.
HELD, JACOB B.
HOREWITZ, JACOB E.
HUMES, JOHN J.
ISHERWOOD, JAMES E.

JONES, RICHARD F.
JONES, THOMAS C., JR.
LEVY, LEO A.
MEGAHAN, H. DOUGAN
MOGILOWITZ, SAM N.
OSMER, GILBERT G.
SCHUTTE, WILLIAM F.
SEEL, CLARENCE W.
SERENA, JOHN R.
SHEA, FRANK J.
SILBERBLATT, MORRIS L.
SOBOL, LEONARD
SPECTER, EDWARD
STEWART, HAROLD A.
STEWART, WILLIAM G., JR.
SWISS, IRWIN A.
THORNTON, THOMAS A.
WALLACE, JAMES B.
WILSON, JOSEPH L.

— Class of —
1924

ARMSTRONG, SAMUEL DALE
BAIR, HAROLD R.
BALTER, ABRAHAM L.
BAUM, WESLEY F.
BOSCIA, ANTHONY A.
BURNSIDE, ETHEL B.
CARMICHAEL, PAUL D.
CARNEY, WILLIAM J.
CARSON, ROBERT, III
COPE, RICHARD P.
ECKERT, WILLIAM H.
EWING, LEONARD L.
FRIEDMAN, DAVID
FRUCHS, LAURA
GELTZ, JAMES A.
GILFILLAN, JOHN
GLEETEN, WAYNE A.
GOLDBERG, ADOLPH
GOURLEY, W. CULLEN
GREENBERGER, ISRAEL
HART, DONALD R.
HAWKINS, CHARLES E.
JONES, MYRON W.
JORDAN, MURRAY J.
KERR, JAMES S.
KIPP, EUGENE H.
LOVE, PRESTON A.
LUKE, RANDALL B.
McCLURE, ROBERT H.
MILBURN, WILLIAM L.J.
MONTGOMERY, HARRY M.
MUNN, CHARLES E.
MURDOCK, FRANK R.

PEARLMAN, EDWARD E.
REID, B. MEREDITH
ROBINSON, DANIEL S.
ROSENFIELD, LOUIS
RUGH, FRANK A.
RUTTENBUSCH, WALTER R.
SCHLEGEL, RALPH C.
SCHRAMM, GUSTAV L.
SHRUM, PAUL L.
SMITH, RALPH H.
SOLOMON, EFFIE M.
WALTER, CHARLES P.
WILSON, EMMETT C.

— Class of —
1925

ADAMS, RUSSELL H.
BALDAUF, VINCENT A.
BARTON, THOMAS E.
BLEADINGHISER, ELVIRA
BLIMMEL, WILLIAM J.
BROWN, ALBERT G.
CAPUTO, EUGENE A.
CARSON, ROBERT M.
CHALLENER, WILLIAM A., JR.
COUSE, J. MILLER
CUFF, ALBERT L.
DILLEY, J. HARTFORD
DILLEY, L. NORMAN
D'IVERNOIS, DON F.
EATON, HOMER T.
FERGUSON, L. BARTON
FOGIE, STANTON C.
FRANK, JACOB
FRANZOS, NATHAN
FRIEDLANDER, GERTRUDE J.
FUSHAN, LOUIS M.
GOLDBERG, CHARLES
GOLDSTEIN, MAURICE H.
GRAHAM, WILLARD D.
GREER, RICHARD W.
HAYS, ESLER W.
HEILMAN, WADE E.
HIGBEE, DONALD M.
JACOBSON, HERBERT
JARRETT, CHARLES B.
JUBELIRER, SAMUEL H.
KEMMLER WILLIAM H.
LEVY, A. SANFORD
LEVY, RUTH L.
LINTON, MORRIS
LYON, HAMILTON
McCULLOCH, FRANCIS X.
MILLER, C. HARBAUGH
MONINGER, RUSSELL Z.

MOSS, CLAIR D.
NOFFAT, WESLEY A.
O'DONOVAN, PAUL J.
PACKER, JOHN L.
PEACOCK, RALPH W.
PRUGER, CHAUNCEY
RICHTER, HARRY E.
ROMITO, ANDREW
ROSSI, A. JOSEPH A.
ROWLEY, R. FLOYD
SANES, SIDNEY A.
SCHOENBERG, JULIUS L.
SHRUM, G. DIXON
SILVERMAN, MARTIN
SMITH, FRANCIS H.
SOLOMON, JEROME
STEWART, MARION S.
TAYLOR, SHERMAN T.
TRUXALL, JOHN D.S.
VOSS, VICTOR E.
WALKER, JOHN M.
WILEY, J. ALEXANDER
WIRTZMAN, JOHN

— Class of —
1926

ALBO, SAMUEL V.
ANTON, FRANCIS P.
BOYER, JAMES McG.
BOZIC, JOHN H.
CALVIN, EVERETT Y.
CORR, PATRICK J.
COUFFER, GRANT
DONALDSON, JAMES B.
ELDER, JOHN H., JR.
EVANS, DANIEL M.
EVANS, OLIVER
FAWCETT, DAVID B.
FULTON, JOHN C.
GLUCK, NORMAN
GRAUBERT, ELLA
GREGORY, THOMAS G.
HECHT, JOSEPH R.
HENRY, WILLIAM L.
HIMEBAUGH, JOHN W.
HITCHENS, FRED S.
KABET, ALBERT E.
KIDNER, HERBERT M.
KLARE, G. RICHARD
KLINESMITH, MERYL B.
KRAUS, MANUEL
LEVY, BLANCHE B.
LUCAS, GEORGE W.
LYNCH, ALLEN G.
MARKOWITZ, JACOB A.

MARSH, DONNELL W.
MILLER, JOHN L.
MOREN, HUGH G.
PETERSON, OSCAR G.
READE, GEORGE L.
RINGSDORF, SAMUEL D.
ROSENSHEIN, MARCUS
SHANE, JACK M.
SHAW, THOMAS E.
SOHN, MORGAN H.
STERN, LAWRENCE H.
TAPTICH, FRANCIS
TAYLOR, GEORGE F., JR.
UNCAPHER, ANDREW G.
VAIRA, LOUIS
WALKER, WILLIAM A.
WEISS, SAM J.
WHITLA, WILLIAM F.
WILSON, LAVELLE A.

— Class of —
1927

ALPERN, ANNE X.
BENEDICT, JOSEPH J.
BERGAD, MAX M.
BERRY, JAMES G.
BONNER, C. HENRY
BOVARD, JAMES M.
BOWYTZ, LOUIS
CANCELMI, LOUIS J.
CLASTER, MAURICE H.
CONLY, JOHN B.
CORBETT, WILLIAM T.
COURTNEY, JOHN O.
CROWELL, DANIEL V.
CUMMINS, GEORGE T.
CURRY, LINFORD G.
DODSON, CHARLES W.
EATON, R. PIERSON
FISCUS, ROBERT G.
FORSCHT, RUTH
FRANCIS, EMRYS G.
GIBSON, DANIEL H.
GOLDSTOCK, SAMUEL
GOLDSTON, MILTON W.
HANMER, HAROLD M.
HARRIS, BURTT
HELMRICH, DAVID S.
HERBSTER, WILLIAM S.
HILL, IRA R.
HINDES, MARTIN J.
HUNTER, FRANK H.
JANAVITZ, DAVID M.
JONES, FRANK S.
KANE, E. KENT

KAUFMAN, LOUIS L.
KRAUS, ISADORE E.
LEVY, ELEAZER L.
LEWIS, MAHLON E.
LUELLEN, FRANCIS D.
LUTTRELL, GEORGE W.
MATTHEWS, ARCHIBALD M.
McCREARY, GEORGE B.
MITINGER, ROBERT B.
MODRAK, GEORGE J.
MONTGOMERY, EDWARD A.
MORELAND, CARROLL C.
NEELY, THOMAS W., JR.
OEHMLER, HERBERT K.
PALKOVITZ, DAVID S.
PASSAFIUME, JOSEPH P.
PRATT, ROBERT W.
PURMAN, RALFORD B.
ROBB, JOHN S., III
RODGERS, BENNETT
ROSSER, EVERETT A.
RUBY, JAMES K.
SHUMAKER, CRESSWELL S.
SNYDER, RALPH H.
SPOTTS, EDWARD O., JR.
WASSON, HENRY G., JR.
WRIGHT, JAMES A.

— Class of —
1928

APPLEBAUM, MAX U.
BAIR, HARRY V.
BAIRD, HARRY A.
BALTER, OSCAR M.
BALTER, WILLIAM H.
BECK, CLARENCE W.
BELL, RALPH T.
BERGER, MORRIS M.
BIELSKI, ALEXANDER J.
BLUMBERGER, BEN A.
BUCKLEY, MILDRED R.
CAMPBELL, BRUCE H.
CAPUTO, VIRGINIA N.
CARMICHAEL, MELDRUM K.
CASACCHIA, ANGELO J.
CATANZARO, MICHAEL E.
COBAU, WILLIAM D.
COLE, WILLIAM F.
CONNOLLY, J. WRAY
COOPER, RALPH A.
DALE, WILLIAM J.
DEFIBAUGH, ELLIS R.
DEMMLER, RALPH H.
DIERST, JOHN R., JR.
ENGLAND, DONALD C.

FAHRINGER, ROBERT W.
GRAY, JAMES D.
GREENBERG, MORRIS B.
GRIGGS, THOMAS N.
GROBSTEIN, JACOB
HAMBLIN, WILLIAM K.
HANKEY, DONALD L.
HEARD, CHARLES C.
HENRY, DONOVAN H.
HERSKOVITS, EMIL
HERWITT, HAROLD H.
HIRSCHFIELD, MORRIS H.
ITTEL, FRANK W.
JONES, GLENN C.
JORDAN, FRED J.
JUBELIRER, BEN P.
KAMINSKY, HAROLD
KEAST, DAVID S.
KENYON, BERTRAM H.
KOSTMAN, LEO
KRIEGER, LEONARD H., JR.
LAMOREE, JOHN G.
LATTA, CUTHBERT H., JR.
LIAS, DALE T.
LIGHTCAP, JOHN S., JR.
LOMASK, MILTON N.
MARINO, PATSY V.
McBRIDE, LOIS D.
McCLURE, GEORGE W.
McVICAR, JOHN W.
MILLER, ROLAND I.
MOFFATT, JOHN D.
MORELAND, RAYMOND F.
MULLEN, HACKETT J.
OLBUM, DAVID
O'MALLEY, RUSSELL J.
ONYSHKEW, BASIL
PHILLIPS, JOHN S.
RECHT, JOSEPH
ROLSTON, DONALD M.
ROSENBLUM, SIDNEY E.
ROSENZWEIG, SAMUEL M.
SHAPIRO, LEONARD J.
SISMONDO, AUGUST L.
SMITH, RALPH E.
SMITH, ROBERT W., JR.
STEPHEN, PAUL A.
STEVENSON, ALLEN B.
THEOPHILUS, WAYNE
WILSON, VOYT M.

— Class of —
1929

ASHE, ROBERT E.
BECK, NATHANIEL I.

BEST, JOSEPH L.
BRAUN, ROBERT H., JR.
BRENLOVE, RUDOLPH R.
BROWN, JAMES W.
CARROLL, HERBERT R.
COLDREN, I. BURDETTE
COLL, CHARLES D.
COOPER, PETER
COST, JOHN W.
DAVIS, ISRAEL A.
EWING, THOMAS, JR.
FAUST, GOETHE
FAY, WELLS
FRANK, HARRY H.
FRIEDMAN, BENJAMIN
GAULT, WILLIAM G.
GEISER, DIXON H.
GESSLER, RALPH L.
GREER, ROBERT B.
HARR, S. RICHARD
HARRIS, MILTON E.
HASSON, RICHARD R.
HAWES, EDWARD M.
HUMPHREY, RAY W.
JOHNSTON, WILLIAM K.
JONES, FLOY C., JR.
JONES, PERCY K.
JORDAN, J. WILLIAM
KESSLER, WILLIAM T.
KLABER, ELMER G.
KRAMER, DAVID H.
LAMOREE, THOMAS G.
LICHTER, SAMUEL A.
LIDDLE, RAY A.
LONG, GILBERT E.
MASTERS, HAROLD L.
MATSON, WILLIAM W.
McALLISTER, PAUL W.
McALLISTER, RALPH J.
McCANDLESS, LEE C.
McCONNELL, RICHARD A.
McCORMICK, CHARLES L.
McKINLEY, ROBERT B.
MOKE, WILLIAM T., JR.
MOON, EDWIN C.
NEGLEY, PAUL T.
PER, JOEL
PERSHING, AYRA N., JR.
PURPURA, LAWRENCE J.
RAY, JOHN D.
REPP, ROBERT M., JR.
RICHMAN, BEN H.
RILEY, ROBERT B.
ROSS, CHARLES V.
ROUTMAN, NATHAN
RUDISILL, RALPH E.

SACK, FRANK R.
SCHADE, STANLEY G.
SCHEIF, CHARLES J.
SCHMIDT, THEODORE H.
SEIF, CHARLES L.
SILVERBLATT, DAVID
SINGER, WILLARD
SLESINGER, GEORGE P.
SMITH, GEORGE W.
STADTFELD, HAROLD R.
STANTON, WILLIAM W.
TRIMBLE, THOMAS P., JR.
TROUP, FRANK F.
WEBB, WILLIAM H.
WEISE, KARL E.
WOODWARD, LLOYD W.
YUDIN, HARRY M.

— Class of —
1930

BANE, EUSTACE H.
BARRANTE, ANTHONY A.
BELL, JOHN G.
BLAIR, CHARLES D.
BOLAND, JOHN R., JR.
BOWYTZ, HARRY
BRENNAN, JOSEPH P.
CAMARINOS, ANARGYROS E.
CHAPLIN, DAVID C.
CLARK, LAWRENCE O.
COHEN, SAUL
COLL, ALFRED W.
CRAIG, HAROLD E.
DALE, ROBERT M.
DALTON, DONALD G.
D'AURIA, LEWIS M.
DINSMORE, WILLIAM N.
DOYLE, JULIA
EVANS, J. KING
FISHKIN, ABRAHAM
GATES, FREDERICK H.
GEER, WESLEY G.
GILFILLAN, ALEXANDER B.
GORDON, JOHN B.
GREER, SAMUEL W.
GROSSMAN, SAMUEL H.
GRUBBS, BARTON, II
GUFFEY, JAMES M.
GUFFEY, WILLIAM F.
HARTER, ELMER E.
HIGBEE, W. BROWN
INGRAM, ROBERT M.
IRELAND, ROBERT H.
JOHNSTONE, WILLIAM G.
KANN, BESSIE A.

KAUFMAN, HERMAN W.
KEEHAN, JAMES E.
KEIZLER, EDWARD A.
KELLY, EDWARD A.
KESSLER, MAURICE L.
KRIMSLY, SAMUEL
LIZZA, MAXWELL E.
LONG, LEWIS R.
MacFARLANE, MALCOLM F.
MAROHNIC, LOUIS Z.
MARSH, RABE F., JR.
McCLUNE, EARL F.
McFARREN, FRANCIS L.
McGREGOR, CONSTANTINE F.
McNERNEY, CATHERINE C.
MEDOFF, ABRAHAM D.
MORCROFT, GEORGE E., JR.
MORRIS, LEONARD M.S.
MUZZEY, ALEXANDER A.
POLKABLA, NICHOLAS
ROSENFARB, JOSEPH
ROST, ANDREW J.
SAFIER, MILTON
SCHERMERHORN, FRED M.
SMITH, ALLEN I.
STADTFELD, JOSEPH, JR.
TEITELBAUM, ELVIN
WAGNER, DOROTHEA M.
WAGNER, SAMUEL G.
WASHABAUGH, WILLIAM B., JR.
ZELT, WRAY G., JR.
ZUFFANTE, MICHAEL
ZWIBEL, MAXWELL B.

— Class of —
1931

BASH, JOHN M.
BAUR, BYRON
BIEBEL, GEORGE J.
BOHORAD, JAMES
BOWERS, ROBERT H.
CAMPBELL, BERNARD M.
CAMPBELL, DAVID B.
CHILCOTE, SANFORD M.
COHEN, JULIUS B.
COHEN, OLIVER C.
COHEN, SAMUEL S.
COLKER, LEONARD B.
CRAWFORD, JAMES W.
CRAWFORD, MATTHEW A.
DIERST, GLENN V.
EBBERT, DONALD W.
EDGECOMB, WALLACE E.
EISENFELD, HARRY
ELLIOTT, WILLIS K.

ENDSLEY, ROBERT G.
EPSTEIN, THEODORE A.
EWING, STEPHEN B.
FINKELSTEIN, LOUIS
FISCHLER, JACOB
FRALIN, MAXTON N.
FRIEDMAN, SAMUEL S.
GAMBATESE, ANTHONY L.
GINSBURG, PAUL
GOLDSTEIN, PHILIP
GORDON, MEYER W.
HALL, GEORGE F.
HARPER, HAROLD E.
HERSKOVITZ, SIDNEY J.
HOFFMAN, HYMAN I.
JACKSON, KENNETH G.
JAMES, WILLIAM P.
JOSEPH, LEE F.
KAUFMAN, DAVID M.
KELLER, WILLIAM H., II
LAYTON, LAWRENCE A.
LEONARD, BRESCI R.P.
LIBSON, SYLVAN
LIEBERMAN, HARRY
LIPPARD, ALVIN I.
LONG, C. HAYS, JR.
LOUGHREN, JOSEPH M.
LOUIK, MAURICE
LOWENSTEIN, SAMUEL A.
MARETSKY, SAMUEL
McCLAY, DAVID G.
McCOMMON, ISAAC E.
McDONNELL, J. ADELAIDE
McNAUGHER, ALEXANDER L.
MEIZLIK, HARRY H.
MENDELSON, BEN
MERCUR, SOL R.
MILLER, THOMAS G.
NORRIS, J. BURTON
O'NEILL, JAMES
ORRINGER, JOSEPH M.
PARKER, WALLACE M.
PUTNEY, DAVID
RACK, ARTHUR R.
RASKIN, GEORGE
REID, WILLIAM K.
REIFSNYDER, T. GREGG
ROSEN, BENJAMIN H.
ROSENWASSER, SIGMUND
ROSS, J. THEODORE
ROTHMAN, HAROLD L.
SALMON, JACOB Q.
SAVAGE, HARRY
SCHERMERHORN, EARL J.
SCHERMERHORN, FRED M.
SELKOVITS, MILTON

SIMON, CLEMENS
SILVERBLATT, SIDNEY
SPEER, EUGENE R.
SPELLMAN, EDWARD M.
TENOR, THEODORE E.
THOMAS, J. RANDALL
UMANSKY, EYER
WEISS, DAVID H.
WEYAND, PAUL R.
WILSON, HIRAM B.
WILSON, JOHN L.

— Class of —
1932

ALLISON, EDGAR L.
ANDERSON, W. NILES
BAVOLACK, ADAM D.
BECK, MARY V.
BINSTOCK, ISADORE E.
BROTHERS, FRED L.
CABLE, C. DICK
CARSON, RALPH W.
CASTEEL, HARLAND I.
CHRISTIANSEN, CHRISTIAN
    M., JR.
CHRISTMAN, THOMAS L.
CHUDOFF, EARL
COHEN, ABE
COHEN, ROBERT J.
COLUMBUS, PREMO J.
DANIELS, LEO
DAVIDSON, JOHN H.
DIEHL, ANDREW S.
DONALDSON, LEROY K.
DOWNIE, ROBERT C.
DUFFEY, LEO S.
EDMINDSON, IRA H., JR.
EHRENWERTH, HERMAN C.
EMERY, STEPHEN
FELDMAN, MEYER
FELDMAN, NATHAN
FERRERE, PHILLIP G.
FITCH, GEORGE F.
FRICH, GEORGE H., JR.
FRITCHMAN, H. VERNON
GIBSON, PAUL K.
GIFFORD, DAVID S.
GINSBURG, A. MORRIS
GOLDBERG, HARRY
GORDON, IRVING D.
HALLER, HAROLD S.
HENRY, C. JEWETT
HOWELL, CHAUNCEY D.
IRWIN, FOREST B.
JUBELIRER, BERNARD

KAPLAN, BERNARD
KNORR, CHARLES W.
LEVEN, ALBERT E.
LIDDELL, ALBERT G.
LOEFFLER, KENNETH D.
MacDONALD, WILLIS A.
MAGRAM, SAMUEL
MARKER, HENRY E., JR.
McCASKEY, IRVING W.
McCLAY, DAVID G.
McDONOUGH, JOHN F.
McILVAINE, JOHN W.
McKEE, WAYNE, JR.
McKENNA, J. FRANK, JR.
McKIM, JOHN R.
McLAUGHLIN, STEPHEN J.
McWILLIAMS, JOHN W.
McWILLIAMS, PHILIP A.
MILLER, WILLIAM J., JR.
MOORE, HARVEY E.
MUIR, D. STANLEY
NEGLEY, RONALD D.
NESTA, JAMES A.
PALKOVITZ, ROBERT
PATTERSON, WILLIAM E.
PENNSYL, J. METTLER
PETTLER, LYNN R.
PHILLIPS, JOSEPH V.
POLLOCK, HARRY
RALSTON, JOSEPH C.
ROSEN, HARRY H.
ROSENBERG, HARRY
ROSENZWEIG, AARON
RUTHERFORD, IRA B.
SABLE, LOUIS E.
SABLE, SIDNEY J.
SAMUELS, DAVID
SANDERS, ADAM L.
SANIEL, JAMES
SCHADE, NORMAN R.
SCHMIDT, NORMAN G.
SENSENICH, LOUIS E.
SEYMOUR, FRED T.
SHERMAN, HARRY A.
SILVERMAN, JULIUS L.
SOLOMON, SAMUEL
SPERO, MINNIE E.
STEDEFORD, JOHN D.
STEINER, A. FRANK
STEVENS, HOWARD O.
STRUB, ROBERT H.
SULLIVAN, JOHN B.
SUSMAN, MILTON K.
WALLACE, JAMES H.
WALTENBAUGH, ARTHUR A.
WARREN, LYNNE

WECHSLER, MAURICE B.
WEIN, SAMUEL B.
WEIR, FREDERIC G.
WEISBERG, LEWIS
WESSEL, ARTHUR

— Class of —
1933

ARTUSO, LOUIS H.
BLATT, EDWARD J.
BRAHAM, LUTHER C.
BRANDT, PAUL W.
CALARIC, PETER
CIBULA, ALVIN M.
COOPER, LOUIS D.
COX, JOHN F.
D'ANDRADE, KENDALL
FEE, ROBERT C.
FEIGUS, SAMUEL J.
FIGERT, FREDERICK M.
FINK, CHARLES M.
GELMAN, JOSEPH M.
GLEASON, JAMES J.
GOLDSTEIN, SAMUEL J.
GRAHAM, HENRY L.
GREENBERG, LOUIS
GREER, ROBERT B., JR.
GROSSMAN, BERNARD L.
HANNA, JOHN C.
HAY, MALCOLM
HOFACKER, ERNEST H.
HOFFMAN, JOSEPH L.
HOLLANDER, HERMAN M.
HUNTER, DAVID A.
HUNTER, SAMUEL K., JR.
KLEIN, LOUIS
LANSBERRY, THOMAS F.
LAWRENCE, EDWARD R.
LEWIS, JOSEPH I.
LIPSITZ, HERMAN
LOMASK, HERBERT
LYNCH, J. DONALD
MAHANEY, WILLIAM J.
MANDEL, ISADORE W.
MARSH, JAMES E.
MARSICO, CLEMENT W.
MATHENY, MARSHALL G.
McCABE, ALFRED D., JR.
McDOWELL, WILLIAM J., JR.
McELDERRY, JOHN B.
McKEAN, GEORGE H.
McQUILKIN, FRANCIS S.
MENDLOWITZ, MORRIS A.
METZ, JOHN A., JR.
MILLER, BERNARD J.

MOLDOVAN, WILLIAM
MOORE, WILLIAM D.
MOORHEAD, JOHN R.
MORETSKY, ABE R.
MORGAN, J. HERBERT
MUNNELL, GEORGE W.
NASSAU, RICHARD
NEELY, JOHN H.
NORTON, PAUL W.
PARANSKY, WILLIAM D.
PETTIT, WILLIAM C.
RENNEKAMP, KENNETH E.
RICHARDSON, JASON
RIESTER, ALAN D.
RIVA, VICTOR E.
ROSENBERG, JACK J.
ROTH, HAROLD L.
RUBENSTEIN, MORRIS B.
RUDIN, MAURICE E.
SCHLEIFER, MARY L.
SCHLESINGER, SYLVIA
SCHMIDT, H. GILMORE
SCHOVE, CHRISTIAN Z.
SCHROTH, RAUL P.
SEIGER, BENJAMIN M.
SHAFFER, ARCUS F.
SIEGEL, ARTHUR
SNEE, JOHN V.
SOBIEN, ANDREW J.
SOLOMON, J. LEONARD
STANDISH, THOMAS A., JR.
STEINBACH, SAMUEL B.
SURMA, PETER J.
SWARTZ, HOWARD M.
SYKES, WILLIAM A.
TRYON, IRWIN I.
VENGER, JACOB
VOORHIES, ARCHIE C.
WALD, LEON
WAHL, KATHLEEN C.
WATSON, WILLIAM ATWELL
WEST, RICHARD H.
WINNER, FLOYD V.
WOLF, LESTER K.
WORLEY, RAYMOND M.

— Class of —
1934
AMDUR, SIDNEY A.
ANDERSON, ROBERT E.
ARMOUR, WILLIAM D.
BARBOR, THOMAS S.
BARCO, GEORGE J.
BARNETT, LAWRENCE
BARTHOLD, RALPH W.

BENACCI, LOUIS R.
ROSS, EDWARD S.
BOROVETZ, HYMAN
BUCHMAN, R. HERBERT
BUSH, WILLIAM A.
CAMPBELL, WILLIAM L.
CHESS, ROBERT S., JR.
CLASPER, CLARENCE H.
COHEN, JOHN J.
COHEN, MORRIS F.
CONNELL, JAMES H., JR.
COOPER, HENRY II
CURRAN, ALEXANDER R.
DAWSON, GEORGE A.
DeFOREST, WALTER P.
DILLAN, HOWARD W.
DOCKTOR, FRANKLIN J.
DOM, WILLIAM T., III
DONALDSON, JAMES R.
DRAKE, HIRAM M.
EHRMAN, ROLLAND L.
FELDSTEIN, NORMAN G.
FLAHERTY, JOHN B.
FLEISHMAN, MARTIN J.
FOSTER, JOHN K.
FULLERTON, ERROL
FULTON, CHARLES H.
GOLDMAN, SAMUEL N.
GOLDSTEIN, SAMUEL
GOODMAN, SAMUEL H.
GORDON, ALLEN S.
GRAHAM, HUGH D.
GRIER, ROBERT J., II
HADAS, ROBERT B.
HARRIS, ISADORE
HAZLETT, HOWARD J.
HEILER, S. ZOLA
HICKEY, JOHN P.
HINKES, HARRY R.
HOOD, RICHARD B.
HOUSTON, JAMES M.
IFFT, JAMES P., JR.
JACQUES, CHARLES J.
JAMES, LOUIS R., JR.
JONES, ALFRED E., JR.
JORDAN, JOHN H.
KELIHER, JOSEPH P.
KELLER, ALLEN D.
KERBER, ELEANOR R.
KLEEB, ROBERT H.
KNAPP, DONALD C.
KOESLING, PAUL F.
LARE, EDGAR W.
LEMBERSKY, JACOB H.
LEONARD, LEE L.
LeVINE, JACQUES R.

LINDUFF, SAMUEL M.
LIPMAN, SAUL S.
MAGRAM, HERMAN H.
MATAN, M. JOSEPH
McCLURE, JANE H.
McEWAN, ROBERT C.
McLURE, KENNETH M.
McMICHAEL, FRANCIS S.
McNAIR, WILLIAM H.
MENZER, HARRY
MILLER, EDWARD C., JR.
MILLER, RAYMOND C.
MORETSKY, ABE R.
MORRELL, EDWIN J.
NUGENT, JAMES H.
PERRIN, HARRY M.
PRATHER, FRANK D.
REITER, SAMUEL
RIPP, JOSEPH D.
RITCHIE, ROBERT, JR.
ROSE, J. EVANS
ROSENFELD, SAMUEL
ROYSTON, JOSEPH R., JR.
RUTHERFORD, JAMES
SCHULTZ, EDWARD A.
SHAFFER, MAURICE E.
SHORE, HENRY
SMITH, J. HOWARD
SOOST, WILLIAM J.
STEINBERG, BERNARD A.
STONE, JACOB M.
SUFFOLETTA, FRANK A.
TAYLOR, ROBERT C., JR.
TOEPFER, MARGARET A.
UHL, SIMON K.
VANDER VOORT, ROBERT
WEISS, SEYMOUR
WHITSETT, FRANK A.
WILLIAMS, VINCENT E.
WRIGHT, JOHN M.
ZUPANCIC, LUDVICK A.

— Class of —
1935
BABIC, VLADIMIR W.
BAER, MARTIN C.
BAILY, JOHN E.
BARNA, MARY LOU
BERG, GUSTAV
BERGER, SYLVAN S.
BIGGS, CLARENCE W., JR.
BOWMAN, JOHN R.
BOYD, CHARLES H.
BURDEN, MORTON
BURLEIGH, WILLIAM S.

COLL, JOHN M.
COOPERMAN, THEODORE E.
CORT, DAVID A.
COWAN, LEONARD J.
CRONIN, HAROLD M.
CUMMINS, ANDREW W.
FERGUS, HAROLD V.
GOLDFARB, SAMUEL
GRAFF, HENRY
GRAVER, HYMAN M.
HASTINGS, ANDREW P.
HENDERSON, THOMAS J.
JAFFE, EMANUEL D.
JUBELIRER, HERBERT J.
JUDD, PEARSON M.
KALSON, HARRY S.
LANDAU, MORTON S.
LANGE, ARNOLD S.
LEMON, W. ERNEST
LESKO, EDWARD J.
LEVIN, ROBERT F.
LEVINSON, MAURICE
LEWIS, WILLIAM C.
LOCKHART, GEORGE D.
MacALISTER, ROBERT G.
MAKRAUER, SHERMAN W.
MARCUS, ISADORE R.
McCLURE, JOSEPH M.
McKEAN, GEORGE H.
MERWITZER, MEYER W.
MEYER, WILLIAM A.
MILLER, W. McCOOK
MINCH, GEORGE I.
MORCROFT, GILBERT E.
MUNSCH, THOMAS J.
MUSULIN, RADE R.
PALAHUNICK, ANDREW G.
PASQUARELLI, SAMUEL M.
PORTER, ALLEN S.
RECHT, HERMAN
ST. PETER, JOHN M.
SCHOENBERGER, JOHN J.
SCHWARTZ, JEROME J.
SELIGSOHN, SOL A.
SHORE, MILTON P.
SIKOV, IRVING
SOLOW, NORMAN J.
STAUFFER, THOMAS D.
STEINER, EDWARD J.
STEWART, WALLACE D.
SUFFOLETTA, FRANK A.
TAYLOR, JOB, II
THOMPSON, ROSS W.
VATZ, S. ALLEN
VAUX, JAMES E.

WALD, HARRY J.
YOUNG, WILLIAM G.

— Class of —
1936

ADAMO, VITO W.
AGRESTI, JOSEPH V.
AGRESTI, RICHARD D.
ALTMAN, HERMAN B.
BALDINGER, MILTON I.
BALDWIN, GEORGE A.
BEHAN, LUCILE M.
BLATT, JEROME I.
BLAXTER, HENRY V., JR
BOREMAN, LEONARD
BURKE, JAMES V., JR.
CAPLAN, HARRY
DAVIS, PAUL A., IV
DONALDSON, CLYDE E.
EFRON, MORRIS
FREEDMAN, ARNOLD A.
FRIED, CARL B.
GEISELHART, RICHARD F.
JARVIS, ROBERT A.
JOHNSON, ROGER B.
KASPER, EDWARD L.
KRAUSE, DANIEL
LEVENSON, YETTA
LEVIN, EDWARD H.
MAITLAND, JOHN B.
McCREIGHT, JOHN B.
McKENNA, ROBERT A.
McSORLEY, ROBERT
MOONEY, JAMES T.
MUSTIN, HENRY
ORR, ROBERT L.
PATTERSON, JAMES A.
POLLACK, MORRIS
REUTER, HOWARD P.
RICE, KENNETH W.
RITTS, WILLIAM E.
ROBB, JOHN A.
SCHUTZMAN, HERBERT
SHEEDY, CHARLES E.
SIEGEL, SHERMAN H.
SMITH, JAMES F.
SMITH, JOSEPH G.
STEPHENS, MARLIN B.
STEWART, CLARENCE E.
STINE, JOHN F.
THORN, JAMES M.
VANCE, ROBERT D.
WEISSER, EDWARD A., JR.
WILLIAMSON, J. WOOD
WILSON, ELMER R.

WOLFE, EMANUEL B.
YARD, WILLIAM S.
ZELT, SAMUEL D.

— Class of —
1937

BLATT, GENEVIEVE J.
BRANDT, HERMAN CARL
BROWNLEE, HERBERT V.
CAPLAN, MELVIN
COWLEY, CHARLES D.
COYLE, NORTON V.
CRAWFORD, JAMES S., III
CROWN, JACK
DANAHEY, JAMES A.
DAVIES, JOHN T.
DAVIS, ROSS B.
DILLON, JAMES J.
DOUGLASS, THOMAS V.
DREHER, WILLIAM M.
FISHER, ALVAN H.
FOSTER, WILLIAM
FOUST, RAYMOND K.
FREY, THEODORE E.
FRIEDMAN, PAUL L.
GILES, RICHARD T.
GRAHAM, JAMES R.
HANSON, MARJORIE
HOLLAND, JOHN R.
HUTSON, JESSE E.
IVILL, WILLIAM J.
JOHNSTON, J. ROLAND
KELLER, WILLIAM V.
KENNEY, WILLIAM J.
KOCHER, NORMAN E.
LANDY, NORMAN
LARRY, RALPH HEATH
LIPPERT, MARY JO
MADDEN, MARY E.
NEGLEY, ALEXANDER
OLIVER, AARON
OSTROW, J. LEONARD
PAGE, MERRITT G.
RICH, VETO J.
ROCKENSTEIN, WILLIAM J.
SAYERS, ALBERT A.
SCHMIDT, HAROLD R.
SCHWARTZ, GEORGE
SCOLIO, VIOLET J.
SKODOL, C. HAROLD
SNEE, WILLIAM H.
UNVERZAGT, WILLIAM K.
WILSON, ROBERT S.
WOLKEN, NORMAN P.

— Class of —
1938

ABRAMS, SOL
BROWN, FRANK J., JR.
BROWN, JOHN T.
CERASO, JOSEPH W.
CLAY, W. RODES
DIXON, DANIEL B.
DUFF, JOHN M.
FRANCE, JAMES L.
GERACI, PASQUALE A.
GREGG, DARRELL L.
HALF, RICHARD S.
HERD, WILLIAM A., JR.
HILDEBRAND, MERLE H.
HUSBAND, HOWARD O.
IRWIN, JOHN C.
IURLANO, AUGUST A.
KECK, WARREN R.
KILNER, KENNETH J.
LEWIS, LEROY L.
LINCOFF, AARON L.
LINDSAY, ALEXANDER H.
LITTLE, S. SYLVAN
LUCE, WAYNE S.
LUCENTE, FRANK S.
MACKEY, JOHN F.
MAMULA, JOHN WILLIAM
MARION, ANTHONY J.
MARKS, LEONARD H.
McCOY, GAUIN H.
MOORE, JAMES B.
O'CONNOR, THOMAS B.
PATTERSON, DAVID W.
PETRILLO, EDWARD G.
POE, THOMAS E., JR.
RIESER, JOSEPH A.
ROCHE, JOHN P.
SACHS, HERBERT B.
SCHREINER, C. BRYSON
SOLOMON, JOSEPH
STIRLING, JOE PORTER
TROUTMAN, JAY W.
WANICK, JOSEPH A.
WEISBERG, SAUL
WILNER, ARNOLD D.
WINTERS, RICHARD R.
WORLEY, RAYMOND M.
ZEIDEL, WILLIAM

— Class of —
1939

BARNES, MARY DILWORTH
BEST, PAUL W.

CAMARINOS, TASSO E.
CARNEY, EDWARD H.
CHASE, ROBERT H.
CONNOLLY, RUSSELL G.
CRITCHLOW, PAUL N., JR.
DODDS, AGNES A.
DORAN, EDWARD B.
DORNENBERG, WILLIAM L.
ENGEL, ROBERT
FISCHER, WILLIAM J.
GARROW, JOHN L.
GLUCK, LLOYD E.
GREGORY, WALTER W.
GROTE, DOROTHY K.
HESS, EMERSON G., JR.
HIRSCH, PAUL K.
HOLT, CLYDE
KELKER, JOSEPH F.
KIGER, FRED L.
LARKIN, EDWARD M.
LEFF, MYRON D.
LEVINE, GILBERT D.
LEVINE, HOWARD B.
LUTTRELL, ALBERT E.
MAHONEY, PAUL V.
MARGOLIS, MILTON D.
MARTIN, BRUCE R.
McGHEE, SAYLOR J.
McGUINNESS, ROBERT F.
MEYER, MARY E.
REICH, FRANK
ROBINSON, HENRY E., JR.
ROSENBERG, ROSE SCHORR
SAWYER, JOHN N.
UNKOVIC, ALEXANDER
WHITE, JAMES L.

— Class of —
1940

ANDERSON, D. MALCOLM, JR.
AULD, HOWARD S.
BEESON, HENRY R.
BERLIN, ABE M.
BLUM, HARRY P.
BRANDEN, ALBERT D., JR.
COOK, J. DONALD
COONEY, PATRICK F.
CRISS, NICHOLAS R., JR.
DEVLIN, JOHN H.
EBERLE, ROBERT B., JR.
FIOK, ALBERT A.
GOEHRING, ROBERT L.
GROUDINE, NORMAN A.
HILSENRATH, EUGENE I.
HOPKINS, JOHN M.

HOYE, JOHN R.
HUGHES, JOHN J.
JACKSON, HENRY A., JR.
JACKSON, PHILIP F.
MADDEN, JOSEPH W., JR.
MALONEY, CHARLES J.
MARSHALL, JOHN H.
NEELY, KATHRYN D.
NEWCOMER, EWING K.
NUGENT, RICHARD M.
RIGGS, ROBERT L.
ROTHMAN, SAMUEL
RUFFNER, JAMES S.
RUSLANDER, JULIAN H.
SCHEIB, RAYMOND L.
SCHWARTZ, NATHAN
SIEFF, LEONARD T.
SNYDER, DANIEL J., JR.
TEITELBAUM, HUBERT I.
WELLING, KENNETH O.
WELLINGTON, JOHN S.
WILLS, JAMES D.

— Class of —
1941

BEARER, ROBERT J.
BRODER, LEROY E.
CUNNINGHAM, C. WILLIAM
DAVIS, GEORGE N.
DUFF, WILLIAM R.
ENTWISLE, ROBERT M.
FOREMAN, HERMAN L.
GLASSER, ROBERT L.
GORDON, NORMAN
GRAPP, VALERA
HANNA, MICHAEL A.
HECHT, ROBERT C.
HILL, JOHN C.
HODEL, CHARLES F.
KAMIN, MARION RUTH
LAMPROPLOS, MILTON W.
LEWIS, DONALD A.
LINTON, RICHARD W.
LOWE, WILLIAM T., JR.
LUTZ, E. ELIZABETH
MARSH, EDWARD W.
MASICK, JOHN G.
McKELVEY, JOHN E.
MINDLIN, MORRIS
MORRIS, PHILLIP E.
NEWLON, HOMER T., JR.
PERILMAN, MEYER C.
PORSCHE, ALVIN J.
SHIMSHOCK, FRANCIS H., JR.
SLEASE, CLYDE H.

WEBB, SIDNEY R.
WEINER, SAMUEL C.
WINSCHEL, PAUL J.
WISHART, JOHN W.

— Class of —
1942

ALTON, JAMES H.
ANDERSON, FRANK M.
BEST, JOHN K.
BIELEK, MELVIN S.
BLACK, JEROME
BROCKWAY, PHILIP E.
CAVALIER, WALTER A.
CIMINO, EUGENE L.
COHEN, DAVID E.
COLBERT, WILLIAM H.
CONICK, CHARLES B.
CORBOY, JOHN G.
COULTER, WILLIAM A.
DARLING, LEON E.
DOYLE, ROBERT A.
FORD, EDWARD C.
GUTTMAN, JESSE B.
HARPER, S. KNOX
HARRIS, HERMAN
HASELTINE, BENJAMIN W., JR.
HIRSCH, ARNOLD W.
JOSEPH, GEORGE J.
KOEGLER, WALTER A.
MANTZAROS, GEORGE C.
MARSHALL, WATSON C.
McARDLE, PAUL J.
MILLER, HARRY W.
NOWOTNY, WALTER S.
O'CONNOR, STEPHEN P.
PARKER, MAURICE
PUNZAK, KARL W.
RIETHMULLER, ROBERT C.
RYAN, TICE F., JR.
SCHAUFFLER, HARVEY E.
SCHOLL, CHESTER B.
SCHROECK, GEORGE W.
SHAVER, J. WARREN
SIEGEL, BEN M.
SLOAN, HARVEY F.
SPINA, JOHN P.
SPITLER, CALVIN D.
SPROWLS, ROGER G.
WALTHOUR, CHRISTOPHER
    C., JR.
WHITEHEAD, HOWARD M.
WICK, PAUL A.

— Class of —
1943

BONAVITA, SAMUEL FRANCIS
BRAHANEY, DANIEL THOMAS
CARSON, HOWARD F.
COSTELLO, JOHN EDWARD
DLUGOKENSKI, CHARLES H.
FERGUS, NELLIE MARGARET
FLINN, GEORGE EDWIN
FRANKSTON, ARTHUR S.
FULLERTON, JOHN EDWARD
GEER, THOMAS PAUL
GREENWALD, GERALD
    BENJAMIN
HEIGHTS, EDWARD A.
HERGENROEDER, CHARLES
    WILLIAM
HESTER, JOHN PATRICK
HIRSCH, JOANNE WHITE
HOBART, EDWARD PAINTER
HOEVELER, JOHN WISHART
MADVA, JOSEPH EDWARD
McKEE, MURIEL JANE
MURACCA, FRANCIS A.
MURRIN, VIRGINIA DOUBET
NESCOTT, LEWIS JOSEPH
SCHAFER, GEORGE JACOB
SHAKESPEARE, FRANK JACK
SHAPIRO, HAROLD J.
SIMON, STANLEY MAGNUS
SMITH, J. LEONARD, JR.
STETTER, WILLIAM JOHN
STRASSBURGER, JANE S.
ZEMAN, ROBERT LEWIS

— Class of —
1944

HETHERINGTON, FLORENCE
LIEBER, JEROME B.
MARION, WALTER
MUSULIN, DRAGA
PARKE, DONALD M.
SAMS, NORMAN H.
WOLCYRZ, OLGA M.

— Class of —
1945

BARTLEY, MARGARET E.
COSTA, JESSE D.
DALE, VIRGINIA R.
DISKIN, ARTHUR J.
FELLO, WILLIAM P.
GRAMMIS, ROBERT T.

LOYND, JACK S.
MANLEY, HARRY S.
MARTIN, MELVIN R.
O'BRIEN, THOMAS B.
SOSKA, MICHAEL

— Class of —
1946

TOMLINSON, DONALD R.

— Class of —
1947

BERNSTEIN, SAUL JASON
BOWMAN, JAMES LEON
CAMPBELL, RUTH BENEDICT
CATALANO, LOUIS WILLIAM
COLVIN, WILLIAM HENRY
HAHN, JEROME
HARMAN, RICHARD W.
KING, HOMER WEBSTER
McKENNA, CHARLES
    FREDERICK
MOORE, HENRY SCOTT
O'LAUGHLIN, JOHN MARK
PUGLIESE, MICHAEL JOSEPH
THOMPSON, ARTHUR
    HERBERT
WEISEL, CLIFFORD ALLEN

ALDISERT, RUGGERO J.
CAMPBELL, CHARLES W.
CANNON, DANIEL W.
COPELAND, WILLIAM J.
CORE, DANIEL H., JR.
EGLER, FREDERICK N.
ELLIS, EDWIN F.
LAMPROPLOS, MYRON W.
MILLER, HARVEY A., JR.
SCHWARTZ, LOUIS I.

— Class of —
1948

AIKEN, WILLIAM J., JR.
AIKMAN, JOHN E.
ALLEN, PAUL E.
ANGEL, WILLIAM C.
ANGEVINE, GEORGE B.
BERRY, GEORGE E., JR.
BLUMENFELD, HERBERT
BLYSTONE, CHARLES L.
BRANDT, CHARLES A., JR.
CHAFFO, JOHN L.
CLELAND, DALE

COHEN, AARON
DANIELS, ROBERT Y.
DILL, WILLIAM A.
FELDMAN, HERMAN L.
FISHER, CARL E.
FURLONG, ROBERT R., JR.
GAZETOS, JOHN N.
GEORGE, AUSTIN L., JR.
GOLDSMITH, STANLEY
GREGG, LOYAL H.
HERSKOVITZ, ARTHUR S.
HITCHENS, JAMES W.
HOWARTH, WALTER O.
HOFFMAN, SIDNEY
ICARDI, ALDO L.
KERR, JOSEPH C., JR.
KERR, ROBERT S.
KING, NICK C.
KRZTON, WILLIAM J.
KUHN, JAMES C., JR.
LIEKAR, JOHN P.
LOGAN, FRED E.
LUXENBERG, MARVIN A.
MARGOLIS, GUSTAVE S.
MARR, FRANK W.
MAST, YATES
McCANCE, JAMES ROBERT
McCUE, JOHN BERCHMANS
McDANIEL, LAWRENCE D.
McGOUGH, WALTER T.
McMANUS, OWEN B., JR.
McNAMEE, HARRY K.
McWHERTER, JAMES L.
MILNES, WILLIAM W.
MONTGOMERY, HUGH G.
NELSON, JOSEPH J.
NOEL, JOHN M.
PRIOR, ROBERT L.
REEHER, PERRY L.
RIDDLE, HENRY A., JR.
RIEMER, ROY F.
ROBINSON, JOSEPH R., JR.
RODGERS, SAMUEL L.
SCIGLIANO, AMELIA ANN
SILVESTRI, SILVESTRI
STARR, CHARLES H., JR.
STEEL, MAURICE N.
STERLING, LEWIS P.
STONE, CHARLES D.
STONE, NICHOLAS R.
STRANAHAN, JAMES A., III
TAYLOR, MORD C., JR.
WEIDLEIN, ROBERT B.
WEIL, ANDREW L., III
WOLFE, CHARLES HOLMES, JR.

— Class of —
1949

COFFROTH, TAYLOR BROWN
GILES, CHARLES E.
PARKER, HOWARD KERR
STILES, EZRA CLARKE, JR.
ZISKIND, GERALD

ACKER, WILLIAM MITCHELL
ARBOGAST, FLOYD LEON, JR.
ARONSON, ROBERT STUART
BAIRD, ROBERT DEAN
BARCO, YOLANDA GERALDINE
BLAXTER, GEORGE HAROLD
BROSKY, JOHN GEORGE
BROWN, KNOX
BURGWIN, GEORGE
    COLLINSON, III
BUTLER, RUSSELL JOHNSON, JR.
CAMPBELL, JOHN EARL
CARROLL, ROBERT EARL
CASSIDY, ROBERT JOSEPH
CITRON, EDWARD MARVIN
COOKE, EDGAR JACKSON
CRITCHFIELD, ROBERT WAYNE
CROMER, RAYMOND WALTER
CUSICK, ROBERT EMMETT
DAVIS, J. HUBBARD
DEMAS, PETER JAMES
DeMEDIO, ACHILLIO JOHN
DiCENZO, FRANK D., JR.
DICKIE, WILLIAM GRAFF
DUFF, JOHN HOSACK
DUNN, JAMES W., JR.
EDWARDS, HOWARD
    DILWORTH
FINDLEY, JOSEPH WARREN
FORSYTH, ANDREW
    WATSON, JR.
GILE, DAVID EMERY
GONDELMAN, HAROLD
GREENWALD, IRWIN LEONARD
HEILMAN, HARRY
    ANDERSON, JR.
HERCHENROETHER, HENRY
    CARL, JR.
IRWIN, WILLIAM DeVERNE
JONES, RONALD EMERSON
JOYCE, WILLIAM JOSEPH
KALLOCK, RALPH NEVILLE
KELLER, CHARLES CLAYTON
KENNEDY, JAMES FRANCIS, JR.
LEDEBUR, LINAS
    VOCKROTH, JR.
LEWELLYN, GREGG HIGBEE

MAMULA, MICHAEL M.
MARKOVITZ, HARRY
MARTIN, L. WESLEY, JR.
MATSON, WILMER EUGENE
McCLAIN, EDWARD JOSEPH
McCREIGHT, JAMES CARRELL
McDONALD, GENE EMERSON
McELFISH, JAMES MORGAN
McKEE, WILLIAM RAY
MELDON, EUGENE MORRISON
MICHALSKI, NORBERT
    ANTHONY
MOORE, GRACE DANLEY
NIXON, CLARENCE
    BOVAIRD, JR.
O'FRIEL, PAUL GREGORY
OLMES, MAJOR DONALD, JR.
PANKUCH, JOHN CHARLES
PANNER, ORAN WESLEY, JR.
PERFILIO, ANTHONY
PFADT, WILLIAM EDWARD
PHELPS, J. PAUL, JR.
POLLOCK, EWING BAILY
PRINKEY, OTIS HAMPTON
REED, EDGAR ALLEN
ROSS, GEORGE HARRY
ROTHMAN, MARTIN EDWARD
SAPP, RALPH SAMUEL
SCOTT, HOWARD IRWIN
SEMPLE, HARTON SINGER
SHAHADE, ROBERT EDWARD
SHAMP, CLINTON A.
SHAW, IRA DAYNE
SHEARER, THOMAS PARK
SMILEY, ROBERT WILSON
SOFIS, ALICE HELEN
STAHL, DAVID
STEFL, ROBERT WILLIAM
STEGENGA, GEORGE
    BENJAMIN
STEIN, ARTHUR G.
TAIT, EDWARD THOMAS
THOMAS, HORACE J., III
THOMAS, JAMES KENNETH
UMBERGER, HORACE MILES
WEBBER, WILLIAM SLOAN
WELFER, NANCY
WHITE, MARTHA DUNNE
WILLIAMS, DAVID
    HAMPSON, IV
ZEMPRELLI, EDWARD PHILIP
ZIEGLER, CHARLES IRWIN

— Class of —
1950

BURR, FREDERIC WILFORD
GUNST, CYRIL CURTIS, JR,
SIMONS, R. ERIC
WELSH, THOMAS HARRY
WICKS, JOHN OLIVER, JR.

AZORSKY, MORLEY M.
BASKIN, SEYMOUR
BEHREND, KENNETH W.
BOERIO, JOSEPH
BRADFORD, IRA FRANKLIN, JR.
BURKARDT, ROBERT F.
BURNS, THEODORE
    MORGAN, JR.
CALVIN, JAMES ARTHUR
COHEN, HAROLD MORTON
COHEN, LESLIE IRWIN
CONNELL, CHARLES EDWARD
CRAIG, DAVID WILLIAMSON
DAMRAU, EDWARD ALLAN
DITHRICH, CHARLES WOOD
DODD, MARCUS WILLIAM
DONALDSON, LEE A., JR.
EARLY, JEROME ANTHONY
FAWCETT, HARRY WILLIAM
FINE, MILTON
FISHER, JOSEPH PAUL
FITZGERALD, WILLIAM
    JOSEPH
FLICKINGER, RICHARD J.
GARFINKEL, NORMAN
GLICK, ABRAHAM JACOB
GOLDBERG, SAUL W.
GREGORY, ROBERT EUGENE
HAIMOVITZ, NED
HANNA, GEORGE KENNETH
HANSEN, WILBUR VAUGHN
HARRINGTON, DENNIS
    CORNELIUS
HERMAN, MEYER J.
HIRSCH, DAVID NEWELL
HOUSE, ROY ALEXANDER, JR.
JACOB, WILLIAM LAWRENCE, JR.
KNOELL, WILLIAM
    HOLVERSTOTT
KRAMER, HARRY A.
LAMPL, SANFORD MARK
LAUBACH, JOHN LEROY, JR.
LEVIN, GEORGE
LORENZI, JULIUS JOSEPH
LURIE, HERBERT MANNING
LYNCH, GENE KELLOGG
MATERA, VINCENT LEONARD

McBRIDE, JOHN LAWRENCE
MELLOTT, CLOYD ROWE
MENDLOW, WILLIAM HOWARD
MENTZER, BLISS REES
MIKLAS, HENRY T.
MILLER, JOHN LEE
O'DONNELL, PATRICK M., III
PEPICELLI, VINCENT JOHN
PERRY, LEROY FLOYD
POSA, PAUL P.
RAPHAEL, ROBERT
REDING, WARREN SHERRILL
REED, EARL F., JR.
ROBINSON, WILLIAM CHARLES
RUBENSTEIN, LESTER SHERMAN
SCIULLO, SAMUEL RALPH
SIKOV, SEYMOUR ALLEN
STEWART, JOHN GORDON
SUCKLING, DAVID CRAMER
SUGARMANN, NORMAN J.
TRACY, THEODORE
    McCORMICK
VESLEY, ERNEST V.
WALKER, WILLIAM H.
WALTZ, HENRY B., JR.
WEIS, JOSEPH FRANCIS
WILL, JOHN FRANK, JR.
WILLIAMS, JOSEPH ANTHONY
ZAMOS, DANIEL THEODORE

— Class of —
1951

ASKEY, WILLIAM HARTMAN
ELLROD, FRED EDWARD, JR.
HUDACSEK, JOHN JOSEPH
KELLY, WILLIAM PATRICK, JR.
KERCHNER, CARL MARTIN
TIVE, RALPH DAVID

AGNEW, WILLARD FISCHER
ASHTON, JAMES ANTHONY
BACHRACH, JEROME CHARLES
BELL, EDWARD M.
BIENO, LORRAINE LUCILLE
BRACKEN, AUDREY OLIVE
BROWN, ELIZABETH SUYDAM
CLARKE, JAMES F.
COOK, DAVID WILLIAM
COOPER, RUTH FAY
DAVID, EDWARD GEORGE
DAY, EUGENE FRANCIS
DEASY, JOHN ANTHONY, JR.
DEMPSEY, THOMAS JOSEPH
DiSALLE, RICHARD
DUGGAN, ROBERT WARD

EGAN, JAMES MURRAY
FITZGERALD, JAMES RICHARD
FLINN, RICHARD DeCAMP
FORSYTH, THOMAS
    GORDON, III
GARLAND, ROBERT WILLIAM
GILL, JAMES POWELL
GOOD, JOHN G., JR.
HAYMAKER, JAMES
    GALLAGHER
HOLLINSHEAD, EARL D., JR.
JOHNSTONE, WILLIAM VERNON
KANE, LEONARD PATRICK, JR.
KENNEDY, LAWRENCE JOHN
KORSAK, TADEUSZ ZBIGNIEW
LITMAN, S. DAVID
LUCIANA, JOSEPH LEONARD, JR.
LYONS, JOHN DAVID, JR.
McBRIDE, ALBERT, JR.
McKEE, RALPH DYER, JR.
McKISSOCK, CHARLES EDWARD
MEANS, JOHN M.
MEBS, FREDERICK W.
MELANEY, DONALD HOWARD
MOORE, LAWRENCE E., JR.
MORITZ, DONALD IRWIN
O'BRIEN, JOHN WILLIAM
O'LEARY, FRANCIS ST. CLAIR
OSGOOD, HERBERT I.
PALKOVITZ, JACK
PEARLMAN, ROBERT C.
PERLOW, EDWARD A.
PLUSKEY, RAYMOND SICKLES
REED, HAROLD FRANCIS, JR.
RHODES, JOHN DAVID
RIDALL, EDMUND
    WAINWRIGHT, JR.
RODGERS, THOMAS
    LIVINGSTON
ROEBUCK, RAYMOND
    HENRY, JR.
ROGERS, ROSS, JR.
ROSENBERG, HERBERT A.
ROSS, EUNICE LATSHAW
RUANE, THOMAS PATRICK
RUMISEK, EUGENE T.
RUSSELL, BARBARA ANNE
SCHARAR, ROBERT BARKLEY
SCHLESINGER, ROBERT
    FRANCIS
SEWALL, GEORGE OLIVER, JR.
SHORALL, GEORGE JOHN
SWEET, BERNARD J.
WEBSTER, ROBERT LOUIS
WELTY, PAUL
WILLIAMS, NED STOWE

— Class of — 1952

JACOBY, WILLIAM U.
KECK, HARRY BYRON
SAUL, IRVING ISAAC

ANTON, THOMAS T.
APPLE, MARVIN J.
BARTKO, NORMAN M.
BASHOR, EWING C.
BASSI, MELVIN B.
BLACKSTONE, FRANKLIN, JR.
BOLLINGER, JOHN J.
BOYLE, EMMETT C.
CARSON, ROBERT M., JR.
CAVANAUGH, EARL J.
COLLIE, JAMES T., JR.
CONFLENTI, FRANKLYN E.
COURTNEY, PAUL E.
D'AMICO, JOHN R.
DeMAY, JOHN A.
DUERRING, BURTON C.
ESPER, JOSEPH U.
FEENEY, WALTER S.
GEDDIS, MAVE V.
GOLDFARB, EDGAR J.
GREEN, RICHARD J., JR.
HERRINGTON, EDGAR P., JR.
HUDSON, L. IVAN
KENNEDY, JOHN J., JR.
KERR, WILLIAM G., JR.
KINGSLEY, ROBERT I.
KIRSHNER, CHARLES
KUYAT, EDWARD G., JR.
LEWIS, ROBERT W.
LINZNER, GILBERT C.
LITMAN, ROSLYN M.
LOEBIG, GEORGE E., JR.
MARGOLIS, HERBERT
MAST, FRANK
McDERMOTT, CLARE B., JR.
McKEE, LOIS J.
MEYER, GREGOR F.
MICELI, VICTOR L.
MURPHY, AUSTIN J., JR.
MURPHY, JAMES P.
O'MALLEY, JAMES F.
PAPA, ALFRED V.
PURCELL, THOMAS J.
REA, HENRY E., JR.
RHULE, JOHN D.
RICHARDSON, JOSEPH A., JR.
ROWLEY, JAMES E.
SHEINBERG, HERBERT G.
SMITH, RALPH H., JR.

SNYDER, EDGAR L., JR.
STONE, JEAN V.
TUROSKY, EDWARD A.
WALKER, ALEXANDER H., JR.
WALKER, WILLIAM C.
WARDZINSKI, WALTER T.
WEAVER, GERALD W.
WEIS, THOMAS F.
WITWICKI, RAYMOND T.
YOUNG, MARJORIE P.
ZEHNER, LISLE A.

— Class of — 1953

COOPER, JAY P.
KOVACH, ALBERT A.

ACKELSON, ROLAND D.
BARTIROMO, ANTHONY P.
BERMAN, MYRON J., JR.
BLAUFELD, SAMUEL S.
BLENKO, WALTER J., JR.
BRAUNSTEIN, MAURICE M.
BRISELL, ELIZABETH B.
CAPOZZI, ALVIN D.
CARROLL, FRANK C.
COHEN, MARK I.
CRUM, ROBERT M.
DAVIS, SAUL
DIGBY, DAVID L.
ERVING, ANNE H.
FAWCETT, DAVID B., JR.
FEENEY, JOHN M., JR.
FEINBERG, HERBERT S.
FLOOD, HENRY C., JR.
GUINEY, THOMAS M.
HART, WILLIAM C.
HECHT, JAMES B.
HENDERSON, HOMER M.
HLADIO, MICHAEL
HOLAHAN, FRANCIS E.
HOTCHKISS, HENRY J.
JACOBS, NORMAN H.
JOHNSTON, KENNETH S.
KAPLAN, LAWRENCE W.
KIMMEL, WILLIAM L.
KOHLER, EDWARD L.
LABBIE, HERBERT G.
LANDIS, JERRY B.
LICHTENSTEIN, DAVID L.
LIND, JOHN W.
LUBIC, ROBERT B.
LUKE, JOHN R.
MARGOLIS, CHARLES W.
MARKON, ROY

McCRADY, ALLEN D.
McDANIELS, JOHN H.
McGUIGAN, JAMES L.
McLAUGHLIN, ARTHUR L., III
McMILLIN, EDWIN R., II
MERMAN, MARY M.
MESSINA, JOHN J.
MOORE, JOSEPH W.
OBERT, PAUL R.
PATTON, JAMES M.
PEABODY, ROBERT B.
POTASHMAN, JEROME M.
PRICE, LEONARD E.
RIEHL, ROY W.
ROSENBAUM, JOSEPH I.
RUDDOCK, WILLIAM P.
SABEL, ROBERT H.
SCANLON, EUGENE F.
SCANNELL, RAYMOND F.
SHEINMAN, MARTIN M.
SMITH, RALPH E., JR.
STALEY, WILLIAM J.
STEEDLE, JOSEPH A.
STUCKRATH, ROBERT W.
SWEENEY, JOHN J., JR.
TERPUTAC, THOMAS J.
THOMSON, WILLIAM W.
URLING, WALTER C., JR.
VanGORDER, ANDREW C.
WENDEKIER, LEOPOLD J.
ZANOLLI, STELVIO W.

— Class of — 1954

ROGERS, DONALD EDWARD
SCHURGOT, PAUL DANIEL, JR.

ABBATANGELO, DAVID D.
ALBAUGH, HENRY J.
AMBROSE, JAMES W.
BAGLEY, JOSEPH B.
BERMAN, NORTON L.
BOWSER, JOHN V.
BRUECK, CARL W., JR.
BUCAR, THOMAS N.
BURTELL, EDWARD G., JR.
CINDEA, NICHOLAS M.
CLARK, DAVID K.
COFFROTH, FREDERICK F.
COWIE, NORMAN J.
DORN, KENNETH J.
EDDY, THOMAS R.
ELLIS, JO ANN M.
EMBICK, MERRILL C.
FATULA, EDWARD A.

FURMAN, MELVIN D.
GEORGALAS, MICHAEL J.
GRIFFITH, BLAIR A.
GRODIN, JACK
HARPER, JAMES G.
HEARD, CYRUS R.
IRVIS, K. LEROY
JARRETT, CHARLES B., JR.
KAUFMAN, RICHARD A.
KOERTH, CLIFFORD J.
KOUNTZ, JOHN R.
LANGUE, EDWIN D.
LAUFE, DAVID M.
LAWSON, ERIC F., JR.
LeWINTER, WILLIAM J.
LOEFFLER, JOHN P.
LOVE, MURRAY S.
MAHER, WILLIAM F.
MASSCO, FRANCIS P.
MASTERS, ROBERT J.
McGOWAN, BERNARD J.
McLAUGHLIN, JAMES E.
MILIE, ROBERT J.
MORTON, JAMES D.
NEISH, CLARENCE D.
O'MALLEY, MICHAEL J.
PIPER, ROBERT W.
POLONSKY, GILBERT N.
REGULE, JOHN J.
ROBERTS, WINSTON T.
RODGER, WILLIAM R.
ROTH, SAMUEL B.
SCHUCHERT, JOSEPH S., JR.
SMITH, ASA W.
SMITH, WILLIAM C., JR.
SMITH, WILLIAM H.
STANTON, JOHN
STONE, ROBERT R.
SUTO, ALEXANDER L.
THISTLE, RAYMOND A., JR.
THORPE, LAWRENCE I.
WALSH, ROBERT E.
WARREN, FLOYD R.
WEATHERWAX, DAVID E.
WEIS, GEORGE M.

— Class of —
1955

BLISSMAN, GEORGE C., JR.
CROSBY, WILLIAM IRWIN
DUPLAGA, EDWARD
   THEODORE
IANNUZZI, JOSEPH MICHAEL
LISSFELT, WALTER
   NORMAN, JR.

LOCHNER, RAY NELSON
STROH, SAMUEL Y.
WILLIAMS, DON RUSSELL

ARBUCKLE, JOHN H.
BALZARINI, EDWARD J.
BARBOUR, JOHN B.
BARRETT, EDWARD M.
BRENNAN, THOMAS P.
BYERLY, JOHN A., JR.
CAMPBELL, JOHN W., JR.
CASSOL, ROBERT Y.
COHEN, ALLAN H.
CONLEY, JOHN A.
COOPER, WILLIAM J.
CORBIN, PHILIP, JR.
CURTIS, ERIC J.
DIAMANT, WILLIAM
DOLBY, ARNOLD E.
DONALDSON, HARRY W.
EDWARDS, DANIEL R.
ELCHIK, WILLIAM A.
ELLIS, A. RALPH, JR.
GALLAGHER, RAYMOND J.
GANNON, EDWARD J.I., JR.
GOLDMAN, HAROLD H.
HOUCK, IRA C., JR.
IRVIN, W. ARCH, JR.
KACHULIS, PAUL G.
KRESTEL, ROBERT D.
LYNCH, RALPH, JR.
MADAR, MICHAEL A.
MARTIN, HENRY A.
McLEAN, JAMES H.
MOREAU, LAWRENCE J.
MORGAN, JOHN H.
O'CONNOR, JOHN P.S.
PENTECOST, ALEXANDER JOHN
POWELL, NORBERT J.
PRENY, SIDNEY
RILEY, HENRY A.
RIZZO, LAWRENCE A.
SMITH, ROBERT BANKS
STEPANIAN, LEO M.
STRAYER, B. THOMAS
TUTHILL, DAVID F.
WALLACE, D. HERBERT

— Class of —
1956

MANDELBLATT, LEONARD
   SYLVAN

BAILEY, CARROLL M.
BAILEY, JOHN L.

BEYMER, JAMES P.
BIRCH, DONALD M.
BLATT, CAROL M.
BURR, EDWARD M.
CHEW, CHARLES T.
CLAYPOOL, DENORIS D.
COHILL, MAURICE B., JR.
CONN, MARSHALL J.
CRISANTI, VINCENT A.
CRONE, RICHARD S.
CURRY, ROBERT L.
DAUER, ROBERT E.
DOUDS, JOHN P.
ECKER, RONALD D.
EWART, DONALD L.
FOX, KENNETH E., JR.
FRANKS, WILLIAM J.
FUGE, LLOYD H.
GEORGE, GEORGE J.
HARRIS, STEVE J.
HUMMEL, LEE W.
KNEPP, LARRY F.
LENCHNER, HERBERT L.
LIPPERT, LUDWIG E., JR.
MANLEY, JAMES F.
McQUEEN, ROBERT G.
MORROW, CHARLES S.
NAKLES, NED J.
NELSON, RICHARD S.
O'TOOLE, LAWRENCE E.
PLOWMAN, JACK W.
PLUM, ARNOLD V.
PORTNOY, HAROLD A.
POWDERLY, WILLIAM H., III
ROTH, HARRY E.
SCHMITT, HARRY J.
SCHWARTZ, MELVIN
SCIULLO, JOHN J.
SEIDELSON, DAVID E.
SHORALL, THOMAS J.
SPIEGEL, JOHN L.
STURGEON, JOHN S.
SUPOVITZ, ALLEN M.
VELTRI, RAYMOND G.
VOLK, CHARLES R.
WARMAN, GUY LEE
WENTLEY, RICHARD T.
WHITEHEAD, S. WAYNE
WHITEHILL, CHARLES R.
WOOD, BARRY E.
YOUNG, NELSON P.
ZAVARELLA, PAUL R.

— Class of —
1957

LIVINGSTON, THOMAS A.
MIHALICH. GILFERT M.

ALLEN, NORMAN RICHARD
ARCORACE, THOMAS
BAIRD, ROBERT ROYCE
BELL, DERRICK ALBERT, JR.
BERTANI, DANTE GULEARDO
BOEHM, FREDERICK ADAM
CONTE, FRANK ANTHONY
DAY, REED BLACHLY
DiFRANCESCO, SAMUEL
    RAYMOND, JR.
FERGUSON, GLENN WALTER
FULTON, ARTHUR BOHSE
FULTON, ROBERT EDGAR, JR.
GARDNER, WILLIAM
    MARSHALL, JR.
HECK, HOWARD VINCENT
JENKINS, GEORGE BRUCE
JIM, RICHARD LOUIS
KMIECIK, THADDEUS JACOB
    (now TED JACOB)
LaMARCA, RUSSELL
LENCH, RONALD G.
LOCKE, PAUL EDWARD
LONG, BARRETT EARNEST
McGREGOR, JAMES RUSSELL
McHUGH, RICHARD C.
McKENNEY. SAMUEL
    SCOTT, III
McNELIS, GERALD
    AUGUSTINE, JR.
NARDELLI, JAMES LOUIS
O'KICKI, JOSEPH FRANCIS
PODOLSKY, MALVERN PAUL
POPOVICH, ZORAN
POST, GORDON
    CHRISTOPHER, JR.
RAUSCHENBERGER, FLOYD
    ARTHUR, JR.
REDLICH, BERNARD
REPCHECK, JOHN JOSEPH
RUBASH, NORMAN JOSEPH
SCHANO, JOHN FRANCIS
SCHELLHAMMER, EDWARD
    ROBERT
STANICHAK, JOSEPH
    MICHAEL
STOCK, ROBERT JOSEPH
THOMAS, BENJAMIN ELMO, JR.
THORNBURGH, RICHARD
    LEWIS

TOCCI, EDWARD JOSEPH
VOSS, JAMES VICTOR
XIDES, BYRON D.

— Class of —
1958

ARMSTRONG, HENRY
    HILLIARD
BLOCH, ALAN NEIL
BOYLE, WILLIAM GALVIN
CERASO, THOMAS R.
CONNOLLY, J. WRAY, JR.
CUMMINGS, JOHN FRANKLIN
DAGHIR, GORDON JOSEPH
D'AMBROSIO, LAWRENCE
    ANTHONY
DAVIS, REED JEROME
DeBROFF, ROBERT MAXWELL
DINGMAN, HARRY DALE
DIXON, WILLIAM BERNARD
DOUGLASS, SAMUEL LESTER
FALLAT, GEORGE S.
FISCHER, ROGER M.
FISCHER, THEODORE D.
FLAHERTY, JOHN PAUL, JR.
FRIEDMAN, JON LEWIS
GAUT, JAMES RICHARD
GREGG, JOHN MARSHALL
GRODNER, EZRA DANIEL
HAMMER, EDGAR THOMAS, JR.
JORDAN, HARRY JAMES
KRAYER, WILLIAM LANGFITT
KULICK, ELLIOTT FREDERICK
LIEBER, MARVIN SIDNEY
McVAY, WILLIAM WALTER
MEDONIS, ROBERT XAVIER
MIDDLEMAN, SANFORD
    ALLEN
MILLER, WINFIELD SCOTT, II
MITINGER, JOSEPH BERRY
MULLEN, CLAIR XAVIER, JR.
MYERS, WILLIAM JOSEPH
PERSIO, DINO
PETRO, PAUL MICHAEL
POPE, JOHN HERRION
SCHAFER, SEYMOUR JAY
SIMONI, PETER PAUL
STOCKS, DONALD MACEO
STOOPS, CHARLES
    CRAWFORD, JR.
SWARTZ, BOYD MERLE
TALLMAN, ROBERT PAUL, JR.
THOMAS, WILLIAM PAUL, JR.
TURETS, MAXIM DAVID
VEROSTEK, FRANCIS JAMES

VLHA, JOHN REGIS
WALSH, JOSEPH MICHAEL
WALTERS, ROY FRANCIS, JR.
WEBB, ALAN DANIEL
WILSON, DONALD EARL
WOODARD, RAYMOND STYLES

— Class of —
1959

ACKERMAN, ALAN LOUIS
BOWLES, JOHN RICHARD
CITRON, CARL DAVID
COHEN, DAVID L.
CRAMER, GILBERT B.
DAVIS, WILLIAM REMALEY, JR.
DECKER, ROBERT GEORGE
DeSTEFANO, RALPH THOMAS
FAHEY, WILLIAM JOSEPH
FINKEL, SIDNEY RALPH
FLAHERTY, JAMES JOSEPH
FRIEDMAN, PHILIP RONALD
GREENFIELD, STANLEY
    WILLIAM
HOREWITZ, MURRAY I.
HURON, MARY ANN
LEVENDOS, THOMAS
LYNCH, GEORGE MICHAEL
LYNCH, HILARY GANS
MAKAROFF, STANLEY G.
McKAY, RONALD JAMES
McKENZIE, ROBERT MARK
MEISTER, DAVID LEE
MOFFATT, CHARLES
    KIMBERLEY
ORR, DONALD EUGENE
PANAGULIAS, ROBERT G.
PATERRA, ARTHUR GAETANO
REEVES, LEONARD R.
REYNOLDS, THOMAS A.
ROSE, J. EVANS, JR.
SCHAFFLER, BERNARD
SEDLER, ROBERT ALLEN
SPECTER, GEORGE RONALD
STEWART, WILLIAM POWELL
STILLEY, CHARLES
    CHAMBERLIN
WEIN, PHILMAN LEE
WINSON, DONALD CARROLL
YURCON, GEORGE EDWARD
ZIONTS, BERKLEY

— Class of — 1960

BARLEY, DONALD J.
BEARD, PHILIP EDWARD
BOYD, KIER T.
CHRISTNER, RICHARD SLOAN
GROGAN, VINCENT JEROME
KATARINCIC, JOSEPH A.
LAY, JAMES PLEASANT, III
LOUGHREN, CHARLES HILL
MARCUS, ALAN RICHARD
McCABE, LAWRENCE JAMES
McCABE, ROBERT FOURCE, JR.
McCRACKEN, STANLEY
   GLENN, JR.
McMILLIN, BLAIR STEELE
MILLER, LAWRENCE ALAN
NELSON, THOMAS FREEMA
NOLENDER, JACK HARVEY
PASTEWKA, EDWARD
   ANTHONY
PELAEZ, ALFRED STEPHEN
REINBOLD, EUGENE JOSEPH
SCHMITT, JOSEPH EDWARD
SMITH, RICHARD J.
SOLOMON, GILBERT STANLEY
SPENCER, RALPH WILLIAM
STEINITZ, SIDNEY ABRAHAM
WASHINGTON, DAVID BUSCH
WELTY, ROBERT LOHR
WYMARD, JOSEPH MICHAEL

— Class of — 1961

BERMAN, ALAN
BLOOM, SIGMUND L.
CAIAZZA, FRANCIS XAVIER
CARR, RICHARD RUSSELL
FARLEY, ANDREW NEWELL
FISCHER, RICHARD LAWRENCE
FULTON, HENRY W., JR.
GOLD, DAVID RICHARD
HOLLANDER, THOMAS
JACKSON, THOMAS JAMES
KINNUNEN, VICTOR JOHNSON
KLABER, RICHARD DOUGLASS
LAUGHLIN, PAUL FRANCIS
LEWIS, MORRISON FRANCIS, JR.
MacVAY, CLYDE THOMAS
MADDOX, JAY RUSH
McCONNELL, STEWART
   PHILLIPS, JR.
NERNBERG, A. RICHARD
PAWLOWSKI, BLAIR V.

REDLICH, LEONARD ALLEN
SALLACH, WAYNE NORWOOD
SCHUMACHER, GEORGE EMIL
SEIAVITCH, STUART ERWIN
SUPOWITZ, RICHARD STUART
TAMBURO, VINCENT
   ANTHONY
TUCKER, ROBERT EDWARD
WHITE, THOMAS SULLIVAN
WIDMAR, JOSEPH HENRY

— Class of — 1962

ARNOLD, GENE EDWARD
ASKIN, DAVID JAMES
BLOCK, PETER HAROLD
BOWYTZ, ROBERT BERNARD
COMAY, SHOLOM DAVID
COOPER, THOMAS LOUIS
FOWKES, GEORGE EDWARD
GORDON, GORDON
HATCH, ORRIN GRANT
HERRINGTON, WILLIAM KIRBY
KRAFT, RALPH FRANKLIN
LANGHAM, ROBERT ALLAN
LEBOVITZ, ROBERT ALAN
MANDELL, ROBERT WARREN
McGREGOR, JACK EDWIN
McNEISH, PETER F.
O'HANESIAN, DAVID
PRUGER, JOHN RAOUL
REED, GRETCHEN SOHN
REED, ROBERT CLARK
ROYSTON, JOSEPH ROLAND, III
SEGAL, STANFORD ALAN
SHUST, ROBERT BURTON
SILVERMAN, ARNOLD BARRY
STEIN, IRWIN MANUEL
SWENSEN, JAN CLOVI
SWECHT, CYRIL HARRISON
WITTLIN, CHARLES EMIL

— Class of — 1963

BIRMINGHAM, ROBERT LEWIS
CALDWELL, JAMES ALLEN
CERASO, LOUIS H.
COLIANNI, VINCENT A.
CONWAY, JOSEPH WILLIAM
FEIN, MARVIN ABRAMS
FOREMAN, PAUL S.
GREENBERG, DAVID JEROME
GUTHRIE, WILLIAM WHARTON
HEAZLETT, ELIZABETH

HEMPHILL, JAMES TIERNEY, JR.
HUDSON, HENRY AMMANN, JR.
LICHTER, BARBARA MAE
MAJESKO, RAYMOND THOMAS
MATTERN, CLARA LOUISE
McINTYRE, DINA G.
McINTYRE, RICHARD S.
MEAD, EARL ALEXANDER
MORAN, GERALD ROBERT
MUSICA, LOYIS DONALD
NEWCOMER, JOHN LINDLEY
ODDI, ARCHI SAMUEL
PAPUGA, JOHN PAUL
ROSE, ROBERT PORTER
RUDDOCK, DONN McCLAVE
THOMAS, JAMES HALL
WELSH, EDWARD FRANCIS

— Class of — 1964

ACKERMAN, DANIEL JAMES
ANSTANDIG, LOUIS
ARCH, JOHN GEORGE
BALSINGER, DANIEL FRANCIS
BARMEN, STEWART B.
BUCKI, LEONARD JOSEPH
BUTLER, ERNEST BRUCE
CLOKEY, FRANK RAYMOND
COOK, DAVID LeMOYNE
EWALT, ROBERT MORRISON, JR.
FOLAN, THOMAS JOSEPH
GARFINKEL, ALAN A.
HARBAUGH, JOSEPH DELBERT
JACOBS, JOAN M.
LUCCHINO, FRANK JOSEPH
MASTERSON, JOSEPH OWEN
MAURY, SAMUEL LEWIS
MAY, CHARLES KENT
MAYER, THOMAS CARLIN
MEFFE, DOMENIC ANTHONY
MESAROS, JOHN GEORGE
MEYER, WILLIAM A., JR.
NERNBERG, MAURICE A., JR.
PETERKA, CALVIN OLIVER
SELKOVITS, LAWRENCE DAVID
SHRAGER, DONALD IRVING
SMITH, BRUCE LaVERNE
SMITH, NORMAN WILLIAM, JR.
SPECTER, HOWARD ALAN
STEINBERG, NORMAN LESLIE
THOMPSON, HARRY
   ADDISON, II
WATSON, DAVID STEPHEN
WATZMAN, RONALD N.
YELOVICH, JAMES BRIAN

— Class of —
1965

ARONSON, MARK B.
BEACHLER, EDWIN H.
BEILSTEIN, ROBERT W.
BERNSTEIN, JOSEPH J.
BINGLER, JOHN H., JR.
CORSE, CHESTER C., JR.
COVIELLO, VINCENT F., JR.
CURRAN, J. ROGER
DANIELS, ROBERT S.
FERGUS, HAROLD V., JR.
FLICKINGER, RICHARD F.
FOX, CYRIL A., JR.
FUERLE, RICHARD D.
GALLOWAY, RICHARD H.
HILL, EDWARD A.
HOILES, WILLIAM M.
JACQUES, CHARLES J., JR.
KLUG, WILLIAM F., IV
KNAPP, LAWRENCE M.
LAVELLE, WILLIAM J.
LERACH, RICHARD F.
LIGHTCAP, ROBERT P.
MALONEY, THOMAS E.
McCLURE, WILLIAM C., II
McKEAN, EDWIN L.R.
MEYER, JOHN S.
NEWLIN, WILLIAM R.
ROWLEY, ROBERT D., JR.
ROSSETTI, DONALD D.
SALAMON, LOUIS R.
SILVERHART, LOUIS
SHULICK, WILLIAM T.
STEFF, ALFRED LOUIS, JR.
STEWART, WILLIAM A., III
STRADER, JAMES D.
TIMCHAK, LOUIS J., JR.
TOWNSEND, JOHN A.
WATKINS, CHARLES B.
WHITE, THOMAS O.
YABLONSKI, JOSEPH A.

— Class of —
1966

ANDREWS, W. THOMAS
ANTKOWIAK, MICHAEL JERRY
BALFE, MICHAEL W.
BAROZZINI, ROBERT D.
BAUR, BYRON D.
BELDEN, H. REGINALD, JR.
BLACKWOOD, JAMES E.
BLAIR, THEODORE T.
BODNAR, RAYMOND L.

BRECK, LAWRENCE D.
BUA, RONALD J.
BULL, D. MICHAEL
CLARK, EDWIN M., JR.
CONNER, ANDREW J.
COOK, JOHN R.
CULLEY, JAMES KENT
DEAN, JOHN J.
DORAZIO, MICHAEL
DREXLER, ELLIOTT M.
DRISCOLL, JOHN J.
ECKEL, WILLIAM K.
FINEBERG, LIBO B.
FINKELSTEIN, EDWARD S.
FOSSEE, CHESTER S.
FOX, JAMES A.
GALLAGHER, JOHN O.D.
GOLDBERG, RICHARD T.
HOGAN, THOMAS R.
KENNEDY, GARY B.
KETTERER, WILLIAM G.
KNOX, WALLACE J., III
KOPELMAN, JAMES E.
KOSGLOW, JAMES JOHN
LAFFERTY, FRED B.
LAVERY, MICHAEL J.
LEVENSON, STANTON D.
MacMULLAN, THOMAS D.
MILLS, RICHARD J.
MINSKY, HOWARD A.
MOLINARO, CARMINE V.
O'LOUGHLIN, DAVID L.
PAULICK, LOUIS R.
ROBINSON, OTTO P.
ROSENFIELD, ARTHUR B.
ROSENZWEIG, RICHARD L.
RUFFNER, JAY S.
RUSH, RICHARD E.
SCHWARTZ, WILLIAM J.
SHOOP, ROBERT H., JR.
SNYDER, EDGAR
STEDEFORD, JOHN D.
STEWART, LEONARD L.
STITT, ROBERT K., III
TAYLOR, CHARLES R.
VEEDER, PETER G.
WESTERHOFF, RICHARD V.
WIEGAND, PHILLIPS

— Class of —
1967

AGRESTI, CHARLES DAVID
AURITT, JON JAMES
BECK, ROBERT D.
BEILSTEIN, JAMES R.

BELIN, DORRANCE REYNOLDS
BENEDICT, COLEMAN JOSEPH
BOWYTZ, STEVEN HARRY
BRADLEY, WAYNE ALLEN
BUKES, JAMES SPEROS
CILLO, DANIEL PETER
COHEN, HOWARD ROD
COHEN, ROBERT EVAN
COHEN, STEPHEN L.
COUSINS, JEFFREY LEE
CRITES, ROBERT VERNON
DAVIDSON, JOHN H., JR.
FRIEDMAN, ARNOLD MORRIS
GUTNICK, H. YALE
HAMMER, PAUL LUDVIG
HECHT, ROBERT GARY
HEENAN, MICHAEL TERENCE
HEIMAN, RONALD TOD
HOFFMAN, GARY RODGER
HUFNAGEL, FREDERICK
    BERNHARD
JULIAN, EUGENE JOSEPH
KAAR, RICHARD MICHAEL
KARNS, JOHN FRANCIS
KLEE, JOHN PAUL
KOCH, HENRY MATTHAIS, JR.
KOSINSKI, J. GARY
KRAKOFF, JERE
KUSHNER, LOUIS BERNARD
LASNER, RICHARD FISCHER
LAWRENCE, EDWARD ROSS, JR.
LEBER, FRANK JOHN
LEEBOV, LINDA ELLEN
LEISAWITZ, ALAN GARY
McKEE, ROBERT EARL, JR.
MITCHELL, ROBERT CHARLES
NYCUM, PETER STIVANSON
POOL, HENRY SPRUANCE
REED, ROBERT ALAN
REESE, THOMAS MICHAEL
REITER, SANDRA RENEE
ROBERTS, GEORGE THOMAS
RUDNITSKY, MARVIN JAMES
SCOTT, RICHARD SUMNEY
STARBUCK, CHARLES, III
TOSH, JAMES CLYDE
TREEGOOB, WARREN
    FREDERICK
VENABLE, GILBERT
    TUCKERMAN
WASSON, DAVID BOYD
WHITE, HOWARD WILLIAM, JR.
WHITE, MARY RANSFORD
WYMARD, JAMES ANTHONY

— Class of —
1968

BAGNELL, JAMES FRANCIS, III
BAILY, WILLIAM M.
BASTIAN, ROMAIN FREDERICK
BAUM, RAYMOND NATHAN
BLAXTER, HENRY VAUGHAN
BONISTALLI, JOSEPH JAMES
CAPPY, RALPH JOSEPH
CIMINO, RONALD ALLEN
CINDRICH, ROBERT JAMES
CURRY, DAVID MILO
DELANEY, DANIEL ROBERT
DETWEILER, JOHN CURTISS
DUFF, DANIEL S.R.
DUNN, DAVID FRANCIS
FISCH, EDWARD CARL
GIBBONS, ALFRED BRUCE
GOLDHABER, MARTIN
    EDWARD
GRAFT, ROBERT RUSSELL, III
HAGUE, PAUL CHRISTIAN
HARPER, JACK HAROLD
HARRIS, EARL LEROY
HARRIS, GRACE SALZMAN
HINDS, DOUGLAS PAUL
HOPKINS, THEODORE
    SHELDON, JR.
IVILL, WILLIAM JONES, III
JONES, T. WARREN
KAY, JEFFREY A.
KOCH, EDWARD NICHOLAS, III
LEWIS, ROBERT GARY
LIBSON, ROBERT
LOEB, ROBERT LOUIS
MOLDOVAN, BERT M.
NEIL, BURTON
PRESTIA, JOSEPH
RESNICK, ALVIN MARK
RINGLER, VERNON LEE
RODKEY, RANDALL C.
ROSEN, LAWRENCE JAY
SADOWSKY, BARTON R.
SINGER, PAUL MEYER
SMITH, WILLIAM SCHAFFER
STYLE, ROBERT PHILIP
TATE, ROBERT JAMES
TIGHE, WILLIAM REGIS, JR.
VIERTHALER, JOHN JOSEPH
WASHINGTON, PATRICK HUGH
WEINGART, EDWARD
WEINSTEIN, ANDREW H.
WISEMAN, STEPHEN KENNETH
WOLLESEN, WOODROW DAVIS
WRIGHT, TIMOTHY CLARK

— Class of —
1969

BERGER, WILLIAM M.
BROOKS, THEODORE W.
BURDMAN, LOUIS A.
CALIOR, JOHN EDWARD
CARN, DANIEL LEWIS
CLEMENTS, JOHN K.
COFFEY, LOUIS
DAVIS, RICHARD
DeGUILIO, FELIX J.
DeLUCA, WAYNE
DICE, EUGENE F.
EBERLY, ROBERT E., JR.
ENGLESBERG, ROBERT S.
ERIKSEN, DONALD
FAWCETT, MICHAEL S.
FELTY, THOMAS PETER
FOSTER, ROBERT G.
FOX, MICHAEL D.
GREEN, NORMAN A.
GRUENER, HARRY JOSEPH
HARRIS, LEONARD CRAIG
HECHT, MICHAEL
HORGAN, JOHN J.
HUHTA, ROBERT G.
JOHNSON, WILLIAM A.
KAPLAN, CARL H.
KELLY, MICHAEL R.
KELSO, JOHN McNARY, JR.
KERLAVAGE, MARGARET
LEVENTON, LAWRENCE F.
MALONE, JAMES F., III
MARCOVSKY, GERALD
MARCUS, BERNARD D.
McBRIDE, ROBERT R.
McCONNELL, WILLIAM G.
MEILTON, ROGER B.
MURRAY, ROBERT W.
NASSAU, RICHARD
ORR, SAMUEL J., IV
PETERSON, WILLIAM G.
QUINN, PAMELA KAY
ROEDER, RICHARD W.
ROST, DAVID M.
SENICK, MARK A.
SKIRBLE, JOEL H.
SLEASE, CLYDE H., III
SPAGNOLLI, RICHARD G.
SPECK, NANCY L.
STEIN, BERNARD
STEIN, MELVIN P.
SYMONS, EDWARD L., JR.
TOKER, JOHN A.
TRICE, HARLEY N., II

TUTTLE, JON F.
WEBB, RICHARD W.
VAUGHAN, JAMES
WILSON, ARTHUR M.
WILSON, WILLIAM
WITT, HELEN M.
YOURICK, FRANK E., JR.

— Class of —
1970

ABRAHAMS, HOWARD
AMES, HOWARD NATHAN
ALPERN, CHARLES HARVEY
BALSLEY, DONALD JEROME, JR.
BARTOLOTTA, VINCENT
    JOHN, JR.
BOOTE, ROBERT McLAURIN
BOWEN, ALDEN EARL
BOWMAN, JAMES JOHNSTON
BROOKING, FREDERICK
    RUSSELL
CAREY, FRANCIS JAMES
CATALANO, RICHARD JAMES
COFER, DAVID THORNTON
COHEN, CHARLES IVAN
DEMASE, LAWRENCE ALFRED
ECKHOUSE, MARCUS LEE
ENTWISLE, ROBERT
    MORGAN, III
FERGUS, SCOTT HARSHA
FERN, JOSEPH JACOB, III
FISHER, GORDON DAVID
FLYNN, EDMUND GERALD
FRANK, FREDERICK NEWMAN
GLASSER, JAY DAVID
GOLDBERG, LEE HARVEY
GOLDBERG, THEODORE
GROSSINGER, HOWARD
HALLORAN, THOMAS
    FRANCIS
HANSON, MARCELLA PHELPS
HARTLEY, ROGER CHARLES
HELLERSTEDT, CARL
    HENRY, JR.
HOFFMAN, FRANKLIN DAVID
JACOBSON, PETER DAVID
JESSUP, RICHARD
KEDDIE, ROLAND THOMAS
KLEPAC, GLENN EDWARD
LEETE, JOHN BRUCE
LEMMON, FLORENCE F.
LERACH, WILLIAM
    SHANNON
LIPECKY, WAYNE STEPHEN
LOGAN, JAMES HOWARD

LYNCHESKI, JOHN EDWIN
MALAKOFF, MICHAEL PAUL
McARDLE, PATRICK FRANCIS
McCLAIN, ALLAN
McGINLEY, BERNARD LEO
McINTYRE, JAMES JOHN
McKELVEY, DANIEL EVERETT, JR.
McKENZIE, MARY URSULA
MERCER, H. FRED, III
MORAN, JOHN DOUGLAS
MURCKO, THOMAS CYRIL
NELSON, FREDERIC CHARLES
NEMEC, MICHAEL ANTHONY
PARKER, ELISSA ANN
PEARSON, GREGORY ALAN
PEEL, RICHARD ANDERSON
PICADIO, ANTHONY PETER
PINKUS, RALPH
PRATT, RALPH DOMENICK
RATCLIFFE, TEMPLE LINLEY
RUBENFIELD, HOWARD LOUIS
SHAFFER, HENRY ROSCOE
SHARON, LEONARD IRWIN
SHAVER, DIANA SUZANNE
SHERMAN, CARL LEON
SINGER, HOWARD ROBERT
SNODGRASS, STEWART
    RICHARD
STIBICH, MICHAEL LAWRENCE
TAYLOR, JAMES ALLAN
TAYLOR, ROBERT JOSEPH
THOMAS, HARRY KAY

— Class of —
1971

ADAMS, JAMES EDWARD
AIKENHEAD, DAVID STEWART
AMERICUS, BRUCE ALFRED
BAKER, KENNETH LEE
BARLETT, CARL EDWARD
BENYAK, JANET MARTHA
BLIWAS, STUART MARK
BRANDON, BARBARA H.
BROWN, EILEEN DONNELLY
BROWN, JUDITH A.
CAMERON, FRANCIS X.
CAMILLO, WILLIAM MICHAEL
CAMPBELL, THOMAS
    LEAKE, JR.
CASHDOLLAR, J. LAUSON
CHIODO, MARY HELEN
COHEN, FELIX ASHER
CONNORS, THOMAS HENRY
CORBETT, JOHN HARRY, JR.
COULTER, WILLIAM KIRK

CRAYNE, LARRY RANDOLPH
CREIGHTON, MICHAEL JOHN
DERENZO, RICHARD CARMEN
EHRMAN, JAMES STRENG
EITEL, JOHN ALBERT, JR.
ERENSTEIN, JERRY HILLEL
FINGERET, JAY LEIBER
FLEEGER, DAVID WALTER
FREED, MICHAEL RICHARD
GENTILE, GARY GEORGE
GERHOLD, WAYNE DOUGLAS
GIBBONEY, ALLEN EUGENE
GILKES, ARTHUR GWYER, JR.
GLADSTONE, RICHARD
    WILTON
GLASS, L. EDWARD
GLAUBACH, PETER MICHAEL
GOLDBERG, JAMES KALMINE
GREEN, LAURENCE B.
HARPER, ROBERT BERKLEY
HARTUNG, ROBERT JOHN, JR.
HAVEY, JOHN ALAN
HOWARD, RAY SCOTT
JENISON, ROBERT JUDE
JOHNSON, WAYNE GUSTAVE
KAISERMAN, MARK S.
KALSON, HOWARD JOSEPH
KAPLAN, DAVID STEPHEN
KELLER, JOHN JOSEPH
KIME, ROY CALDWELL
KING, PAUL MARTIN
KINTER, LAWRENCE LLOYD
KOTJARAPOGLUS, GEORGE
    ANGELO
KRAYBILL, JOHN KENT
KUDZMA, JOHN HARVEY
LEADBETTER, BONNIE
    BRIGANCE
LEADBETTER, GARY
    RAYMOND
LEVENTON, PAUL JAY
LINDSAY, ALEXANDER
    HEILMAN, JR.
LINN, JOSEPH WELSH
MARKOVITZ, ROBERT S.
McNAMARA, DANIEL LEO
MENDELSON, GILBERT ALAN
MERRITT, GILBERT STANLEY, JR.
MESSER, HOWARD F.
MIKESIC, NICHOLAS JOSEPH
MILLER, JOHN A.
MOSIER, CHESTER JOSEPH
NIEMI, FORREST WILLIAM
O'CONNOR, PHILIP PATRICK
PATRONO, ALAN KIM
PONTON, ROBERT DARRYL

PORT, WAYNE HOWARD
PURCELL, JEROME JAMES
RACUNAS, ROBERT VINCENT
RICHARDS, MARTHA EMMA
ROBERTS, LEE HAROLD
ROE, GORDON ADAMS
SARTORIS, JOSEPH ANTHONY
SCHEIMER, ALAN JEFFREY
SEIF, JAMES MICHAEL
SHILOBOD, DENNIS STEPHEN
SHOR, J. ELLIOT
SHOSTAK, ROBERT JOSEPH
SMITH, ROBERT BUCHMAN
STRASSBURGER, EDWIN J.
STURGEON, GREGORY W.
TAAFFE, GEORGE ANDRESS, JR.
TEACHER, PAUL THOMAS
THOMAS, JAMES, JR.
THOMPSON, JOHN WILSON, JR.
TRIMM, THOMAS W.
TROY, BERNARD EMERY
TYSON, CHARLES CLINTON
VASILIADIS, CONSTANTINE M.
VILLANOVA, JAMES ARTHUR
VITARO, SAMUEL ALFREDO
WANETIK, LEONARD IRE
WATKINS, NORMAN JOHN
WHITTINGTON, THOMAS
    DAVID, JR.
WILSON, ARTHUR GARY
WILSON, JOHN WAKEFIELD
WOLLETT, WILLIAM RALPH
WRIGHT, ROGER ELLERTON
YURCHESHEN, MICHAEL J.

— Class of —
1972

ADAMS, JAMES DREW
ALFORD, JOHN GRANT
ALMASY, KURT DAVID
AUSSENBERG, MARTIN
BAHL, DAVID RAYMOND
BALTER, ROBERT SIMON
BATSON, ARTHUR GLYNN
BEGLEY, ROBERT JAMES
BENNETT, WILLIAM REED
BIERBACH, CHARLES ALAN
BOAS, PAUL DAVID
BRESNAHAN, MICHAEL
    JOSEPH
BURKE, THOMAS MICHAEL
BURNS, MICHAEL WILLIAM
BUSH, JAMES WILSON
CAVANAUGH, TERRY
    CHARLES

— 253 —

CEFOLA, RICHARD ANTHONY
CHERELLIA, PETER PAUL
CHESIN, RONALD M.
CLEMENTS, FRANK JAMES
COCHERES, LOUIS GABRIEL
COLE, JAMES BROOKE
COOK, MICHAEL
	WELLINGTON
CRAWFORD, JAMES LOWRIE
CROSBY, JUDD F.
CULLEN, JAMES DONALD
CURRY, PETER JAMES
CYPHERS, JOSEPH ALBERT
DAVIS, STANFORD GERALD
DeJULIO, LEONARD ANTHONY
DELUZIO, VINCENT CHARLES
DICKEY, WILLIAM HUGUS, JR.
DILORETO, DENIS MICHAEL
DREELAND, ALLAN EDWARD
ECHARD, ALEXANDER
	EDWARD
ENGLISH, JAMES HARRY
ERB, W. PETER
FLINT, ROBERT L.
FRIEDMAN, JOSEPH
FRIEDMAN, SHELLEY
GARODNICK, FRED DAVID
GILTENBOTH, JEFFREY LLOYD
GOLDBECK, JOSEPH
	ANTHONY, JR.
GORDON, JAMES RICHARDSON
HALLER, LEON P.
HAMILTON, WESLEY FREDERICK
HANDLER, MICHAEL
HARHUT, CHESTER T.
HARNER, JANET GAIL
HAUSHALTER, WILLIAM REGIS
HEINEY, GEORGE GARY
HEMMINGS, JANE REBECCA
HENDERSON, SCOTT
	EDWARD
HERGENROEDER, CHARLES
	WILLIAM
HERROD, DAVID JARRET
HORVAT, HENRY MARTIN
HOYE, JOHN RAYMOND, JR.
HUDSON, WILLIAM LEE, JR.
HYMAN, MARSHAL JAY
ISAAC, ANN MORRIS
JARGIELLO, THOMAS
	RAYMOND
JEFFREY, JOHN WILLIAM
JOHN, FREDERICK LUDWIG, II
JOHNS, CLIFFORD ALLEN, JR.
JUNG, BERNARD MICHAEL
KALMEYER, GARY HAROLD

KAUFFMAN, WILLIAM RAY
KELSON, RICHARD BARRY
KEPPLE, GEORGE REA
KIGER, JEROME WILLIAM
KILGORE, FRED E.
KING, ROBERT A.
KISCADEN, LEO MICHAEL
KLEIN, DANIEL LOUIS
KLIMESZ, MARIE EVELYN
KNIGHT, JOHN HENRY
KOERBER, DWIGHT LEWIS, JR.
KRINER, WILLIAM CURTIS
LAUVER, EARL EUGENE
LEDERMAN, STANLEY BRUCE
LENNIG, EDWARD NICHOLAS, III
LERACH, RICHARD HARWOOD
LEVINE, MAX ALLEN
LEVINE, SANDRA BECK
LEWIS, JON MARK
LINDQUIST, THOMAS ELLIOT
LINEBAUGH, STEPHEN
	PATRICK
LONGO, ROBERT ANTHONY
LUBIN, NORMAN MARTIN
MacMILLAN, TIMOTHY
	BERNARD
MASON, EDWARD FRANCIS
MARNEN, JAMES
McADOO, GARLAND HENRY, JR.
McAULEY, DAVID
McFADDEN, R. LEE
McNALLY, MARK KEATING
MEDWICK, GEORGE MICHAEL
MICHAELIS, KENNETH LEE
MILLER, CLYDE GEORGE
MILLER, TED GRANT
MOLLICA, JAMES ANTHONY
MORRIS, FRANKLIN DAVID
MOUNTZ, DAVID THOMAS
MULVIHILL, DENNIS ST. JOHN
MURPHY, ARTHUR JOSEPH, JR.
NYDES, LARRY BRUCE
OLIVER, PERSIFOR SMITH, JR.
O'MALLEY, RUSSELL JAMES
OMBRES, RICHARD SAMUEL
PAGANO, CARMEN VINCENT
PANDORA, FRANK T., II
PAUL, SYDNEY WILSON
PIETRAGALLO, WILLIAM A.
PINNEY, PETER R.
PORTER, RUSSELL WILLIAM, JR.
PORTERFIELD, JAMES D.
POSNER, DAVID SMITH
POTTER, ROBERT LINCOLN
REVAK, LESLIE DENNIS
ROANTREE, THOMAS CHARLES

ROSE, RONALD BLANE
ROTHMAN, LEE GARY
SABOL, GERALDINE
	GEORGEANNA
SCAFETTA, JOSEPH, JR.
SCHAPIRA, JEFFREY ALAN
SCHMIDT, EDWARD CRAIG
SHAFFER, PETER HENRY
SIMON, STEVEN PAUL
SIMPSON, BARRY MICHAEL
SIMPSON, LESTER
	ALEXANDER, JR.
SMITH, DORIS A.
SOKOLOW, BARRY B.
SPRY, DONALD FRANCIS, II
STEBBINS, GEORGE
	LAMBERTON
STEFANIK, DENNIS JOHN
STRAPAC, PAUL A.
STROUD, D. MICHAEL
STROYD, ARTHUR HEISTER, JR.
SZAFRAN, JAMES JOSEPH
SZUCH, PAUL ANDREW
TECKLENBURG, JOHN
	CHRISTIAN, II
THOMPSON, LEWIS LEROY, JR.
TOMB, MYRON HAY
TOOLE, DANIEL ALBERT
UPSON, DIANNE MATTHEWS
WAGNER, JOHN FREDERICK, JR.
WALSH, ROBERT LOUIS
WECHSLER, BENJAMIN
	BERNARD, II
WHITEHILL, ROBERT STUART
WIGGINS, THEODORE EDWARD
WOZNEY, GEOFFREY PAUL
YELLIG, TERRY RUSSELL
YOUNG, PETER SEATON
ZRUST, FRANK JOSEPH
ZUZIK, DENIS PHILLIP

— Class of —
1973

ALM, STEVEN WILLIAM
ANANIA, FRANCIS ANTHONY
ANDERSON, ERIC NORTH
ANDERSON, JOHN RICHARD
ANDERSON, JUDITH LOREN
ANDREWS, WILLIAM CHARLES
ANTIS, MARC DAVID
ARON, PETER
AUSTIN, ROBERT DALE
BABST, CHESTER ROWLAND, III
BAKER, TOMMY
BALLA, G. ALAN

BARGERSTOCK, CHARLES THOMAS
BECK, DAVID LEE
BEGLEY, WILLIAM JAMES
BENEDICT, THOMAS SAMUEL
BLUM, JEFFREY S.
BODEK, MILTON ALAN
BOGATY, RAYMOND HARRY
BONYA, JOHN A.
BOOCOCK, STEPHEN WILLIAM
BOSICK, JOSEPH JOHN
BOWEN, PAUL HENRY, JR.
BRANCA, THOMAS C.
BROOKS, HOWARD D.
BROWN, BURRELL ALFORD
BUKAC, JAMES EDWARD
BUNSON, ALEXANDER B.
BURKE, LINDA BEERBOWER
BURKE, TIMOTHY FRANCIS
BURR, KEITH J.
CASCIO, JOHN MATTEO
CAULEY, MICHAEL A.
CHALNICK, LEONARD PAUL
CHARLSON, ALAN EDWARD
CHERVENAK, MICHAEL PHILIP
CHILDS, WADE DOUGLAS
CHRISTIANSEN, MICHAEL ERIC
CHRISTIANSON, ROBERT ANDREW
CHRISTIANSON, SANDRA SCHARDING
CLAUS, LAWRENCE NEFF
CLEMENTS, BARBARA
COHEN, MELVIN CHARLES
COHN, STEVEN LAWRENCE
CONRAD, RALPH D., III
COOPER, CLIFFORD C.
COOPER, PAUL RONALD
COSTANZO, AUGUST JAMES
CREMEN, FRANK J.
CROTHERS, ROBERT TOVELL
CUNNINGHAM, ROGER STATON
CURRY, PAUL FRANKLIN
CZELEN, JOHN C.
DeCOMO, PATRIC JOSEPH
DeHAAS, ERNEST PREECE, III
DeMARCO, MICHAEL DAVID
DiRENZO, JOHN JOSEPH, JR.
DOLFI, GLENN DOUGLAS
DONALDSON, DAVID MICHAEL
DOREZAS, JERRY MICHAEL
DUFFY, JAMES MICHAEL
EDWARDS, TREVOR

ELOVITZ, SHELLEY W.
ESTOCK, HOWARD GORDON
FALTENOVICH, RICHARD ANDREW
FELLHEIMER, ROBERT MAYER
FOLTZ, JOSEPH WADE
FORSYTHE, LYNN MAUREEN
FRAMPTON, THOMAS THORNE
GAZZA, BEVERLY ANNETTE
GELMAN, I. LAWRENCE
GELNETTE, JEFFREY ALTON
GENTRY, EDWARD F., III
GEORGALAS, JAMES G.
GILBERT, ALAN RICHARD
GILTENBOTH, JUDITH KLASWICK
GRAUL, PLIMPTON LEECH
GRAY, WILLIAM ALBERT
GREGG, WALTER EMMOR, JR.
HAGG, KATHERINE LOUISE
HAGGERTY, JOSEPH KEVIN
HALLER, DANIEL LEE
HELD, ERIC J.
HELLER, MERVIN A., JR.
HELZLSOUER, WILLIAM JAMES
HERSH, CHARLES SYLVAN
HOROVITZ, ARNOLD MARTIN
HUDZIK, JAMES BERNARD
HUTZLER, JOHN L.
ISACKE, ROBERT NELSON
ISACKES, PAMELA M.
IURLANO, JOHN P.
JAMES, JOSEPH M.
JOHNSON, ROBERT L.
JONES, HERBERT LAWRENCE
JORDAN, JOHN WESLEY, IV
JURCIC, JAMES THOMAS
KALMEYER, BRIDGIT
KALYVAS, JAMES THOMAS
KING, MICHAEL JOSEPH
KISSANE, DENNIS PAUL
KITT, JONATHAN MICHAEL
KLADITIS, NICHOLAS STEVEN
KLEMEYER, JOHN HENRY
KOHL, CHRISTINE NOEL
KOVACH, RICHARD ALBERT
KRANSON, MARC
KUHNS, DAVID LINDLEY
LADOV, EDWARD DONALD
LaMANNA, EUGENE CHARLES
LANDIS, RICHARD MARK
LATSKO, JOHN MATUSCAK
LEMME, CHARLES DAVENA
LESTITIAN, JAMES JOSEPH
LEWIS, KENNETH EDWARD

LICHTENSTEIN, ROBERT JAY
LILLY, THOMAS MORE
LITTLE, WALTER RICHARD
LOCKWOOD, WILLARD KELLY
LUDWIG, GILBERT HAGGERTY
MABON, JAMES MONROE, JR.
MAGAR, KENNETH ANTHONY
MALAKOFF, LOUISE REIBER
MANGOLD, NEAL DONALD, JR.
MARTI, JON P.
MATTHEWS, ROGER S.
MATWICZYK, PETER
McCORMICK, JAMES FRANCIS
McCORMICK, PETER JEROME
McDOWELL, MICHAEL DAVID
McENERY, JOHN FRANCIS
McGINLEY, MICHAEL PATRICK
McKENNA, JAMES FRANCIS
McQUOID, EDWARD ARTHUR, JR.
MEARS, SCOTT OLLETT
MERUSI, JOYCE THERESA
MILLER, GLENN M.
MILLER, JAMES ALAN
MILLER, JOSEPH McCORD
MILLER, KENNETH RICHARD
MILLER, RANDALL BRUCE
MILLER, THOMAS JAY
MONTAGUE, ROBERT TAYLOR, JR.
MORRISON, DAVID RITTENHOUSE
MOSS, DARIUS G. C.
NASUTI, JAMES FRANCIS
NEFF, RICHARD L.
NOVAK, RAYMOND A.
OBER, RUSSELL JOHN, JR.
OBLICH, DAVID
O'DONNELL, JOHN M.
OGDEN, W. EDWIN
O'LOUGHLIN, JOHANNA G.
PERFILIO, ANTHONY JOHN
PLATTER, LAWRENCE
POTTER, CHARLES L., JR.
QUICK, ROBERT JACKSON
RAWSON, RICHARD LAYTON
RERKO, FREDERICK JOHN
RIAL, ELIZABETH LOWRY
RIDDLE, FRANK RANDOLPH
RIZZO, SAMUEL FRANCIS
RODGERS, LINDA RICE
ROSE, ANDREW
ROSEN, LAWRENCE JEFFREY
ROSENWASSER, MARC RICHARD
ROSS, BERT ALAN

RUBIN, JAY YALE
RUNDORFF, WILLIAM J., JR.
SCHILDNECHT, C. WILLIAM
SCHMIDT, WILLIAM MICHAEL
SCOTT, HARRY WESTLEY
SEGAL, EARL LESLIE
SENICK, MICHAEL RICHARD
SHELAPINSKY, PHILIP N.
SILVERMAN, GARY PAUL
SIMON, ROGER MICHAEL
SKIBA, GARY VINCENT
SMITH, JOHN RENNIS
SMITH, PETER A.
SAIDER, TIMOTHY JAN
SOLOMICH, THOMAS
    RICHARD
SOLOMON, JACK ERWIN
SPISAK, KENNETH JOHN
SPRENKLE, STEPHEN
    DOUGLAS
STEIN, GREGORY ALAN
STEINER, JACK JULIUS
STREIFF, CHARLES JAMES
STUDENY, JOHN MICHAEL
STUMP, HARRY HOWARD, II
SULLIVAN, RODERICK
    PHILLIP, JR.
TANSKY, EVA
TERRINONI, VAUGHN
    ANTHONY
TROGLIO, PETER FELIX
TUITE, JAMES REGIS
TUPLIN, FRANK PRESTON
TURNER, THOMAS MITCHELL
UNKOVIC, DENNIS
VALENTINE, WILLIAM
    EDWARD
VETICA, JOHN PAUL, JR.
WADE, CHARLES F.
WALLACH, S. HOWARD
WELDON, DARLA J. COVELL
WHALEN, KENNETH CHARLES
WIEGAND, BRUCE
WINTER, BRUCE EDMUND
WISE, ROGER L.
WITCHKO, RICHARD KEITH
YATES, ALFRED GLENN, JR.
ZALESKI, CHARLES EDWARD
ZEMAN, DAVID WILLIAM
ZERA, RONALD JOSEPH
ZOMNIR, RICHARD MICHAEL

— Class of —
1974

ACHMAN, ANDREW JOHN
ALLMAN, ROBERT LEE, II
ALSTON, ROBERT A.
ALVIN, LOUIS CHRISTOPHER
ANDREWS, LINDA SHARON
ANTHES, JOHN ALLEN, JR.
AYERS, WALTER N.
BANKERT JOSEPH EDWARD
BASINSKI, ANTHONY JOSEPH
BERGER, SHELDON PHILLIP
BERLIN, MICHAEL DAVID
BERMAN, DIANE LOUISE
BOUFFARD, ALAN JOSEPH
BOULD, SHELLEY ANNE
BRATIC, ALEXANDER
BRYSH, PAUL JOHN
CAIN, JOSEPH DUANE
CAMPBELL, LOUDON L.
CASSIDY, MARY SHARON
CASSIDY, PATRICK S.
CLARK, RICHARD ALLYN
COGAN, DANIEL E.
COHEN, EARL S.
COHEN, FREDERICK M.
CONNELL, PATRICIA
CRITTENDEN, CLAIRE R.
CROWE, JOHN C.
CUSICK, CHARLES STEPHEN, JR.
DAGUE, LAURENCE WILLIAM
DALCANTON, CAROL L.
DEAN, VERDELL
DEELEY, JAMES PATRICK
DODSON, F. BRIAN
DONAHUE, JOHN
    CHRISTOPHER
EBERT, FREDERICK CLARK
ERTESCHIK, LOUIS
ESARY, GARY S.
FIELDS, PARTHENIA ELAINE
FLINN, MICHAEL JAMES
FRANCALANCIA, NICK
FRANK, MARK STEPHEN
FRICK, DENNIS DUANE
GALLAGHER, ALAN L.
GREEN, STEPHEN ROSS
GUFFET, WILLIAM BUTLER, JR.
HARPER, ROBERT E.
HARPER, THOMAS J.
HARTMAN, DAVID RICHARD
HARTWIG, ELIZABETH ANN
HEMMINGS, RICHARD
    ANDREW
HENRY, DEBORAH J.

HOGUE, JON GEOFFREY
HORTON, ROSS GARRETT
HUCKESTEIN, THEODORE F., JR.
HUNT, JOYCE FRY
HYMAN, LEWIS N.
JACKSON, MATTHEW
    EDWARD, JR.
JAFFE, JOSEPH ALLEN
JORDAN, JAMES V.
KADUNCE, DARRELL LEE
KALUZA, MICHAEL EDWARD
KASENTER, ROBERT ALBERT
KEARNEY, MICHAEL JOSEPH, JR.
KENNEDY, JAMES E.
KIEFER, WILLIAM R.
KNUTSON, CAROL K.
KRAWITZ, MICHAEL F.
KUHN, JAMES C., III
LAMPL, ROBERT O.
LANCASTER, GARY LEE
LASKOW, MARK J.
LAWLOR, J. GARY
LEVINE, STANLEY E.
LUCCHINI, ALLAN CHARLES
LUTZ, THOMAS PHILIP
LYONS, THOMAS J.
MacLEOD, ALAN EDWARD
MAHON, MORGAN BARTLEY
MAHOOD, JAMES EDWARD
MARTIN, ANTHONY GEORGE
McCORMICK, J. MICHAEL
McMILLAN, RICHARD
    LAMONT
McVEY, DAVID ALLEN
MESSINA, JOSEPH DANIEL
MILLER, LESLIE DAVID
MUSCATELLO, BRUNO A.
O'BRIEN, JOSEPH J.
O'CONNELL, JAMES P.
OBRECHT, JOHN LOBB
PARKER, ROSS GAIL
OAYNE, JESTYN GYLDAS
PEPPER, RICHARD
    HUNTINGTON
POHLAND, DAVID C.
PRISELAC, DAVID M.
RAFFERTY, DENNIS B.
REED, MARY CATHERINE
    SKOOG
REED, THOMAS C.
REITER, DENNIS O.
RICHEY, PAUL JEROME
ROSENBAUM, SUSAN PAT
RUSINAK, RONALD PETER
RUSSELL, RICHARD JOSEPH
SABLOWSKY, STEVEN LARRY

SCHALL, JAMES M.
SCHLOTTER, CHARLES JOHN
SCHREIBMAN, TED MICHAEL
SEETHALER, ANTHONY
    ANDREW, JR.
SEFTON, KEITH THOMAS
SHILLIDAY, JAMES MYLES
SIEGEL, DAVID PAUL
SLONE, ROBERT HENRY
SMADES, IRA
SMITH, CHARLES RAYMOND, JR.
SNODGRASS, TIMOTHY JAMES
SPILLAS, KENNETH GEORGE
STANTON, DOUGLAS READ
STATON, WILLIAM GARRETT
STRAUSS, EDWARD K.
SULLIVAN, ARTHUR BERNARD
VALASEK, KENNETH GEORGE
VEENIS, AUDREY FULCOMER
WEISS, EDWARD PAUL
WHATLEY, ARTHUR LEE
WICKSTROM, MICHELE
    HOREW
WILSON, LINDA SUE
WOOD, JAMES ARTHUR
WOODS, ARLENE JOHNSON
WOODSKE, BRUCE E.
WORSTELL, DAVID L.
YOUNG, JAMES W., JR.
ZEGLIN, DONALD E.

— Class of —
1975

ABRAMS, IVAN SAFYAN
ANDERSON, JANICE
    HARTMAN
BABB, W. MICHAEL
BARRETT, JEANNIE
    ANTOINETTE
BAUGHMAN, MICHAEL
    JOSEPH
BEMILLER, JAMES BERNARD, JR.
BELLIVEAU, JAMES DENNIS
BENSON, STUART WELLS, III
BERGER, CYNTHIA CURRENS
BERTSCH, GENE CLAIR
BLANAR, ANDREW CHARLES
BORING, KIRBY LEE
BOSCHINI, PETER CARLO
BUCHWACH, MICHAEL DAVID
CAFARDI, NICHOLAS PATRICK
CARRA, RICHARD
CASCIO, JAMES RILL
COMAY, DEBORAH E.
COMAY, ESTELLE FISHER

CONWAY, NEIL L., JR.
COUGHENOUR, BRIAN PAUL
CRAIG, CHERYL ALLEN
DAS, EVA BORSODY
DASHOFF, ALAN DAVID
DeWITT, CHARLES BRADY
DONAHOE, THOMAS PATRICK
DUGAS, STEPHEN
DURRANT, ROBERT EDWIN
EICHLEAY, JOHN WILLIAM, JR.
EPSTEIN, JAMES PETER
EVANS, SUZY
FABIAN, GARY ARTHUR
FELDMAN, JOAN PHYLLIS
FLAHERTY, ROBERT DAVID
GAINOR, CARL
GARRIS, CHARLES EDGAR
GEARY, TIMOTHY JOEL
GLASSER, PHILIP RUSSELL
GOLDHAMMER, FLORIE
    BRETTLER
GRAUER, MYRON C.
GREENE, DOUGLAS T.
GRUBOR, JOHN MARTIN
HAMILL, RAYMOND LLOYD
HANSEN, KEVIN CARL
HART, JOHN KANE
HARTLINE, JAMES RALPH
HARTMAN, RONALD GEORGE
HEINTZ, FREDERICK WILLIAM
HEINTZMAN, MICHAEL DAVID
HENNESSY, TIMOTHY PATRICK
HERSH, JEFFREY MARTIN
HOLLAND, FLORENCE MAE
HRUSKA, MARK ALLEN
HUGHES, MICHAEL DAVID
JACKSON, FRANK ANDERSON
JONES, ALBERT JAMES
JONES, FLOYD PAUL
JONES, GREGORY ADAMS
JUDSON, KENNETH
    GALLAGHER
JUNKER, THOMAS MORSE
KASENTER, KENNETH ALBERT
KATZ, JONATHAN GARBER
KEFALOS, GEORGE JOHN
KELLER, CHARLES WHITESELL
KEMP, KENNETH LAWRENCE
KENNEDY, MARK WILLIAM
KING, DAVID PETER
KLAVONIC, LEONARD P..
KNAPP, WILLIAM CHRISTIAN
KORULAK, RICHARD
    MICHAEL
KOZLOFF, DAVID BRUCE
KRASNOW, RONALD S.

KREY, JOAN FRIEDMAN
KUSHNER, PHILLIP JAY
LEE, JOHN A.
LEEPER, CHARLES SAMUEL
LITTLE, FRANK EDWARD
LUNN, ROBIN REED
MANN, A. KENNETH
MANSELL, CHARLES YOUNG
MARCUCCI, DONALD ROY
MARTIN, THOMAS FRANCIS
MATLOWSKI, NANCY KISHEL
MATLOWSKI, PETER EDWARD
MATTERN, HARRY PAUL
McANENY, JAMES LEO
McCRORY, MARY JOAN
McCUE, JOHN FRANCIS
MEGNIN, DAVID FREDERICK
MEISTER, FREDERICK
    WILLIAM
METOSKY, SANDRA
    ROSECRANS
METZ, LEROY LAWRENCE, II
MURDOCH, DAVID ALAN
MURPHY, TERRANCE
    HERRINGTON
NEWBORG, JOHN DAVID
NEYLAND, KEITH WALLACE
OTTO, GREGG PETER
PANNETON, JOHN PAUL
PASKOFF, STEPHEN M.
PERSKY, JOEL IRA
POHL, PAUL MICHAEL
POOLEY, THOMAS JOSEPH
PRICE, JOHN LLEWELLYN, JR.
PURVIANCE, EDWIN MERRILL
QUIGLEY, MICHAEL
    NEEDHAM
REED, DOUGLAS WAYNE
REINHARTSEN, LAURENCE JOE
ROGAL, ANDREW LAWRENCE
ROME, ERIC CHARLES
ROSS, CHARLES GRIFFITH
SABLE, KENNETH LEE
SAMUELSON, WAYNE PAUL
SCHMIDT, GORDON WILLIAMS
SCHROEDER, NORMAN JAMES
SCRABIS, RICHARD JOSEPH
SHAFFNER, WILLIAM G.
SHANE, ILENE W.
SHEEHAN, CYNTHIA ALICE
SIEGEL, RUTH MARJORIE
SILVESTRI, JOHN M.
SIMPSON, REXFORD CHARLES
SMITH, EDGAR ACTON
SMITH, RICHARD FREDERICK
SPANGLER, JOHN HOLLEY

STANTON, THOMAS
STAUDENMAIER, RICHARD
    ERNEST
STERN, SHARON G.
STETS, JOHN ALBERT
STUBNA, MICHAEL
    THEORDORE
TAYLOR, LORRAINE DARLENE
TOLHURST, FREDERICK LOUIS
TRAVALIO, GREGORY
    MICHAEL
VADNAL, MATTHEW LEE
VATER, CHARLES J.
VERDUCI, ALEXANDER
    COSMO
VOLLMER, CHARLES JOSEPH
WADEM, JACK, JR.
WEBER, E. MICHAEL
WEIN, HOWARD JAY
WENNICK, GEORGE DARYL
WERFEL, GERALD HOWARD
WOLAK, MICHAEL
    ALEXANDER, III
WOLF, BRUCE MARTIN
WOODS, AARON, III
WRIGHT, NEIL DENNIS
WYNN, CRAIG EDWARD
YANG, WESLEY
YOST, MICHAEL ANDREW, JR.
YOUNG, DAVID LORRAINE

— Class of —
1976

AGRESTI, THOMAS P.
ALEX, HOWARD M.
ALEXANDER LEE A.
ALLISON, WILLIAM T., JR.
ALLSHOUSE, DAVID H.
ALSTADT, LYNN JEFFREY
ANNELIN, JAMES SCOTT
AYRES, JOHN ALLEN, JR.
BACKER, RONALD GEORGE
BANOS, ROBERT P.
BASH, ROSS SEANOR
BAUMGARDNER, RICHARD
    JAMES
BENJAMIN, MICHAEL DAMIEN
BLAHOVEC, JOHN EDWARD
BROWN, RONALD JAMES
BURIANEK, FRANCIS PAUL
CAMPBELL, ROBERT PAUL
CAMPBELL, WILLIAM HOWARD
COHEN, DAVID IAN
COOK, VIRGINIA IRENE
DEMPSTER, MICHAEL JOHN

DePAUL, LOUIS ANTHONY
DINEEN, JOHN WILLIAM
DODD, ROGER JAMES
DOUGHERTY, FRANCIS
    MICHAEL
EDMINDSON, ROBERT CLAUDE
ENGELHARDT, BRIAN C.
ENGLAND, THOMAS FRANK
FARRELL, CHRISTOPHER
    FRANCIS
FASULO, DAVID JOSEPH
FAZEKAS, ERNEST F., II
FITZSIMMONS, JAMES N., JR.
FLOWER, DAVID JEFFREY
GASKIN, MARY JANE
GEER, THOMAS LEE
GENTILE, ROBERT NICHOLAS
GERHOLD, CATHERINE CLARK
GRAHAM, THOMAS JEFFREY
GRASBERGER, JOHN EDWARD
HEBEN, LAWRENCE WAYNE
HEPTING, DAVID ALAN
HILL, FRANK FULTON, JR.
HOGUE, LINDA HADDAD
HUBER, JOSEPH WILLIAM
HUGHEY, MICHAEL KEVIN
HUNT, GARY PATRICK
JACKSON, GERARD JOSEPH
JOHNSTON, JEFFREY MARTIN
JONES, CRAIG WARD
KALINOSKI, EILEEN RIORDAN
KELLY, MICHAEL JOSEPH
KENDALL, WILLIAM R.
KESSLER, STEVEN FISHER
KOTLER, HELEN R.
KRUPER, PAUL DAVID
MARICONDI, CAROLYN WOOD
McCONNELL, MARY ANN
MERKAMP, PATTY ELLEN
MILLER, PATRICIA GOYETTE
MISTICK, D. THOMAS
MLINAC, STEPHEN RICHARD
MOSER, MELVIN L.
NASH, STEPHEN PAYN
NELSON, LARRY N.
NEUHART, DAVID MICHAEL
O'NEIL, SHARON MARIE
OLDS, EDWARD ANDREW
PALMQUIST, ROBERT FRED
PERER, ALAN H.
PERER, DIANE LEE
PETRO, SUSAN
PETTRONE, GEORGE JOSEPH
POLAND, PETER JAMES
PORT, LARRY NEIL
QUINN, JOHN M.

REGEN, MARK JONATHAN
ROCHFORD, REBECCA
    STUART
RODGERS, WILLIAM, JR.
ROSEN, NEIL R.
RUBENFIELD, ALLEN JAY
RULONG, ROGER G., JR.
SABLE, MICHAEL HARRY
SAUL, WILLIAM ROSS
SCHULTZ, ROBERT FRANCIS
SCHWEIGHARDT, THOMAS
SESTAK, REGINA MARIE
SHEARER, HARRY JACK
SIKORSKY, JOSEPH EDWARD
SINCLAIR, HOWARD KNOX, I!
SMALES, SANDRA LEE
STATON, LYNELL NUNN
STEMBER, JOHN EDWARD
STEVERMAN, BENJAMIN W., JR.
TABAKIN, LORRAINE SMITH
TORIE, CHARLES CARLETON
VALENTINE, GEORGE HENRY
VATER, JOSEPH ADAM, JR.
VENDER, JOSEPH LOUIS
WALLACE, DONALD ALAN
WEINBERG, LEE SNYDER
WERT, JAMES NORMAN
WILKISON, ROBERT PAUL
WINKLER, RICHARD
WOOD, ANN BELL
XIDES, ROBERT GUST

— Class of —
1977

AFRAME, CARL D.
ALLMENDINGER, JAMES
    FRANK
ANDERSON, PATRICIA JANE
ANGEL, MARGARET BICKEL
APPELBE, TIMOTHY DANIEL
ARNOLD, JEANNINE TURGEON
AUGUST, JERALD DAVID
AYERS, MINEKO SASAHARA
AYERS, PHILIP ASHLEY
BANKENSTEIN, BRUCE
    CALDER
BELINKY, MARK ALLEN
BEOZZO, SYLVESTER A.
BETZ, KARL WILLIAM
BLACKMUND, BARBARA ANN
BOBBY, THEODORE NICHOLAS
BOYLE, THOMAS EDWARD
BRAUNSTEIN, JONI BETH
BRAVERMAN, BEVERLY ANN
BRIDGES, JAMES STEEL

— 258 —

BROWN, DAVID McCRAY
BROWN, EDWARD GEORGE
BUSH, LUCINDA ANN
BYER, ROBERT LEWIS
CANCILLA, MARK PHILIP
CANNON, DAVID CYRIL, JR.
CANNON, DENNIS
  NATHANIEL, JR.
CAPUTO, LOUIS EUGENE
CARLAND, TIMOTHY M.
CARR, LOUIS J., JR.
CASSIDY, MICHAEL ALLEN
CHESNIK, RICHARD A.
CHOMAS, JAMES LOUIS, JR.
CLAAR, BENJAMIN
  HARRISON, JR.
COOPER, JOHN EDWIN
CORDTS, APRIL LYNN
CORSETTI, ROSEMARY
  LORRAINE
COX, ALLAN M.
CRISS, MARK A.
CROMER, ROBERT JOHN
CUNNINGHAM, DONALD
  MARK
CURRAN, M. SCOTT
CURRY, KAY O.
DEWALT, JOHN W.
DICKINSON, Q. TODD
DIEHL, JAMES PRESTON
DiMARTINI, DENNIS MICHAEL
DONEY, WILLIAM PATRICK
DOYLE, DON BARTON
DURIGON, ALBERT PETER
EDGECOMBE, RICHARD
  ALLISON
EISMONT, DIANE SHUTT
EMERY, STEPHEN, JR.
ENTWISLE, ELIZABETH
  BRADBURY
EPSTEIN, IRENE R.
EVAN, GEORGE MICHAEL
FALLER, FREDERICK BRICE, JR.
FELLENBAUM, NEAL
FERGUSON, DAVID S.
FRIEDENBERG, JAY SAUL
FULTON, WILLIAM JOHN
GALIE, LAWRENCE P.
GALLAGHER, DAVID C.
GASPER, WILLIAM CHARLES, JR.
GEARHART, RICHARD
  DENNING
GERJUOY, EDWARD
GILBERT, DOUGLAS EDWARD
GORDON, JAMES GERARD
GORDON, MARK

GREENFIELD, JAMES MILTON
GREGOR, JAMES PAUL
GREIF, ARTHUR JOHN
GRONINGER, JOHN EDGAR, JR.
GUARRIERI, FRANK SAMUEL
HAINES, DENNIS J.
HARMUTH, JOHN CARLISLE
HAYS, PATRICIA CARSON
HAYS, THOMAS ROBERT
HELWIG, DAVID PARKER
HENDERSON, THOMAS JOHN
HENKE, THEODORE ROBERT
HENKEL, WILLIAM F.
HEPTING, JANE FAY LARRICK
HOUSER, HAROLD NEIL
HUDOCK, MICHAEL THOMAS
ISLER, JEROME
JACKSON, PAUL REUBEN
JONES, DENNIS WILLIAM
JONES, LINDA HEISERMAN
KABLACK, WAYNE ANDREW
KACZYNSKI, WILLIAM
  CHARLES
KENNEDY, RICHARD THOMAS
KLOTZBAUGH, GEORGE
  ROBERT
KOCHERZAT, STEVEN
KRUK, GREGORY MICHAEL
KUBINSKI, THOMAS STEPHEN
KUBRICK, KENNETH W.
LANDMAN, WILLIAM ALAN
LEVICOFF, AVRUM
LEWIS, CLAUDE JAMES
LEWIS, ROBERT W., JR.
LIGHTBURN, ROBERT
  CHARLES
LONG, CHRISTINE MATHEWS
LONG, DANIEL JOSEPH
LUBER, JOEL STUART
MAGONE, FRANK DAVID
MARTIN, WILLIAM GILMORE
MAY, THOMAS HERBERT
McFARLAND, EDWARD A.
McGARRITY, JAMES PATRICK
McGRANN, GEORGE EDWARD
McHUGH, MARILYN
  SCHUSTER
McKNIGHT, MARCUS
  ACHESON, III
McNALLY, REGIS JOHN
McTIERNAN, ROBERT L.
MECHLING, ROGER TRUMAN
MILLER, CHARLES
  FREDERICK, III
MYERS, MARLEE
O'HARA, CHARLES GABRIEL

OLSON, GREGORY ALLEN
OLSZEWSKI, EDMUND LUCIAN
PARKS, CHARLES GARFIELD, JR.
PATTI, DEBRA D.
PEELOR, PAMELA KAUFFMAN
PEREGO, CHARLES FRANK
PERFIDO, RUTH SPIRER
PFERDEHIRT, RONALD HARRY
PRETZ, LAURENCE DALE
PROROK, ROBERT FRANCIS
PROZZI, JAMES ANTHONY
PYLE, ANTONION DOUGLAS
QUINN, JOHN DAVID
RAFFA, MARK STEVEN
RAFTERY, LAWRENCE
  MICHAEL
RAIZMAN, DOROTHY
  LOWENTHAL
RAPHAEL, PHYLLIS
RAPPOPORT, LARRY JAY
REILLY, THOMAS E.
REMALEY, WILLIAM JAMES
REMSBERG, STEVEN ALLEN
ROSENZWEIG, MARTIN
  SAMUEL
SCHALL, MICHAEL AMES
SCHEINGROSS, ALEX
  BERNARD
SCHIFFMAN, RONI SHARON
SCHULTZ, ALEXANDER
SCHWARTZ, STEVEN GARY
SHEFFEY, TIMOTHY DAVID
SHILTS, RICHARD DEAN
SIEGEL, RONALD L.
SINGER, SUE FRIEDBERG
SLESNICK, DAVID JOEL
SMITH, LON B.
SMITH, TEMPLETON, JR.
SONOSKI, PAUL BERNARD, JR.
SPIEGEL, BETH ELLEN
SPIRO, LAURIE SUE
STELLATO, LOUIS EUGENE
STEMLER, DAVID McFARLAND
STEVENSON, WILLIAM
  BRADDOCK
STEWART, MICHAEL JOSEPH
STONER, CHARLES TIMOTHY
STRAUSS, STEVEN BRIAN
SUSKO, PAUL JOHN
SUSTERSICH, MERLE FRANK
SUTTON, RUSSEL V.
SYLVANUS, JOHN JAMES
THIEMAN, FREDERICK
  WARREN
THOMAS, JOHN MARK
VALETICH, STEPHANIE

VANDERMAN, KRIS A.
VITA, MARK WILLIAM
WALKER, JOEL MARTIN
WATSON, DENNIS
    ALEXANDER
WATTERSON, ALFRED V.
WEINRICH, DOUGLAS
    EDWARD
WEKSELMAN, WILLIAM
WOLKEN, DANIEL F.
WOOD, EDWARD BOSS
YINGLING, NATHANIEL D., JR.

— Class of —
1978

AARONSON, JOEL P.
AMBLER, THOMAS W.
ANDERS, JERROLD P.
ANTOUN, JAMES M.
ARMSTRONG, CATHY
ARNOLD, PAMELLA J.
AUSLANDER, AMY M.
BAK, BRAFFORD DLAIR
BANKS, WILLIENARD
BARKER, WILLIAM F.
BECK, CHRISTOPHER A.
BELL, PAUL A., II
BELLISARIO, DOMENIC A.
BELLISIMO, ELIZABETH L.
BERGSTEIN, STEVEN A.
BERGSTROM, ALAN L.
BERLIN, ANNE FEENEY
BILHEIMER, JOHN
BIRSIC, JAMES S.
BLEWETT, NANCY T.
BLOUGH, MARGARET D.
BRABENDER, RICHARD F., JR.
CAPRIO, CHRISTINE W.
CARDAS, MARIANNE
CASANO, WILLIAM C.
CATTANEO, ROBERT M.
CAVANAUGH, TERRANCE P.
CHAMBERLAIN, GEORGE K.
CICITTO, JOSEPH A.
COGNETTI, MARIA P.
COHEN, CARL A.
COHEN, ILENE D.
COHEN, PAUL E.
COLEMAN, PAULA W.
CULP, JAMES E.
CURTIS, LEE P.
DANNHAUSER, ROBERT
DEMBLOWSKI, DENIS A.
DILLON, BETTY A.
DISSEN, RICHARD

DIXON, JOSEPH J.
DORKO, JEFFREY
DULAC, DONALD T., JR.
DUNN, MAUREEN I.
EGLER, FREDERICK N., JR.
EHRMAN, PHILIP B.
ELBLING, HOWARD BURTON
ELLIOTT, CHARLES W.
ELLIOTT, THOMAS RICHARD
EVANS, JOHN K., III
FELDMAN, ARTHUR D.
FIESCHKO, JOSEPH E., JR.
FOA, PAMELA S.
FORNELIA, LEONARD
FRIEDEMAN, LAWRENCE K.
FRIEDMAN, PHILIP B.
GARRAUX, JAMES D.
GERMAN, ROBERT D.
GERMINARO, SAMUEL J.
GILCHRIST, RICHARD D.
GILLESPIE, TOMMIE L.
GINOZA, DONN
GISMONDI, JOHN P.
GLASSMITH, SCOTT D.
GOTTLIEB, JOANN
GRAMC, DANIEL F.
GRATER, PAUL T.
GUEHL, JOHANNA C.
GUNN, JOSEPH N.
GUNN, RAYMOND F.
HARPER, LEO C., JR.
HARVEY, WILLIAM T.
HELMS, ERNEST E.
HERB, JAMES M.
HILL, FREDERICK W.
HOLLIN, EDWARD J.
HOOVER, MICHAEL E.
HOWIE, IRENE E.
HUNTER, CHARLENE C.
HUNTER, JAMES
JEFFREY, ADRIENNE O.
JONES, KATHLEEN M.
JONES, WILLIAM A., JR.
JORDEN, WAYNE M.
JOY, MARGARET P.
KABLACH, PATRICIA
KAUFMAN, GEORGE B.
KELLY, CRAIG E.
KELLY, J. MICHAEL
KINCAID, JOHN A., JR.
KING, BRUCE C.
KORSMEYER, MARY D.
KOVACH, DENNIS
KRAYER, NICHOLAS H., III
KRONENWETTER, PATRICK
    JOHN

KUKITZ, GERALD A.
LAING, ANITA M.
LAMPL, DAVID W.
LANG, ROBERT H.
LAUBACH, EDWARD J., JR.
LEIBOWITZ, STANLEY H.
LEICHTY, LINDA C.
LENNOX, RICHARD S.
MAHFOOD, GEORGE
MAKOUS, DAVID N.
MARGOLIS, EZRA DAVID
MARKLEY, B. HELEN
MARSHALL, ANNE M.
MARTIN, CATHERINE T.
MARTIN, THOMAS C.
MAUTE, JUDITH L.
McCANDLESS, JOHN W.
McMULLEN, JOAN D.
McPOLAND, MICHAEL E.
MEANS, CHARLES M.
MEDVED, GEORGE
MENEILLY, BRAD A.
MERICLI, KEMAL A.
MILLER, R. JAMES
MOCNIAK, MICHAEL J.
MOON, RUSSELL F., JR.
MRKOBRAD, MILAN K.
MUDRICK, RICHARD C.
MULHOLLAND, DANIEL M., III
MYERS, EDWARD D.
NEELY, BRUCE
NEELY, JOHN J.
NELSON, GARY P.
NEUSTEIN, STEPHEN ALAN
NEWSTADT, HOWARD M.
NYCHIS, PETER G.
NYE, STANLEY T., JR.
OPSITNICK, ALLAN J.
PALMER, ALLEN L.
PAPAS, WILLIAM E.
PARKER, ANNE R.
PARKER, SUMNER L.
PELHAM, WILLIAM JAMES
POOLE, WILLIAM H., JR.
POVILAITIS, JOHN F.
PRESTIA, CLAYTON J.
QUARLES, DWIGHT
REVELL, MARY
RICHARD, SUSAN B.
RILEY, STEVEN E., JR.
ROCK, SALLY SPOTTS
RODGER, BRUCE E.
ROSEN, GREGG M.
ROSS, GARY E.
ROTHENBERGER, CARL E., JR.
RUTT, DAVID N.

RYDLE, REBECCA L.
SABADISH JOSEPH S.
SABOURIN, DENNIS H.
SALERNO, WILLIAM J.
SALVATORI, DOMINIC D.
SANTEE, DALE W.
SCHADEL, JAMES R.
SCHLUTZ, MARJORIE A.
SCIOSCIA, MARK
SERENE, DAVID C.
SHAKES, DAVID L.
SHELLY, CARL H.
SHUCOSKY, MICHAEL A.
SIMMONS, WILLIAM T.
SIMON, MICHAEL J.
SIMPSON, KATHRYN L.
SMITH, BRADLEY E.
SPATZ, HILARY A.
SPEAKS, DENISE D.
STABLER, STEPHEN J.
STECKLAIR, FRANCIS X.
STEIN, ARTHUR W.
STELMACH, MARK R.
STONER, OLIVIA H.
STRATTON, DAVID
STRAUB, CHRISTOPHER
SUKENIK, JEROME
SWIGART, SUZANNE N.
SZELIGO, VINCENT P.
TERRY, MICHELLE
TOMASSETTI, TERRENCE E.
TOY, MARGIE A.
VAN der VEER, HUGH G., III
VERES, JOSEPH A.
VIDELOCK, ERIK N.
VOGEL, ALBERT E., JR.
VREELAND, THOMAS O.
WALKER, JOHN L., JR.
WALLACE, S. JAMES
WARD, DAVID HERMAN
WATSON, ROBERT R.
WEISS, ARLENE R.
WHITE, STEPHEN L.
WITHEREL, MICHAEL JOSEPH
WOLF, STEVEN
WOLFF, CASEY
ZAHREN, THOMAS J.

— Class of —
1979

ABRAMS, NANCY BETH
ANDERSON, MARC ANDREW
BACH, PETER H.
BARRY, W. TIMOTHY
BAUMANN, THOMAS C.

BEARDSLEY, ALBERTA RAE
BEHREND, BERNHARD MORRIS
BENDER, GARY CARL
BENNETT, CHARLES
    FREDERICK, JR.
BIRSIC, THOMAS E.
BIRT, CECIL JEROME
BITTNER, LORRAINE M.
BLUMEN, KAREN L.
BOBINIS, CHARLES E.
BODNAR, JOHN ALEX
BOWES, MARY JANE
BOWMAN, SUSAN D.
BRAUN, HILARY WEDNER
BRAUTIGAM, DAVID C.
BREWER, CHRISTOPHER B.
BRNILOVICH, DAVID
BROZ, GEORGIA ANN
BRUMMER, GEORGE L.
BUI, HUY NHAT
BUTLER, MARIA M.
CHERVENAK, M. FRANCESCA
CHESTAK, KENNETH DEAN
CHRISTIN, STEPHEN LINK
CICOLA, DAVID A.
CLAIR, PATRICK J.
CLARK, PHILIP L.
COHEN, HARRY SAMUEL
CONTURO, MARY KATHERINE
CONWAY, CHARLES R., III
CORNELIUS, ANDREW J.
COSGROVE, THOMAS M.S.
COUNCIL, CLAUDE C., JR.
COYLE, CHRISTOPHER J.
DAWSON, JAY WESLEY
DEVECKA, JOSEPH M.
DeAUGUSTINO, DEBORAH
    ANN
DeGEORGE, WENDY ELAINE
DeMAY, PATRICK J.
DePASQUALE, JAMES E.
DiGREGORY, KEVIN V.
DOMBROWSKI, MICHAEL G.
DONAHOE, ROBERT J.
DONNELLY, DAVID
EBERT, MARK C.
ECKLE, DAVID JOSEPH
EDWARDS, MICHELE
EMORY, JEFFREY RAY
ENGLERT, RONALD G.
ENGLESSON, NICHOLAS E.
ENZEL, DAVID HOWARD
FELDMAN, JOEL F.
FENTON, BRIAN S.
FERRIN, MICHAEL J.
FIORENTINO, JAMES R.

FLEMING, WILLIAM S.
FLOM, RICHARD ALAN
FORD, SHEILA MAUDE
FOREMAN, ROBERT L.
FREEBURN, RICHARD EUGENE
FRIES, JOHN J.
FUNSTEN, LAWRENCE D.
GAERTNER, GARY J.
GALLAGHER, KATHLEEN JOAN
GASDICK, MICHAEL J.
GEIGER, WILLIAM D.
GLORIUS, EDWIN G., II
GOLDEN, WILLIAM LANE
GOLDMAN, RICKY S.
GONANO, DOUGLAS E.
GOODEMORE, DANIEL R.
GOODMAN, MURPHY
GRAHAM, MARK STEPHEN
GREENE, BEVERLY M.
GREENFIELD, CARLA H.
GRISWOLD, JAMES R.
GROMIS, SUSAN A.
HAMILTON, MARK R.
HANZEL, MICHAEL COLLINS
HARRIS, ANDREA S.
HARVEY, MICHAEL
HATHAWAY, GERALD T.
HENRY, MICHAEL J.
HERZL-BETZ, LOUISE
HILL, PETER J.
HIMMELREICH, DAVID BAKER
HOMYAK, MARK J.
HORAN, MARILYN J.
HORGAN, ROGER D.
HORNEY, PETER E.
HUDDLESTON, JAMES
IORFIDO, GARY A.
JOHNSTON, FRANCES COOK
JOHNSTON, HENRY R., III
JORDAN, SANDRA D.
JOSEPH, ROSEANN B.
KANE, RICHARD S.
KASUBICK, GIRARD
KEELY, ARLENE J.
KEENAN, CHARLES R., III
KENNEDY, DANIEL B.
KLAYMAN, MURRAY A.
KOCHUBA, EDWARD L., JR.
LAMM, ROBERT E.
LAMPL, MARLENE R.
LEBOW, LARRY J.
LEE, GARY W.
LEHMAN, STANLEY J.
MALLICK, CRAIG D.
MALONE, SUSAN HILEMAN
MANN, PETER

MANNE, JASON W.
MARKS, MICHAEL H.
MARLETT, CHARLES P.
MARSHALEK, MARY T.
MATERA, BARBARA
    FRANKART
MATERA, MARK V.
MAUSER, ROBERT E.
McCANN, KENNETH K.
McCOMMON, PATRICIA A.
McCORMICK, TIMOTHY J.
McKENNA, JAMES L.
McMASTER, JOSEPH
    SHANNON
MERSKY, CHARLES
MILITA, VINCENT J., II
MIODUSZEWSKI, MARK E.
MOORE, CARL N.
MORRIS, JEFFREY T.
MORSE, DANIEL W.
MOSES, L. DAVID
MOWRY, DAVID F.
MUCHOW, RICHARD L.
MULLIGAN, KATHLEEN R.
MUNSCH, JOHN L.
MURPHY, ROBERT L.
MURPHY, WILLIAM S.
MUSE, SUSAN A.
NESTLER, GILBERT C.
NIEDERRITER, EDWARD R.
NUCCI, EDWARD C.
O'HANLON, PAUL W.
PACACHA, MARY ANN
PEMRICK, KEITH M.
PENNY, M. ANN
PERLOW, CHARLES S.
PERRY, JOHN E., JR.
PICKENS, DAVID W.
PIETROSIMONE, FRANCIS W., JR.
PITONYAK, JAMES ANDREW
POLLOCK, MARK H.
PROGOFF, SUSAN
PUSHINSKY, JON S.
PUTT, TONI-RENEE
RAGSDALE, RANDOLPH VAN
RAMSDEN, MARY S.
RAYMAN, ROBERT C.
RAYNAK, JAMES A.
READIE, W. ALLEN
REITMEYER, MARY
RICHARD, JOHN T., III
ROB, SAMUEL JOSEPH
ROCK, CHRISTINE A.
ROKOSKI, RAMONA J.
ROONEY, ROBERT DAMIEN
ROSE, WENDELL A.

ROSENTHAL, LEE
ROUSOS, PETER C.
ROUSSEAU, ROBERTA M.
ROYSTON, ROBERT D., JR.
RUSSELL, RICHARD A.
SALLER, LESLIE B.
SANDERLIN, WILLIAM W.
SAUL, AMY JO
SCHAEFER, ERIC ANDREW
SCHINDLER, ELLEN M.
SCHLUETER, BONNIE G.
SCHORNER, JAMES A.
SCHWARTZ, MARK D.
SEGUR, DAPHNE LOUISE
SHAFFER, GARY L.
SHAFFER, WILLIAM R.
SHAW, NANCY R.
SHEAFFER, CHRISTINE H.
SHROYER, DONALD R.
SINGH, JOAN
SKEEL, PETER B.
SMITH, CARL J., JR.
SPEARS, ROBERT D.
STEARNS, FRANKLYN C.
STONE, HARLAN S.
STUCZYNSKI, JAMES J.
SWICK, JEFFREY D.
TAYLOR, KATHLEEN JO
THOMPSON, JANE A.
TILY, GIL C.
TREMONT, HELEN M.
TROFINO, RALPH J.
TUCKMAN, ERIC A.
VARDARO, ANTHONY J.
VERES, JUDITH H.
WALKER, KENNETH E., II
WALLIS, RICHARD J.
WALSH, EDWARD J.
WECHSLER, ELLEN IRENE
WEINFELD, DAVID M.
WEISBERGER, STEVEN
WEST, RONALD D.
WHEELER, PAUL W.
WHITE, HARRY F., II
WINTERSTEIN, DAVID C.
WISER, LESLIE G., JR.
WITZIG, MARC W.
WOLFE, FRANK ALLAN
WOLKIN, GARY L.
WOOLLS, ARTHUR PAUL
YOHE, SUSAN
ZALEVSKY, HARVEY A.

— Class of —
1980

ADAMCZYK, JOSEPH R.
AFFINITO, HOWARD J.
AMRHEIN, RICHARD J.
ARCH, MICHAEL E.
ASHLEY, JOHN W.
BABCOCK, WAYNE A.
BARRETT, JAY E.
BARTHOLOMEW, JOHN J.
BAXMEIER, CHERYL L.
BENZ, JOHN E.
BERG, FREDDIE J.
BERRY, EUGENE G.
BETTS, MICHAEL J.
BLACKSTONE, WILLIAM M.
BLANDINO, ALAN G.
BLUE, DONALD S.
BOCCHER, EDWARD J.
BOWERS, KENNETH R.
BOYLE, MARK S.
BRAUN, JANET L.
BRODE, KEVIN
BROK, RICHARD E.
BROWN, ROBERT W.
BURKE, KIM K.
CAMPBELL, CATHY D.
CARUTHERS, WILLIAM F.
CECH, ALAN E.
CERAUL, DAVID J.
CHABAN, LAWRENCE R.
CILLI, GABRIEL P.
CONNOLLY, JAMES G.
CONTE, RICHARD M.
COONER, JAMES R.
CORNELL, JOHN W.
COX, J. CRAIG
CRAWFORD, THOMAS F.
DAVIS, JEFFREY W.
DEFIORE, PAUL P.
DEMBERT, DAVID C.
DiGIORGIO, JOSEPH M.
DIULUS, ADELINE P.
DOBSON, THOMAS R.
DRIER, MARC S.
EICHER, JEFFREY D.
ESKIN, HAROLD S.
FASISKA, BARBARA
FEDERLINE, ROBERT L.
FISS, PETER L.
FOURNIER, KEITH A.
FRIEDMAN, KENNETH P.
FYALKOWSKI, FRANKLIN J.
GALPER, MARK S.
GERSON, ARTHUR S.

GETSINGER, BRUCE L.
GIRIFALCO, SANDRA A.
GLEASON, GREGORY
GLICK, JONATHAN
GOCKLEY, JAMES M.
GOODWIN, MICHAEL S.
GOODWIN, PAMELA S.
GREENE, JANET
GROSS, THOMAS B.
HALLER, JO ANN
HALLER, MARCIA H.
HAMILTON, KIMBERLY
HANNA, MICHAEL K.
HARPER, DANIEL J.
HARVEY, JAMES W.
HAWK, MICHELLE M.
HESLOP, JOHN W.
HIGGINS, TIMOTHY J.
HILGENDORFF, ROBERT F.
HITT, LEO N.
HORNER, JOHN J.
HOSKING, RICHARD W.
HOWARTH, HENRY
HUFF, JAMES R.
HUMBERT, DANIEL W.
IMBRIE, CHARITY J.
IANNAMORATO, ARTHUR J.
JACOBSON, DEBORAH
KABNICK, LISA D.
MORITZ, EUGENIA A.
KAUFMAN, MITCHELL A.
KELLY, SIDNEY J.
KLEIN, JEFFREY G.
KNOELL, KRISTIN A.
KNOX, KATHERINE E.
KOPLOVE, JAY S.
KREHELY, KIMBERLY
LANE, LAURA A.
LAPE, ROBERT W.
LARCHUK, STEVEN B.
LATSHA, KIMBER L.
LAZARUS, BRUCE I.
LEARNED, SCOTT J.
LEDERER, HOWARD M.
LEWIS, ANNE H.
LIPTAK, PATRICIA J.
LOW, RICHARD C.
LYDON, JOHN P.
LYNCH, STEVEN J.
MALENKY, JEFFREY C.
MARIANI, ANTHONY M.
MARSICO, LEONARD J.
MASSON, RICHARD A.
MATHENA, LARRY R.
MATTHEWS, ALEXANDRA J.
McARDLE, BERNARD T.

McBRIDE, ROBERT E.
McCARTHY, RANDY L.
McCULLOUGH, CHARLES P.
McDONALD, NANCY E.
McFALLS, MAUREEN D.
McGROGAN, DANIEL C.
McLEAN, THOMAS J.
McQUISTON, DAVID M.
McRANDAL, NANCY E.
MILNES, GARY L.
MORROW, MARK C.
NAGLE, REX A.
NINOS, HELEN M.
O'BRIEN, DAWN C.
O'DONNELL, MAURA E.
O'TOOLE, TIMOTHY T.
PEDEN, KEITH S.
PERRY, DANIEL J.
PETERSON, THOMAS P.
PINGITORE, LINDA
PIPER, DONALD R.
PORTER, BARBARA A.
REDDY, WILLIAM J.
REIBER, JOHN E.
REYNOLDS, MEREDITH B.
RHOADS, BARRY D.
RICH, PETER R.
ROBINSON, DEBORAH J.
ROMAN, DONALD J.
ROSENTHAL, PHILLIP B.
ROY, DANIEL J.
RUPRECHT, RICHARD N.
SAMUELS, JACQUELINE L.
SANCHAS, RAYMOND N.
SARGERT, JANET W.
SAYLES, MICHAEL D.
SCHAFF, MICHAEL D.
SCHMIDT, LYNNE D.
SCHMUCKI, ROSS F.
SCHNEIDER, RONALD A.
SCHNIPPERT, REGIS J.
SCOTT, HENRY
SCOTTI, DAVID A.
SHABBICK, BARRY C.
SHATTEN, DEBORAH A.
SHEARON, ANNE
SHOMPER, JAMES D.
SIDMAN, MARK H.
SILBERBLATT, JAY N.
SILVERMAN, DONALD J.
SIMMONS, JEAN A. M.
SINWELL, JAMES C.
SIROKY, GEORGENE M.
SLOAN, MARTIN C.
SLOMSKI, WALTER D.
SMALLHOOVER, JOSEPH J.

SMETANKA, STELLA L.
SMITH, WENDY E. D.
SMOLKO, SHARON M.
SOSSONG, ANNA M.
STACK, LOUIS J.
STEELE, JAMES T.
STEFFES, WILLIAM A.
STEIN, EDWARD A.
STENGEL, LAWRENCE F.
TAYLOR, MARY L.
TELESKO, TAMARA G.
TISSUE, JOSEPH N.
TISSUE, LOUISE J.
UNDERWOOD, MICHAEL J.
VASKOV, JOHN A.
VEDDER, CLYDE W.
VERGOTZ, JAMES S.
VILLELLA, GERALD J.
VUONO, MARK T.
WALLACE, WILLIAM L.
WALSH, KEVIN W.
WESTERMAN, JEFF S.
WHITE, JACQUELYNE A.
WHITE, ROBERT J.
WILLIAMS, SCOTT T.
WILSON, JAMES R.
WOLOWSKI, STANLEY J.
WORDEN, JOSEPH R.
YARNELL, STEPHEN V.
ZAJAC, SUZANNE E.
ZITTRAIN, RUTH ANN
ZWILLING, THOMAS M.

— Class of —
1981

ABBOTT, KEVIN CHARLES
ACKER, WILLIAM WILSON
ALEY, CHARLES R.
ALLEGRETTI, JON ANTHONY
ALTER, JAMES STANLEY
AMELIO, GARY ALAN
AVALLI, CHARLES JOSEPH
BALDWIN, ANN ELIZABETH
BARRETT, MICHAEL CLARK
BECKMAN, BARBARA RILLING
BECKMAN, GABRIEL
BELKIN, RICHARD STUART
BENSON, TRACEY GRANGER
BERMAN, MITCHELL ALAN
BLACK, BLANE ALAN
BLAIS, SUSAN LYNN
BONAVITA, THOMAS JAMES
BOWDEN, CONSTANCE MARIE
BRADLEY, STUART VAN
    LEER, JR.

BRIGHT, DANIEL E.
BROIDO, JULIE BROCK
BROWN, EDWIN PRUGH, JR.
BROWN, KELLY LEE
BRYANT, RANDY LEWIS
BUBBA, JOSEPH ANTHONY
BURKE, PAUL DAVID
CAMINITE, MARK J.
CARR, NANCY ESCH
CARROLL, ROSEMARY
CASTELLI, ANITA LOUISE
CHENEY, BRIAN JAMES
CHUTZ, MICHAEL JAY
CONKLIN, PATRICIA ANN
CONLEY, WILLIAM VANCE
CONNERS, MARY ANN
CONNOLLY, MICHAEL JOHN
CRONE, ANDREA LEE
CUNNINGHAM, WILLIAM
    RUSSELL
DAVIDSON, CHARLES EDWARD
DAVIS, DOROTHY ANN
DECKER, JOSEPH P.A., JR.
DEER, ROBERT WILLIAM
DeGORY, STANLEY PAUL
DEMPSEY, MATTHEW D.
DERBYSHIRE, JANE FIELD
DICKOS, GEORGE DEAN
DiLUCIA, KIM ELLEN
DODDS, DEBORAH DETCHON
DOWNEY, WILLIAM JOHN
DRISCOLL, JOHN FRANCIS
DURRANT, SALLY HOFFMAN
EATON, KIM DIANE
ECK, MARK ALLEN
EGAN, LUCEILLE MURRAY
EMILI, DENO PAUL
ESCOVITZ, JAMES ALEXANDER
FELDMAN, BRUCE ALBERT
FISS, SUSAN KING
FOX, MARJORIE JOAN
FRAY, JOHN MICHAEL
GALE, CHRISTINE ANN
GESTRICH, RICHARD GLENN
GINN, RAYMOND EDWARD
GLEIXNER, SANDRA MARIE
GLOGOWER, GARY ILAN
GOLDEN, LEE ROBERT
GORDON, DAVID ISRAEL
GOWELL, JOHN ROBERT, JR.
GREGO, SAMUEL ROBERT
GREGORY, SHARON LENZE
GRIFFIN, PATRICIA ANN
GROSSMAN, JOAN CAROL
HAHN, PETER I.
HANNA, MATTHEW

HANNON, MICHAEL JOHN
HARRELL, VALERIE L.
HART, WILLIAM MAXWELL
HASTINGS, DENNIS MARK
HAYDUK, JUDITH LYNN
HEWITT, DANIEL J.
HICKTON, DAVID JOHN
HIGH, WILLIAM PENN
HILTON, STANLEY EDWARD
HINCH, LORINDA L.
HINDIN, MARK DAVID
HODSON, THOMAS JAMES, JR.
HOLLEN, WILLIAM LYNN
HORNAK, MARK RAYMOND
HOUSTON, MARGARET FERRY
HUBBARD, BARTON AUSTIN
HULL, PAUL EDWIN
HUMMEL, RANDY ALAN
IGNELZI, PHILIP ANTHONY
ISAACMAN, ILENE LOUISE
JACKSON, DAVID BRYAN
JESION, PAULA JEAN
JOHNSON, MARGARET RUTH
JONES, JONATHAN EDWARD
KAHOE, BARBARA STRATTON
KAHOE, FRANK CODY, JR.
KAISER, LINDA SUSAN
KAMENETZKY, DEBORAH
    MORRISON
KAMINITSKY, STEPHANIE
    KAREN
KARAS, JOSEPH MICHAEL
KATUCKI, CHRISTOPHER
    THOMAS
KEMP, KATHLEEN NAGY
KENDRICK, KIM
KILBERT, KENNETH KEITH
KIMES, STEPHEN LEE
KING, BRYAN WEBSTER
KING, MARY ELIZABETH
KIPP, DONNA LOUISE
KLEIN, CHRISTOPHER JOHN
KLEIN, SARA JEAN
KNEZEVICH, MINA
KUHL, ROBERT WILLIAM
KULAKOWSKI, GEORGE D.
KUREMSKY, LAWRENCE
    JOSEPH
LASH, SCOTT EDWIN
LAZO, ANN ELIZABETH
LEE, WALTER
LEONE, HENRY
LETCHFORD, KATHRYN DEE
    BURGCHARDT
LIPRANDO, THOMAS
    EDWARD

LITTLEFIELD, MARY LOU
LOWMAN, WILLIAM LYLE
LUPTAK, DAVID ALAN
LUTZ, LAWRENCE PAUL
LYNCH, MAURA JANE
MANNE, BEVERLY ESTHER
MARKEL, JOHN FRANCIS
MARKLE, SPENCER
    GRANVILLE
MARTIN, DAVID CHARLES, JR.
MARTIN, MELINDA ELIZABETH
MASTOVICH, GEORGE B.
McBRIDE, CHERYL L.
McCARTHY, GLENN CHARLES
McCLINTOCK, LISSA
    LIEBERMAN
McCOMB, DAVID FORBES
McINTOSH, ROBERT KEITH
McNAIR, TIMOTHY DEAN
McNULTY, SIBYL MAE
    SHEPARD
MEARS, BEVERLY JEAN
MELIA, JAMES PATRICK
MEREDITH, JEFFREY SCOTT
MINEO, CHARLES WILLIAM
MOORE, GREGORY CHARLES
MULOCK, MARY HAHALYAK
MULVIHILL, KEITHLEY DAVID
MULZET, CHARLES KURT
NADEAU, MARK ALLEN
NAPOLI, SAMUEL FRANK
NEGLE, WILLIAM IRWIN, JR.
NEUROHR, JOHN BEST
NEWTON, WENDELYNNE JOY
NIEDZIELSKI, DENISE TESSIE
NORKUS, NANCY JEAN
NUBANI, JOHN IBRAHIM
OBOZIAN, MARGARET
OGG, GARY JAMES
O'MALIA, PATRICK J.
O'SHEA, THOMAS DANIEL
OWLETT, EDWARD
    HOWLAND, III
PALMORE, ARCHIE LEE
PAPPAS, JAMES
PARK, BARBARA JEANNE
PAVETTI, JEFFREY ARMAND
PAVSEK, EDWARD JOSEPH, JR.
PECK, HARRY EDWARD, III
PELLOW, JAMES ALFRED, III
PERKINS, KENNETH DONALD
PETRIKIS, STEVEN MICHAEL
POERIO, JAMES MARK
POLLEY, RICHARD CLAYTON
PONTON, LISA STAMPER
REDDING, KENNETH ALAN

REED, MICHAEL DONAHOO
REYNOLDS, HARRY RAND
RHOADES, RANDY RAY
RIPPEL, SHERRY ANN
ROBERTS, MARC ALAN
ROVINSKY, JOHN VICTOR
RUBIN, ALAN
SAUER, JEFFREY FRANCIS
SCHAUB, ROSS JOSEPH
SCHERTZ, PHILIP ROBERT
SCHWARTZ, SAUL Y.
SERRATTA, SHERYL ANN
SHEPPARD, JAMES POWEL
SHORE, DOUGLAS TOD
SIMS, HOWARD LEONARD
SINGER, GARY S.
SMITH, JESSIE LOUISE
SMITH, JOHN HONEYMAN
SMITH, RALPH HARRY, III
STADLER, MARK
STEELE, SUSAN ELAINE
STROME, WILLIAM FREDERICK
SZABAT, RONALD PAUL
SZEMANEK, CATHERINE ANN
TAYLOR, WENDY SHARON
TISHOK, JOHN MICHAEL
VANDERGRIFT, CRAIG LEE
VOGLER, PHILIP WILLIAM
WALLACE, PAUL DELWOOD, JR.
WARD, JEFFREY PAUL
WARNER, RUSSELL STEVEN
WELCH, ALLEN COMPTON, JR.
WELSH, JEFFREY DALE
WERTKIN, ROBIN STUART
WESOLOWSKI, TED
WHALEN, LINDA LONG
WIMER, DAN PHILLIP
WINSCHEL, WILLIAM FRANCIS
WOLFE, MICHAEL GEORGE
ZEGLEN, JOHN M.

— Class of —
1982

ABZANKA, DOROTHY JEAN
ACKERMAN, GRANT R.
ALBERT, BRIAN MICHAEL
ALBERTS, MARK ROBERT
ALLEN, LARAINE REA
BACON, SONYA JORDAN
BAHN, CINDY L.
BARBIN, BRYAN EDWARD
BARNHART, DEBRA
    McCLOSKEY
BARTOLOTTA, BRUCE
    ANTHONY

BAUER, DREW JOHN
BAXTER, DAVID ARTHUR
BECKWITH, ROBERT WARREN
BEISLER, DANIEL PAUL, JR.
BIRMINGHAM, VIRGINIA
    WILLEY
BITTNER, EDWARD AUGUST
BOND, C. JAMES
BOND, ROBIN FRYE
BORTNER, PETER ERNEST
BOYLE, RICHARD FRANCIS, JR.
BROCKETT, DANIEL
    LAWRENCE
CAMPBELL, CHARLES W.
CAMPBELL, THOMAS LIONEL
CARL, MATTHEW JOHN
CARUSO, JOSEPH FRANK
CLOFINE, ROBERT
COLABRESE, CAROL ANN
COLE, JEFFREY LAWRENCE
CONBOY, GERARD TIMOTHY
CONSEVAGE, JOHN B.
CORBETT, FRANCIS E., III
CORE, PHILIP KENNEDY
CORTESE, ANTHONY
    VINCENT
COSTO, JOHN THOMAS
COULTER, JAMES P.
CURRIE, ROBERT ANDREW
CURRY, E. BRUCE
DANIEL, DAVID EMERSON
DAVEY, JOHN C.
DAWSON, TIMOTHY PAUL
DePASQUALE, CARL JOSEPH
DINNEY, MICHAEL SETH
DIVELY, MELISSA KAY
DOBRAN, JAMES MICHAEL
DOUGLAS, LAURA GAIL
DOWNEY, LAURIE EILER
DOYLE, PATRICIA EILEEN
DREWITZ, MARY JACQUELINE
duPONT, WILLIAM BAYARD
EDEN, ROBIN
ERSHLER, AMY FRANCES
FALLERT, THOMAS MARK
FAVISH, BRUCE IAN
FAYE, TERRANCE GILEO
FERBER, PEGGY LYNN
FERRELL, ROBERT WALTON, III
FITZSIMMONS, DANIEL
    EDWARD
FLANNERY, JAMES LLOYD
FLANNICK, NICOLETTE
    PATRICIA
FLECK, JOHN PAUL, JR.
FOLEY, THOMAS JOSEPH, III

FONTANA, MARK ALLAN
FURNESS, PETER JOYN
GEFSKY, JAMES BARNETT
GIBEL, MARSIA LEA
GORROW, SUSAN GORMAN
GOSS, DOUGLAS DAVID
GOULD, ISABEL WILLIARD
GOWER, ROBERT JOHN
GRAHAM, DONALD PAUL
GRAYNOR, ANDREW DAVID
GREEN, ROBIN CHERYL
GRIFFITH, DOUGLAS JOHN
GUCKERT, CAROL ANN
HAJDUK, LARRY JOHN
HAMMERSCHMIDT, JUDITH
    LYNNE
HARTMAN, ANDREW L.
HARTZELL, JAMES FREDERICK
HAY, AMY REYNOLDS
HELLEIN, BRADLEY KEITH
HELMREICH, MARTHA
    SCHAFF
HERRERA, ANN JOSEPHINE
HILL, THOMAS WILLIAM
HIRSCHLER, PHILIP
HISCOX, DAVID BRADLEY
HOELLER, MARY JANE
HORNE, ERIC LORIN
HUNKELE, EDWARD GERARD
HYATT, THOMAS KARL
JENNINGS, RICHARD O.
JOHNSON, SELINA PEDERSEN
KATZ, OWEN WILLIAM
KENDALL, JEFFREY DONALD
KIFER, STEPHEN CHARLES
KINZLER, THOMAS MICHAEL
KRAMER, ELLEN MINDY
KUFTIC, VICKI LYNN
KUNTZ, PAUL SAMUEL
LABRIOLA, LISA LOUISE
LABUSKES, BERNARD
    ANTHONY, JR.
LANDIS, LAURENCE ROSS
LANE, MARYL A.
LAVELLE, JOSEPH PHILIP
LEINO, ROBERT GILBERT
LeSUER, ROBERT CHARLES
LEVINE, RICHARD CHARLES
LIEBENGUTH, CAROLINE
    PUCCIANI
LILLIS, JAMES MICHAEL
LINKES, MARYANNE MICHELE
LISKO, JOHN MICHAEL
LOLL, JAMES JOSEPH
LUBIMIR, JOHN ANTON
LUDIN, ERIC ELLIOT

LUNDBERG, ALLAN CLAIR
LUSZCZ, CHESTER ANTHONY
LUTINSKI, JAN ELIZABETH
MacBETH, LYNN ELLEN
    SCHOLZE
MAGHRAK, MONICA
MARCHETTI, CAROLYN LEE
MARKOVITZ, LEE
MARSHALL, JULIE ANNE
MARUCA, WILLIAM HAROLD
MATHER, RICHARD PAUL
MATTHEWS, DAVID JOHN
McALLISTER, DAVID JOHN
McCAGUE, JOHN MICHAEL, JR.
McCREA, CHRISTINA
McKAY, MARGARET MARY
McKEEGAN, KEVIN FRANCIS
MEDOFF, JAN IRA
MILES, CHRISTOPHER EARL
MILLER, ALAN SCOTT
MILLER, ROBERT MYERS, JR.
MITCHEL, ROBERT STANLEY
MOMICH, HOPE
MOOSEY, JOAN MARIE
MORGAN, ROBERT PATRICK
MORGENSTERN, DENNIS
    MICHAEL
MORISON, JANICE LEIGH
MORROW, JACQUELINE RENEE
NEBEL, CHRISTINE MARIE
NOGA, COLLEEN MARIE
O'CONNOR, PATRICIA ANN
PANKOWSKI, DONNA JEAN
PATTERSON, JUDITH ELLEN
PEACE, REBECCA L.
PEARLMAN, RICHARD MARK
PELCHER, STEPHEN RICHARD
PEPICELLI, LISA GAIL
PERKINS, KEVIN MICHAEL
PERRY, LESLIE ECOTRLYN
PILEGGI, AMES JOSEPH
POWELL, ROY ALAN
QUIGLEY, PETER JAMES
QUINN, JOSEPH FRANCIS
REED, JEFFREY
RHODES, MANUEL EUGENE
RIEBER, MARK VINCENT
ROBISON, JONATHAN
    BENJAMIN
ROSEN-MOY, CAROL LYNN
ROSENBERG, DAVID JOHN
RUBENSTEIN, PHILIP HOWARD
RIBINOFF, MYRON RICHARD
RUGGIO, MICHAEL FRANCIS
RUSSELL, MEGAN ELIZABETH
SANDERS, RUSSELL RONALD

SCHAFER, GERARD THOMAS
SCHARPF, MARJORIE JEAN
SCHENCK, EDWARD ALLEN
SCHERMER, LELAND PAUL
SCHMIDT, WILLIAM JAMES
SCHRECKER, BILLIE
SENCAK, JOHN LEE
SHAFFER, THOMAS RICHARD
SHAPIRO, MINOR HOWARD
SHUTTER, WALTER DAVID
SILVA, ZOILO ITTAI
SINKO, GLENN STEPHEN
SITTIG, WILLIAM ROBERT
SMITH, SHERYL LEE
SMITH, THOMAS GORDON
SNYDER, KING CLAUDE
SPAHN, G. DANIEL
STASCHAK, MICHAEL
    CARMEN
STAUB, PATRICIA LOUISE
STRUNK, DONALD JAMES
TELL, MELINDA GALE
TENO, CAROL A.
THIEL, DENISE LYNN SNYDER
TOBIN, LINDA F.
TOCCO, DONNA JEAN
TOMALIS, MATTHEW WILLIAM
TRAUB, PETER PEARSON
WARD, CHRISTINE ANN
WEBER, GARY LEE
WHALEN, JAMES WALTER
WONG, PATRICIA KAY
WORKMAN, DENNIS DALE
YAUGER, DOUGLAS PAUL
YOUNGS, CHRISTOPHER JAY
ZACHARY, JANE ELIZABETH
ZIMMERMAN, BETSY A.
ZOTTOLA, JOHN ANTHONY

— Class of —
1983

ABBOTT, DAVID LLOYD
ABRAMS, DANIEL DAVID
ADAMS, DOROTHY DAWN
ADELSON, BRUCE
    LAWRENCE
ALLEN, BEVERLY ROSE
ALLEN, JOSEPH W.
ALTMEYER, HELEN CAMPBELL
ALTMEYER, HENRY BRANN
AMRHEIN, BARBARA ANN
ANTHONY, MICHAEL JOHN
APFELBAUM, JAY MARTIN
AGENTO, L. JOHN
ARNOLD, JANE KAREN

ARRINGTON, CHRISTINE
    DENISE
BAHR, LAURIE JEANNE
BEATTY, VICKI LINN
BELL, LYNN ELLEN
BEN-AMI, RAPHAEL Z.
BERGSTEIN, SCOTT JEFFREY
BERRY, CAROL JEAN
BEST, DONALD LOUIS, JR.
BETZ, THOMAS
BEVIS, JOHN WAYNE
BINGHAM, JEANNE J.
BOOKER, VAUGHN ANGELO
BUCEY, WENDY ANN
BURGESS, VICTORIA MARIE
CAMPBELL, BRYAN B.
CAMPBELL, KELA DAYTON
CARUTHERS, JAMES DAVID
CELLER, VANESSA F. BELL
CERCONE, SUSAN SHELDON
CHIAFULLO, JAMES DANIEL
CICCONI, RICARDO JOSEPH
CILLO, ANTHONY
CITRON, STANLEY ROBERT
CLEMENT, MARK THOMAS
CODY, STEPHEN WILLIAM
COLETTA, JAMES PAUL
CONFLENTI, ROBERT F.
CONTES, PHILIP WILLIAM
COSS, LESLIE RAE
COSTIGAN, RICHARD
    ANDREW
CUSICK, PATRICK T.
DATESH, LU ANN RUSSO
DAVIS, DAVID MICHAEL
DAY, VINCENT
DEDIANKO, PATRICIA ANN
DiGIORNO, RONALD JOSEPH
DiPERNA, BRENDAN JOSEPH
DiSALLE, FRANCIS J.
DRAGO, LINDA SUSAN
DREYFUS, RICHARD BAECK
DUNLAP, GREGORY EUGENE
DUNN, ROBERT A.
DUVALL, MARTHA JEAN
EARLE, MICHAEL JAMES
ECKMAN, ALEXANDER LACEY
EDWARDS, ALAN HITCHCOCK
EDWARDS, PAULA ANNE
EISNER, EVAN SPENCER
ELLSWORTH, LAURA
    ELIZABETH
ETHRIDGE, CHRISTINE
    ROBERTA
FAIGEN, JANICE McSHERRY
FANCHER, BARBARA JEAN

FEENEY, THOMAS CHARLES, III
FEINBERG, GREGG MICHAEL
FELDER, MURRAY ALAN
FINNEGAN, MICHAEL JOSEPH
FOSTER, EDWARD GEORGE
FRATTO, LINDA MARIE
FRENZE, JENIFER
GALLISHEN, WILLIAM
    CHARLES
GASDICK, JEFFREY JOHN
GHILARDI, MELINDA
    CHRISTINA
GIBSON, SHEILA ANN
GLIMCHER, SUSAN D.
GLOWACKI, BRIAN
GOBOS, JOY
GONGAWARE, WAYNE
    BOWMAN
GRIFFIN, GREGORY
    OSWALD-JAMES
GRIMES, MARCIA LUCIDI
GUADAGNINO, FRANK
    THOMAS
HABER, DAVID LEE
HAMMOND, GREGORY JAMES
HARVIN, JAMES EDWARD
HAVER, RONALD J.
HERTZBERG, ALAN DAVID
HILL, J. PETER
HILLDORFER, JOSEPH PETER, III
HOFFMAN, DAVID ROBERT
HORNER, CLARE DAHLBERG
HOROSZKO, KYNDA WEBER
HOURIGAN, JAMES KEVIN
HUNKELE, DENISE DIANE
IURLANO, PAUL ANTHONY
JACKSON, JEFFREY JOSEPH
JACOBS, JAMES MELVIN, JR.
JOHNSON, JAMES ANDREW
JOHNSON, KAREN SUE
JONES, LYN EGLI
KABBERT, WILLIAM JOHN, II
KAPLAN, DAVID N.
KATRON, BARBARA AMY
KEARNEY, JAMES PATRICK
KELLY, DANIEL JOHN
KENNEDY, JAMES ANTHONY
KENNEDY, JOHN STODDART
KIMMEL, CLAIRE ANN
KING-SEIDEL, DEBBIE GRACE
KISTLER, DENNIS ALLEN
KLINK, JEFFREY MERLE
KUIS, SUSAN GRAGSON
KUKURA, THOMAS VINCENT
KUNKLE, KARL WAYNE
KUTZ, THOMAS MICHAEL

KUYAT, CRAIG EDWARD
LASSMAN, DONALD R.
LERNER, BARRY ROBERT
LESKO, DEBORAH LEE
LEWIN, MARY ODREEN
LINDQUIST, JOHN ARTHUR, III
LISLE, CANDACE RUTH
LONGYEAR, MICHAEL J.
LUNDBERG, DALE ANDREW
MACK, DAVID JOHN
MALLOY, MARIANNE SARA
MANGUS, DEBRA ANN
MARBURGER, DAVID LINDSEY
MASON, DAVID CHARLES
MATTHEWS, BARBARA LYNN
McCLAIN, THOMAS JUDE
McCLENNEY, YVONNE
    CHARLENE
McCOLLOM, DAVID PUTNAM
McDERMOTT, ROBERT
    THOMAS
MEAD, JOHN JAMES
MIHELCIC, JOHN P.
HILLMAN, CHARLES J.
MONSOUR, ROBERT
    DISHINGTON
MORRISON, BRIAN RAY
MURPHY, MARK JOSEPH
MYERS, WILLIAM SNEATH
NEIDERHISER, VIRGINIA
    HOLLY
NELSON, MICHAEL GERARD
NIKOLOFF, DAVID KEITH
NORTON, JEFFREY JOSEPH
ONDECHEK, CHERYL ANN
OWLETT, THOMAS MASON
PALUMBO, JOSEPH JAY
PASSODELIS, WILLIAM
    CHRISTOPHER
PERINIS, JANE O'CONNELL
PETRAKIS, JONATHAN MARK
PETRILLO, MARY ANN
PIETRZAK, RONA L.
PILLOW, MICHAEL F.
POLING-KALIS, BEVERLY A.
POWELL, DEBORAH P.
PUNTURERI, LARRY JOSEPH
PUPO, LISA MICCIO
RADEL, RICHARD MARK
RAFFERTY, FRANCES M.
REPCHECK, KEVIN RONALD
RHODES, BARBARA LYNN
RITZ, SUSAN ELIZABETH
ROCHE, JEANANN
ROCKWELL, RAYMOND PAUL
ROGERS, WILLIAM JAMES

RODNEY, RITA MARIE
ROSEBERRY, CATHERINE
    MEADE
ROSS, F. ANNE
RUSSIAL, THOMAS JOHN
RUVANE, ANNE JULIE
SABOL, MARY WILSON
SALZMAN, DAVID BRUCE
SANTILLI, MARIO, JR.
SASSANO, MARY ELIZABETH
SCHOFF, PAUL J.
SCHWABEDISSEN, ELIZABETH M.
SCHWARTZ, ANSEL MARTIN
SCHWARTZ, ARNOLD MARVIN
SCHWENDINGER, JO ANNE
SEANEZ, FRANCIS MICHAEL
SEPANSKI, DAWNE EILEEN
SIEGEL, DANIEL ISAIAH
SILVERMAN, PHYLLIS NOVICK
SIPUS, LAWRENCE JOSEPH
SLAMON, JANIE
SMITH, MICHAEL WATERS
SMITH-DELACH, KATHLEEN
    CLARE
SOLOMON, VERNADEAN L.
SPROWLS, LAURA DAWN
STRADER, ANN WALLACE
SULLIVAN, KEVIN MICHAEL
SULLIVAN, MARK ROBERT
SUPINKA, MICHAEL JOHN
SZYMANSKI, LINDA ANN
TAYLOR, DANIEL KENNETH
TAYLOR, MARY BETH
TERIS, SHARON FRANCES
THOMAS, JACQUELYN LEE
THOMPSON, DOUGLAS ALAN
TOMPKINS, MARY
    EVANGELINE
UBER, JAMES GROTE
VALENTINO-CAPRARO, RITA
    ANNE
VASSAMILLET, LAURA ANNE
VERBOFSKY, HOWARD ISRAEL
VIDI, JAMES EDWARD
VON WALDOW, ARNO
    NORBERT
WALKER, JOHN ALBERTSON
WAMSER, THOMAS JOHN
WEAVER, CAROL JEAN
WEAVER, KEVIN LAMAR
WEEKS, ANGELIQUE G.
    EUPHEME
WEINROTH, JOSEPH
WEPPER, CAROLYN L.
WERNER, RICHARD EDWARD
WILLE, DANIEL EDWARD

WILLIAMS, CAROL ANN
WILLIAMS, SUSAN NOLAN
WILSON, LEE
WISEMAN, RUTH RACHEL
WOOD, RICHARD EUGENE
WRAY, JAMES HAROLD
YARNELL, PETER HEWLETT
YENERALL, PAUL MATTHEW
ZYTNICK, JOEL HOWARD

— Class of —
1984

ACKERMAN, MARILYN H.
ADAMS, JOSEPH E.
AL KHAFIZ, MARILYN
ALBUERME, AMARILIS A.
ANTOL, MICHAEL S.
ANZALONE, VERONICA R.
ASHER, JAMES F.
ASKEW, DELPHINE
ATCHISON, CYNTHIA J.
BALZER, BETH L.
BAROCCHI, LINDY T.
BARR, LINDA H.
BASICHAS, MARK
BELLEW, JOSEPH M.
BENUCCI, PAULA J.
BERKOWITZ, JANET L.
BINCZEWSKI, NEAL E.
BLATTER, ELAINE
BLISS, RICHARD E.
BOURKE, MARY WEBB
BOZIK, MARGARET J.
BROWN, DOUGLAS K.
BROWN, LORRAY S.
BURK, HOWARD J.
CAIN, ESTA L.
CAIRONE, MATTHEW C.
CAMERON, DOUGLAS E.
CAMPANA, ANGELA M.
CANNON, ELLIS G.
CANTER, LEANN R.
CAPLAN, ARNOLD R.
CARDWELL, GAIL C.
CASALE, HENRY M.
CHA, JASON S.
CHAMBERS, JUSTINE F.
CHERVENICK, DAVID P.
CHOUAI, KATHLEEN
CHRISTIAN, DOUGLAS Y.
CHRISTMAN, EILEEN
    HOFFMAN
CIBIK, MELANIE S.
CLICKNEW, M. JEAN
CLINE, JACK W.

CLOKEY, JANE F.
COLWELL, SUSAN D.
COMER, RHONDA L.
CONNOLLY, MARK L.
COOPER, JODI L.
COVITCH, CAROL A.
CRIBBINS, KATHLEEN A.
CRISSMAN, DAVID A.
DAMICO, DAVID A.
DEASY, KEVIN M.
DEEB, PETER J.
DEGIULIO, FRANK P.
DESIMONE, DAVID R.
DESPOY, TERRY W.
DIGIROLAMO, SUSAN M.
DISALLE, JOHN P.
DODGE, ARTHUR B., III
DUNLOP, SCOTT G.
DUNMIRE, BELINDA J.
EDDY, MARIANNE A.
EDWARDS, PHILIP J.
ELLIOTT, LORI K.
ENSMINGER, ELIZABETH A.
EVANS, ROBERT B.
FALK, ERIC K.
FERRAND, FREDERICK O.
FONNER, DAVID K.
FOOR, ROBIN J.
FORSYTHE, KEVIN C.
FOX, GREGORY S.
FUCHS, BRUCE C.
GANDRUD, JOHN T.
GERMAN, WILLIAM R.
GLICKMAN, ILENE R.
GNAZZO, MELANIE J.
GOLDSTEIN, ALAN S.
GREER, MARTHA J.
GROSS, CAROL S.
HADLOCK, SUSAN M.
HAUSMAN, JOEL E.
HECKATHORN, CYNTHIA S.
HILL, MARCELLE P.
HODESBLATT, ALAN H.
HOLMES, BARBARA E.
HORVATH, ANDREW L., JR.
IMBLUM, GARY J.
ISLAND, ELIZABETH M.
JEFFRIES, GARY A.
JOHNSON, STEPHEN W.
JORDAN, GREGORY B.
KALEMON, LINDA M.
KALSON, DAVID J.
KAPUT, JOSEPH K.
KARNOFF, K. LARRY
KLEIN, ANITA T.
KLINK, GREGORY L.

KRAMER, FREDERICK P., II
KRZTON, NANCY L.
KWITOWSKI, KATHRYN A.
LAPIDUS, MELANIE S.
LEECH, ANTHONY P.
LEHMAN, HOWARD R.
LEWIS, DAVID A.
LIEBER, THOMAS K.
LIPINSKI, JOHN M.
LIVINGSTON, CATHERINE S.
LOVECCHIO, MARC F.
MACKEY, STEVEN E.
MAIONE, ANGELA
MANILOFF, HOWARD R.
MANOGUE, DAVID J.
MARTIN-NAGLE, CAROL R.
MASTON, WILLIAM H.
MATTIOLI, MARISA
McDANIEL, PATRICK C.
McGILL, ROGER D., JR.
McMANAMON, PETER M.
McWILSON, FRANK B.
MILBERGER, PATRICK A.
MILLER, V. COLLEEN
MINNO, MATTHEW F.
MIZAK, GEORGE A.
MOHAJERY, BARBARA A.
MOIR, JAMES H.
MOLTER, PAUL R.
MUNSCH, KATHERINE A.
MUNSON, J. MARK
MURRAY, TIMOTHY
NAPOLEON, VINCENT J.
NEFF, MARK J.
NICOLA, JOSEPH P.
NIKSA, THOMAS
O'BRIEN, TERRY A.
O'FARRELL, MICHAEL J., JR.
O'HARA, SALLY E.
O'MALLEY, MARGARET A.
PARRISH, MICHAEL K.
PATARINI, CHRISTOPHER
PELINI, CRAIG G.
PETROCCIA, MALCOLM W.
PINKSTON, GALE B.
POLIVA, ROBERT E.
POLLOCK, ADAM N.
POST, LINDA C.
POWANDA, ALLEN P.
PUNTIL, RONALD M., JR.
QUINLAN, MADELINE N.
RAYNOVICH, ANDREW
REEHL, JAMES R.
ROBERTS, REID B.
RODGERS, SALLIE A.
ROOS, KENNETH A.

ROSENZWEIG, MICHAEL H.
SAIDMAN. SHEILA
SCARBOROUGH, KATHLEEN G.
SCHNABACKER, SCOTT D.
SCHENCK, WILLIAM J.
SCHILLER, PAMELA M.
SCHUMANN, GEORGE M.
SHAFER, ALEXANDRA M.
SMITH, ANDREW C.
SMITH, SCOTT C.
SMITH, STEPHEN C.
SMITH, WILLIAM B.
SOBOCINSKI, JOSEPH S.
SOREK, PATRICK
STEPHENS, DAVID P.
SUDINA, RHONDA J.
SWAN, RAYMOND A.
TEREK, DAWN C.
THOMPSON, GLENN A.
TOLL, JEFFREY B.
TOPOLOSKY, GARY P.
UMBEL, JANICE L.
VALAW, BARBARA L.
VEON, MARIE T.
WARMBRODT, JAMES C.
WASSALL, DONALD B., JR.
WEAKLAND, BRIAN L.
WEBB, JANE M.
WEISS, DAVID P.
WENDOLOWSKI, RAYMOND P.
WEST, CANDACE
WIECZOREK, GARY E.
WILSON, GERI KIVINSKI
WISE, LORINA W.
WOOLLEY. HELEN P.
WRIGHT, JEFFREY D.
YAKOPEC, STEPHEN
YOUNG, MARY E.
ZACCARELLI, LAUREN
ZAWADZKI, PAULA A.

— Class of —
1985

ACKERMAN, LAWRENCE H.
ALEXANDER, EFFIE G.
ALLEN, ANDREA C.
ANDERSON, RHONDA D.
BACH, MARY ANN
BAKER, JOHN K.
BALL, GEORGE L.
BARNES, JANE S.
BASSO, RONALD
BEZEGO, WILLIAM J.
BILICKI, BYRON A.
BLANCO, ALAN C.

BLOCH, BARRY H.
BRADLEY, SCOTT
BRAUNSTEIN, ROBERT L.
BRLETIC, DEBRA L.
BROSKY, DAVID J.
CAMPANELLA, MICHAEL F.
CAPLAN, LORRAINE S.
CAREY, DOUGLAS G.
CARLOS, JOHN
CARSON, CHRISTOPHER
CASELLA, LAWRENCE J.
CETLIN, ILENE L.
CHAKERES, ANDREW A.
CICCONE, VINCENT A.
COLANGELO, ANTHONY T.
COLARUSSO, MICHAEL J.
COLE, SHARON K.
COTLER, ROBIN
CRABTREE, MICHELLE R.
CRISANTI, ROBERT A.
CRUM, WILLIAM R.
CUMMINGS, GLENN P.
CUTRIGHT, SUSAN E.
CYR, HOWARD M.
D'ERAMO, FRANCIS J.
DENNIS, CHARLES E.
DEROY, HELEN M.
DEVITT, H. WILLIAM, III
DISMUKES, SCOTT R.
DODD-O, JAMES J.
DOODY, PATRICIA A.
DUGGAN, ANNE J.
DUPRE, LYNDA M.
ENG, JUDY M.
EYSTER, CHRIS R.
FABRIANO, PHILIP A.
FANGMAN, KARIN K.
FAWCETT, DAVID B.
FELDMAN, HOPE R.
FERRY, MARION L.
FEUSTER, LINDA S.
FLECKENSTEIN, STASIA
FORNEY, DAVID L.
FRANKFURT, SHARI L.
FRASER, STUART W.
FRYE, VIVIAN L.
FUHRER, SUSAN D.
FURE, BARBARA A.
GAUGLER, NELSON B.
GIANNUZZI, GREGG
GILLIAM, JEFFREY D.
GINGRICH, KURT
GOLDBERG, DANIEL L.
GOLDBERG, MICHAEL R.
GOLDBERG, RANDI L.
GREINER, JOHN K.

GRIEWAHN, ROBERT D., JR.
GUTHRIE, MATTHEW L.
HACKETT, NORA ANN
HARTLEY, LESA L.
HENRY, DAVID W.
HERBERT, KIM L.
HERBERTSON, THOMAS C.
HIGHTOWER, JANET R.
HINDMAN, KIMBERLY
    HANDLAN
HIRSCH, VELMA B.
HODGES, CLEMON H., II
HOFFMAN, MATTHEW M.
HOWARD, LINDSAY P.
HOWES, DAVID A.
HULL, EUGENIA
ILER, DANIEL J.
JACOBS, STEVEN D.
JOHNSTON, KATHRYN
JONES, CYNTHIA B.
KACHUSLIS, GEORGE P.
KADILAK, SUSAN
KASABACK, JOHN
KEARNS, JOHN B.
KELLEY, BRENDAN R.
KELSEY, ANDREA N.
KINSKEY, GREG T.
KIRSHENBAUM, STANLEY A.
KLEMENS, ROBERT M.
KLINE, MICHAEL J.
KLINE, TERRY A.
KNAPP, BRUCE D.
KNOX, JOSEPH J.
KRAMER, MERLE S.
LABRIOLA, SUSAN D.
LAPENTA, SUSAN M.
LEASURE, KEVIN P.
LEHMAN, DAVID J.
LEHR, MATTHEW B.
LIGHT, ERICA L.
LIVINGSTON, PATRICK M.
LOFTUS, MAUREEN A.
LOVE, LINDSLEY W.
LUNDY, TODD L.
LUPOVITZ, LAURA F.
LYND, ALICE
MALLEY, COLLEEN C.
MANOGUE, LINDA A.
MARCUS, PHILIP H.
MARGOLIS, ALAN D.
MARTINELLI, LESLIE L.
McCAHILL, JOHN W., II
McCLELLAND, DIANNE J.
McGINTY, KEVIN M.
McLAUGHLIN, CHRISTINE D.
McMANUS, MARY E.

McMASTER, DAVID E.
MILTON, ELISABETH A.
MITCHELL, MILES H.
MONAHAN, JANE T.
MOORE, PAMELA A.
MORGADO, MARY E.
MUSSMAN, SUSAN M.
NEHRING, PAMELA
NICKEL, THOMAS C.
NORRIS, KEVIN A.
NORTON, GARY E.
NOZIGLIA, DAVID A.
NUNEZ, RICARDO J.
O'HARA, KATHLEEN F.
OSWALT, WALTER L., III
PAGE, THEDA W.
PALADIN, LAWRENCE G., JR.
PAPA, SUSAN M.
PASTORE, DANIEL J.
PAVLICK, DONNA L.
PEABODY, MARK B.
PFEFFER, JOEL
PFEIL, CHARLES E.
PHELPS, GAIL B.
PONTICELLO, CHRISTOPHER
POTTER, JAMES W.
PRIN, CLAIRE
PROCOPIO, PHYLLIS T.
PUTINSKY, THOMAS F.
RATTNER, STEVEN C.
REGULA, MAX A.
REIDBORD, TODD F.
PEITENAUER, RUTH
RIDGE, DAVID G.
ROBINSON, DEBORAH L.
ROBINSON, MICHAEL S.
ROMIG, JEFFREY L.
ROGUE, BARBARA B.
SAMIOS, GUS D.
SAUNDERS, KURT M.
SCHREIBER, SHEILA R.
SCHWAB, GREGORY G.
SCIBETTA, JEFFREY D.
SCOTT, PATRICIA J.
SERPA, JOHN R.
SETCAVAGE, JUSTINE R.
SHADER, DONNA L.
SHEARER, GAIL R.
SHEPHERD, THOMAS D., JR.
SHIRE, MARK J.
SHOWALTER, DONALD S.
SIKON, GREGORY M.
SODINI, GREGG S.
SODOMSKY, ALLAN L.
SPENCER, JAMES
SPERLING, LAWRENCE I.

STANFORD, DENISE J.
STEIN, MITCHELL J.
STEIN, SHERRY J.
STEWART, ARTHUR B.
STEWART, MICHAEL T.
STONEMETZ, KAY L.
STREILY, MICHAEL W.
SYMONDS, ROBERT L., JR.
THOMAS, CHARLES E.
THOMAS, PETER H.
THOMAS, RICHARD J.
THOMPSON, ROSSMAN D.
TISCHUK, GLORIA A.
TOKARSKY, DIANE M.
TOOMEY, TERRY
VARGO, BRIAN S.
WADE, MARK G.
WAIN, REBECCA L.
WALKOW, RONALD H.
WEINER, SHEILA C.
WEIS, PHILIP J.
WEISBERG, LISA B.
WOLSTONCROFT, BRUCE J.
ZANIC, EVAN M.
ZUBROW, STEPHEN S.

— Class of —
1986

AARON, WAYNE JAMES
ARCHER, VICTORIA LEIGH
AZMOUN, AFSOUN
BABCOCK, GRETCHEN ROSE
BELINKOFF, DALIA E.
BERGER, JOSHUA L.
BIRSIC, DANIEL J.
BLACKMORE, STEVEN CRAIG
BLECHMAN, JAY A.
BLUEDORN, DONALD CARL
BOCIANOSKI, LOUIS G.
BOUGHNER, JAMES R.
BOURNE, ELAINE MARIE
BRENNEMAN, KEITH ORR
BROWN, VANESSA THORNTON
BUDDIE, JAMES ANTHONY
BURKE, ALMON STITH, JR.
CAMPBELL, PAULA ANNE
CANTER, JACQUELINE H.
CANTERNA, PAUL E.
CARL, BARBARA BALLING
CARNEVALI, RONALD P.
CARRARA, SHELLEY ANN
CASALNOVA, CHARLES C.
CAVANAUGH, SUZANNE M.
CERASO, AMY
CESARE, BRENDA

CLOUSE, MARY C.
COLEMAN, CATHERINE BAINE
CONNOR, JACK W.
CONWELL, WILLIAM MICHAEL
CRAIG, DENNIS PATRICK
CRIBBS, GREGORY D.
CUBAN, BRIAN
D'ALFONSO, GINA M.
DALY, ERIC A.
DANAHER, MARIA GRECO
DANFORTH, BARBARA JEAN
DAPPER, ROBERT E., JR.
DEAN, MARY FRANCES
DEMPSEY, KEVIN J.
DENTICE, JEANNE LYNN
DIETRICH, MARIAN FAYE
DOLLASE, ELLEN K.
DUFFY, CHARLES MARION
EARLY, CLIFFORD THOMAS
EBERLE, ROBERT ALAN
EDGECOMBE, WALLACE E., JR.
EINHORN, RUTH MARY
ESPOSITO, STEVEN MICHAEL
FELDMAN, BRIAN J.
FERGUSON, MICHAEL DAVID
FIELDS, JULIE LYNN
FINE, ROBERT PETER
FINGERET, ILENE H.
FIORE, JOHN ROBERT
FRISCHMAN, CRAIG E.
GALLA, KAREN VICKLESS
GASIOR, MARIANNE FRANCES
GEEVER, MARY BRIDGET
GERACIMOS, JOHN N.
GILLIAM, ANTHONY
    CHARLES
GOERN, GILLIAN LEE
GORDON, ALAN BENNETT
GREENE, ALBERT, JR.
GRENEN, JAMES FREDERIC
HAAK, MARK F.
HABOVICK, MICHELE M.
HANCOCK, DAVID L.
HARTMAN, SUSAN DiMARCO
HATFIELD, WILLIAM J.
HERMAN, KATHY E.
HOEL, CHRISTOPHER
    CHARLES
HOFRICHTER, JOHN THOMAS
HOKE, PAMELA RENEE
HOLZMAN, JAMES A.
HOOPER, MICHAEL EDGAR
HOPKINS, TINA GWENDOLYN
    ANN
HOWEY, TARA ANN
IOLE, JOHN EDWARD

JOHNSON, RICHARD, JR.
JOSEPH, STEVEN
KATZ, MICHAEL S.
KEIM, AMY L.
KELLEY, CHRISTOPHER P.
KENNISON, JUDITH L.
KIMBALL, ANDREW GEORGE
KINGAN, ALBERT RICHARD
KIRSCH, SUSAN MURPHY
KIRSHNER, MILES ANDREW
KLEIN, ARNOLD I.
KNAPP, MARK TIMOTHY
KOCZAN, PAULA ANN
KOEPKA, JENIFER
KOHLER, JANET SUE
KONIECZKA, DANIEL JOHN, JR.
KUHN, DAVID RICHARD
KUHNSMAN, DAVID WILLIAM
KURTZ, ANDREA LYNN
KUTZ, JAMES WILLIAM
LAMPENFELD, GARY DAVID
LANG, CHERYL ANNE
LAPCEVIC, JAMES S.
LAUDA, KATHI J.
LAWRENCE, STEWART BRYAN
LEVENSON, JOAN AMY
LEWIS, GARY W.
LIEBER, PENINA KESSLER
LINES, KAREN R.
LLOYD, MICHAEL EDWARD
LOAIZA, JACQUELINE
LONGER, FRED S.
LOY, JOSEPH MICHAEL
MADIGAN, THOMAS JOHN
MAGOVERN, FRANCES A.
MALECKI, DONALD E.
MARKLE, MARGARET L.
McCARTHY, CHRISTOPHER J.
McCARTHY, KEVIN FRANCIS
McCRARY, NINA YVONNE
McDONACH, JOSEPH MICHAEL
McDONNELL, TYRONE M.
McGINNIS, THOMAS PATRICK
McHUGH, JAMES JOSEPH, JR.
McKENNA, C. KIM
McMAHON, MARJORIE LYNN
McNALLY, CHRISTOPHER
    KEVIN
McNULTY, SEAN JOSEPH
MEYER, GREGOR F., JR.
MIKLOS, ROSEMARY
    NAKONEZNY
MILAVEC, STANLEY J., JR.
MIRBAGHERI, LEDAN
MOLCZAN, WILLIAM
    THOMAS

MORAN, JOSEPH THOMAS
MORRIS, DONNA J.
MURTHA, SHARON CMAR
NAZZARO, SAMUEL G., JR.
NULTON, KEVIN L.
OBERDICK, DAVID GLENN
O'HARA, ROBERT J., JR.
OLUP, JEFFREY THOMAS
PAPPAS, LIA MICHELLE
PATTON, STEPHEN RICHARD
PETERS, JEFFREY DAVID
PETERS, JOHN CALVIN, JR.
PETERSON, BETTIE JANE
PETTIT, D. BRADLEY
PLUM, LINDA CATHERINE
PODHEISER, IRA L.
QUINN, JEFFREY HUGH
RELPHORDE, COLIN B.
RIBACK, SCOTT HUNTER
RICH, JANET LOWRY
RIELLY, EILEEN REGINA
RODELLA, PATRICIA BRADY
RODGERS, MARY JO
ROSENBERGER, MOIRA BETH
ROYER, CHARLES P.
RUNCO, PAMELA ANN
RUSCHAK, MARY JO
RUYMANN, JOHN ANDREW
RYAN, GEORGANN ELIZABETH
SALPIETRO, FRANK
    GUGLIOTTA
SAMBOL, STEPHEN B.
SANFORD, MICHAEL JAMES
SCOLIERE, MICHAEL EDWARD
SCOTT, RAY H.
SEDORY, RICHARD T.
SHAW, KANESSA MARYSHOW
SHERMAN, CAROL JEAN
SHOLL, TROYER JOSEPH
SIEGEL, DAVID M.
SILKO, ALAN THOMAS
SISCA, JOSEPH S.
SIVAK, STEPHANIE ANN
SMITH, KENNETH EUGENE
SMITH, WALLACE W., III
SPILKER, LAWRENCE J.
STONER, EUGENIA CHAMBERS
STOUT, LAUREN PREE
STUBBLEFIELD, WILLIAM H.
SWEENEY, MICHAEL T.
TENAGLIA, MARCY LYNN
THREET, GERALD LEE
TOLWIN, NATHANIEL LEVI
TUTOKI, JANE ANN
TYLINSKI, LORI KAYE
VALYO, CARY W.

VERONIS, NICHOLAS A.
VISNIC, MARK GEORGE
WALSH, COLLEEN ANNE
WEBSTER, BONNIE PEARCE
WEIS, JOSEPH F.
WESDOCK, MARY ANNE
WILDER, BRUCE LORD
WILLIFORD, DONALD
WILSON, LLOYD ELLSWORTH, II
WILSON, LORI ELIZABETH
WIRFEL, EMANUEL W.
WITHEREL, MATTHEW LOUIS
WOLFE, BARRY HALL
YUHAS, JOSEPH A.
YURKO, AMY JO NAPONIC
ZARR, JOHANNA C.

— Class of —
1987

ABRUZZO, MARK DAVID
ACKERMAN, LINDA S.
ADAMCHIC, JOSEPH PAUL, JR.
ADAMS, JEROME M., JR.
ADOMITIS, ANDREW FRANK
AIGNER, PAULA M.
ANSA, O. DANIEL
ANTHONY, G. DOYLE
BAMONTE, ANNA M.
BARKUS, MARIANNE
    ELIZABETH
BARNISIN, DEBRA BONDI
BARTOLACCI, JOSEPH C.
BAUMAN, JEFFREY PAUL
BEERS, LORIE RAE
BELAK, JOHN PAUL
BELAN, LAURIE ANN
BETZNER, ERIC PAUL
BICKERSTAFF, CHRISTINE L.
BIRDY, DEAN ALAN
BISOGNI, GARY
BLACKWELL, CHRISTOPHER L.
BLOOM, DAVID STEVEN
BOEHMAN, MICHAEL PAUL
BOYLE, ROBERT G.
BOYNTON, PAUL D.
BRAND, JUDITH P.
BRENNER, MICHAEL L.
BROWN, STEPHANIE ELLEN
BRUNO, JUDY ANN
BRUNORI, DAVID ERIC
BURKE, TIMOTHY CHARLES
BURKHARDT, JAMES MICHAEL
BUTKO, DIANA M.
BUTTENFIELD, PHILIP M.P.

CAMPBELL, DONALD BRUCE
CANTOR, JILL DEBRA
CARY, MARY SUE
CERMINARA, KATHY L.
CHAFFO, JOHN L., JR.
CHAJSON, HOWARD A.
CHAVIS, DIANE HERNON
CHIODO, GAIL M.
CIRBA, RONALD EDWARD
COHEN, SUSAN AMY
COLE, WILLIAM CHARLES
COLWELL, CHRISTOPHER J.
COOPER, WILLIAM MARION
COPPOLA, VINCENT A.
CORNEY, SUSAN TYLER
CORNIBE, TRACY L.
COX, KEVIN FERGUSON
CREAGH, MARY THERESA
CRUM, ELIZABETH
D'EMILIO, DEANNE HORNER
DAILEY, JOYCE CULLINAN
DAILER, PETER JOHN
DAYICH, LOUIS MARKO
DEANER, MARJORIE JANE
DEMASE, PATRICIA
DENMAN, ANN McKINSTRY
DEORAS, MONICA BHANU
DEPAUL, MICHAEL R., JR
DETTORRE, COLLEEN ANNE
DETWILER, ELIZABETH C.
DiCICCO, CARLA M.
DiVENCENZO, CHARLES J., JR.
DOEPKEN, KATHLEEN MILLER
DOUDS, VALERIE SUE
DUZYK, DAVID MICHAEL
EVAN, KRISTEN MICHELLE
EVANS, JULIE A.
EVANS, SHARON M.
FELDMAN, KENDRA D.
FERRETTI, JOSEPH R.
FIORE, KEVIN J.
FRANC, BRADLEY J.
GABRIEL, ARTHUR
GEDRICH, ALAN ROSS
GEMEINHARDT, ELISE A.
GENTILCORE, EDWARD
    BERNARDON
GENTILE, FREDERICK JOSEPH
GIUNTA, JAMES THOMAS
GOLDBERG, MINDY KAE
GOLDSTEIN, TAMMIE L.
GOODERHAM, JEFFREY P.
GRABOSKI, EDWARD
    THOMAS JOSEPH
GRECO, MARIA L.
GRIFFITH, RODNEY B.

GROSSMAN, NANCY SUE
GROSSO, KAREN LYNN
HAAGENSEN, JANICE
HACKETT, MARY JOAN
HALL, PATRICIA MARIE
HARNISH, DAVID LEE
HART, MELISSA ANNE
HARTMAN, RHONDA GAY
HECKATHORNE, HOLLY ELICE
HEILMAN, NANCY LAUFFER
HENKE, CORNELIUS JOSEPH
HERMANN, PETER W., JR.
HERSH, JEFFERY LEE
HETRICK, MICHAEL R.
HICKS, MICHAEL WADE
HINKLE, ANTHONY WAYNE
HLAFCSAK, JUDITH J.
HOPPE, JON ALEXANDER
HORWITZ, JEFFREY SCOTT
HUDAK, TIMOTHY QUALEY
IRVIN, JANET G.
JACKSON, LEE STEVEN
JAMES, AARON NATHANIEL
JOHNSON, DANIEL P.
KALSON, SUSAN FRIEDBERG
KALYVAS, PAMELA
    PANAGIOTA
KENDAL, JODI AILEEN
KERR, SARAH
KIESLER, THOMAS EUGENE
KING, BENJAMIN WEEMS
KINLEY, MARK E.
KOHOUT, EDWARD R.
KOOSER, JOHN H.
KOROSTOFF, JEFFREY A.
KOROWICKI, KAREN
KOTCELLA, MARY BETH
KRAMER, KATHERINE E.
KRASIK, ELAINE BELLE
KREY, CLIFFORD ALLEN
LANCE, MARY KATHRYN
LANDAU, ABBY HARLAN
LANGER, JERROLD I.
LANUTI, FRANK JOHN, JR.
LANZILLO, RICHARD A.
LAUER, HARRISON S.
LAVELLE, MARCELINE A.
LEAHY, STEPHEN GERARD
LEBOWITZ, LAWRENCE MARK
LECCE, DANIEL J.
LEE, KENNETH W.
LESNOCK, JOAN ELAINE
LIJEWSKI, TIMOTHY S.
LINGERNFELTER, DAVID BLAIR
LINN, CHARLES ALLEN
LOMEO, JAMES J.

LONDON, ERIC H.
LUDDY, ROBERT JOSEPH
LYNCH, BRIAN P.
MAHDAVI, MARYAM
MAIOLO, ROBERT NICHOLAS
MASTERSON, CHARLES
    VINCENT, III
MASTERSON, J. BRUCE
MAYCHECK, KAREN MARIE
McCARTHY, SHEILA H.
McCORMICK, JUDITH
McGREGOR, JAMES RUSSELL, JR.
McHOLME, NANCY J.
McMARLIN VATER, SUSAN
    MARY
MEADEN, LAURA A.
MEHALKO, ANNA MARIE
MEHNO, CHRISTOPHER D.
MIDDLEMAN, LISA G.
MORELLA, JEFFREY J.
MORRISON, LAURA WINTON
MUOLO, JOHN E.
MURRMAN, FRANCIS ROBERT
MYERS, GAIL ALISON
NAPIERKOWSKI, EDWARD
    MICHAEL
NOGAY, ARLIE R.
NORD, MICHAEL DAVID
O'DONNELL, NEIL TANEY
OLSON, RICHARD KARL, JR.
OLSZEWSKI, JEFFREY MICHAEL
PACILLA, FRANKIE JO
PALKO, PATRICIA P.
PALMIERI, ANNE MARIE
PALUTIS, ALEXANDER J.
PALUTIS, MICHAEL J.
PANIAN, MICHAEL G.
PANZARELLA, JAY L.
PASSODELIS, BARBARA LYNN
PATTERSON, GEORGE M., II
PATTERSON, PETER ROSS
PAWLOWSKI, MARGARETE
    EMILIA
PECSENYE, TIMOTHY D.
PERELMAN, SHARON WITTLIN
PERLOW, LESLIE A.
PETERS, ALBERT C., II
PETRARCA, JOSEPH
    AMERICO, JR.
PHILLIS HERB, JANA LEE
PICCIRILLO, JULIE KAREN
POGARSKY, GREG
POLENTA, ROSEANN
    MARIE-DeGEORGE
POLLOCK, JEFFREY
    LAWRENCE

PORCELLI, JAMES GERARD
PORTER, JOHN J.
POULOS, KATHLEEN JOANN
POWERS, GREGOR JAMES
POYTHRESS, ELEANOR JANICE
PRISTAS, TINA MARIE
PUCHNICK, WILLIAM L.
QUINN, JAMES MICHAEL
RANDAL, BARBARA TOOHEY
RAU, SHARON TERESE
RAY, GREGORY ROBERT
REAGLE, CYNTHIA LEE
REICH, STEPHEN F.
REISMAN, MARC S.
REITZ, RONALD E.
RENO, DAVID SCOTT
RIBACK, KATHERINE IRWIN
RICKABAUGH, DAVID EUGENE
RIEFLE, ROBERT HOAK
RIELLY, WILLIAM WHITFIELD, JR.
RITTER, MICHELLE IVY
ROMPALA, KAREN ELIZABETH
ROMUALDI, JOHN P.
SAUCHIN, JANICE ANNE
SCHIEVE, MARY AGNES
SCHRAG, SUSAN EMILY
SCOULOS, GARY M.
SEGERDAHL, JAMES R., JR.
SENNETT, BARBARA ELLEN
SHAPIRO, CYNTHIA D.
SHAW, MARK JOHN
SHEPARD, MICHAEL DREW
SHEPLEY, DAVID L.
SLOAN, TIMOTHY JAMES
SMITH, DEBORAH L.
SMITH, SUSAN KAY
SOKOLOSKI, ROBERT GARY
SPINA, MARIA L.
SPUNGEN, CLIFFORD E.
STANZIOLA, CARMEN R.
STEWART, PAULA G.
STORM, NICHOLAS GERARD
SWEENEY, MICHAEL T.
SWEET, BARRY N.
SZUCH, RICHARD COLEMAN
TALADAY, MATTHEW B.
THEIS, MARCELLE M.
TORRANCE, W. ALAN, JR.
TYLINSKI, LORI K.
ULINE, MOLLY
UPDYKE, SALLIE ANNE
WALK, TRACY ANN Q.
WALLA, NANCY ANN
WASSER, THERESA LYNN
WEBSTER, DEIRDRE LOUISE
WEIS, GREGORY T.

WEIS, JOSEPH FRANCIS
WEIS, MARTIN JAMES
WENDEL, GLORIA
    ALEXANDRA
WHITE, SUSAN S.
WILLIAMS, GOMER T.
WILLIAMSON, TINA LOUISE
WIRTZ, STUART PAUL
WITTENBERG, ERIC JAY
WOHLGEMUTH, ANN MULROY
WYMARD, ELLIN H.
YOAKAM, TED G.
ZATSICK, EDWARD T.
ZIEGLER, ELIZABETH ANN

— Class of —
1988

ADELKOFF, STEVEN JAY
ANDERSON, WILLIAM H.
ASHDALE, KAREN MARIE
AULT, AMY EMERICK
BAE, TANYA
BALZARINI, MICHAEL
BANCKS, DARYL ANN
BARBER, RONALD D.
BARE, ROBBIE W.
BARNA, STEPHANIE ANNE
BASON, ERNEST F.
BAUER, JACQUELINE M.
BEARD, PHILIP EDWARD
BENDER, ELENA DURONIO
BENTZ, JAMES WORTHINGTON
BERGER, MATTHEW H.
BERNSTEIN-RUDOV, HOLLIE A.
BLAND, DONA
BLISSMAN, RODGER J.
BLOCH, CAROLYN JEAN
BLUME, CHARLES EARL
BORDEN, DIANE L.
BRENNAN, THOMAS JOHN
BROWN, GLADYS MARIE
BROWN, RICHARD ROBERT
BRUBAKER, LISA ANN
BUKSTEIN, YVONNE F.
BURKARDT, MEG L.
BURKE, MAUREEN ANN
BURKE, SALLY LOUISE
BURNS, MICHAEL E.
BURZACHECHI, NANCILEE
CAHILL, SUSAN LYNNE
CARROLL, BRIAN PATRICK
CHISNELL, JANICE HOFFMAN
CLEARY, DENISE M.
COHEN, KIP
COHEN, MICHAEL ALLAN

COHN, JACOB CHARLES
COLEMAN, SEAN MICHAEL
COOK, V. SUSANNE
COPP, PAULA JEAN
CORDES, SAMUEL JOHN
COSTELLO, AMY LOUISE
CRAY, PATRICIA
CURRIER, JAMES D.
DEVINE, JILL A.
DICE, MARY A.
DIULUS, GREGORY P.
DOCTORS, RACHEL
DOLPHIN, ARLETTE T.
DORMAN, MICHAEL C.
DORR, JOHN CHRISTOPHER
DRYJANSKI, ANDREW L.
DUDZINSKI, CHESTER A.
DUGAN, MITCHELL HUNTER
DUNCAN, GILBERT HUFFMAN
DUNST, KATHLEEN A.
DUPLAGA, EDWARD
    KAZIMIERZ
EDWARDS, ALICE RIEDMAN
EGLER, MARGARET MARY
EHRMAN, KURT GERARD
EISMAN, ANDREW B.
ELLENBOGEN, NANCY GAIL
ELLIOTT, PATRICIA LYNN
ELLISON, WALTER LEE, JR.
EMIG, MARIANNA GAIL
EVANGELISTA, JAMES PAUL
FABRIZI, JOSEPH W.
FARBER, ALAN I.
FARNETH, GEORGE R., II
FARWELL, THERESA M.
FAWCETT, DANIEL McKAIN
FAZIO, LINDA R.
FENCHEL, JAMES RICHARD, II
FENNER, JOHN WINN DANA
FERGUSON, CHRISTINE RAE
FERGUSON, DWIGHT DAVID
FIRESTONE, NATHAN N.
FISCHER, ERIC ANTHONY
FLEMING, PATRICIA ANN
FREY, JAMES MICHAEL
FRIONO, ALFONSO, JR.
GABLE, KAREN L.
GAERTNER, DOROTHY
    ELIZABETH
GATES, MARTIN STANLEY
GEBELOFF, STEPHEN
    BENJAMIN
GELMAN, CATHERINE M.
GEORGE, STEPHANIE LEE
GILMORE, ANGELA DENISE
GINDLESPERGER, BARRY B.

GOLDMAN, LESLIE AYN
GOTTLIEB, CHARLES
    BENJAMIN
GRAYSON, ZACHARY LOUIS
HADLEY, THOMAS J.
HAECKLER, MATTHEW XAVIER
HAMMALIAN, JOHN BOYD
HAMMER, MICHAEL CHARLES
HARRINGTON, MOIRA cm
HELEEN, MARK LOUIS
HENDLER, SCOTT MARTIN
HENRY, PAUL M.
HERRERA, FREDERICK M.A.
HERRUP, DIANE M.
HILL, LYNN FISHER
HITT, MARY ELIZABETH
HOOTON, LUCILE CLEMONS
HOTIS, PETER DEAN
HUNTER, RACHEL LEA
HYMAN, CAROLINE L.
IGNASIAK, CHERYL ANN
INGERSOLL, DIANA K.
JEFFREY, COLEEN ANNE
JOHNSON, MICHELE P.
JOSHOWITZ, JAMES H.
KARAMANOS, NICHOLAS
    CHRISTOPHER
KAY, PAUL GERARD
KEATING, JOHN HOBART
KEISER, KIMBERLY J.
KELLEY, MICHELE M.
KEMPIC, ANNAMARIE
KENNEDY, MICHAEL
KIRLEIS, ALYSON J.
KOCEVAR, FRANK CARL
KOMOROSKI, KENNETH
    STANLEY
KRATZ, CAROLYN MARIE
KROPF, JOHN WHITWORTH
KUCK, MARY MARGARET
KUNKEL, GREGORY T.
KUPFERSTEIN, RONNI CAROLE
LACKATOS, JOHN C.
LADAS, CHRISTOS
LAUBACH, GREGORY L.
LAUN, MAX WALTER
LAWTON, CHARLES P.
LEHMAN, SHARON F.
LEVENSON, ELLIOTT I.
LEWIS, JOSEPH M.
LOFTUS, MARY ELLEN
LORENZO, OLIVIA J.
LUCAS, LAWRENCE
    LIVINGSTON
LUCHOK, REBECCA RUTH
MALLOY, MARY GENE GARRITY

MARKS, MELANIE S.
MARSHALL, WESLEY ROBERT
MATHIAS, KAREN E.
MAZZEI, MARK E.
McCARTHY, LAWRENCE B.
McCARTHY, MARGARET
    EVANS
McCLAM, SHANNON D.
McCULLOUGH, KAREN KEMP
McDONNELL, THOMAS
    ANTHONY
McGINNESS, CATHERINE
    SCULLY
McGRAW, CANDACE SERAFINI
McGRAW, JOSEPH EDWARD
McKENNA, MAUREEN ELLEN
McNALLEY, MARSHA L.
McQUILLAN, ARTHUR T.
MEISNER, MARY M.
MERCHANT, CHARLES A.
MERCOLINI, JAMES
    ALEXANDER
MEYERSON-BENTZ, AMY
    ERIKA
MICKA, MARY JO
MILLER, KATHY D.
MILLER, MARVIN
MIZNER, JOHN F.
MOORHEAD, WILLIAM J., JR.
MORITZ, J. KENNETH
MORROW, MARK B.
MULLANEY, MARTIN PETER
MURPHY, RACHEL
NEWMAN, KENNETH TODD
NORD, MARCY LEE
NOVAK, DAVID JOHN
NOVAK, GEORGE DAVID, II
O'CONNOR, DONNA MARIE
O'DONNELL, SEAN R.S.
OSBERG, LINDA MARGUERITE
OWENS, GARY RONALD
PAMPENA, DENISE MARIE
PARIS, DAVID
PATTON, DONNA J.
PATTON, WILLIAM J.
PAUL, JONATHAN W.
PENNER, NANCEY G.
PERESS, SASSON DAVID
PFATTEICHER, CARL
    THOMAS GEARHART
PLUNKETT, CAROL M.
RAYMUND, FRANK JAMES
RENDE, BRUCE EDWARD
RENWAND, SANDRA MACKEY
RINGEISEN, WAYNE WILLIAM
RIPEPI, CATHERINE ROSE

ROCHE, CHRISTOPHER
    CHARLES
ROGERS, DAVID J.
ROLLINS, TRACI HOPE
ROSE, RICHARD D.
ROSENBERG, JAMES F.
ROSENBLATT, STEPHEN MARK
ROSS, ROSALIND MARON
ROSSO, GERARD THOMAS
ROTHERMEL, FRANK A.
RUSHFORD, ROBERT H.
RUSSELL, JEFFREY J.
SANCHEZ, ANTHONY G.
SCHECHTER, SUSAN
SCHUSTER, JEANNINE ANN
SCURFIELD, SCOTT A.
SEEKINGS, MICHAEL
SILVAGGIO, ANNA MARIA
SNYDER, GEORGE T.
SOCCI, PHILIP L.
SPRINGER, DENISE BABLAK
STACHOWIAK, CATHERINE
    ANN
STADTMILLER, STEVEN
    MICHAEL
STAFFORD, CAROLINE
    JEANETTE
STANZIOLA, MARK BERNARD
STILL, ELLEN CATHERINE
STRAM, KENNETH MICHAEL
STUCK, GREGORY ARTHUR
STYSLINGER, MARGARET R.
TAULBEE, GEORGE M.
TEMPLE, CHRIS MICHAEL
THOMAS, JOSEPH ROBERT
TOLLERTON, MARGARET M.
TROTZ, CHRISTINE MARIE
TUKAN, IBRAHIM J.
WALDMAN, IVAN MARC
WALLACE, DERRICK L.
WALSH, COLLEEN ANNE
WALSH, GARY WILLIAM
WALTERS, ANNE ELIZABETH
WEBBER, DON L.
WEINER, CHARLES
WEISS, CYNTHIA LAURA
WELSH, DANIEL JOSEPH
WEST, ANN ZUBERBUHLER
WEST, JOSEPH ROBERT
WHELAN, MARGARET FRIED
WILBURN, MELISSA LYN
WILLIAMS, ANGELA MARIA
WILLIAMS, RONALD LYNN
WILLIG, ROBERT A.
WILSON, PAMELA SHIRLEY
WOLFF, GREGG MICHAEL

WU, BENJAMIN H.
YABLONSKI, JOSEPH MICHAEL
YARD, JOHN SCHUYLER, JR.
YOFFE, JEFFREY NORMAN
ZOTTER, JOHN WRIGHT

— Class of —
1989

ADAMS, DANIEL ALLEN
ADAMS, WILLIAM MICHAEL
AMATO, ANITA J.
AMDUR, BRETT
AMES, RICHARD L.
AUDLEY, SEAN PATRICK
BARCHIESI, JOHN ERIC
BARTLETT, CYNTHIA M.A.
    BULL
BARTOSZEWICZ, JOSEPH
    EDWARD
BEDORTHA, JAMES J.
BEGG, TODD MASON
BELLO, ROBERT G.
BERKUN, FLORA MARCUS
BERTOVICH, TERESA ANN
BLUMENFELD, MARTIN L.
BOGDANOFF, MICHAEL S.
BRAY, ROBERT CHARLES
BRENNER, LORI ELLA
BROWN, ELIZABETH
CAMPBELL, PATRICIA ELLEN
CAPLAN, MICHAEL SINGER
CARDUCCI, LINDA R.
CARLSON, R. BRUCE
CARR, ALISA NICOLE
CARTWRIGHT, THOMAS
    WILLIAM
CASEY, MARIA TERESA
CAVALIER, MICHAEL JEFFREY
CHEN, MARY F.
CLAUNCH, KATHLEEN MARIE
CLEARY, KATHLEEN A.
COCHRAN, JEROME
COLECCHIA, THERESA J.
CONN, JEFFREY J.
CONNELL, ELIZABETH WARD
COOPER, MARCIA LYNN
CORBELLI, JAMES VINCENT
CRAWFORD, LESTER
DANIELS, KEITH ALLAN
DAVIS, PETER JUSTIS
DeFRANK, VICTORIA LYNN
    DOMENICA
DIAS, ANTONION F.
DLUTOWSKI, JOSEPH
    ARTHUR

DRANE, LINDA A.
DUER, D. HOLBROOK
ESPOSITO, CHERYL L.
ESTEY, JOHN HARPER
FEDEL, LIONEL CHARLES
FEIGENBAUM, MICHAEL D.
FERRIS, COLETTE ELIZABETH
FINK, N. LEAH
FINLEY, AMY JENE
FIORA, GLEN E.
FISHER, KAREN SUSAN
FOLLETT, KENDRA S.
FRENEY, SANDRA MARIE
FROHLICH, MINDY BETH
GAVLIK, LISA K.
GEORGE, DIANE F.
GERLACH, GREGORY DONALD
GERMAIN, REGINA
GILBERT, EDWARD E.
GIOVANNELLI, JOHN G.
GIRDANY, PAUL
GLADDEN, THOMAS
    DOUGLASS
GLEESON, ROSEMARY
    KATHERINE
GOLD, RONALD ERIC
GOLDBLUM, PHILIP A.
GOODMAN, NANCY J.
GRACE, MAUREEN ELAINE
GRAY, GEORGE RICHARD
GRAZAN, LISA V.
GREENWALD, MARK DAVID
GREER, SANDRA T.
GRODEN, MAUREEN PATRICIA
GRUBER, DAVID J.
GUIDAS, ELIZABETH W.
HAHALYAK, JOHN ALBERT
HALLORAN, RICHARD A.
HAROUSE, DAVID KYLE
HARRIS, NANCY MARY
HECETA, W. ELGINE
HENDERSON, HERBERT
    PALMER
HENDERSON, ROBERT JAMES
HENRICH, CAROLINE ANN
HENRY, DEBRA LYNN
HESS, CATHERINE ANN
HIRSCH, BARRY I.
INNAMORATO, MARY FRANCES
IWINSKI, DAVID, JR.
JAEGER, EDWARD ABBOTT, JR.
JIN, PHYLLIS ANN
JOHNSON, DENISE RENETTE
JOSHI, JUI M.
KASPERKOSKI, KATHLEEN
    MARIE

KATZ, MARTIN BERNARD
KECSKEMETHY, JOSEPH M.
KEENAN, BETH E.
KIRSCH, ERIC D.
KNEE, KATHRYN
KLANICA, KENNETH F.
KOEHLER, MICHAEL JOHN
KOLAN, JAMES STEPHAN
KORDING, NICCOL D.
KUNSELMAN, HARRY F.
KUTSCH, ANTHONY JOHN
LAMPENFELD, ELIZABETH L.
LAZZARO, JOSEPH W.
LEBOVITZ, STEPHEN HOWARD
LESHER, AMY JOY
LeSCHACK, MARK ELIOT
LIBERTY, SUSANNA
LINDSAY, THEODORE D.
LIVINGSTON, KATHLEEN
    MARIE
LOCH, ROBERT A.
LOGAN, TIMOTHY NEIL
LOVE, FREDERICK AARON
LOWERY, TERRI ANN
LUBA, DIANE MARIE
LUPAS, DAVID W.
LYNCH, GARY F.
MAGGIO, MATTHEW G.
MALLINGER, JEFFREY DAVID
MALONEY, RAYMOND MARTIN
MANGOLD, ROBERT GREGORY
MARUCCI, JAMES CAMILLO
MATTIONI, MICHAEL
MAZZA, SHERRI L.
McCAGUE, RICHARD JENKINS
McCLAIN, LISA DENINE
McDERMOTT, THOMAS
    PATRICK
McKENZIE, GLENN C.
McMAHON, J. ROBERT
MENTZER, PAUL
MERVAN, LORRAINE WELTY
MIESNER, JOHN THOMAS
MILLER, JEFFREY B.
MITCHELL, GREGORY JAMES
MITINGER, ALICE
    BIRMINGHAM
MONDIK, SUSAN HELENE
MOORE, JOHN NELSON
MORAVITZ, BARBARA
    BLOTNICK
MORRIS, ROBIN FIGUREL
MORRIS, ROGER N.
MUELLER, PATRICIA ANN
MURPHY, MICHAEL A.
MYERS, JAYMI LYNN

NICHOLS, KENNETH LEE
NOLAN, STEVEN M.
NOONAN, PATRICK THOMAS
NOREIKA, GLORIANA
O'CONNELL, EDWARD
ONORATO, DANIEL ANTHONY
OVACIK, TURHAN M.
PANTELIS, MELANIE FALLONE
PAPAZEKOS, THEODORE
PASTRICK, TRACY L.
PETERSON, JEFFREY SCOTT
PICCININI, MARSHALL J.
PRINGLE, MARY F.
RAMSER, JOSEPH ANDREW
RANIERI, MICHAEL THOMAS
RANTOVICH, G. SCOTT
RATTNER, DAVID LEONARD
RAY, GREG A.
REIDBORD, AMY E.
REINHART, ANDREW WILLETT
RITCHIE, CAROL EVADNE
ROSENFELD, MAURA AVA
ROUSSOS, DAVID G.
RUPP, CATHY DIANE
RYAN, KAREN ELIZABETH
SAPIRA, LEE
SCHAIN, STEVEN MATTHEW
SCHEUERMANN, JAMES E.
SCHOOLEY, ELIZABETH
    WALTER
SCHWARTZ, JEFFREY A.
SCHWARTZ, NATHAN
    ALDRICH
SCOTT-ROEBUCK, RUTH A.
SHEEHAN, MARK ANDERSON
SHEPARD, ANNE M.
SHERIDAN, THOMAS W.
SHUMLAS, ALICE WARNER
SILVERMAN, MICHAEL ERIC
SILVERMAN, STEVEN BRETT
SIPPER, MARK A.
SLIFKIN, NEAL LOUIS
SOLES, CARLENE A.
SPEAR, JEFFREY WAYNE
SPOOL, TRACY L.
STAGG, LINDA LARSEN
STIEHM, RAFAEL G.
STRONG, SANDRA JEAN
SUNDBERG, KURT
SUPOWITZ, PAUL A.
SZEJK, LAUREN S.
TAYLOR, W. BRETT
THOMAS, DERRICK
THOMAS, GWYN ANN
TINKO, JOSEPH WILLIAM
TUMMONS, BERNADETTE K.

VOELKER, EDWARD
    FRANCIS, JR.
WASHINGTION, WYCESSA
    DOREEN
WASSEL, DAVID
WEBBER, DALE STAFFORD
WECHT, SIGRID RONSDAL
WEISMANN, DONALD JOSEPH
WOJCIK, MICHAEL H.
WOLFE, FREDERICK JAMES
WORLEY, LETITIA W.
WORMER, SUSAN LYNN
WYMAN, HEATHER ANNE
YAO, JEFFREY B.
YOUNG, IRA L.
ZANIC, MICHAEL G.
ZEREGA, DIANNE H.
ZICHERMAN, DAVID L.
ZINSKI, KEVIN R.

— Class of —
1990

ABRAMS, AVERY R. (Dec., 1989)
ADAMS, CECELIA A.
ANDERSON, ROBERT J.
ANGELELLI, MICHAEL D.
ARNOLD, CRAIG J.
AROMATORIO, JEFFREY G.
ARTMAN, EDYTHE A.
BANE, SCOTT E.
BARLOW, JEFFREY D.
BEAUREGARD, MICHAEL R.
    (Dec., 1989)
BECH, PAUL B.
BECK, SUE A.
BELDECOS, ARIADNE
BERCIK, KARRIE L.
BERGMANN, WILLIAM C.
BLACK, THEODORE N.
BLOCH, JAMES J.
BLUCHER, PAUL A.
BLUMENTHAL, LISA
BOJSZUK, SCOTT J.
BOOTH, CHRISTOPHER R.
BRADLEY, DENISE R.
BRAHAN, JEFFREY P.
BRICMONT, DANIEL K.
BROWDIE, STACY L.
BROWN, CARLA I.
BROWN, TERRYL L.
BRUNI, JOHN W.
BRUSTEIN, SHARON E.
BURGER, KEVIN S.
BURGESS, DAVID K.
BURNS, GERALD E.

BURNS, JAMES W.
BUZZINOTTI, ELAINE M.
BYRNES, DAVID F.
CABLE, STEVEN S.
CAMPBELL, DAVID D.
CAMPBELL, JILL A.
CAMPISANO, GINA
CAPPELLA, KERRI I.
CARSON, JACK A.
CHAMBERLAIN, APRIL L.
CHAMPION, AILEEN M.
CHETLIN, NATALIE K.
COHEN, HERBERT B.
COHEN, JUDITH M.
CORREA, DIEGO F.
COYLE, JANE E. (Dec., 1989)
CROWLEY, JAMES B.
CRUM, MICHAEL T.
CUNNINGHAM, HOWARD S.
CURLEY, JOHN F.
DAVIS, MICHAEL E.
DeCECCO, LISA L.
DeCICCO, EMILY K.
DIAMOND, MARGARET A.
DODDS, GEORGIA L.
DUFER, CAROL L.
DUFFY, JOHN M.
ECKERT, ROBERT N. (Dec., 1989)
EWING, PAMINA G.
FEDEL, SABRINA C.
FERGUSON, THOMAS M.
FICERAI, KENNETH
FIDDLER, THOMAS B.
FIELDING, JOHN R.
FIORILLA, JOHN L.
FISHMAN, CRAIG L.
FOX, JAMES M.
FRANKLIN, JEFFREY A.
FRENCH, KAREN S.
FRIEDKEN, LAWRENCE J.
FUCHEL, THOMAS K.
FULLER, CONSTANZE K.
FURRY, MARK W.
GAMBINO, MONICA P.
GARDA, CYNTHIA L.
GARDNER, MARNY A.
GARVER, KAREN A.
GERBER, MICHAEL L.
GLASSER, DANIEL H.
GOMPERS, MICHAEL F.
GOURNIC, KENNETH P.
GRAF, JOHN E.
GREENBERG, BENJAMIN H.
GREGG, ADELLA J.
GROSICK, GLENN J.
GROSS, LINDA M.

GUIDOS, ROBERT J.
HAMMER, THEODORE M.
HAMPTON, JEFFERY C.
HANNON, SEAN P.
HARKINS, KEVIN C.
HARRIS, GWENDOLYN W.
HARRIS, STACY J.
HENRY, AUGUSTINE P.
    (Dec., 1989)
HENRY, CAROLAYNE E.
HERSKOWITZ, JEAN E.
HIGGINBOTHAM, LISA M.
HOBSON, WILLIAM T.
HOSAY, CRAIG T.
HOULLION, JEFFREY R.
HOWARD, DERRICK
HOY, PAMELA E.
HOYER, MARK A.
HUETTER, GLENN A.
HUNTLEY, DAVID M.
IMPINK, ANNALIESE
JAMESON, BRUCE E.
JOHNSON, DAVID J.
JONES, SUSAN
JONES, WALDO D.
KAHN, LISA H.
KAHN, SUSAN L.
KATZ, BRUNO W.
KENAWELL, JOHN W.
KLABER, ANDREW B.
KORANDA, MICHAEL A.
KRAEMER, THOMAS R.
KRALL, ROBERT J.
KROLL, MAUREEN S.
KUBIT, JOSEPH E.
KUHN, JOHN M.
LEDEBOHN, KARL
LEE, YOUNG NA
LEECH, GORDON R.
LESTITIAN, WILLIAM E.
LEVY, SAMUEL D.
LINEMAN, JOSEPH E.
LOOP, PATRICIA K.
MAFRICE, LOUIS P.
MAGEE, BARBARA G.
MAGLEY, STEPHEN J.
MAHBOD, DEBORAH S.
MAHR, ERIC J.
MARCINCUK, ROBERT E.
MARTIRANO, JOHN M.
MASON, PAUL H.
MAYER, CHARLES F.
MAZESKI, MARK J.
McCORD, EDWARD L.
McDEVITT, DANIEL D.
McKEEVER, CONSTANCE Y.

McMANUS, CATHERINE G.
McNAMARA, FRANK V.
MERLIN, DEBORAH S.
    (Dec., 1989)
MERTZ, WILLIAM L.
MESSINA, CHRISTOPHER M.
MEYERS, RICHARD D.
MICHEL, LISA G.
MILLER, EDWARD A.
MITCHELL, ZANFORD A.
MLAWSKY, DAVID R.
MOFFATT, LORA A.
MONAHAN, PATRICIA A.
MONAHAN, RICHARD A.
MOORE, FRANCIS M.
MOORE, RICHARD D.
MULGRAVE, ANNE E.
MULROY, JOHN A.
MURPHY, GLENN E.
NESPOR, SHERYL
NYKYFORUK, PHILIP W.
O'CONNOR, EMILY I.
ORMOND, ELLEN N.
OTTO, CHRISTIANN
PASEK, MELISSA A.
PATERNOSTRO, ANDREW L.
PEDERSEN, BIRGIT
POSER, JOSEPH J.
QUINLAN, PATRICK P.
QUINN, THOMAS F.
RADMAN, DIANE R.
RAUSCHENBERGER, FLOYD A.
REED, SHERRI S.
RESNICK, JOHN A. (Dec., 1989)
ROBERTSHAW, NATALIE H.
ROSO, GINA J.
RUSCHEL, REBECCA J.
RUSHFORD, JOHN H.
RUYLE, BRIAN L.
SADOFF, JULIE B.
SALTZGIVER, LAURIE A.
SANTORI, MARGARET H.
SCAGLIONE, VINCENT
SCHAFFNER, CLARK F.
SCHESSLER, MICHAEL J.
SCHOLLE, PAUL R.
SCHOTT, DAVID C.
SCHUMANN, ERIC M.
SECUNDA, DAVID S.
SHERIDAN, SEAN O.
SIMPSON, SHAWNDYA L.
SINGLETON, TAMMY J.
SKEES, TONY D.
SLAGLE, BETH ANN
SMITH, NAMOSHA J.
SMITH, ROBIN A.

SOCHATS, LaVERNE L.
SOLOMON, ROBERT H.
SPILLER, DAVID G.
STEFAN, DENNIS M.
STOLAR, MARGARET M.
STRAKA, JOHN A.
SUSZKOWSKI, GEOFFREY J.
TOBIN, DANIEL R.
TOMASKO, RONALD T.
UISELT, THOMAS R.
VALVO, JACQUELINE
VENESKEY, CATHERINE A.
VOLK, TIMOTHY M.
WACHTEL, JONATHAN M.
WADDELL, DANIEL L.
WAGNER, MARYLOUISE
WAINWRIGHT, DIANNE S.
WAKULCHIK, LISA K.
WALKER, PAMELA L.
WALSH, PAUL J.
WARGO, RICHARD T.
WEBB, LISA D.
WEIS, ELIZABETH A.
WEISS, DANIEL L.
WEZOREK, LISA M.
WHITE, DAVID E.
WHITE, DAVID W.
WIDRIG, BARBARA L.
WILLIAMS, JOHN H.
WILLIAMS, SARA M.
WILLIAMS, SERENA M.
WITKOWSKI, ELIZABETH A.
WRIGHT, SHAWN N.
ZAKOWITZ, HILARY S.
ZANGRILLI, JOAN C.
ZENTZ, ROBERT
ZUCK, WALTER M.

— Class of —
1991

AGATE, DEBORAH L.
AKIN, LILIAN ALEXA
ALBERT, LORRIE K.
ALBRECHT, EDWARD M.
AMCHIN, JESS DAVID
ANTINOFF, STEVEN
ARGENZIANO, JON MICHAEL
ARMONDINO, SCOTT ALLEN
    (Dec., 1990)
ATHEY, ERIC N.
AVERY, EUGENIA CHRISTINA
BARRISH, KENNETH S., JR.
BASILE, MICHAEL JOHN
BECK, MARK EDWARD
BENKEN, JACQUELINE G.

BERKEBILE, KAREN KAY
BERNSTEIN, PAUL
BILLEY, EILEEN CHELLMAN
BLOCH, EVAN A.
BONN, BARBARA DARRAH
BORNSTEIN, PHILIP J.
BOZIK, GILLIAN T.
BRADLEY, GREGORY L.
BROWN, BETH ANN
BROWN, SANDRA ALBRIGHT
BROWNLEE, KAREN M.
BRYAN, JOHN K.
BULLOCK, SCOTT G.
CABRERA, KAREN R.
CAHOUET, ANN P.
CARLISLE, JAMES R., II
CARNINO, GINA M.
CAULFIELD, THOMAS PATRICK
CHILCOTE, KAREN ELIZABETH
CHRISTIN, JOHN JOSEPH, JR.
CLARK, JAMES R.
COHEN, DAVID SEAN
COLE, JAMES LAWRENCE
CONSTANTINE, AMY
    ELIZABETH
COSTA, ROSALIA J.
CRESTON, DONALD PAUL
CUNNINGHAM, LORI K.
CUSCINO, GLEN R.
DALEY, JOHN M.
DAUER, ROBERT EARL, JR.
    (Dec., 1990)
DEASY, JOHN FITZGERALD
DeMARCO, MARK STEVEN
DEUTSCH, LISA ANN
DIAZ, RODRIGO JOSE
DiCARLO, DAVID J.
DICK-HURWITZ, REBECCA
    JANE
DiNARDO, SHEILA SMITH
DONLEY, GARRETT
    CHRISTOPHER
DuBOIS, JEFFREY SCOTT
EARLY, MICHELLE MARGARET
EVANOFF, JOHN MICHAEL
FATO, LUCIANA
FINOLI, VINCENT JAMES
FISCHER, JEFFREY A.
FORD, J. STUART
FOX, JAN L.
FRANCISCUS, JOHN JOSEPH
GAFFNEY, RICHARD C., JR.
GIARRUSSO, LISA M.
GILL, MARY KAY
GIUSTI, LYNN CHRISTINE
GORCZYCKI, HENRY J.

GRACE, THOMAS R.
GRADEL, JOHN NEUMANN
GREENBERG, STEPHEN R.
GREENSTEIN, MICHAEL B.
GROSSMAN, COLBY H.
HALLOS, GREGORY P.
HAMBURG, WALTER, III
HAPPEL, DOUGLAS IAN
HARSHMAN, JOHN GIBSON
HARTLAND, CHRISTINE ANN
HARTLAND, JEFFREY D.
HAUSER, THOMAS A.
HARVEY, JESSE FERREE
LUKE, PAUL BRYSON
LUND, KENNETH JOHN
LYNCH, PAUL PATRICK
MARIANI, WARNER L.
MARQUIS, JEAN M.
MARTIN, BARBARA GRUSCH
MARTIN, THOMAS HOWARD
MARTINUCCI, ARTHUR DALE
MASELLI, MICHAEL CARMEN
MATHIAS, ANN G.
MAXSON, THOMAS DRAPER
McCURDY, DENNIS WILLIAM
    (Dec., 1990)
McELWAIN, STEPHANIE ANN
McLAUGHLIN, RAYMOND
    GRAHAM
MEDDIS, EILEEN JOYCE
MEDSGER, PHILIP ROSS
MEGHNOT, HEDYE
MENDELSON, ANN
MENGINE, ANTHONY
    CHARLES
MERVAN, STEPHEN C.
MEYERS, DIANE R.
MICHAILENKO, ANN
MORTAKIS, BRIDGET KHRISTIE
MULLER, MARIE MARGARET
MURPHY, MICHELE A.
NATALE, ANTHONY, III
NEIMEYER, PAUL CRAIG
NEISH, LAURENCE ADLAI
    (Dec., 1991)
NEWTON, JOEL D.
NG, CHERYL ANN
NORTHEY, JANET VIRGINIA
OAKES, KIMBERLY ANN
O'HARA, ANDREW S.
O'HERN, DANIEL J.
OSTERHOUT, PATRICIA M.
PARRISH, GEORGE C.
PFIRRMANN, JAMES
    RICHARD
PHILLIPS, JEFFREY K.

PICKERING, KATHYRINE S.
TURICI, MELINDA B.
UHER, PHILIP JAMES
UNCAPHER, LESLIE JACKSON
WALKER, CHRISTINA S.
WALSH, KATHLEEN A.
WASHINGTON, LISA Y.
WATTERSON, KIM M.
WESSELL, MICHAEL
    ANTHONY
WESTWOOD, SCOTT E.
WHITE, SONYA ANNETTE
WILLIAMS, CAROLYN V.
WILLIAMS, HEATHER A.
WILSON, ALAN TODD
WISHART, SCOTT SHERIDAN
    (Dec., 1991)
WITHERUP, JANICE M.
WOJNAROSKI, EDWARD PAUL
    (Dec., 1990)
WOOD, REBECCA C.
WYLER, MARCUS R.
    (Dec., 1990)
YOUNG, JONATHAN B.
YOUNG, JONATHAN PHILLIP
ZANONI, ANTHONY JOSEPH
ZICCARDI, DAVID C.
ZIMMER, BARBARA PALKOVITZ
ZIMMERMAN, DAVID M.
ZIMMERMAN, LORI C.
ZOLFAGHARI, PAUL N.

— Class of —
1992

ABBOTT, RICHARD
ABROMATS, PHILIP
AIELLO, JAMIE RENEE
    (Dec., 1991)
ALUKO, PHYLLIS LaJUANA
ANGELINE, PETER M., JR.
APPLEBY, ELIZABETH C.
    (Dec., 1992)
ASH, MICHELLE
BABLAK, JASON
BACHY, DENNIS R.
BAILEY, TAUNULA C.
BANSAI, MANISHA
BARTLETT, CHRISTINE H.
BARRETTE, KATHLEEN
    (Dec., 1992)
BEAMON, MARTINE M.
BEARD, NATHANIEL B.
    (Dec., 1992)
BERNSTEIN, MICHAEL
BLACK, CRAIG WILLIAM

BOSCH, GERARD R.
BOYER, CATHY S.
BOZICH-DiLUIGI, MARYANN
    (Dec., 1991)
BROSTOFF, TERESA KISSANE
    (Dec., 1991)
BROWN, MICHAEL JOHN
BRYANT, JEANA RASHEEDA
BUCK, THOMAS E.
CAIN, PAMELA LYNN
CARAWAY, TODD A.
CARTER, PATRICIA HASER
CARUSO, ALBERT PHILLIP
CHIESA, LISA ANN
CHO, KYUNG-HEE
CLEMENT, HENRY
    LITTLEFIELD, III
COLLINS, JANE
CORNELL, STEVEN CURTIS
COX, JOHN NEEDHAM
CRIST, MARJORIE ELLEN
CROFT, MARK SCOTT
CROSBY, DEBORAH NATHAN
CROSS, MARY ELIZABETH
HAAS, MICHAEL W.
HABER, KENNETH J.
HACKBARTH, MARGARET A.
HALASA, MARI-NELA
HARNER, HEATHER J.
HARRIS, ZACHARY DAVID
HAZEN, MARIELLE F.
HIMMEL, BRIAN T.
HITCHINGS, JOSEPH LANCE
HOFFMAN, KEITH MICHAEL
    (Dec., 1991)
HUBER, JENNIFER M.
HUDOCK, JOSEPH A., JR.
HUDSON, HOPE L.
HUSSON, JULIA SNOW
IMBARLINA, TERRI JEAN
ISSENBERG, ADAM DOV
JEFFRIES, SCOTT THEODORE
JOSEPH, TAMMY L.
JOYCE, HOLLY MARIE
JUBELIRER, MARNIE A.
KARLEWICZ, DEBORAH A.
KELLEY, LOREY A. (Dec., 1991)
KELLY, LISA R.
KHAN, MOHAMMED M.
KIM, HYUN SUN
KISSLINGER, PAUL WILLIS
KNELL, KEITH R.
KOENIG, CRISTEN LEIGH
KRAUS, BRADLEY J.
KRIEGER, TIMOTHY A.
KRUTZ, LISA MARIE

KUNDIN, JOEL B.
LAMBERTSON, ANDREW
    WILLIAM
LANDON, LUDD
LaROSA, CHRISTOPHER H.
LAUN, PETER DAVID
LAWRENCE, JOSEPH ROBERT
LEVENSON, MICHAEL JAY
LEVINE, DAVID A.
LEWIS, ELAINE E.
LEWIS, GERARD J., JR.
LIPPS, PAMELA ELAINE
    (Dec., 1991)
LITTS, JEFFREY D.
LLOYD, LINDA S.
LORENZI, HARRY LOUIS
LOWECRAYTON, SHERRY D.
LUND, DONALD M.
MARCHESE, JOHN JUDE
MARTIN, ALLISON LINDEN
MARUCCI, VICTORIA
MASSUCCI, LAUREN M.
MATSON, JENNIFER HALE
MATTINGLY, AMELIA FIELD
McCORMISH, KRISTEN M.
McELLIGOTT, MICHAEL J.
McGONIGAL, ALAN GORDON
McGOUGH, HUGH
    FITZPATRICK
McINTYRE, JOHN D.
McINTYRE, RICHARD J.
McMAHON, PATRICK B.
McMILLS, MICHELE (Dec., 1991)
McMINN, ROBERT SPENCER, II
McNICHOLAS, KEVIN
MERINAR, JOHN R., JR.
METZGER, THOMAS LLOYD
MILLER, JAMES PETER
MILLER-WEIN, DONDRA J.
MINKLER, MARJORIE ALICE
MINNICH, STEVEN L.
MONTOURO, LAURA ANN
MOTLEY, JULIE L. (Dec., 1992)
MOUTSOS, RAYNI
MOYE, MARQUITA N.
NEISH, LAURENCE ADLAI
    (Dec., 1991)
NIKLAUS, ROBERT CRAIG
NYBERG, PAMELA L.
OVERSTREET, KEITH A.
PARKER, STANLEY JOEL
PASSODELIS, CONSTANTINE
    JOHN
PATBERG, ROLF LOUIS
PAVLICO, MARY JO MARIE
PEASE, JOHN JOSEPH, III

PECORI, EMIL R., III
PEIFFER, DAVID A.
PEPPER, WILLIAM (Dec., 1992)
PHILLIPS, AMY JO
PIERSON, MICHELLE STIRMAN
PINTO, SUZANNE MARIE
PLANT, MARIANNE CHRISTINE
PONTZER, DAVID STEPHEN
POWER, PATRICIA CATTRELL
POWERS, ALEXANDER LEWIS
RANKIN, CONSTANCE G.
RAPHAEL, NATHAN MARC
RIZZA, SUSAN JEAN
ROBERTS, JAMES BARTON
ROBERTS, SUSAN
    TARABORELLI
ROBINETTE, JOHN SCOTT
ROGALSKI, ROBERT J.
ROLLINS, JOHN LEWIS
ROSENTHAL, MICHAEL DAVID
    (Dec., 1991)
ROTEMAN, RONALD BRIAN
ROTH, STEVEN J.
RUDMAN, AIMEE PAULA
    (Dec., 1991)
RUSSELL, JANICE Q.
SALON, CHRISTINE LYNNE
SCHMID, BARRY CHARLES
SCHOEPPNER, CYNTHIA
    WILLIAMS (Dec., 1991)
SCHRANGHAMER, DANIEL
    FRANCIS
SCIARRINO, ANTHONY J.
SCOTT, WILLIAM PATRICK
SEEL, STEVEN H.
SELINGO, DAVID JOHN
SHARIF, LINDA C.N.
SHEFFIELD, JULIE CUTTING
SHELDON, ROBIN
SHERER, LEONARD C.
SHERMAN, EDWARD ROBERT
SHIN, SEUNG-WOOK
SIEGEL, HANS LINGER
SMARTS, BETH
SMITH, AMY E.
SMITH, LISA LYNN
SMOKELIN, JENNIFER ANN
SOLLER, ERIC G.
SPANGLER, REBECCA D.
SPELLS, NED L., JR.
SQUIRES, JOHN ARTHUR
STAFFORD, LISA MARIE
STEFANIS, THEONA
STEINBERG, GAIL A.
SUMEY, BENITA J.
SWITZER, JANE ANN

TAFT, JEFFREY PETER
TOBAK, MICHAEL J., III
TOSH, JOSEPH N. (Dec., 1992)
TRANQUILLI, MARK V.
TROTZ, KAREN
TUCKMAN, DEAN S.
ULMER, K. GRETCHEN
UZARSKI, NANCY JANE
VELISARIS, ELAINE (Dec., 1991)
VENTRESCA, KENNETH
    MICHAEL
VERTZ, BRIAN CHRISTOPHER
    (Dec., 1991)
WAGGONER, PAMELA
WALKER, NANCY ANNE
WEIS, SHEILA M.
WEISS, PAUL
WHITE, DONNA ALLAIN
WILLIAMS, RICHARD
    TIMOTHY
WININSKY, NICHOLAS A.
WINSLOW, WILLIAM H.
WISHART, SCOTT SHERIDAN
    (Dec., 1991)
WISZ, WALTER A.
WOLFSON, TIMOTHY COOPER
WOODINGS, ROBERT THOMAS
WRIGHT, PAMELA J. (Dec., 1991)
WRIGHT, VIRGINIA A.
WYMARD, JOSH THOMPSON
YARUSSI, JILL ANN
YOUNG, MARGUERITA
    TIMBERLAKE MU-LAN

— Class of —
1993

ALBERTS, MICHAEL JOHN
ALLISON, JERRY C.
ANDERSON, RONALD W.
APPLEBY, ELIZABETH C.
    (Dec., 1992)
ARNOLD, ROY WILLIAM
AULD, JANE PATTERSON
AUSTIN, G. LINELL
AUSTIN, HEATHER ALEY
BACHMAN, STEPHEN J.
BAILEY, NATHAN DOUGLAS
BALCHUNAS, GEORGE C.
BALDAUF, KENT EDWARD, JR.
BARBERA, ANNETTE L.
BARRETTE, KATHLEEN M.
    (Dec., 1992)
BARRY, MICHAEL JAMES
BARTHOLIC, MARY E.R.
BARTIFAY, GLENN R.

BASHAW, WALTER R., II
BATES, ROBERT CREW
BATURIN, MADELAINE NINA
BAXLEY, JAMES A.
BEARD, NATHANIEL
    (Dec., 1992)
BECKMAN, STEVEN C.
BELLISSIMO, JOSEPH S.
BELOFF, GREGG
BERARDINELLI, JAMES F.
BERGER, PETER G.
BERGER, ROSLYN
BLAHO, JOELIE
BRILLMAN, SUSAN L.
BRINGE, KAREN S.
BROWN, LESLIE JEANNE
BUNVILLE, KATHRYN LEE
BURT, JOHN G.
BUSSWOOD, KERRI S.
CAMERON, ROBERT WILLIAM
CAMPBELL, CARLA L.
CASEY, PATRICK JOSEPH
CASSIDY, MARGARET M.
GARLAND, ROBERT C.
    (Dec., 1992)
GARRIS, VIRGINIA L.
GAUL, MICHAEL A.
GAVLIK, ROBERT R.
GERSTNER, R. THOMAS
GILLESPIE, BRIDGET M.
GLASER, TAMARA L.
GLEASON, LAUREL SUZANNE
GOTTSCHALL, CANDICE
    KENNEDY
GROSS, RACHEL ANN
HADJIS, ALEXANDER J.
HANNA, CHARLES H., III
HARDIMAN, JASON ERIC
HARRISON, GINA CECEIL
HAY, AMY CHRISTIAN
HELLING, KATHLEEN AMES
HILDENBRAND, NORMA L.
HILDICK, JUDITH ANN
HOCHFELD, ERIC D.
HOFFMAN, ANDREW DAVIES
HOROWITZ, SCOTT B.
HUFFMAN, BRIAN EDWIN
JACQUES, CHARLES J.
JOCHIMS, JEFFREY THOMAS
JONES, JOHN D.
JOSHIE, SAILY MANOHAR
JURBALA, MARIE FRANCES
KASENTER, ROBERT A.
KATZ, STEPHANIE
KENDALL, DAVID JAY
KENT, MARIAN

KIRK, KIMBERLY SUSAN
KIRKWOOD, KOLEEN S.
KLAPKOWSKI, KURT EDWARD
KNUPP, JACQUELYN A.
KOHLER, MARY R.
KUBISIAK, AMY B.
KUCHEK, DONALD R., JR.
KYPER, ANGELA M.
LACY, ELIZABETH
LAMPERSKI, BLAINE A.
LARSEN, PATRICK HOWARD
LEE, LAWRENCE C.
LIESEMER, JEFFREY A.
LIGO, WENDY
LINDAUER, PATRICIA
LOUTTIT, ERIC JAMES
MacVAY, LAUREN MARIE
MALKIN, BRIAN SAMUEL
MALMSTRÖM, RICHARD
    HAYDEN
MALMSTRÖM, THERESA A.
MARCUS, DAWN W.
MARSH, JOHN W., JR.
MATESIC, RICHARD STEPHEN
McALLISTER, MARGARET A.
McKAVENEY, CHRISTINA E.
MEDER, JULIE WILLIAMS
MEDLIN, W. ERIC
MEEHAN, EDWARD J., JR.
MEISNER, GREGORY JOSEPH
MERSKY, DAVID W.
MILLER, ERIN L.
MILLER, MAX FREDERICK
MITCHELL, KAREN LEIGH
MOSES, MATTHEW IAN
MOTLEY, JULIE L. (Dec., 1992)
MOYER, EMILY JANE
NOREIKA, MARYELLEN
NOVAK, JEAN E.
NUBY, MELANIE ROSE
O'BRIEN, ROBERT W.
O'MAHONY, WILLIAM JAMES
O'MALLEY, CHRISTOPHER S.
PANNAMAN, MICHELLE
    ELIZABETH
PARKER, VIRGINIA
PASQUAL, MARY ANN
PAUL, DAVID McCAFFERY
PAUL, LAURIE CAROL
PEEPELS, D. STEPHEN
PEPPER, WILLIAM (Dec., 1992)
PERRY, JAMES O.
PETERS, LAUREL ANN
PETERSEN, ANGELA B.
PETRUNA, JOHN G.
PETRUSH, JOHN J., JR.

POTOKA, JUDITH A.
PURTELL, BRIAN R.
RANKER, JOHN M.
REED, SHAWN LYNNE
RIDENOUR, STACEY LYNN
RITCHIE, JILL ELLEN
ROBINOWITZ, MATTHEW S.
ROBINSON, DEBORAH ANN
ROSENBERGER, REBECCA M.
RUCKER, MARSHA LYNN
RULLO, MARIA N.
RUST, MICHAEL (Dec., 1993)
SAFERSTEIN, BENNETT LEE
SALTZMAN, MATTHEW DAVID
SALZMAN, MICHAEL R.
SCHIENEMAN, KARL A.
    (Dec., 1992)
SCHWAB, CHRISTINE M.
SCHWARTZ, BRIAN M.
SEITANAKIS, NICHOLAS J.
SHELBY, JOSEPH DAYTON
SHERIDAN, ROBIN M.
SHIDERLY, HEIDI
SHORISH, BETH HALL
    STROM
SHULTZ-BUNDE, SELINA J.
SILVER, GREGORY FRANK
SILVERMAN, RANDI J.
SIMPSON, TERESA LYNN
SINCLAIR, DANIEL J.
SLAVKIN, ROBERT EDWARD
SMITH, LISA MICHELLE
SOKOLOVICH, NATASA
SONNTAG, PAMELA J.
STOKES, DANIEL LAWTON
SUROLUCEYWIEC, GERALD S.
SWEENEY, MAUREEN
    ELIZABETH
THOMPSON-COLDREN, JUNE R.
THOMSON, ALEXANDER W.
TIBERI, TODD J.
TIMPERIO, NICHOLAS
    EDWARD, JR.
TOKARSKY, MICHELLE LYNN
TOSH, JOSEPH N., III
    (Dec., 1992)
TRBOVIC, MARGO ANN
TWYMAN ELIZABETH R.
VEHEC, KELLY R.
VENNUM, MICHAEL K.
WAHL, JOSEPH ANDREW
WARE, JACQUELINE SARITA
WASSON, GERARD J.
WATT, CARRIE E.
WEISS, MELISSA JANE
WHALEN, KARLA D.

WHITE, CHRISTOPHER A.
WHITE, H. WILLIAM, III
WHITE, ILONA LAUREN
WILLIAMS, FRANKLIN A.
WILLIAMS, MELANIE E.
WOJDAK, LISA KARIN
    (Dec., 1992)
WOLF, DARREN E.
WOLF, F. ANDREW
WOODWELL, DAVITT B.
WYRICK, WILLIAM J.
YOUNG, KENNETH B.
ZEYHER, LANCE H.

— Class of —
1994

ABRAMOWICH, PATRICK L.
AMATO, PAUL (December, 1993)
ANDERS, KRISTIN L.
ANDERSON, DEBRA Z.
    (December, 1993)
ANKE, JENNIFER A.
ANSANI, AL C.
ASHCOM, SUSAN RINEHART
    (December, 1993)
AVEDIAN, SHAHAN
AXELROD, ERICA D.
BARNES, STACEY MARIE
BARR, BRENDA J.
BARTELL, THOMAS
    MICHAEL, JR.
BAYHAN, HOLLY SUZANNE
BECKER, LAUREN JENNIFER
BEDWICK, JOSEPH CHARLES
BEETEL, CHRISTOPHER
    PATRICK
BEIRIGER, TRACEY DIANE
BEREXA, KATHLEEN MARIE
BERGSTROM, LUKE JAMES
BERMAN, MICHAEL CURTIS
BERTOCCHI, JOHN GUIDO
BIANCHERIA, CHRISTINE
BRANDEIS, DANIEL
    OPPENHEIMER
BRAUN, JEFFREY L.
BREWER, ALISON E.
BRINKMAN, JENNIFER LAURA
BUCKNER, CELESTE MAUREEN
BURGER, MATTHEW
    FREDERICK
BURKOFF, NANCY M.
BUZARD, DANIEL PAUL
CALABOYIAS, DIANNA
CANTY, GEORGE ROMUALO, III
CAREY, ROBERT THOMAS

CARROLL, JULIE H.
CLINE, ELIZABETH M.
COCO, AMY J.
COLBURN, CRAIG P., JR.
COLLADO, LYDIA L.
COOPER, STEPHANIE LYNNE
COOPER-SILVIS, DEBORAH M.
COPELAND, ROSA ALEASE
CORCORAN, RICHARD M.
COSTANZO, VALARIE S.
COVIELLO, KATHRYN CLARE
CRANE-HIRSCH, AUDREY
    CELESTE
CRAWFORD, SHAWN JAMES
CREW, SHANNON L.
CUNNINGHAM, THOMAS M.
DAVIDSON, BRIAN R.
DAVIS, MICHELLE RENE
DECKER, SCOTT EUGENE
    (December, 1993)
DEMBOSKY, LUKE E.
DIANTONIO, JANET VICTORIA
DIANTONIO, MARK
    ALEXANDER
DIGIACOBBE, KIMBERLEY L.
DIMAGGIO, MICHAEL
    ANTHONY
DIPAOLO, SHARON
    FITZGERALD
DIPAOLO, WILLIAM J.
DONOHUE, PATRICK JOHN
DOOLEY-BEIER, MARY
DOUGHERTY, THOMAS S.
DOWLER, MICHAEL H.
DUCRUET, VERA KOEPPEL
DYER, MICHELE L.
DZIALGA, DANIEL
EDGE, BRENDAN C.
ENGEL, STEVEN P.
EPSTEIN, MARK N.
ERIKSEN, KAREN ANNE
ETTER, SCOTT C.
FARRELL, MARC JOSEPH
FAWCETT, KENNETH GILBERT
FIORENTINO, KAREN
FONTECCHIO, JOHN
    MATTHEW
FORBES, MATTHEW EDWARD
FORINO, CHERYL MARIE
FREEMAN, ROBIN LYNN
FRIEDMAN, SUSAN ALLISON
GABRIEL, BRIAN P.
GALLAGHER, HELEN
    MARGARET
GARBER, PATRICIA A.
GAUL, STUART CRAWFORD, JR

GENNAULA, PAMELA M.
GILLICK, JOEL WILLIAM
GLADSTEIN, BRUCE PETER
GOODMAN, CYNTHIA LOUISE
GROVES, KEVANNE M.
GUBINSKY, MARK K.
HAKIM, JOHN
HALL, K. MARK
HAMMOND, MARK
    CHRISTOPHER
HANSBERRY, JENNIFER
HANSBERRY, JOHN CHARLES
HARRIS, CHERYL T.
    (December, 1994)
HAWKINS, MICHELE
HAYLES, SHERON
HELEEN, WENDY DENTON
HENDERSON, PAUL THOMAS
HERILLA, SUSAN L.
HITE, CHRISTOPHER DAVIS
HOGAN, MAUREEN P.
HONG, KIMBERLY J.
HOVIS, CURTIS D.
HUFFMAN, JANET MARIE
    (December, 1993)
HURD, ELIZABETH ANN
IAGNEMMA, KRISTEN M.
JACOBS, JOHN JAMES
JAFFE, DAVID A.
JERGE, MARTIN R.
JOHNSON, AVERY L.
JOHNSON, CAMPBELL
    STEPHEN
JOHNSON, PRISCILLA SPILLERS
JONES, JOHN PAUL
KANDOR, DIANE E.
    (December, 1993)
KAUFMAN, REBECCA
KAYE, SALLY KATHERINE
KAZISKA, DAVID
KEENAN, CATHERINE L.
KELLY, ELIZABETH
KELLY, JOAN ANNETTE
KHOURY, MICHAEL K.
KIM, MIKYUNG CHOE
KINARD, KEITH D.
KINSLEY, PETER ANDREW
KIRK, THERESA MARLENE
KIRKLAND, ANN MARGARET
KLAPKOWSKI, KRISTIN RENE
KLUNK, WENDY LYNN
KOERTH, JONATHAN R.
KOSINSKI, CHARLES EDWARD
KOTWA, FRANK R., JR.
LARSON, FRANCINE VILLA
LAUTEN, HEATHER LIDDELL

LAYNE, DEBORAH E.
LEA, DIANA E.
LEIT, CANDICE C. BAKER
LENT, MATTHEW WILLIAM
LEVINE, ROBIN ADAMS
    CUTLER
LEVY, PHILIP ERWIN
LEWIS, BARRY A.
LEWIS, J. STEPHEN
LIEBER, MICHELE E.
LINDT, MARKETA
LLOYD, BETHANN R.
LOCHMILLER, BETH ANN
MAGERA, GEORGE FRANK
MAKUTA, SHIRLEY ANN
MARSHALL, MATTHEW
MATTEI, RENE CATHERINE
MATTHEWS, SCOTT A.
MATVEY, THOMAS R.
MAURER, LORI ANN
McGANNON, JACQUELINE
    KELLEHER
McGILL, BARBARA ELLEN
MEINERT, JAMES MARTIN
METAL, RENEE A.
    (December, 1994)
MICHALKA, ANNE M.
MIKOVCH, ERIC J.
MIKUSH, KEITH JOSEPH
    (December, 1993)
MORITZ, STEPHEN DAVID
MOSKOWITZ, DANIELLE
    KATHRYN
NICKERSON, DIANA
    CANTWELL
NORRIS, JEFF
NYGARD, TIMOTHY WILLIAM
O'CONNOR, TERRENCE PARKER
PARRISH, MICHAEL J.
PATEL, BAKU N.
PEKICH, MARIA LYNN
PERALTA, MARIANELA
PETTLER, STEPHEN L., JR.
PEYSER, RHONA
    (December, 1993)
PIETROPAOLO, RENEE
    DOMENIQUE
PITTLER, ALAN M.
PIXLEY, STACEY L.
PROVOST, THOMAS W.
    (December, 1994)
PRUGAR, TODD P.
QUINLAN, RENE DAVID
QUINN, KELLY ANNE
REUBEN, MINDEE JILL
    (December, 1993)

RIBAR, LYNN C.
RICHARDS, JENNIFER L.
RIDEOUT, JAMES K.
RIDOUT, BETH ELLEN
RINALDI, GEORGE HENRY
RIZZA, THOMAS MICHAEL
ROBERTSON, JAMES J., JR.
ROSENTHAL, ALAN B.
RUSNAK, GEOFFREY C.
RYCHCIK, CARL JOSEPH
SACCO, TODD ANDREW
SAILER, DONALD R.
SANDOE, SUSAN JOAN
SCANLON, ERIN ELIZABETH
SCARLOTT, KERRY T.
SCHWERHA, JOSEPH JOHN, IV
SCOTT, RODERICK
SEGALL, JENNIFER ANNE
SEIFERT, ROBIN ELIZABETH
SHARPE, JAMES M.
SHAW, JOHN W.
SHENKIN, TODD STUART
SHERER, DIANE ADELE
SHUCKROW, ALAN T.
SHUFFSTAL, DEARALD
SHULTZ, THOMAS M.
SHUMAKER, THOMAS A., II
SIFORD, JOHN F.
SIMPSON, SLOANE
SINGER, JAMES MICHAEL
SINSHEIMER-WEEKS, ANN
SITKOWSKI, ROBERT JOSEPH
SLIVINSKA, DIANA
SMITH, HEATHER ROSE
SPANGLER, BRIAN
STANEK, BERNARD W., JR.
STEFANKO, TRACY ANN
STORMS, AMY ELIZABETH
STUBENHOFER, GERALD J., JR.
SUBAK, MICHAEL PAUL
SUTCLIFF, KRISTIN A.
SWAN, DAVID I.
SZUCH, JAMES (December, 1993)
SZYMANSKI, CHARLES
    FRANCIS XAVIER
TAYLOR, JENNIFER L.
TAYLOR, JOHN L.
TELEK, MARCIA L.
TINNEMEYER, JAMES
    WILLIAM, JR.
TORLIDAS, IPHIGENIA
TRABOLD, CHRISTIAN ANTON
UNDERWOOD, CAROLYN E.
VAN CARA, PAMELA A.
VOTA, LAURIE JO
WACHSMAN, ELIZABETH E.

WALSH, DONNA A.
WEBB, SHARON E.
WEISBERG, STACY LYNN
WEISBERGER, CAROLYN
WEST, CAROLINE S.
WHALEN, JOHN JARRETT
   KENNEDY

WIEGAND, ROBERT S.
   (December, 1993)
WILLIAMS, TOINETTE DIANA
WILLIAMS-LASTER,
   LEAHTINES
WILSON, CHRISTOPHER
   FARRELL

WU, CHORNG-MING
XIAO, JACK Q.
YUHASZ, DEBRA MARY
ZEIDEN, MARK A.
ZIMMER, DAVID H.
ZUPANCIC, JOSEPH

−TABLE SIX−
Presidents of the University of Pittsburgh
Law Alumni Association

YEAR	NAME	YEAR	NAME
1930-31	Harold Obernauer, '13, Founder	1980-81	Homer W. King, '47
1931-32	Honorable William H. McNaugher, '17	1981-82	Blair S. McMillin, '60
1932-34	Honorable W. Heber Dithrich, '12	1982-83	Vincent C. Deluzio, '72
1934-36	William S. Moorhead, '09	1983-84	Robert J. Cindrich, '68
1936-37	Leonard S. Levin	1984-85	Dennis Unkovic, '73
1937-38	Thomas N. Griggs, '28	1985-86	Robert Buckman Smith, '71
1938-39	William J. Eckert, '24	1986-87	Carl W. Brueck, Jr., '54
1939-40	J. Boyd Duff, Jr., '14	1987-88	Russell J. Ober, Jr., '73
1940-41	Patrick J. Corr, '26	1988-89	Thomas P. Lutz, '74
1941-42	Samuel G. Wagner, '30	1989-90	Jeffrey S. Blum, '73
1942-45	Honorable Thomas Marshall, '11	1990-91	Diane W. Perer, '76
1945-46	G. Dixon Shrum, '25	1991-92	Robert F. Burkardt, '50
1946-47	Honorable Alexander Cooper, '22	1992-93	John H. Morgan, '55
1947-48	John D. McIntyre, '21	1993-94	W. Gregg Kerr, '52
1948-49	Paul Kern Hirsch, '39	1994-95	Joseph T. Moran, '86
1949-50	Honorable Sara N. Soffel, '16		
1950-51	Honorable Russell H. Adams, '25		
1951-52	S. Knox Hunter, '33		
1952-53	Alan D. Riester, '33		
1953-54	Benjamin W. Haseltine, Jr., '42		
1954-55	Honorable Thomas F. Lansberry, '33		
1955-56	Walter T. McGough, '48		
1956-57	Robert F. Burkardt, '50		
1957-58	Howard I. Scott, '49		
1958-59	Carl Brandt, '37		
1959-60	Tice F. Ryan, Jr., '42		
1960-61	William J. Copeland, '47		
1961-62	Honorable J. Frank McKenna, Jr., '32		
1962-63	I. C. Bloom, '22		
1963-64	John Spiegel, '56		
1964-65	Jack Plowman, '56		
1965-66	Harold R. Schmidt, '37		
1966-67	Joseph A. Richardson, Jr., '52		
1967-68	Honorable David Stahl, '49		
1968-69	William Unverzagt, '37		
1969-70	Andrew N. Farley, '61		
1970-71	Honorable David Olbum, '28		
1971-72	Abe R. Cohen, '32		
1972-73	William B. Washabaugh, Jr., '30		
1973-74	James M. Houston, '34		
1974-75	Milton W. Lamproplos, '41		
1975-76	James D. Morton, '54		
1976-77	Franklyn E. Conflenti, '52		
1977-78	Samuel N. Goldman, '34		
1978-79	J. Lawrence McBride, '50		
1979-80	Grace S. Harris, '68		